PEG LEG

PEG LEG

The Improbable Life of a Texas Hero,
Thomas William Ward, 1807–1872

By David C. Humphrey

Texas State Historical Association
Denton

This is Number 1 in the
Watson Caufield and Mary Maxwell Arnold Republic of Texas Series.

Library of Congress Cataloging-in-Publication Data

Humphrey, David C., 1937–
    Peg Leg : the improbable life of a Texas hero, Thomas William Ward, 1807–1872 / by David C. Humphrey.
        p.   cm. — (Watson Caulfield and Mary Maxwell Arnold Republic of Texas series ; no. 1)
    Includes bibliographical references.
    ISBN 978-0-87611-237-3
    1. Ward, Thomas William, 1807–1872. 2. Texas. General Land Office—Officials and employees—Biography. 3. Consuls—United States—Biography. 4. Texas—History—Revolution, 1835–1836. 5. Texas—History—Republic, 1836–1846. 6. Texas—History—1846–1950. I. Title. II. Series: Watson Caulfield and Mary Maxwell Arnold Republic of Texas series ; no. 1.
    F390.W322H86 2009
    327.730092—dc22
    [B]   2009009848

Published by the Texas State Historical Association.
Design by David Timmons.

To

Rebekah Connally

and the memory of

Sara May Meriwether

Contents

Illustrations follow page 180.

Acknowledgments

WHAT HAS MADE WORKING on this book such a joy over the past decade is not only the two fascinating people who are its subject, Thomas William Ward and his wife, Susan Ward, but also the many people who have so generously helped me along the way. Above all, I am grateful to Rebekah Connally and the late Sara May Meriwether, Ward's great great-granddaughters, for their enthusiastic support and for the freedom they gave me to mine the rich collections of Ward materials in their possession, in particular Thomas William Ward's papers, owned by Ms. Connally.

I first became interested in Ward while living in Austin but did the research and writing for this book after moving to Northern Virginia. My repeated research trips to Texas as well as trips to Ireland and New Orleans were financed in part by grants from the Summerlee Foundation in Dallas and the Texas State Historical Association, for which I am most appreciative. My thanks in particular to John Crain of the Summerlee Foundation and to Ron Tyler and George Ward, formerly of TSHA. I am also indebted to Biruta Kearl, former director of the Austin History Center, Austin Public Library, for administering the Summerlee Foundation grant and to the staff members of the Austin History Center for their able assistance not only on this project but over the past thirty years.

Given Ward's significance as Texas Land Commissioner, research in the holdings of the Texas General Land Office has been a major focus, and the directors and staff members of the Archives and Records Division have been enormously helpful, in particular Susan Smith Dorsey, Jerry Drake, Galen Greaser, John Molleston, James Harkins, and Rob Jones. I would also like to express my appreciation to the staff members of the Center for American History, University of Texas at Austin, and the Texas State Archives for unfailingly courteous and knowledgeable assistance. Special thanks go to Alison Beck, associate director at the Center for American History, for her help with illustrations for this book.

In Dublin, Ireland, staff members at the National Library of Ireland, Trinity College Library, and the Representative Church Body Library were most obliging. I am especially indebted to Eileen O'Byrne for her genealogical discoveries, to Professor David Dickson of Trinity College, Dublin, for his insights and advice, and to Richard Corrigan of County Carlow, for enlightening me about Beechy Park Cottage. In New Orleans I benefited from the expert guidance of Sally Reeves of the Notarial Archives, Pamela Arceneaux of the Williams Research Center, and the staff members of the Louisiana Division of the New Orleans Public Library. At the Houston Public Library's Metropolitan Research Center, Will Howard shepherded me through the collections, while in New Hampshire, Edward Holden of the New Hampshire State Library in Concord and Jon Godfrey of the Smyth Public Library in Candia were especially helpful. Archivists Wayne DeCesar and David Langbart helped me find my way through Treasury Department, State Department, and other records at the National Archives in College Park, Maryland, and Margaret Kieckhefer of the Library of Congress provided crucial assistance with illustrations for this book.

My gratitude also to the following: cognitive psychologist John Riskind, Ph.D., orthopedic surgeon Geraldine Richter, M.D., and the late John Lawson, M.D., rheumatologist, for their insights into the psychological and physiological implications of Ward's injuries; my friend and former colleague Barry Beyer for reading early drafts of most chapters and providing much needed encouragement; Jim Ely, longtime friend and professor at the Vanderbilt University Law School, for his advice on legal aspects of Susan Ward's lawsuits; Tina and Will Houston for several times making their lovely Austin home available to me while I was doing research; Professor Jerry Thompson of Texas A&M International University for his enthusiastic review of my manuscript and his suggested revisions; Janice Pinney, until recently Director of Publications at the Texas State Historical Association, for her guidance, support, and responsiveness, and her creative ideas for enhancing the book's appeal; David Timmons for a striking dust jacket and a handsomely designed book; and Ryan Schumacher for his deftness and care in managing production of the book and his responsiveness to my many queries and concerns.

Finally, I am profoundly grateful to my wife and best friend, Jan, for the many ways she made this a better book. A professional editor, she gave the manuscript a much-needed careful reading. But I particularly remember the countless times during the past decade she helped me clarify my thinking, resolve a stylistic issue, or move forward when I was struggling. It was Jan, for instance, a former volunteer and board member at the Center for Battered Women in Austin (now SafePlace), who helped me understand Susan Ward and the troubles she faced. Thank you, my love.

Part One

Peg Leg,
1807–1845

Introduction

DAWN BROUGHT A COLD, dreary, sad morning to Austin, Texas, on November 25, 1872. Just three hours earlier, Thomas William "Peg Leg" Ward had breathed his last, succumbing to typhoid fever in his sixty-fifth year. The flag atop the Texas capitol was lowered to half-mast. Tributes poured forth to this "brave old hero" of the Texas Revolution, "one of the marking men of the early history of Texas." The next day state offices and many businesses closed to honor his memory. At the State Cemetery his friends and admirers gathered for his burial.[1]

They had much to remember him by. As land commissioner during the 1840s, at a time when land was the principal asset of the Texas Republic and the magnet that attracted immigrants, he had brought "order and system" to the General Land Office and had fought to remedy the land system's many defects—all with the goal of fulfilling the promise of free land to those who settled and fought for Texas.[2] As an ally of Sam Houston, he played a critical and controversial role in the celebrated Archive War. In the mid-1850s, while serving as a U.S. consul in Panama, he represented the interests of the thousands of adventurous Americans who crossed the Isthmus yearly on their way to and from California. At least he did until he charged two of shipping magnate Cornelius Vanderbilt's captains with mistreatment of seamen and refused to back down when told to do so by the Secretary of State. Upon receiving a presidential appointment as a U.S. customs official following the Civil War, he earned plaudits for administering a sprawling new federal customs district that stretched more than 140 miles from Corpus Christi to the Rio Grande. Of meager means when he first arrived in Texas, by 1850 he had become one of Austin's two wealthiest residents. Three times during the town's formative years he served as mayor, coping in 1865 with the lawlessness that followed disbandment of the Confederate army and with the racial tensions that followed the emancipation of the slaves.

Above all else, his mourners remembered the momentous days in December 1835 when Ward and his fellow volunteers stormed San Antonio in the first major engagement of the Texas Revolution and subdued the Mexican Army holding the town. And they remembered the cannon shot that shattered Ward's right leg, necessitating its amputation. That he nonetheless proceeded to New Orleans and recruited more troops for the Texas Army, returning in 1836 as second in command of a volunteer brigade, enhanced his reputation for "extraordinary courage and endurance, and an indomitable will." He demonstrated these qualities anew in 1840 following a grievous accident that required the amputation of his right arm. Though conscious of his "peculiar appearance" and often beset with pain in his residual leg (his stump), he nevertheless pursued public office with undiminished fervor for the next thirty years. "'Old Peg-leg' is on the 'stump,'" cheered one veteran of the revolution when Ward declared once again for land commissioner at age sixty-two.[3]

Many of Ward's fellow Austinites, however, could not have helped but recollect another side of his life, his failed marriage to Susan Ward, her accusations of verbal and physical abuse, and his vigorous denials and countercharges of infidelity. Married to Ward in 1844 when she was a young widow with two children, Susan confided to a friend in 1854 that her marriage the past ten years had been full of "horrors" but for the sake of her children she had endured silently the "agony and intense suffering" he had caused her.[4] She refused to join her husband in Panama, and two years after his return she left him, taking with her their two youngest children and her two children by her first marriage. Seeking to establish a life of her own, she sued for legal separation and alimony in New York (where the Wards had resided since 1856), charging cruelty, and won. But by then Thomas William Ward had resumed living in Austin. Not to be outdone, she followed him to the Texas capital and sued him again, this time for divorce and half their community property. As the Civil War between North and South escalated during 1861, so too did the civil war between the Wards. When he refused to pay alimony awarded by the court for her support during the suit, she prevailed upon the court to jail him for contempt. The lawsuit was still not resolved when Thomas William Ward died in 1872. Among his many mourners at the State Cemetery, Susan Ward was not to be found.

Thomas William Ward was a man "of strong passions, fervid in his friendships and unrelenting in his dislikes," observed one obituary, and unrelenting he had been in his resistance to Susan Ward's lawsuits. He was a man who rarely gave in to anything, whether it was an enemy on the battlefield, severe physical disability, a powerful adversary like Vanderbilt, or a wife backed by courts in two states. But on that November morning, "like the weather-beaten oak, which has been shorn of its limbs, and then prostrated by the storm," he had fallen.[5]

CHAPTER 1

From Dublin to New Orleans

THOMAS WILLIAM WARD was born on June 20, 1807, into a thriving Irish family that fell on hard times. "My dear Tom," his sister wrote him years later, "what a Change has been in our family, [once] Healthy Wealthy and *most happy*, now separated *far far* from each other." The fortunes of the Ward family, like those of the city of Dublin in which they lived, plummeted during the 1820s. Thomas's father entered the decade a prosperous builder but ended it with his property "in embarrassment." By 1830 Thomas and his three brothers had either migrated to North America or "taken to the sea."[1]

How different the future had appeared to Thomas's parents in the years following his birth. Dublin at the time numbered close to 200,000 residents and was the second city of the British Empire and linchpin of British rule over the Emerald Isle. It was a city of "inexpressibly graceful" appearance, observed an English visitor in 1810, with its wide streets, splendid homes, and the River Liffey flowing through its heart. Dublin was proudest of its many elegant public buildings, such as architect James Gandon's two neoclassical masterpieces fronting on the Liffey, the Custom House and the Law Courts. Yet Dublin was also a city of stark contrasts, of magnificence and misery. If there were pots of geraniums in the windows of many homes, there were beggars in many doorways. The exquisite mansions on fashionable Rutland Square seemed a world away from the squalid, fearfully crowded slums in the Liberties, the center of Dublin's industrial activity.[2]

In June 1807 Dublin was a city consumed by distant events. The Napoleonic Wars raged on the European continent as Britain and its allies of the moment, Austria and Russia, struggled against the surging forces of the French emperor. The *Dublin Evening Post* reported on June 13, a week prior to Thomas's birth, that the Russians had just surrendered Danzig in Prussia (now Gdansk, Poland), a "calamitous event" thought "likely to be decisive of the fate of the Continent." As it turned out, the struggle against Napoleon was forever in the background of Thomas's early years. The fate of the continent was not settled until 1815, when the French emperor was defeated at Waterloo just two days short of Thomas's eighth birthday.

For Thomas's parents there were far more pressing matters following his birth than distant military strife. On June 23, 1807, he was baptized at the parish church, St. Mary's, a few blocks from the Ward home.[3] St. Mary's had a rich history, as one might expect in a parish that comprised some of the most fashionable parts of Dublin. Dramatist Richard Brinsley Sheridan and Irish patriot Wolfe Tone had been baptized there; John Wesley, the founder of Methodism, had first preached in Ireland there; and just a few years earlier Arthur Guinness, head of the Dublin brewing family, had been married there.[4] What mattered most to the Wards, however, was that it was Protestant.

Henry Ward, Thomas's father, traced his ancestry in Ireland back a century and a half to an adherent of Oliver Cromwell's who had come to Ireland from England in the heyday of the Puritan leader, possibly with Cromwell's punitive expedition to Ireland in 1649. By heritage the Wards were Anglo-Irish: of English descent, Protestant, and loyal to the English crown, but Irish nonetheless.[5] Just where in Ireland Henry and his wife, Frances, grew up and married is uncertain. They do not turn up in Dublin records until 1792 when the first of their eleven children was baptized at St. Mary's. Their affiliation with the church lasted thirty-five years, and their steadfast Protestantism brought distinct advantages.[6] For Dublin was a Protestant city, not in numbers—Protestants composed one-third of the population, Catholics two-thirds—but in the city's domination by the Protestant elite, the Protestant municipal government, the Protestant trade guilds, and the legally established Protestant church, the Church of Ireland. When Thomas was three his father was admitted as a freeman of one of Dublin's twenty-five guilds, a privilege denied to Catholics. Guild membership still could have economic benefits, but more importantly by this time, it carried with it the right to vote in municipal and parliamentary elections. The Protestant guilds had become political clubs whose 3,000 to 3,500 members composed more than 80 percent of Dublin's electorate and thus controlled the outcome of elections. Candidates beat a path to guild meetings and those in office provided favors. For Henry Ward, his admission to the carpenters guild in 1810 was a sign of his rising status and a harbinger of opportunities to come.[7]

Several years prior to Thomas's birth the Wards had taken up residence on Moore Street, a short side street north of the Liffey. The family lived there until about 1827, when Thomas was twenty. Like the Wards themselves, the residents of Moore Street were tradesmen and their families—tailors, wine merchants, bakers, provision dealers, a glass stainer, a bookseller, and a coach maker—some 600 people living in 55–60 houses. They were middling people in a city with a pyramid-like social structure topped by a privileged elite with an enormous lower-class base.[8] Households on Moore Street were big, and at the Ward home children were plentiful. Thomas was born into a family with three daughters and a son who was barely a year old. By the time Thomas was eight, Frances Ward had given birth to five more children. Although she "had her little faults," remarked one son after his mother's death, "if ever a saint lived on earth she was that one."[9]

Thomas and his older sister Caroline became very much attached, and Thomas's profile hung over the mantel in Caroline's home in Dublin long after his departure for North America. He was "always a rogue," she recalled of their youth together. Years later she still remembered that his favorite piano tune as a boy was *The College Horsepiper*, and thinking of him she played it on the piano for her husband. Three decades after Thomas left Ireland she would join him in New York, and Thomas's life and her son's would become intertwined. Thomas's youngest brother, Samuel, recalled that he was "a great favourite" as a youth. How extraordinary, marveled Samuel in an 1855 letter to Thomas, that he now lived on the very spot, a mile from Moore Street on the outskirts of Dublin, where the two of them had gone as boys to fly a large kite. Thomas, reflecting on his youth in Dublin, remembered particularly his fondness for "athletic exercise" and field sports. The little evidence available suggests that Thomas grew up in a relatively harmonious household ruled with a firm hand by his father, who, as a relative put it, was "somewhat positive in the exercise of his domestic authority."[10]

A century later, in 1916, Moore Street would become known for its role in the Easter Rising, a week-long armed insurrection against British rule. Insurgents who had taken over the General Post Office, around the corner from Moore Street, sought to establish a new head-quarters after attacks by British forces set the General Post Office ablaze. But, as a dozen rebels headed up Moore Street they were cut down by soldiers massed behind a barricade at the other end of the street, not far from where the Wards had lived.[11] Events on Moore Street were not so dramatic in Thomas's days, yet it was so situated that a youth could not have escaped immersion in Dublin's vibrant life. Just one block east was Sackville Street (now O'Connell Street), Dublin's premier street, 150 feet wide and lined with prestigious business establishments and the residences of doctors, barristers, and solicitors (see illustrations). Horse-drawn wagons and carriages moved at an easy pace along the spacious avenue. Men in top hats and women with parasols strolled and shopped. On Sunday evenings people enjoyed music played by military bands.[12] Towering in the middle of the street was the recently constructed Nelson Pillar, a Doric column almost as high as the street was wide crowned with a statue of Horatio Nelson, the heroic British admiral who had died in action in 1805 while winning a spectacular victory against the French and Spanish fleets. It could not have helped but inspire a boy whose natural tastes, as he later acknowledged, led him toward martial pursuits.[13]

Just around the corner from one end of Moore Street was Dublin's famous Lying-In Hospital, the first maternity hospital in the British Isles; but Thomas was undoubtedly more fascinated by the construction of the General Post Office around the corner from the other end of the street. It took more than four years, from 1814 to 1818, to erect the massive three-story building fronting on Sackville Street. It was not just that youngsters are drawn to construction projects, but that construction was the lifeblood of the Ward family. Eventually Henry Ward would decide that he wanted Thomas to follow in his footsteps as a builder and would give Thomas a role in his work.[14]

While the General Post Office was under construction, Thomas's father was engaged in his most substantial building project to date, at Trinity College, Dublin, down Sackville Street and across the Liffey. One of Ireland's most venerable and renowned institutions, the college experienced a surge in student attendance during the first two decades of the nineteenth century and a corresponding shortage of student accommodations. It was decided to complete the square on campus known to generations of students ever since as Botany Bay, first by doubling the length of the four-story building on the east side and then by constructing an entirely new four-story building on the north side. College architect Richard Morrison designed the plans, and Henry Ward submitted the lowest construction bid. Little did he realize that he would be digging in reclaimed land and that beneath the surface lay the eastern extremity of an old mud-filled quarry extending towards the Liffey. Construction began on the east side addition in the summer of 1813, but as Ward's workers dug down to lay the foundation they came upon so much water they had to man pumps day and night for five months, fortified by the spirits Ward provided to persuade them to work in water and mud for hours on end. Banks collapsed and were shored up. More than 100 piles—lengthy beams of timber—were driven into the ground by dropping a heavy weight on them. Finally the foundation was secure, only to have the process start over when Ward took on the north side building in the summer of 1814. This time the men pumped and scooped water for seven months. Six hundred fifty-five piles were driven into the ground. But by 1817 the buildings were finished and open for use. Plain but practical, they provide accommodations for students to this day (see illustrations).[15]

Henry Ward had survived a difficult test as a builder, and it may have helped him win the favor of Dublin's Wide Streets Commissioners. Established by act of Parliament to transform narrow streets into wide ones, the commissioners demolished houses and created broad streets like Sackville Street that forever altered the appearance of Dublin. In 1817, shortly after Ward had completed his work at Trinity College, the commissioners leased to him for 999 years a very promising property across College Street from Trinity College in an area recently blessed with wide streets and new buildings and shops. He promptly built three substantial brick "dwelling houses" and leased two of them for long terms. In 1821 he had the satisfaction of seeing his daughter Margaret marry a physician, a profession high on the social scale (though he had to pledge his College Street property as collateral to secure her dowry). But then things began to go sour for Dublin and for Henry Ward.[16]

Dublin's economy, which had slumped following the end of the Napoleonic Wars in 1815, suffered depressions in 1822 and again in 1825–26 that had a devastating impact on the city's industrial base of textile manufacturing. Thousands of laborers were thrown out of work, and the middle class also suffered as incomes fell. People in the service industries struggled. Property values declined, as did the demand for middle-class residential housing. The "oomph" went out of the real estate market, and those engaged in speculative development found themselves in deep trouble.[17] Dubliners who had leased land and buildings adjacent to Ward's College Street property began pleading with the Wide Streets Commissioners to lower their rent because of the "continued Badness of the Times" and "the present unparalleled decay of Trade in this City." Ward soon found himself overextended and suffering from illiquidity. In 1825 he began mortgaging his property, including the College Street property and the property near the Liffey on Lower Exchange Street. Not only was he indebted to the Bank of Ireland, but he could not pay off the £500 dowry he had guaranteed Margaret's husband.[18] Several years later his property was "still in embarrassment." In fact, at his death in the 1840s whatever property remained was "fearfully encumbered through law and other matters," his youngest son reported. In 1857 the College Street property was sold under the Encumbered Estates Act.[19]

Thomas Ward had probably begun working for his father by the early 1820s. Though his future membership in the carpenters guild was assured by right of birth, Thomas was by no means committed to a career as a carpenter and builder. More than likely he had benefited from some formal schooling, judging by how literate he was as an adult and by how much he valued education as a parent—he told his wife that education was "the richest gift that parents can bestow upon their children." While Dublin had no public school system, there were many small private schools. Usually they consisted of a single teacher, often a clergyman, who billed his school in the newspapers as a "Classical and Mercantile Academy" or a "Classical and English Day-School" or, in the case of one especially ambitious pedagogue, an "English, Commercial, Mathematical, and Classical Day and Boarding School."[20] But Thomas's most promising alternative to a career as a builder came by way of an unidentified relative and friend of his mother who offered him a cadetship in the famed British East India Company, long a dominant commercial and political force in India. Here was an opportunity to attend the prestigious military seminary at Addiscombe in England, where cadets were trained for service in the company's military forces in India. It is difficult to believe that a youth who was attracted to martial pursuits and who later ventured to North America and joined the

Texas army did not find the offer tempting. But Henry Ward would have none of it. He did not want his son, then still in his teens, to go so far from home or from his oversight, and he insisted that Thomas follow the career as a carpenter and builder he had chosen for him.[21]

About 1827 the Wards left Dublin, where they had resided for the previous thirty-five years. They never returned to Moore Street. It was an enormous change for the family, presumably forced upon them by the deteriorating situation in the Irish capital. From the heart of one of Europe's major metropolises they moved to a cottage amidst meadows and pastureland outside the village of Rathvilly in County Carlow, about fifty miles south of Dublin. What drew them to the area is unclear—perhaps a construction job or possibly a family connection to the Hutchinsons, who owned the estate on which they now resided. Beechy Park Cottage, as their new home was known, was a longish one-story farmhouse built of granite with a slate roof. In front was a cobblestone yard. Inside, the kitchen had a large open fireplace. The setting was bucolic, with green fields, stone fences, verdant trees, and the Wicklow Mountains in the distance. Nearby the Ward's cottage was Beechy Park, the Hutchinson family's three-story country home built in the mid-eighteenth century.[22]

Henry and Frances Ward moved to Beechy Park Cottage with their four surviving sons and one unmarried daughter, Grace. Three years later only Grace remained at home. The exodus began in 1828. In his twenty-first year Thomas made the momentous decision to go to North America. By then he was a lad of imposing physical presence: almost six feet tall, with broad shoulders and light blue eyes. He was an intelligent, adventurous fellow, well versed in a trade, and, one suspects, worldly-wise for his age. He gambled that his future would be brighter in the New World than in Ireland, facing as he did his family's and his own diminished prospects. What lay ahead would certainly be different from what his family anticipated. "Who would ever think the morning we parted in County Carlow that you would be a Consul of the United States," his brother Samuel remarked years later.[23]

Between 1815, when the Napoleonic Wars ended, and 1844, the eve of Ireland's Great Famine, 800,000 to 1,000,000 Irish emigrated to North America. Some, like Thomas, were propelled by limited opportunities and dashed hopes, others by oppression, exploitation, and severe hardship. They were drawn by the promise of a better life portrayed in letters home from those who preceded them. The decision to emigrate was just the beginning of a precarious venture for all. For Thomas the difficulties were probably eased by the companionship of his twenty-two-year-old brother Henry, who we know left home about the same time and, like Thomas, settled in New Orleans. Thomas's first stop was Dublin, where he boarded a vessel for Quebec, the primary destination at the time for ships carrying Irish emigrants across the Atlantic. Judging by the transatlantic voyages of the *Dublin Packet* in 1828, Thomas may have found himself in agreeable company. Close to two-thirds of the *Packet*'s passengers were between sixteen and thirty years of age, many of them single men and women. The voyage to Quebec routinely took four to six weeks, for the most part one tedious day after another, but music, dancing, and games alleviated the boredom. Seasickness and homesickness were rife. The occasional storm frightened and sometimes terrorized passengers, who were shut up in the dark below decks while their small ship was tossed about— the typical vessel was one-hundredth the size of the Titanic. Some emigrant ships sailing from Dublin to Quebec in 1828 boasted that they carried ample supplies of water and other necessities and had "excellent accommodations." By the latter they meant there were six feet between decks—just enough room for Thomas to stand up. Even if these claims were true, passengers still confronted days on end of overcrowding, poor ventilation, and inadequate sanitation.[24]

For many Irish emigrants Quebec and Canada were not destinations but way stations. After a few weeks' stay in Canada, Thomas moved on to the United States. Then he gradually made his way to New Orleans, probably by descending the Ohio and Mississippi Rivers. Upon Thomas's death in 1872, the Austin *Statesman*'s obituary recalled his years in New Orleans—how he had "pursued his inherited profession of engineer and architect," "acquired a handsome fortune," and, with Texas on the verge of war against Mexico, "raised and equipped, with his own resources, a company of volunteers," the New Orleans Greys, "at the head of whom he marched to Texas." Not a word of it was true. Instead, upon reaching New Orleans he plunged into obscurity. "Yes, he is a great man now," commented a Texan years later, "but when I knew him in New Orleans he was shovin' a jack plane."[25]

Whether Thomas headed for the Crescent City or simply ended up there remains a mystery, but its reputation as an El Dorado could not have helped but appeal to a city-bred young man on the make. New Orleans during the 1830s was a boomtown that attracted thousands of job-seeking newcomers like Thomas every year. Explosive growth turned it into the country's third most populous city by 1840 and a commercial beehive that challenged New York City as the nation's leading exporter. Steamboats and flatboats by the hundreds carried cotton, flour, tobacco, and myriad other products of the vast Mississippi River valley system to New Orleans. There they were loaded onto oceangoing ships departing for the eastern seaboard and Europe and onto sloops and schooners sailing to Mexico and the Caribbean. The business of the city was transacted on the levee, a large earthen dike several miles long lined with sailing vessels and steamboats four or five abreast.[26]

New Orleans's commercial success sparked a wave of new construction—office buildings, banks, hotels, shops, and elegant homes for the newly enriched—and created work for carpenters. In 1831 Dr. Joseph Martin, a socially prominent physician who owned a one-story home on Royal Street in the French Quarter, decided to turn his modest residence into a mansion. He contracted with a builder to add a second story and a garret plus a two-story kitchen at the rear and gave him eight months to complete the job. But the builder fell behind schedule and hired Thomas, then twenty-four years of age, to help out. Constructing the second story took much of their time since Martin's plans called for an elegantly crafted dining room and parlor with five fireplaces and a balcony onto which opened three doors from the parlor. Thomas was paid $365 for his efforts. The building is still there at 709–711 Royal Street (see illustrations).[27]

The renovation of the Martin home was probably typical of the kinds of jobs that came Thomas's way during his stay in New Orleans, but finding traces of his life is difficult. He does not appear in any surviving records of New Orleans, other than the release he signed upon completion of the Martin project. He was never listed in a city directory; nor was a plaintiff or defendant in a case before the district, parish, or commercial courts; nor owned any real estate or slaves; nor signed any contracts. Nor does he appear in the surviving records of nearby parishes. Even his sister Caroline had trouble tracking him down. As "many letters as I have written I cannot obtain one answer," she wrote in an 1832 letter to Thomas in New Orleans—the only extant piece of correspondence from his pre-Texas life. "For Gods sake my Dr Thomas if you have any affection left for me (which indeed I do not doubt) write to me without delay." It is particularly striking how much emotional distance Thomas seems to have put between himself and his family in Ireland. Fragmentary reports of his doings in New Orleans and Texas reached them in the years ahead, probably by way of his brother Henry in New Orleans but not from Thomas himself. From the mid-1830s to the mid-1850s he was out of touch, an aloofness that suggests he may have parted on bad terms or perhaps that he just relished his unconstrained life free from family interference.[28]

Caroline's 1832 letter to Thomas bore the sad news of their mother's death from cholera. On her deathbed, Caroline related, "she bequeathed you her last blessing likewise her dear son Henry and hoped you were both minding your duty towards your God as she was given to understand that you were both living in a place where there was every corruption of morals to be found." New Orleans was indeed a racy place renowned for its many gambling houses, barrooms, and prostitutes, and chances are Thomas was not unfamiliar with them. His wife would later accuse him of wanting their sons, as they grew up, to "be taught the vices he himself knew—and especially the vice of associating with impure women." But Thomas was introduced to a great deal more in New Orleans than lasciviousness—heat, humidity, and mosquitoes to begin with. It was also there that he learned about slavery. Slaves and free people of color outnumbered whites. Slaves chained together cleaned the streets. Slaves for sale, in the largest slave market in North America, were housed in high-walled "slave pens" and on market days were lined up in front dressed in blue suits and calico dresses. Thomas probably also absorbed something of the aggressive, unrestrained spirit of the town, especially as expressed in the quarreling, fighting, and dueling that were so common among the young men of New Orleans. In 1834 there were more duels fought in the Crescent City than there were days in the year, fifteen on one Sunday morning alone. A report (unverifiable) reached Thomas's family in Ireland that he had been stabbed with a knife in New Orleans. It was here, too, that he may have developed an affinity for the Southern code of honor, in which dueling was so integral a ritual. Beyond this Thomas was clearly influenced by the Creole architecture that distinguished some official buildings and residences in New Orleans and the many plantations nearby. In 1837 he would build Texas a Louisiana plantation house for its capitol.[29]

But New Orleans was a city in which Thomas failed to make his mark, and at age twenty-eight he was still single and seemingly without roots in the town. Had he ventured across the Atlantic in search of a better life for this, he must have wondered. In October 1835 he suddenly left the Crescent City. His destination was Texas, then a rebellious province of Mexico. This time his venture would transform his life.

CHAPTER 2

The Storming of San Antonio

ONTHS PRIOR TO THOMAS'S DEPARTURE, the smoldering conflict in Texas had become a common topic of conversation in New Orleans and the subject of frequent reports in the newspapers. By early August 1835 the New Orleans *Bee* was predicting civil war.[1] In Texas, Anglo-American settlers bristled at the threat of increased control exercised from Mexico City. Left much to themselves during the 1820s and early 1830s, they had run their own lives and not taken their Mexican nationality seriously. Settlers and government officials clashed occasionally but almost always with words, not arms. Mexico hesitated to force its policies on distant Texas but resented the colonists' disrespectful attitude. Tensions escalated during 1834 and 1835, by which time the number of Anglo-American Texans may have exceeded 20,000. A new regime under Antonio López de Santa Anna took decisive steps to centralize authority and suppress state and local power, abolishing Mexico's federal constitution of 1824, which Texans viewed as a bulwark of their liberties. Texas and the Mexican government eyed each other with heightened suspicion, the former fearing repression, the latter anticipating resistance. In September 1835, Santa Anna dispatched reinforcements to Texas to impose centralist authority and quell insurrection. News of the advancing forces steeled the Texans' will to resist. "War is our only resource," declared Stephen F. Austin, the founding father of Anglo-American Texas. In early October, Texas militiamen skirmished with government soldiers at Gonzales and captured a garrison at Goliad.[2]

New Orleans residents perceived the unfolding crisis much as Anglo Texans did, as a defense of liberty against an autocratic regime. The Texans of 1835 were following in the footsteps of their forefathers in 1776.

They were "determined to maintain their rights," declared the *Louisiana Courier*, and "shake off the yoke of a tyrannical and oppressive government." "Shall Americans suffer their friends and relations in Texas to fall for want of timely assistance?," asked the *Bee* on October 13. The answer came later that day.[3]

Toward 8:00 p.m. on the evening of October 13, Thomas headed for Banks's Arcade on Magazine Street—a spectacular block-long, multi-purpose building with a three-story glass-roofed arcade. Placards on street corners with two-foot-high letters announced the "PUBLIC MEET-ING" that evening. Though intended to be only a preparatory gathering for the immediate friends of Texas, one participant recalled that a "Mississippi-like stream of people" flowed toward the Arcade, so that the meeting, which convened in a committee room, eventually moved to the arcade's large coffeehouse. Once the meeting was under way, speaker after speaker ascended the podium to denounce the usurper Santa Anna and plead for support of the heroic Texans, all to thunder-ous applause. The enthusiastic audience approved seven resolutions calling for assistance "by every means in our power" and subscribed several thousand dollars.[4] Then followed a call for volunteers. Adolphus Sterne, long a champion of Texan independence, promised muskets to the first fifty men who would "go up Red River to Texas" with him. Volunteers streamed to the desk where he stood and signed up. Others were drawn to Orazio de Santangelo, a veteran political activist who years earlier had fought in Napoleon's Italian and Russian campaigns and just months before had been expelled from Mexico for defending the Texans. The pluck of the grey-haired sixty-year-old, starting a new list with his name at the head of it, stirred the crowd. Thomas joined an eager group of men, many known to one another, who followed San-tangelo's lead. Thus the illustrious volunteer force, the New Orleans Greys, was born, and thus Thomas committed his future to Texas. Sev-eral days later he would depart for Texas with his company, not at its head but as a private.[5]

For Thomas the war in Texas offered the prospect of adventure and glory and a chance to fulfill the military ambitions his father had frus-trated a decade earlier. But other considerations also swayed him. Reflecting later on the decision to enlist that night, one of Thomas's fellow Greys explained, "I saw that it was an opportunity for the enter-prising to better their fortunes, and immediately stepped forward and enrolled my name." For Thomas too, it was an opportunity to start over and advance himself after the lean years in New Orleans, and it was a chance to acquire land—not land to farm but land to accumulate for profit and status. In his native Ireland the landed stood high on the social ladder. On the very day that Thomas enlisted, a New Orleans newspaper trumpeted Sam Houston's promise that volunteers who joined their brethren in Texas would receive "liberal bounties of land. We have millions of acres of our best lands unchosen and unappropriated." For Thomas, land was soon to become the focus of his career and the key to his wealth. But first he had a war to fight.[6]

Following the October 13 rally, the Greys were organized into two companies; armed with muskets, rifles, pistols, and knives; and dressed in hunting caps and ready-made grey jackets and pants—the distinctive outfit that gave them their name. Sterne's company boarded the steamer *Ouachita* on the 17th and, after delays to repair a broken shaft, headed up the Mississippi and Red Rivers to western Louisiana. There the men disembarked and set out overland on a three-and-a-half week trek by foot and horseback to San Antonio de Béxar.[7] Soon after the *Ouachita* started up the Mississippi, the schooner *Columbus* started down with Thomas's company aboard—sixty-five men with two cannon and a four-month supply of Navy bread, pork, and beans. They had chosen to go by way of the Gulf of Mexico to get to the action sooner. Once clear of the Mississippi, the *Columbus* sailed at a brisk clip across open water to the Texas coast—a lark for a veteran of the Atlantic like Thomas. On October 25, 1835, the Greys went ashore at the settlement of Velasco near the mouth of the Brazos River to a rousing welcome from the locals and promptly elected their officers. Robert Morris was chosen captain; Thomas remained a private. According to Charles Bannister, one of the Greys, the men then "commenced making war"—not on enemy troops but on the abundant prairie hens and partridges that offered a tasty change from pork and beans.[8]

The Greys' destination—the camp of the Texas army just outside San Antonio de Béxar—was still some 250 difficult miles away, but the next segment of their venture was memorable for its pleasures, not its hardships. They boarded a little river steamer, the *Laura*, and chugged upstream to the town of Brazoria for another, even more exuberant, reception. Flowers were strewn at their feet and a sumptuous feast served. "By the time we had emptied some dozen baskets of champagne," recalled Bannister, we "had in our imagination conquered all Mexico." Judge Henry Andrews administered the oath of citizenship to the men, and Thomas and each of his fellow Greys received a citizenship certificate entitling them to land as a settler. Then their officers informed them that it was time to buckle down, to learn discipline and subordination. With rifles on their shoulders and knapsacks on their backs they set out on foot for San Antonio. Across the prairie they marched to Victoria and then to Goliad, a long and tedious journey made worse by thirst and aching feet. At least at Goliad (where five months later Mexican soldiers would massacre nineteen members of the company) many of the men were supplied with horses. But they were "devilish and wicked" imps, groused Bannister, disposed to "pitching, snorting, biting, [and] kicking."[9] The Greys resumed their march mostly on horseback—Thomas was on a bay—but periodically riders found themselves "unceremoniously brought in violent contact with the ground." By then it was mid-November and the weather turned cold and wet. Rain poured down in torrents "without a tree or shrub to shelter us," bemoaned one Grey. Shortly before reaching the Texan camp they came across the body of one of their own who had ridden on ahead only to fall into enemy hands. They arrived within sight of San Antonio in a vengeful mood, eager for battle against the Mexican army holding the town, but two frustrating weeks would pass before they attacked.[10] While the Texan commanders vacillated over launching an assault, Thomas became an artilleryman. He would soon be promoted to lieutenant and then captain of artillery.[11]

The Greys camped with the buckskin-clad Texan army about a mile north of town, next to an old mill on the west side of the San Antonio River. The company of Greys that came by way of western Louisiana joined them several days later. Between the camp and San Antonio lay a cornfield, barren in November, that extended along the river as it flowed toward town. Within San Antonio, a community of 1,600 souls, the Mexican army waited behind impressive fortifications: log and earthen barricades and a dozen cannon defending the two town plazas and mounted on the walls of an abandoned mission, the Alamo, just across the river east of town. Stephen F. Austin commanded the Texans but was about to leave to seek volunteers, loans, and other support for the Texan cause in the United States. Opposing him was General Martín Perfecto de Cos, commander of Mexican forces in Texas. Sporting long sideburns and a dashing mustache, Cos had risen speedily in the ranks by dint of being Santa Anna's brother-in-law. Cos had 600 to 700 men, Austin 700 to 800. Defeat of Cos seemed imperative for the revolt to succeed, but the Texans hesitated to attack entrenched positions. Throughout November they continued the siege they had laid in late October. The Mexicans maintained the defensive posture they had adopted following their defeat by Texan forces in a clash at Concepción mission south of town on October 28. Skirmishes punctuated the stalemate. By the time the Greys arrived, morale and discipline had deteriorated badly in both camps as a result of inaction, cold weather, illness, and shortages of medicine, food, and clothing.[12]

Also by this time the Texans and Mexicans had begun dueling with cannon. Virtually every day the sound of cannon fire pierced the frigid air, accompanied, one Texan remembered with a smile, by the Mexicans' "fine band of music, which generally performed during these interchanges of salutes." No sooner had Thomas's company reached camp with its two cannon—one a much anticipated twelve-pounder—than Austin ordered immediate construction of an entrenchment for cannonading within 300 yards of the Alamo. His plan was to storm San Antonio the next morning, but he was forced to call it off upon learning that fewer than 200 men (the Greys among them) favored the assault. The cannonading, however, picked up pace with the new battery, and Thomas and the Greys were in the thick of the action. "Everything was lively in the trench," recalled Herman Ehrenberg, a fellow Grey. "All stood around the cannon, and alternatively first one and then another had the pleasure of giving a blow by taking a shot at the old walls. Before firing every man was first required to indicate in advance which part of the Alamo specifically he intended to demolish, and thereby bets were placed accordingly for or against him. 'A hundred ready-made bullets against twenty!' one was heard to call out, 'that I will hit between the third and the four window of the barracks.' 'Accepted!' cried three or four voices simultaneously; the gunner fired. He had to pour bullets all the following day.'" The Greys greeted every good shot with loud applause. The Mexicans returned fire with grapeshot and ball, and the Texans scurried around the cornfield picking up spent rounds to fire back. Despite their enthusiasm, the Texans inflicted little real damage on the old mission, and their shots into town did not fare much better. The mostly novice gunners often missed their mark, with balls intended for more threatening targets hitting trees and knocking down a hen house. It was good training for Thomas and his fellow cannoneers as they gradually mastered the complicated process of loading, aiming, and firing a cannon. But it did little to improve the Texans' prospects for defeating Cos.[13]

Samuel Maverick, a San Antonio resident, recorded the almost daily exchanges of cannon fire in his diary. A thirty-two-year-old South Carolinian, Maverick had settled in town just weeks earlier, lodging at the home of fellow American John W. Smith. Suspicious of their sympathies—rightly so as it turned out—Cos barred Maverick and Smith from leaving town, but Maverick maintained secret communications with the Texans. The cannon duels had barely started, Maverick recorded in his diary, when the Texans directed heavy fire at the Alamo that "took a soldier's leg off" and shattered another's shin bone. Maverick's neighbor, Alejandro Vidal, borrowed Smith's saw and amputated the injured man's leg. "His operation was singular and savage," Maverick wrote, and the man "died at sunset, killed by Videll." It was a gruesome incident that must have been on Maverick's mind when he found himself in Vidal's place not long afterward, helping amputate the leg of another wounded soldier.[14]

On December 1 Cos suddenly relented and permitted Maverick and Smith to depart San Antonio upon their promise to go to the United States. The next day the two men turned up at the Texan camp. At a meeting of officers, both urged an assault and briefed the group on Mexican defenses. Objections were aired, and then Edward Burleson, Austin's successor as commander, ordered a three-column assault at dawn on December 4. However, as the troops formed for attack in the black of night, the skittish officers were unnerved by a shadowy figure, who it was feared had crossed lines and tipped off the Mexicans. Once again the attack was postponed, with demoralizing consequences. When morning came "there was a general breaking up," Maverick wrote in his diary. Dozens of soldiers departed. "All day we get more and more dejected." Burleson called for an orderly withdrawal, but near dusk, with the army in the process of abandoning the siege, the "appalling" spectacle was reversed. A deserting Mexican cavalry officer rode into camp and reported to Burleson that Mexican morale was at a low ebb. At the same time Captain William Cooke of the Greys rallied the still-eager Americans, who had been pleading to storm the town since their arrival. Then Ben Milam, just returning from a scouting mission, confronted the Texan settlers: "Who will go with old Ben Milam into San Antonio?" Maverick believed that Milam's "animating manner and untiring zeal" turned the tide. More than 300 men volunteered and chose Milam to direct an assault the next morning. As night descended, Thomas readied himself for his first day of combat—and his last.[15]

Ben Milam, forty-seven years old, had fought for several months in the War of 1812 and in 1824 had served briefly as a colonel in the Mexican army. His plan of attack was simple, befitting the untrained volunteers who would carry it out. A company of Texans would take a cannon across the San Antonio River to the east side, above the Alamo, and distract Cos by shelling the old mission. Then two assault units would rush down parallel streets into town west of the river and seize footholds from which to carry on the fight. Thomas was assigned to the first division, composed of an artillery company and six infantry companies, with Milam in command. Sam Maverick and Hendrick Arnold, a free man of color, would guide the division as it infiltrated town in the dark. Most of the Greys were in the second division, on Milam's left, led by Colonel Francis (Frank) W. Johnson and composed of eight infantry companies.[16]

Before 3:00 a.m. on December 5 Thomas was aroused by guards who went from tent to tent awakening the sleepers. The men wrapped themselves in blankets against a frigid north wind that blew across the camp. It was "still as death." Thomas and his fellow artillerymen assembled. John Cook, an Englishman, had served as a gunner in the British fleet. Virginia-born William Carey, twenty-nine years old, had already tasted action against the Mexicans at Gonzales; three months later he would command artillery at the Alamo and lose his life. Nineteen-year-old William Langenheim, known as the "Brunswicker" after his birthplace, the town of Brunswick, Germany, would later become a Philadelphia photographer and pioneer in the development of stereopticon slides. There were fifteen men in all commanded by Lieutenant Colonel Nidland Franks. Thomas and Carey were officers under Franks. The men waited shivering in the bitter cold for the signal to move with their two cannon—a twelve-pounder and a six-pounder—each mounted on a two-wheeled carriage. Their ammunition included enough cannon balls to get them through the early action.[17]

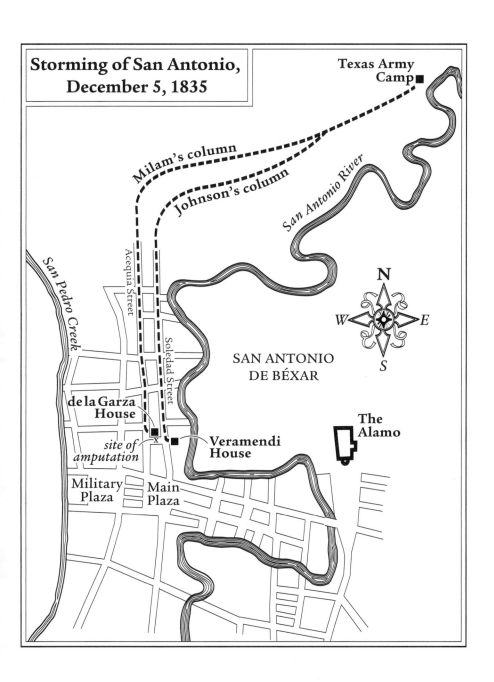

Storming of San Antonio, December 5, 1835

Texas Army Camp

Milam's column

Johnson's column

San Antonio River

San Pedro Creek

Acequia Street

Soledad Street

SAN ANTONIO DE BÉXAR

N
W — E
S

de la Garza House

site of amputation

Veramendi House

The Alamo

Military Plaza

Main Plaza

At 5:00 a.m. the anxiously anticipated thunder of cannon fire shattered the silence as the Texas contingent east of the river fired on the Alamo. "Instantly the enemy drums began to roll and the bugles pealed in motley confusion," Herman Ehrenberg later wrote. From the Alamo "came continuous booming toward the place from where our people with their small guns courageously challenged the entire Mexican army." The feint was working. Falling in behind Milam and his infantry, Thomas's artillery company maneuvered the two heavy cannon in the darkness across the cornfield to the edge of town. Then, with Texan cannon fire and Mexican counterfire still thundering to the east, Maverick guided Milam's division as it rushed down Acequia Street into the heart of San Antonio. Without a shot being fired the entire unit reached its goal—the de la Garza house—but not a moment too soon. Mexican troops detected the second division as it advanced down a parallel street and unleashed a "heavy fire of grape and musketry." Milam's men opened fire to provide cover, and the second division reached its objective—the Veramendi house. Separated from each other by Soledad Street, the two flat-roofed, one-story houses were fortress-like structures, with thick adobe and stone walls, massive oak doors, and few windows. The Texans controlled strongholds only 50 to 100 yards from San Antonio's Main Plaza.[18]

The early morning ruse had worked to perfection, but now it was daylight and the Mexicans knew exactly what they were up against. The Main Plaza and the Military Plaza just west of it bristled with Mexican firepower—at least seven cannon, infantrymen behind breastworks and on rooftops, and snipers in a church tower. "About the time we entered these houses," infantryman Henry Dance recalled, "their cannon were discharged together with other small guns which seamed to set fire to earth and skie kiling every beast in the Sts." The bombardment came not just from the two plazas to the south but also from the Alamo to the east, pinning down the Texans with a devastating crossfire. "We made port holes diches & Breast works," Dance remembered, and prepared to "paly [play] on them with our cannon." Texas sharpshooters returned fire from the cover of the two houses with Kentucky long rifles that were far more deadly than the Mexicans' Brown Bess muskets. "No sooner did a head appear above a wall than it was the target for a dozen hunting rifles," bragged one Texan. With the streets and grounds around the de la Garza house peppered with a "constant shower of balls," finding cover for the artillery tested Nidland Franks and his men. Gun crews did get their two pieces into action, but at no little cost as the battle wore on. Lieutenant William Carey remembered what happened that morning vividly:

> I thought & still think that nothing but fate save[d] me[.] we only had four killed and thirteen wounded [during the five day battle.] three of the wounded & two of the killed received the shots along side of me when discharging their duty at a cannon that was ordered by a fool in the open street immediately before the enemies breastworks within 120 yards of their heavy fires, but he was my Superior and I did obey and when the men was killed & wounded I loaded and fired the gun assisted by two more instead of ten and escaped only slightly wounded, a ball passed through my hat and cut the flesh to the scull bone and my clothes received many shots until by a lucky shot made by me into the port-hole of the Enemy I dismounted their cannon which caused them to cease firing until we got our away.[19]

Thomas lay severely wounded from a cannon ball that smashed his right leg while he was "endeavouring to save the Artillery from being destroyed by the enemy"; according to army officials, he "acted with great bravery" until hit. John Cook, the former British gunner, and artilleryman George Alexander, who was shot through the lungs, received mortal wounds and died several days later. The twelve-pounder was dismounted despite Thomas's efforts.[20]

It was a desperate situation for the wounded. The Texans were still under heavy fire. Getting back to camp was a "very hazardous undertaking" with "a cross fire of grape from the Alamo the whole Route," testified Dance, who returned that morning with a team to get more cannon balls. "We were destitute of supplies, and could not obtain them without exposing ourselves," recalled Thomas Stiff of the Greys. "We did not get water until night." Surgeon Albert Levy of the Greys, shrugging off a slight wound to his forehead, dressed the injured when not fighting the enemy himself.[21] It was decided that Thomas's leg required immediate amputation, under what can only be described as primitive conditions. Even back at camp the medical situation was grim, though possibly improved from a month earlier, when Stephen Austin complained that "there is no medicine in camp—and so far as I am informed, none on the way—There are no surgical instruments nor bandages, nor materials for making lint, nor anything else to provide for the sick and wounded." Fortunately Levy had brought medicine and instruments with him from New Orleans, and he was just one of several physicians and surgeons who participated in the assault, any one of whom might have had some familiarity with amputation, which was the most commonly performed major operation at the time.[22] Standard practice dictated amputation of limbs struck by cannon balls because of the severity of the damage to bone and soft tissue; and immediate amputation was widely believed to be the safest course, especially to prevent inflammation from spreading from the wound to the rest of the body.

Years later Sam Maverick stood near the Veramendi house reminiscing with his son about the storming of San Antonio and Thomas's fate. "There during the fight," he said pointing to Veramendi Street, "I helped cut off a man's shattered leg, and we saved his life." That his action would save Thomas's life would have been a risky prediction that morning. Amputation normally had a mortality rate of about 40 percent at the time, and the circumstances, it is safe to say, were worse than normal. Fearful as Thomas must have been about the outcome, he had first to deal with the agonizing pain of the surgery. Anesthetics had yet to be discovered. At best the pain could be dulled, by alcohol, opium, laudanum, or morphine—if any were on hand. Perhaps Maverick calmed Thomas and held him still as the doctor made a circular cut with a knife perpendicular to his leg, through the soft tissue to the bone. He then retracted skin and muscle from the residual leg to saw through the bone, tied off the arteries, and pulled the skin and muscle down over the stump. It was an operation fraught with potential problems when done in an appropriate setting by an experienced and properly equipped practitioner—none of which may have been the case here.[23] Thomas's fortitude during the ordeal soon was raised to the level of myth. In 1840, while he was mayor of Austin, a local newspaper described it thus:

> Capt. Ward received a shot in the leg, which rendered immediate amputation necessary. While the surgeon was performing the operation, capt. W. saw a number of Mexican soldiers upon

the top of the church; he pointed them out, and a shot from one of our little pieces of artillery carried away a considerable portion of the church, and convinced the Mexicans that a less exalted condition would conduce more to their safety. The operation was soon performed, and without a complain from capt. W. He contended that he should be placed in such a position that he could see the progress of the fight, and told his companions not be discouraged, that he never had for one moment doubted the success of the enterprise.[24]

Later that day, probably after dark, a group of soldiers took the wounded back to camp.[25] Thomas's comrades fought "like devils"—street to street and house to house—until, on the fifth day of the battle, the Mexican army surrendered. Upon leaving the battlefield, Thomas had to fight two new enemies. One was unseen but nonetheless lethal—infection. Infection following surgery was what killed most patients, but before the 1860s no one knew anything about infection and the role of microorganisms, such as bacteria, in disease, so the significance of aseptic conditions for surgery and recovery was unappreciated. Surgeons amputated limbs employing techniques similar to those used today to clean fish. During Thomas's amputation a large area of underlying tissue was exposed under filthy conditions. Surgeon Levy confessed to his sister that during the five days and nights of battle he slept little but was "running about without a coat or hat, dirty and ragged." The situation was no better back at camp, where the troops were strangers to personal hygiene. The issue was not whether Thomas's wound would get infected—battle wounds almost universally became infected—but whether his immune system would combat the infection so that healing could occur or whether the infection would spread and he would die. Thomas was lucky.[26]

Thomas's second enemy confronted him daily—the physical and emotional trauma of his injury in combat and then of losing his leg. Every day he was in physical pain, even, it must have seemed, in his missing limb. And there was emotional pain—at first shock at the mutilation, at the fact that his leg was really gone, then a welter of emotions over the implications: grief, frustration, anger, fear, despair. His life had changed irreversibly, and his future was uncertain and foreboding. He had come so far, from Ireland to Canada to New Orleans and finally to Texas, seeking opportunity and adventure—but now he was crippled and helpless. His horse and his mule were stolen from him because he could not take care of them. His gun was stolen too. It was more than he could bear. He called Sam Maverick over and begged his friend to hand him a pistol so he could end his ill-fated life.[27]

CHAPTER 3

With Green's Brigade

ON THE THIRD DAY OF THE BATTLE for San Antonio Ben Milam was killed by a Mexican sharpshooter. The Texans were stunned. Morale slumped. Later, in the courtyard of the Veramendi house, the Texans buried their commander, the first martyr to the Texas revolution. "There is no name in our revolutionary history to which we can recur with more pride than to that of Milam," the *Texas State Gazette* wrote in 1851. "There was a vitality in his heroism which was worth an army to the Republic, and a moral power in his example more efficient than the sword." When Thomas William Ward died in 1872 his obituary reported matter-of-factly that Milam's "body and Ward's leg were buried in the same grave." The story has been retold time and again in writings about Ward, though often prefaced with a qualifier such as "legend has it." The image of a dual burial, the body of one hero interred with the leg of another, was symbolically important to Ward's reputation both during his lifetime and after his death, associating him closely, in a sense intimately, with the gallant Milam.[1]

Whether legend or fact, how did the story originate? It turns out that the dual burial is not mentioned in any surviving writings, personal or published, during the first twenty-two years after Milam's death. But in 1858 Jacob De Cordova, a Texas land agent who was a good friend of Ward's, introduced the idea in a biographical sketch of Ward in his book, *Texas: Her Resources and Her Public Men*: "The remains of the one hero, with part of the other, were placed in the same grave, as soon as the army had leisure to bestow upon them appropriate military honors." The sketch was written by Ward's nephew Charles Smyth, a Presbyterian minister who idolized his uncle. Embellishing information Ward provided in a letter, Smyth fashioned the sketch with apologies to his uncle for "any blarney." Though the portrayal is a fund of useful information about Ward, blarney abounds. It is possible that Smyth invented the story of the dual burial, but far more likely that he got it from Ward, who, it should be noted, was by no means above taking liberties with the facts. In his 1870 pension application, for instance, he swore that he had commanded his company of New Orleans Greys. It was Smyth's sketch, in fact, that first suggested he played a significant role in organizing the Greys.[2]

The story of the dual burial has survived almost a century and a half, but there is good reason to doubt its validity. Not only did it go unmentioned (even in connection with the exhumation and reburial of Milam's remains in 1848) until the publication of Smyth's adulatory piece, but why would Ward's leg have been buried with Milam in the first place? The two men did not fall within moments of each other, as an Austin newspaper asserted in 1840, or even on the same day. Ward's leg was amputated two days before Milam was killed. Perhaps anticipating the issue, the Austin press provided an answer in an 1865 profile of Ward, then mayor, that was repeated in his obituary: "Ward and Milam had been intimate friends." A reasonable explanation, it would seem, except that prior to the eve of battle the two men did not know each other.[3]

Ward's association with Milam in the minds of his contemporaries enhanced his stature as a heroic figure, but Ward's recovery following his devastating injury provides far more authentic and persuasive testimony to his courage. He somehow found the inner strength to overcome his mutilation, not only pulling back from the brink of suicide but also soon forging ahead with his military career. Within six months of that grim day in December 1835 when he sought to end his life he had become a major in the Texas army commanding several companies. To all appearances he had surmounted, to put it in the language of the time, "his mortified and wounded sensibilities."[4] Later, though, there would be reason to think that his traumatic experience had left a permanent mark on his personality. In subsequent years he would exhibit symptoms comparable to those experienced by Vietnam veterans suffering post-traumatic stress disorder—interpersonal hostility, outbursts of anger, an impulse to violence, marital discord, and alcohol abuse.[5]

It is axiomatic that "a poorly performed amputation almost guarantees poor rehabilitation." In Ward's case his amputation was performed under wretched conditions and his recovery hampered further by dismal postoperative medical care and by infection. The result was lifelong problems with his residual leg, starting with a lengthy period for healing. Eleven weeks following his injury the wound still had not healed.[6] At first he had to endure the crude conditions in the camp north of town. The situation improved in mid-December when General Cos and his defeated Mexican army evacuated San Antonio and marched south. Those Texans still in camp—many had left for home—moved into the Alamo compound, where the second floor of the old stone convent was turned into a hospital and some injured officers were cared for in the headquarters building. But provisions, clothing, and probably medical supplies grew increasingly scarce. By mid-January 1836 the men were "almost naked," complained the commander of the garrison, and his force was down to one hundred or so men, only seventy-five of them fit for duty, and this at a time when enemy troops were reportedly advancing on the town. As it turned out, another month would pass before Santa Anna's army crossed the Rio Grande on its way to retaking the Alamo, but by mid-January families had begun to flee San Antonio. Ward was soon on the move, too, furloughed to New Orleans for medical care.[7]

During the 1830s, New Orleans enjoyed a growing reputation as a medical center that attracted patients from throughout the South and Southwest. Following Ward by a few months, Sam Houston would seek treatment in the Crescent City for the leg wound he suffered at the Battle of San Jacinto. New Orleans boasted a number of able surgeons and the Medical College of Louisiana, founded in 1834.[8] For Ward the challenge was getting there with his mobility severely impaired, his wound tender and still healing, and his stamina depleted by his ordeal. His journey overland to the Texas coast, by way of Gonzales and San Felipe de Austin, took several weeks. At least part of the trip was on horseback, but riding a horse was problematic. The only way he could manage it was to ride sidesaddle, probably strapped in to keep him from falling off, with help required to mount and dismount. Help, however, was readily proffered to a maimed veteran of the battle for San Antonio. He "carries the mark of the part he acted, [and] you will find him a fine gentleman & a brave man," John W. Smith, Sam Maverick's colleague, wrote in a letter of introduction for Ward as he departed for San Felipe. Ward later told friends that Sam Houston offered him money following his injury even though Ward was a stranger to him. In San

Felipe, temporary seat of Texas's provisional government, the governor's advisory committee recommended that in gratitude for his sacrifice "the brave and wounded Capt Ward" be provided with a team and cart and anything else needed "for the comfort and conduct of Capt Ward to this place." The committee on finance decided to compensate him $406 for his services as a volunteer, the loss of his horse, mule, and pistol, and "his expenses & suffering by amputation of his right leg." Upon his arrival in San Felipe the local newspaper saluted him, but despite the warm welcome, Ward did not linger. A few days later, on February 25, an express from William Travis brought the shocking news that Santa Anna's army was in sight of the Alamo and threatened to overwhelm its small force, a disaster that befell the garrison ten days later. By then Ward had departed for Velasco and boarded a vessel for New Orleans. And by then he must also have come to realize that, whatever his anxieties over how people would react, his valor in battle and the resulting mutilation had brought him honor and gratitude and was, in the eyes of his government, a debt to be repaid.[9]

Back in New Orleans, Ward had an opportunity to renew old friendships and see his brother Henry. Despite medical treatment, he hobbled around town on crutches for the better part of two months, his stump still too tender to tolerate a prosthesis. But he was probably fitted for one before he left New Orleans in May 1836, most likely a rudimentary wooden peg leg that was far less accommodating than the innovative prostheses with knee and ankle joints and an articulated foot that he would start wearing in the 1840s. While it was a great help to his mobility he must have found his artificial limb to some degree uncomfortable, an irritant to his skin, fatiguing, and sometimes painful. At first, he probably used a cane in his left hand to steady himself as he put his peg leg forward.[10]

His difficulties with his amputation notwithstanding, Ward resumed his military duties by mid-April, this time not fighting but recruiting. His new commander was thirty-four-year-old Thomas Jefferson Green, an able man and a political veteran (he had served in both the North Carolina and Florida legislatures) but a military neophyte who was full of himself and headstrong to boot. Though Green had attended West Point and looked the soldier, his career at the academy was brief, probably because, as historian Marilyn McAdams Sibley has written, "his temperament was completely alien to the Academy's discipline." As an officer he was oblivious to red tape. A month earlier, in March, Green had proposed to David Burnet, ad interim president of the Republic of Texas (Texas had declared its independence on March 2), that he raise a brigade of volunteers in the United States. Burnet seized the opportunity, reeling as his country was from the debacle at the Alamo and the ravaging advance across Texas of Santa Anna's army. He commissioned Green a brigadier general and authorized him to go to the United States to recruit troops and raise funds—quickly. Green launched a recruiting campaign in Louisiana and Mississippi. He was not shy about dramatizing the cause. "Our women have been insulted, our virgins defiled, and our men treated as devils rather than Christians," he wrote. Upon arriving in New Orleans on April 6 he told Burnet he would shortly march 1,500 men into Texas.[11]

New Orleans residents were already aroused about the fate of their "suffering Brethren in Texas." A report of the Alamo's fall, in gruesome detail, had reached the city several days earlier, news that must have been especially distressing to Ward. The victory for which he had sacrificed his leg had been reversed and many of his comrades "butchered." One of the best-attended public meetings in memory convened at Banks's Arcade to express sympathy and provide support. Green put Ward in charge of a recruiting station, and on the very day that Ward learned Mexican troops had massacred some 350 Texas soldiers at Goliad, a fired-up public meeting named him to a committee to raise funds to send the enlistees to Texas. Undoubtedly stung by the realization that the twin calamities at the Alamo and Goliad had destroyed the New Orleans Greys as a fighting unit, Ward threw himself wholeheartedly into his new job. "Capt Ward has been using great exertions in raising volunteers," wrote William Bryan, general agent for Texas in New Orleans, to Burnet on April 30. Green was also impressed. He commissioned Ward a major in his brigade and instructed him to continue recruiting men in New Orleans. Directly contrary to Burnet's instructions, however, Green liberally distributed other commissions, not as a reward for signing up recruits but as an incentive to do so. His confidence proved misplaced. Though he commissioned colonels and lesser officers for six regiments, he ended up with barely enough volunteers for one regiment, about 400 men. Burnet later refused to confirm many of Green's commissions (but did confirm Ward's). Not one of Green's colonels returned with him to Texas.[12]

By May Burnet was exasperated with Green but no longer hanging on the outcome of his recruiting "crusade." On April 21 the Texans had unexpectedly decimated Santa Anna's army at the Battle of San Jacinto and captured the Mexican president. Green realized he had better hustle to the scene of the action with his undersized brigade before it was too late. He assured his recruits that there were still two Mexican divisions in Texas to be dealt with. In mid-May Green assembled a modest flotilla at New Orleans—the steamer *Ocean*, the bark *Charles P. Williams*, and two schooners—loaded the vessels with provisions, and called on "every man disposed to go" to report for boarding. It was late May by the time the little fleet left the Mississippi for open water through Southwest Pass, escorted by the armed schooners *Brutus* and *Invincible*. Green's only field officer and the brigade's second in command was none other than Major Ward. It was a remarkable comeback for the crippled but still youthful soldier and testimony to his "indomitable perseverance," as Charles Smyth put it in his biographical profile of his uncle. Once again the profile overdid it, however, crediting Ward alone with raising Green's force.[13]

Green's volunteers arrived at Galveston on May 30, 1836, eager to wreak revenge for the Alamo and Goliad, only to discover that hostilities had officially ended. In treaties signed two weeks earlier Santa Anna had agreed to withdraw Mexican forces beyond the Rio Grande and not to take up arms again. Burnet promised in turn to free the Mexican leader, a provision that did not sit well with many Texans and certainly not with Green's volunteers. They soon had an opportunity to make their feelings known. Green dispatched part of his force to Lavaca Bay (a western extension of Matagorda Bay), while he and Ward set out with 230 men in the *Ocean* and the schooner *Pennsylvania* for Velasco, the temporary Texas capital. They sailed into an explosive political storm. Anchored off shore was the *Invincible* with Santa Anna on board—placed there by Burnet to be returned to Mexico. Indignant crowds had gathered on shore to protest, and Green's volunteers, parading menacingly in arms, joined them in "denunciations and violent threats" against those favoring release of the much-hated Mexican leader. Hanging, many insisted, would be far more appropriate. His hand forced, Burnet yielded; Green boarded the *Invincible* with several men, removed the panicky Santa Anna, and put him and his aides in a cabin on board the *Ocean* under the protection of the "Officers of the

Guard": Green, Ward, Aide-de-Camp Leon Dyer, and brigade doctor J. H. Lyons. Santa Anna remained their prisoner for several days.[14]

Though he was a participant in the events that precipitated Santa Anna's forced disembarkation and was charged with his protection, Ward's involvement with the Mexican dictator proved short-lived. Burnet understandably wanted Green's volunteers out of Velasco and issued instructions to that effect. On June 7 Green ordered Ward to Lavaca Bay to take command of the battalion dispatched there earlier and march it to the headquarters of the main Texas Army. Green himself departed with his troops at Velasco to fight Indians. He turned his captive over to Burnet. Santa Anna was finally freed in November.[15]

Looking back on the events of 1836 from today's perspective, it is clear that by the time Green's brigade reached Texas the war for independence was over and Mexico never again seriously threatened to subdue the republic. But during the summer of 1836 some Texans feared that the republic was still in great danger. No one was more convinced of that fact than General Thomas J. Rusk, commander-in-chief of the Texas Army from May to October 1836. The son of a Scotch-Irish stonemason, Rusk had practiced law in Georgia before rushing to Texas in 1835 in hot pursuit of thieves who had absconded with the funds of a company he had invested in heavily—a fool's errand as it turned out. Barely catching his breath he joined the Texas independence movement, was given command of troops though a novice at warfare, and fought bravely in the Battle of San Jacinto. As commander-in-chief he was popular with his soldiers—he had an "easy familiarity with the privates," one veteran commented—but his genial manner and democratic style did not enhance his authority at a time when greater discipline was needed in the ranks.[16]

In mid-June Rusk was sure that Mexican forces were about to invade Texas in overwhelming numbers. Though mistaken, he remained highly suspicious of Mexican intentions. During August he recommended going on the offensive, contending that only if Mexico felt the "horror of the War" would she ever acknowledge Texas's independence. An expedition against Matamoros was planned. Rusk was spurred on by the ever blustery Green, who had been urging him to "strike the enemy a home blow" ever since joining Ward at Rusk's headquarters in mid-July. As major and then lieutenant colonel of Rusk's second brigade—Green's brigade—Ward was directly affected

during the summer by his commanders' views of the Mexican threat. It
started in June a few days after he arrived at Lavaca Bay. Rusk sent him
a series of urgent messages warning him that "a Large number of the
Enemy are rapidly advancing upon us" and ordering him to rush his
troops to headquarters. It ended in September when Ward was detailed
to New Orleans to recruit volunteers and secure provisions for the
anticipated attack on Matamoros. During the intervening two months
Ward was stationed with his men at Rusk's headquarters, first at Victoria and then on Coleto Creek about fifteen miles east of Goliad. It so
happened that neither the Mexicans nor the Texans took the offensive,
but that hardly made for a trouble-free period of command.[17]

Invasions that never materialized and attacks contemplated but
never launched did not provide the kind of action that many officers
and men had signed up for. The army was restless during the summer
of 1836, "impatient under the lassitude of an idle camp," as Burnet put
it. "The volunteers did not yield patiently to discipline, subordination,
or effective organization," historian John Milton Nance has written.
Nor were they reluctant to act on their discontent, as demonstrated
when Burnet appointed Mirabeau Lamar in late June to replace Rusk
as commander and the army flatly refused to accept him. Ward encountered difficulties soon after taking command of the troops at Lavaca
Bay. "Two companies in our Battalion are in a mutinous & insubordi-
nate state," Ward's assistant quartermaster reported to Green in late June
without specifying the causes. "A hostile and low mean Envious feeling
are pervading both the Privates & in several instances officers against
our worthy and I am satisfied much injured friend Majr. Ward." Ward
himself told Green he was having some trouble with one company
over special pay promised them upon enrolling. No less vexing was his
inability to supply Green with the artillery and provisions he had
requested, due in part to "all the public horses & mules having been
stolen. . . . It seems as though the majority of the army has been composed of rogues," he complained. Courts-martial were convened for
some of the more serious offenses. During July, after joining Rusk,
Ward presided over the trial of an officer for neglect of duty and served
on another court that sentenced two enlisted men to be shot for deser-
tion. Then, in August, he was subject to a court-martial himself.[18]

By early August Green had promoted Ward to lieutenant colonel.
The officers of the brigade, however, were not pleased. They met in

protest on August 10—ten captains, fifteen lieutenants, and one hot-head, Major James H. Milroy, a troublesome fellow with an admittedly irritable disposition. Milroy presided. In resolutions presented to Green, they demanded the right to elect field officers (colonels, lieutenant colonels, and majors) as well as company officers and threatened not to obey the commands of those officers appointed over them without their consent (Ward, in other words) until proper redress was rendered. They claimed that "much disorder and discontent" prevailed in the brigade over the issue. That same day Green accepted Ward's resignation as lieutenant colonel. The next day Milroy was made acting colonel.[19]

In the years ahead it would become increasingly clear that Ward was thin skinned and quick to anger. Given Milroy's volatile temper and contentious manner it is not surprising that the events of August 10 and 11 triggered a serious altercation between the two men. Its exact character is not known, but one of them probably challenged the other to a duel. Rusk temporarily relieved both of duty and scheduled a court-martial to consider charges against them. Undeterred, Ward made it known to Milroy that he planned to shoot him when the court martial was over. Milroy decided to seek a reconciliation, but Ward rejected his initial note and the intercession of a "disinterested friend." When Milroy expressed regret at the altercation in a second note, admitting that his anger had gotten the better of him, the matter was settled and the court-martial cancelled. But the event foreshadowed a pattern of aberrant behavior on the part of both men. The very next day, in fact, Milroy drew a pair of pistols on a private he suspected of circulating a report that he had apologized to Ward, for which he was arrested again.[20]

Ward appears to have maintained his equilibrium for the next few months, but it is difficult to know, for it was decided following his "amicable adjustment" with Milroy that it would be best if he proceeded posthaste to New Orleans. As for Ward's colonelcy, it was presumably restored since both Green and Rusk addressed him as lieutenant colonel following the reconciliation. But the promotion was never confirmed by the Texas government. In fact, it was not until Ward visited Velasco at the beginning of September en route to New Orleans that Burnet officially confirmed his appointment (retroactive to May) as a major in the Texas regular army, the highest rank he achieved in the regular army. If to Green and Rusk he was Lieutenant Colonel Ward, to Burnet and Secretary of War Sawyer he was Major Ward. A number of Texans were understandably confused. During the following three years some called him major, others colonel. An 1839 Austin newspaper managed to call him one and then the other in successive paragraphs in the same article. By the 1840s, however, people addressed him exclusively by the more elevated title of colonel, and he enjoyed that honor for the rest of his life.[21]

In early September 1836 Ward was once again back in the Crescent City, but by then the fervor over Texas had dissipated. There were no impassioned meetings at Banks's Arcade, no fiery articles in the press excoriating the Mexicans and calling the Americans to arms. The New Orleans business community was fed up with the Texans—the Texas navy and Texan privateers in particular—for disrupting its commerce with Mexico. Nor was Texas any longer in desperate straits. "It would appear," observed the *Louisiana Courier* in a mid-September article on Texas, "as if there was no further need of the warlike; so that those only who are disposed to plant may expect to reap." Gone, too, was Texas's credit. "It is impossible to raise money here on the faith of the Government," reported Thomas Toby, the new general agent for Texas in New Orleans. Charged with securing troops and desperately needed supplies for the Matamoros campaign, Ward found it tough going despite Burnet's instruction to Toby to "render to Major Ward every aid in your power" and provide funds as needed.[22] Ward once again enjoyed some success at recruiting but reported in early October that there was no chance of getting supplies since Toby had no money. In fact, Ward complained that Toby refused to consult with him on any business. At least he could take satisfaction in meeting one of Green's requests: a full set of "Texas buttons" for his uniform.[23]

By October plans for a Matamoros campaign were floundering. Not only were prospects for supplies nil but support for the operation was dwindling. Sam Houston, the hero of San Jacinto, had long "abhored" the idea, seeing "no benefit" in it. When Houston was elected first president of the republic in September, many of those agitating in favor of the campaign realized it was finished. Green meanwhile had decided to resuscitate his political career, winning election to the first Texas Congress. Rusk left the army to become secretary of war in Houston's cabinet. In New Orleans the *Louisiana Courier* captured the change in spirit as Texas inaugurated its first elected government:

"the Texians altho' prepared to defend the country at a moment's warning, are throwing off the habilaments of war and introducing the comforts, luxuries and recreations of a people freed from the thraldom of oppression." Ward lingered in New Orleans, his lifestyle bolstered by the $460 in pay and reimbursements he had collected before departing Texas, but as far as Sam Houston was concerned he was no longer needed to do the job that had taken him there.[24]

December 1836 brought to a close Ward's active service with the Texas army. His rise had been meteoric, from an unknown private to a lieutenant colonel widely respected for his courage. In the process he had come to know two distinguished Texans, Thomas Rusk and David Burnet, whose patronage would later play a crucial role in his career as a government official. For now, however, he decided to revert to the trade for which he had been trained as a youth in Dublin and that had sustained him in New Orleans before joining the Greys. What triggered the decision was an irresistible opportunity—to build a capitol for Texas.

CHAPTER 4

Launching Houston

"WE HAD AN AFFAIR of *honor* settled here yesterday," reported the Houston *Telegraph and Texas Register* on May 16, 1837. "No blood shed however, all was amicably adjusted by merely shooting into *wood*." The wood was Thomas William Ward's right leg. "If all duels were settled by merely shooting at *blocks* instead of *blockheads*," vented the newspaper's disgusted editor, an implacable foe of dueling, "the practice would be far more consonant with the dictates of wisdom and justice."[1] Ward had initiated the altercation when he discovered a group of aspiring young statesmen debating politics by candlelight one evening in the capitol, his capitol. The building was unfinished, still without even a roof, but Congress had begun meeting there ten days earlier. A visitor to the infant city later recounted the events that led to Houston's first duel.

> Fearing or pretending to fear that the young men would fire the house with their eloquence or something else, [Ward] came furiously into the meeting just at the time the whole was in full blast, blew out the candles, and directed abusive language to the members of the club. One of the members, who was unwilling that their deliberations should be broken up in this manner, retorted the abuse and slapped the intruder upon the cheek. The latter drew a pistol but was prevented from doing mischief by the interference of others.

Judging himself "sorely aggrieved," Ward issued a challenge the next day, which his adversary accepted. They met at the edge of town, very near the capitol, at a spot soon to be known appropriately as the dueling ground (now along Main Street between Texas and Capitol

Streets). Undeterred by the puddles and mud from a drenching rain, large numbers of citizens

> crowded around to witness what really appeared to them an amusing spectacle. Firing at the distance of ten paces, both parties missed. The challenger was not yet satisfied. A second round was fired, and the challenger having received his adversary's shot in his wooden leg . . . came to the conclusion that a bullet in a wooden leg was quite a sufficient apology for a slapped cheek, and expressed his entire satisfaction. Thus ended this "honorable" affair.

Perhaps, but ten months later, according to a report in the *Telegraph*, one of the parties denied that the affair was settled by "shooting into wood." One suspects it was Ward himself, raising the possibility that the ending to the story was a joke at the disabled Ward's expense.[2]

Houston at the time of Ward's encounter was a town of half-finished houses and tents, "puny buildings" over which the two-story capitol towered "like a gigantic live oak amid the prairie bushes," in the words of the *Telegraph and Texas Register*. Ward had agreed to undertake the building of the capitol back in January when Houston was only days old. Its founders—Augustus C. Allen and his brother, John K. Allen—land speculators and consummate wheeler-dealers, had purchased an uninhabited tract on snag-filled Buffalo Bayou in 1836, which they shrewdly named after the hero of San Jacinto and promoted brazenly as the coming "great interior commercial emporium of Texas." What turned the trick for them was persuading the Texas Congress to choose Houston, which did not exist, as the republic's new capital over fifteen competitors that did exist (though some but barely).[3] In making their pitch the Allens offered to build a "State house" and offices for government departments and then, in the heat of competition, upped the ante by promising to do so by April 1, 1837, the day the winning site would officially supplant the town of Columbia as capital. Congress gave Houston the nod and adjourned in late December 1836 to resume deliberations at its new home on May 1. As 1837 opened, the Allens had three months, at most four, to turn prairie grassland dotted with groves of timber into a town with accommodations and a capitol.[4]

It was in New Orleans, where the Allens' business interests and activities in support of the Texas Revolution took them occasionally, that they probably crossed paths with Ward during 1836 and early 1837. It was there in May 1836, for instance, that Augustus Allen accepted a commission as aide-de-camp in Green's brigade at the very time Ward was recruiting for Green in the Crescent City.[5] And it was there in early 1837 that Allen engaged Ward to build a capitol in Houston, which at the time meant handling everything from design through construction. Although it was not until mid-February that they signed a contract, Ward was on the job by mid-January. On January 21 he secured a letter of credit for $4,000 from William Christy, one of New Orleans' leading citizens and an ardent supporter of Texas independence, to purchase lumber for "public buildings" in Houston. By early February Ward had started running a notice in the *Telegraph and Texas Register* announcing "immediate employment and liberal wages" in Houston for twenty carpenters. In New Orleans he signed up carpenters for four months at $55 a month with free board and lodging and free passage to Houston (but not, he insisted, free bedding). Then on February 18, Ward met in New Orleans with Augustus Allen to nail down the details of the capitol.[6]

The two men inked a contract that called for a spacious two-story building for Congress that would be seventy feet wide and sixty feet deep (counting ten-foot-wide galleries along the front and back), with two meeting rooms on the first floor for the Senate and the House. Two narrow one-story "wings" for the executive departments were to extend back fifty-four feet from its rear. Ward agreed to have the House and Senate meeting rooms ready to receive Congress on May 1, with the balance of the work "to be completed without unnecessary delay," a vagueness that both Congress and executive officials would soon come to regret. Allen agreed to pay $15,000 for the job—half of which he had already turned over to Ward in "ready money"—plus the costs involved in transporting building materials and laborers to Houston, no small sum.[7]

By March Houston was a city in embryo of several hundred people, some living in linen tents pitched helter-skelter on the prairie and others sleeping outside on beds of Spanish moss. In the wooded areas along Buffalo Bayou and across the bayou to the north, settlers felled pine and cedar to construct homes of logs and rough sawed boards. Slightly worn paths between buildings gave the first appearance of streets, but spring storms regularly turned them into mud. Everything was expensive—food, clothing, whiskey, lumber, and labor—not good news for a builder working on a fixed contract, though Ward apparently purchased most of his building materials in the United States, including some through his brother in New Orleans. Fearing, with good reason, that Ward might not have the capitol ready for Congress, the Allens erected a long one-story building nearby to serve the purpose in the interim if needed. As it turned out, it was not, but it became a commercial center housing eleven or so stores, a kind of early mall known as the Long Row, whose ownership Ward eventually wrested from the Allens as partial payment for constructing the capitol.[8]

Francis Lubbock, one of Houston's first residents and later governor of Texas, wrote in his memoirs that work on the capitol "was not begun till the 16th of April, but it was pushed with such energy that the capitol, though not finished, was far enough advanced to accommodate Congress and the heads of departments" when Congress convened on May 1. Whatever delayed the start—a shortage of carpenters, a holdup in getting the lumber, work on other projects like the Long Row—Ward's furious efforts did not make up for it. There was the matter of the missing roof, for instance. According to the House journal, the representatives were unable to meet on May 10 "owing to the storm of the preceding night, and the insufficiency of the building, the floor being flooded with water, and the hall unfit for the transaction of business." Another downpour took its toll five days later while also drenching visiting ornithologist James J. Audubon. "We amused ourselves by walking to the capitol," Audubon recorded, "which was yet without a roof, and the floors, benches, and tables of both houses of Congress were as well saturated with water as our clothes had been in the morning." Not having a roof was disruptive, but so was the banging of Ward's crew putting it on and finishing other work. A disgruntled House member introduced a motion to have Ward suspend work while Congress was deliberating, but the motion failed. The congressmen were probably desperate for Ward to be done with it.[9] The department heads had even more to complain about—and complain they did. President Houston and his cabinet had left Columbia on April 16 to take up residence in the new capital. Secretary of the Treasury Henry Smith protested that he then spent months in a "temporary shed" that was "entirely unfit for an office." As for the wings of the capitol, they were unfinished and "in all probability cannot be occupied for some time to come," he declared in frustration five months after getting to Houston. Just why construction dragged on so long is difficult to say, but it was not a job that should have taxed Ward's managerial skills, judging by his success later in administering what for the time were fairly complex organizations, such as the General Land Office.[10]

For all its problems, the building was a landmark in nineteenth-century Houston, first as the capitol and then for thirty-five years as the Capitol Hotel. During its brief life as capitol—until Austin stole Houston's political thunder in the fall of 1839—it was not only home to the Texas government, but also the scene of balls, concerts, regular church services (early Houston had no church buildings), even exhibitions of paintings. Located on the northwest corner of Main and Texas Streets, later site of the storied Rice Hotel, Ward's capitol is often depicted as it looked in a photograph taken about 1857. But by then it had long been converted to a hotel, its roof penetrated by chimneys and dormers, a second story added to its wings, and other alterations undoubtedly made that are difficult to identify because we do not know exactly what it looked like when Ward completed it.[11] Luckily for posterity, Mary Austin Holley sketched it in December 1837, and cursory though her drawing is (she may have done it from memory), it captures Ward's architectural style (see illustrations). Like many other visitors to Houston at the time, she arrived by steamboat from Galveston, docking at the foot of Main Street. It was six blocks up Main Street to the capitol and the beginning of the prairie, about a quarter mile from the landing, she estimated, past two hotels, several stores, the Long Row, and a few two-story houses. The capitol was "painted peach blossom," she observed, and stood "in the prairie making a good appearance." In Holley's sketch the capitol resembles nothing so much as a Louisiana plantation house, with its hipped, umbrella roof sloping down on all four sides and its columned two-story gallery across the front, a style that distinguished many homes in the New Orleans area and was well-known to Ward. Once the one-story wings were completed, the exterior of the capitol remained the same at least into the mid 1840s. Augustus Allen and his wife entertained Holley during her visit, and it may have been Allen who told her the capitol cost $30,000 to construct, far more than Ward had contracted for. The Allens recouped some of their outlay by renting the building to the government for $5,000 a year. Even better for them, the speculative venture of which it was a part, Houston itself, gave every indication of succeeding, unlike so many paper cities in Texas.[12]

The future for Ward, now thirty years old, did not seem so promising. "He is in debt and under a large bond for building the capitol," a Houston acquaintance observed in early 1838. Financing its construction proved far more onerous than he had reason to expect, in part due to the Panic of 1837 in the United States. Banks collapsed, credit dried up, and the economy went into a tailspin that reverberated in Texas. In May and June 1837 the "checks" Ward wrote to purchase lumber bounced in New Orleans—three drafts for $4,100 drawn against William Christy's letter of credit were returned protested.[13] Then later in 1837 the Allens "forewarned all persons" from trading in several promissory notes they had given to Ward for $7,900. He took the Allens into Harrisburg (later Harris) County Court in October and again in January 1838 and won judgments for the $7,900 plus interest and court costs, but he quickly discovered the Allens were tenacious legal adversaries. They appealed the decisions to the district court, which put off consideration of the cases for a year on a technicality. Finally, in June 1839, the district court upheld the county court's judgments, but Augustus Allen (John Allen had died in 1838) appealed that decision to the Texas Supreme Court. Much to Ward's frustration, the county sheriff was forced time and again to postpone the sale of Allen's property that had been ordered by the county court to satisfy its judgments. Two years after initiating the suits, Ward was still was a long way from winning the day, even after the Supreme Court also found in his favor and assessed Augustus Allen damages of 10 percent for "vexatious" conduct.[14]

Ward was not a man who took a blot on his name easily, from the Allens or from anyone else. Francis Lubbock found that out early in 1838 when he "abused" the Colonel publicly, as Lubbock put it; "Ward did not come up to my idea of right in a business transaction between us." Lubbock was a "go-ahead fellow" in his own words—able, ambitious, and newly named at age twenty-two as comptroller for the republic. Ward did not hesitate to challenge him to a duel. But a friend advised Lubbock that Ward was in such debt over the capitol that he could not honorably risk his life dueling until his obligations were settled. So Lubbock ignored the challenge, only to have Ward declare publicly that he would chastise him and make him apologize for his abuse. Lubbock started carrying a derringer in his pocket and another pistol in his belt. The conflict came to head at, of all places, the capitol. The occasion was a joint session of Congress on April 14, convened to hear an address by President Houston. At its conclusion, as the crowd dispersed, Ward struck Lubbock with a stick and knocked him down. Lubbock drew his derringer and fired at Ward but missed when a friend jostled his pistol as he fired. Lubbock later claimed that the incident took place after he had exited the capitol and was returning to his office, but that was not the Senate's view. Two days later the Senate ordered the sergeant-at-arms to arrest both men and bring them "before the bar of this house for trial, for an act of contempt"—fighting in the gallery of the capitol in view of the Senate. Lubbock appeared forthwith, defended himself, and was honorably discharged. Ward at first locked himself in his house and refused entry to the sergeant-at-arms but relented in time to explain his actions to the senators at their afternoon session. Unimpressed, they voted to reprimand him; the senate president, Mirabeau Lamar, did so on the spot. Much in character, Ward was indignant rather than contrite.[15]

Historian William Ransom Hogan has cast this incident as a reflection of the more general disposition to fighting and dueling at that time in Texas and especially in Houston—a propensity for settling disputes without adjudication—which he ascribed to the "rampant individualism" of the Texas frontier. Viewed in the context of Ward's life, however, it provides further evidence of how contentious he was and how prone to expressing his anger through violence. Ward's fiery temper and his penchant for dueling—and his attack on Lubbock in particular—may also have been fueled by resentment at what he considered disrespect due to his physical infirmity. He must have found galling and perhaps humiliating, for instance, his exclusion from one prominent group in 1838 by reason of his injury. Sometime in late 1837 or early 1838, he petitioned for initiation into Houston's Masonic lodge, Holland Lodge No. 1. The secret fraternal order of Ancient Free and Accepted Masons attracted many of the republic's most distinguished figures to its ranks—David Burnet, Sam Houston, Mirabeau Lamar, Anson Jones, Thomas Rusk, Thomas Jefferson Green—and some sixty Texans who participated in the storming of San Antonio. Holland Lodge was so "busy making new members," remarked Francis Lubbock, secretary of the lodge, that he had to work evenings to keep up. Meanwhile Ward's petition was first referred to the Grand Lodge of Louisiana, which failed to act on it, and then to the newly founded Grand Lodge of the Republic of Texas. Finally in December 1838 a committee of the Grand Lodge determined that it must report unfavorably on Ward's petition, though it did so with regret and with sympathy for Ward "on account of the misfortunes which forces us to recommend the rejection of his application for membership." The reason for excluding him was simple: the rules of the order required that any candidate for admission be "free from any physical defect or dismemberment" since, as it was explained, "we can only expect able workmen in able-bodied men."[16]

It is difficult to believe that Ward did not take his rejection, with its implication that he was less than a full man, amiss. He could not help but fear that his mutilation, though often portrayed as a badge of courage, was actually seen by some of his peers as a debasement. "In a sense, all mutilations were equal," historian Kenneth Greenberg has suggested in his study of honor in the antebellum South, because men of honor "read the character of other men through the external physical features of their faces and bodies," and it was "noble features" they admired, while physical defects, in the words of historian Bertram Wyatt-Brown, "carried special opprobrium." Dueling, on the other hand, offered Ward a means of proving his manliness, both to his peers and himself. Seen in this light, Lubbock's brushing aside his challenge to a duel was terribly demeaning, an affront he could hardly ignore without seeming to confirm doubts about his manhood. As for his rejection by the Masons, his undoubted bitterness was at least mollified by his acceptance into another fraternal order that was putting down roots in Texas, the Independent Order of Odd Fellows. In fact, during the summer of 1838 he played a role in organizing the Odd Fellows' first lodge in Texas, Lone Star Lodge in Houston. He remained active in the order for the rest of his life.[17]

Although excluded from the fellowship of the Masons, Ward was hardly an outsider in early Houston. He took an active hand in its civic affairs, perhaps encouraged by the example his father had set as a member of a political club, his guild. When the chief justice of Harrisburg County, Andrew Briscoe, dallied over calling an election of city officials following Houston's incorporation in June 1837, a group of citizens met to press the issue. Ward acted as secretary and was named to a committee of three to raise the matter with Briscoe. He served on a second committee charged with forming a patrol to preserve order in the rough-and-tumble town. In August, Ward just missed becoming Houston's first mayor in a cozy election won by the Allens' agent, James Holman, with twelve votes to Francis Lubbock's eleven and Ward's ten. Late in the year, with citizens growing jittery over the safety of their currency (U.S. bank notes) due to the Panic of 1837, Ward was one of several prominent Texans, among them Augustus Allen, Thomas Rusk, and Anson Jones, appointed by a large public gathering to frame resolutions on the subject. But by far Ward's most significant involvement, foreshadowing his career as commissioner of the General Land Office, was his appointment in February 1838 to the Harrisburg County Board of Land Commissioners.[18]

As Ward toiled away at the capitol during May and June of 1837 he could not have helped but give thought to his future. With the exception of his brief stay at Beechy Park, he had always lived in cities, and Houston certainly held out the promise of becoming one. But was the career his father had chosen for him what he wanted to pursue in a new town in a new country bristling with opportunity, especially given the prominence he had already achieved in Texas following years of anonymity in New Orleans? He did not abandon his trade overnight; as late as March 1838 he was "fitting up" rooms in his capitol with 500 feet of lumber. To what extent he took on other building projects is unknown, but in late 1837 he did build a two-story home a block from the capitol that he sold to Andrew Briscoe for a handsome profit.[19] Nevertheless his days as a builder were soon behind him. By early 1838 he had obtained a license as a lawyer and was administering estates and representing applicants for headright grants of land.[20] Land increasingly became the focus of his attention, not the least because he acquired rights himself to almost 8,000 acres through provisions in the Texas constitution and Texas laws that rewarded settlers who had aided in the struggle for independence and soldiers who had fought in its battles. More than half his land (4,428 acres) came by way of a special grant to all those permanently disabled in the war, legislation that specifically mentioned Ward. His 8,000 acres were still to be located, surveyed, and patented, and even then would have little market value for some time with so many Texans recipients of grants, but it was a start toward building what would eventually become a substantial estate.[21]

Ward first met with the Harrisburg County Board of Land Commissioners not as a member but as an applicant for a first-class headright. The Texas constitution provided that adult males living in Texas on the day the republic declared its independence, March 2, 1836, were entitled to a first-class headright, a grant of one league and one labor of land (4,605 acres) if head of a family and one-third of a league (1,476 acres) if single. Excluded were Indians, African Americans, those who had received land from Mexico, and anyone who had given assistance to the enemy during the war for independence, left the republic to escape military service, or refused to serve. Legislation passed in December 1837 created a mechanism to screen candidates for headrights, a three-person board of land commissioners in each county elected by both houses of Congress. Candidates for first-class headrights were required to swear that they met the qualifications specified in the constitution and produce two witnesses who would testify that they had actually been citizens on Texas Independence Day and had continued to reside in the republic. Ward attended one of the Harrisburg County board's very first meetings—at the capitol—took the oath, produced two witnesses, and was immediately granted a first-class headright of 1,476 acres (see illustrations). Then on February 4, 1838, he began screening other applicants following his appointment by the board as an associate commissioner to replace a member who had resigned—an appointment made official by Congress in May. He served for a year, until Congress reconstituted the boards in early 1839.[22]

Besieged by applicants eager for free land, many obsessed by the prospect, the board worked feverishly at first, meeting some twenty-eight times during Ward's first two months as a commissioner and hearing hundreds of cases, often more than twenty at a single sitting. It was like being set upon "by a pack of wolves," commented a commissioner in a nearby county. Periodically Ward would switch roles and serve as a witness himself for former army friends and other acquaintances. Once the early surge of claimants was disposed of, the board convened far less frequently but, for a while, reviewed an even more imposing number of cases at each meeting, thirty-three on average at the thirteen meetings from April through June. The fact that applicants for second-class head-rights predominated during that period facilitated the task. Second-class headrights (1,280 acres for heads of families and 640 acres for single men, again excepting Indians and African Americans) were conferred on those who had settled in Texas after March 2, 1836, but before October 1, 1837. The time of settlement was not only easier to verify, but disloyalty during the war was not an issue for most applicants. Even so, the board moved through cases at a lightning pace, seemingly taking most claimants and witnesses at their word though required by law "to investigate all claims." The board members were ill equipped and perhaps not sufficiently motivated to probe. It may not have helped that they were paid (by the recipients) for issuing certificates but not for denying them. In 1839 an official inspection of the records of the various county boards turned up extensive evidence of certificates obtained fraudulently. Many claimants had applied for a certificate in more than one county. The Harrisburg County board was faulted in particular for granting certificates without adequate proof to administrators and attorneys representing the heirs of deceased settlers. It should not be thought, however, that the board was just a rubber stamp. Some claimants were rejected, and among them was no less a figure than President Sam Houston. He applied for a first-class headright as a head of family, but was turned down because his witnesses did "not know of any white family of the applicants in Texas." His first wife, Eliza, had left him years earlier in Tennessee, while his second wife, Tiana, was part Cherokee.[23]

Ward's participation on the board not only intensified his involvement in land, but also whetted his appetite for public office, to an extent that, as was once said of a perennial candidate for the U.S. presidency, it was quenched only by an injection of embalming fluid. For the rest of his life he sought public office as a career, a source of income, and a vehicle for exercising leadership, winning a series of government positions and bouncing back from a dozen electoral defeats. "I am urgently solicited to be a candidate for Com[missione]r of the Gen[era]l Land Office. Please to give to me your advice," he wrote a friend a month before his death, despite the fact that his health was in shambles and he had already run four times for the office and lost.[24] During the summer of 1838, while serving as a county land commissioner, he set his sights on election as the representative to Congress from Harrisburg County. But seven others joined the race, Ward fell grievously ill prior to the election with an unspecified "sickness," and he ended up losing badly. Whatever the malady, it obviously put him a foul mood. "No power on earth could have induced me to charge for my services," the acquaintance who attended him day and night for twenty-eight days told him, "but your own unfeeling and ungrateful conduct." Despite the loss, by January 1839 Ward was back in the electoral hunt, this time for the senate seat for Harrisburg and Liberty Counties. The incumbent, Robert Wilson, had been expelled, but Wilson ran again anyway and won.[25]

By February 1839 Ward's service on the land board had come to an end, but he quickly snagged another government appointment, as postmaster for Houston. At his office on Main Street, down two blocks from the capitol, Ward rented mailboxes, collected money for postage, and, most important of all, handled the mail that came in every Wednesday evening from near and far and went out Friday morning on the same routes. The work was part-time, but the duties could be arduous, especially when large packets of mail arrived from the United States for distribution to post offices around Texas. Unfortunately the compensation, mainly commissions on postage sold, was paltry. Not surprisingly, Ward left the job after several months. He left Houston, too, much as he had earlier abandoned Ireland and then New Orleans.[26]

By 1839 Houston was a bustling community of more than two thousand residents, with hundreds more constantly coming and going. A visitor in 1838 who returned nine months later was taken aback by how different it looked. "I discovered more than twice the number of houses. Whole squares had been added." The picturesque appearance of cabins nestled among trees and newcomers camped by fires had vanished. The town was fast becoming "the grand focus of the republic," one resident boasted, despite the repercussions of the Panic of 1837 that made for some dull times for Houston businessmen.[27] Yet there was much about Houston that troubled visitors and residents—yellow fever epidemics, the bottomless mud, the thousands of rats who "made sport by night," the endless drinking, fighting, and gambling. Houston was "a mudhole, a graveyard, an abominable place," grumbled one congressman, and there was the rub.[28] Houston's deficiencies compounded the grievances that a number of politicians had had about its selection as capital in the first place. A movement to displace the Bayou City as capital soon bore fruit, with substantial implications for those, like Ward, who had hitched their careers to the government.

Congress had never promised Houston anything more than a trial period of three years as capital, and it took only months for the legislators to renege on that pledge. In 1837, while Ward was still finishing the capitol, Congress established the first of three commissions to select a permanent location for the seat of government. The die was cast for a western site, rather than an eastern one like Houston, when Mirabeau Lamar succeeded Sam Houston as president in 1838. Envisioning a Texas empire to the west, carved partly out of land still in the hands of Mexico and the Comanches, Lamar believed the Colorado River frontier could become the heartland of that empire and was thus the ideal setting for its capital. In April 1839 the third and last site selection commission, urged on by Lamar, chose Waterloo, a hamlet on the Colorado 160 miles west of Houston, at the very edge of settlement in country virtually unmarred by axe or hoe. Houstonians were aghast. Waterloo possessed "none of the advantages of a city," remonstrated one Houston newspaper, but instead was "at the end of the road" and a sitting duck for attacks by Mexican troops and Indians. Roads to the site were "impassable—not even jackassable," pronounced one critic.[29] Lamar ignored the carping and dispatched his good friend Edwin Waller into the wilderness to plan the town—to be named Austin—and construct government buildings.

The selection of Austin came just a day after Ward signed on as postmaster of Houston. Several months passed before he decided to follow the government westward, and several more before he made it a permanent move. The voters of Harrisburg County may have helped make up his mind. That September they once again turned thumbs down on his candidacy for representative to Congress. Not missing a beat, he landed a position within a week as chief clerk in the stock commissioner's office, the government agency responsible for refunding the public debt. Though he stayed on the job into October, the capitol emptied out within days of his appointment, its contents loaded onto forty or fifty wagons for shipment to Austin.[30] He put a notice in the newspaper that he intended to reside in Austin for some months and would attend to land claims, collection of money, indeed any government business in the new capital entrusted to his care. Before October was out he had joined some 700 settlers living in cabins, shanties, and tents in the frontier village. In Houston, his capitol was put up for rent.[31]

Ward had come to Houston as a builder, but departed with a different view of his future. The government of Texas fostered that career change with several appointments. In return, Texas was to benefit for years from the skills of a man of "unusual capacity for high civil duties," as Texas Governor Peter Bell later characterized Ward. For the republic the appointments were also a means to discharge what was felt to be its obligation for the suffering Ward had endured in the service of Texas. Congress not only provided a special land grant of 4,428 acres, but also passed a resolution for his relief crediting him with an extra year's service as a major, for which he was paid almost $2,300.[32] Reflecting an attitude toward the disabled deeply rooted in Western culture, many of his fellow Texans also viewed him as deserving of pity. As one Texan remarked, Ward won both "the respect and the pity of the people." Sam Houston put the issue less sentimentally in explaining his motivation in 1853 for supporting Ward's appointment to a consulship in Panama: "I had recommended him for his present situation, because, he was mutilated, and I pitied him." Yet if Ward's mutilation aroused people's feelings of pity, he was far from a passive beneficiary of their benevolence. He might have reacted to the stress of his limb loss by becoming withdrawn, timid, and fearful; instead, as glimpsed during his years in the military and in Houston, he was aggressive, ambitious, and competitive. His lofty career aspirations were soon to be fulfilled.[33]

CHAPTER 5

"Autocrat of the Land Office"

M ARCH 2, 1840, THE FOURTH ANNIVERSARY of Texas independence, was to be a day of celebration in Austin. Many of
the several hundred people still in town following the adjournment of
Congress a month earlier looked forward to a stirring oration to be
given at the temporary capitol by E. L. Stickney, president of the Austin
Lyceum, the debating society that provided a veneer of sophistication
for the rudimentary community. Thomas William Ward (together with
Colonel John D. McLeod, a fellow New Orleans Grey) was to direct
the firing of a "national salute." The erstwhile captain of artillery was
the unofficial town cannoneer. Back in October he had supervised a
"salute of twenty-one guns" fired from a six-pounder as President
Mirabeau Lamar and his cabinet entered the town for the first time.
Now the six-pounder was wheeled out again for action. As the citizenry waited in anticipation, Ward rammed the charge down the muzzle. Suddenly and unexpectedly the gun discharged, shattering Ward's
right arm and badly injuring his right side. Ward shouted to have someone bind up his arm to stanch the bleeding. Within hours it was amputated near his shoulder. "Hopes are entertained that he will recover,"
reported the Austin *Sentinel*.[1]

The shock of a second maiming and amputation, once again as a
victim of cannon fire, must have been severe. Infection was again his
lethal foe, the harbinger of death that so often followed amputation and
that two decades later would deprive the Confederacy of General
Stonewall Jackson soon after the amputation of his wounded arm. But
fortune was on Ward's side. As he lay in bed for a month, recovering
from the assault on his body, the pain slowly subsided, the wound
healed, and he had time to contemplate the difficult days ahead. The
practical consequences were not as staggering as those he faced upon

losing his leg, but they were still daunting. From now on—he was just thirty-two—he would be one-handed. A workable prosthesis for an above-elbow amputation had yet to be invented. He would have to make do with a limp sleeve.[2] Moreover, he was right handed. He wrote with his right hand, fired a gun with his right hand (duels were out for now), and depended on his right arm together with his left to use crutches, his means of mobility when his stump was troubling him and he was unable to wear his prosthesis. His appearance was likely to seem odder than ever.

Yet before April was out, Ward was back in circulation. Four months later he was elected the second mayor of Austin, besting three competitors. When Sam Houston rose to take the oath of office in December 1841 following his election to a second term as president, it was Ward, stationed with a cannon on a hill across Congress Avenue from the capitol, who fired the salute.[3] He soon learned to write a very legible backhand and to shoot accurately with his left hand. "Maimed as he was, he was a dead shot with rifle or pistol," testified John Salmon Ford, later mayor of Austin. Dueling was still on his list of possible responses if offended. A longtime antagonist who challenged Ward to a duel in 1841 but then departed for New Mexico with the Santa Fe Expedition withdrew his challenge after returning to Austin in 1842. Ward scoffed that "he challenged when I was like a child in the use of weapons and withdrew it when I became master of my weapon." On one occasion after his injury, Ford related, "he had a quarrel in the streets of Austin with a gentleman; hard words passed; Colonel Ward left. In a short time he returned, followed by a colored man with a basket on his arm. The colonel approached his antagonist and removed a large napkin from the basket, bringing into view a pair of loaded pistols. He politely invited the gentleman to take his choice. The gentleman left in a hurry."[4] Ward's unusual appearance caught the eye, to be sure. Years later, in 1852, U.S. Senator William H. Seward, later Abraham Lincoln's secretary of state, would ask to meet him, as Ward recalled the incident, "because of my peculiar appearance, of having but one leg and one arm." He had the "delapidated appearance" of Admiral Nelson (who lost his right arm in battle), commented an Austin newspaper. Yet Ward was still an imposing figure, "a much larger and finer looking man" than Nelson ever was, the same article went on to say. To what extent a second mutilation and brush with death left new emotional scars is difficult to say.

He was a contentious person afterwards, but not noticeably more so than before.[5]

Ward thus not only survived another close call, but once again made a remarkable recovery. The town in which he was to reside for years to come had survived a close call, too. When Congress convened in Austin for the first time, in November 1839, congressmen from east Texas, led by Sam Houston, bitterly reproached Lamar for putting the capital in such a remote place, deep in Indian country. "This is the most unfortunate site upon earth for the Seat of Government . . . ," declared Houston to a friend, "removed outside of the settlement, and not a house between this and Santa Fe." Unspoken was his resentment at the abandonment of his namesake city. "Western" representatives jumped to Austin's defense. For three days, debate raged over a bill calling for a nationwide election pitting Austin against a more easterly site on the Brazos River. The measure was killed in a close vote, but the opposition to Austin would resurface later and almost extinguish the fledgling town.[6]

Though beset with enemies, Austin still had many admirers. Visitors and settlers alike applauded the picturesque setting with verdant hills "rising abruptly and boldly up towards the heavens" and the Colorado River "dashing down" past the town. The scenery was "rich—varied—beautiful—sublime," enthused one newcomer. A visitor raved, "Austin is handsomely laid out on a still more handsome situation & is susceptible to being made one of the most delightful places in the world."[7] Fronting on the Colorado and nestled between two streams (Waller and Shoal Creeks), Austin was bisected by Congress Avenue, conceived as a grand avenue extending from the river through the heart of town to Capitol Square (though not until 1853 was a capitol built on that site). One-story buildings constructed of hewn logs and plank lumber lined both sides of Congress Avenue, housing the State Department, War Department, and other government offices (see illustrations). Set back from Congress Avenue on a hill (near what is now West Eighth Street) was the temporary capitol, a one-story frame building constructed hurriedly to be ready for Congress. Ward thought it a slapdash job, and it was certainly much plainer than his Creole capitol in Houston. Surrounding the capitol by the summer of 1840 was a stockade pierced with portholes for firing on invaders and encircled by a five-foot-wide ditch, testimony to the pervasive fear of attack by hostile Indians and Mexican troops. Though built by Lamar to provide a refuge for the citizenry, the citizenry was far from reassured. Wags ridiculed the fortifications as playthings for children and nicknamed them "Lamar's Folly." If Mexican troops reached Austin, it was said, "a few sticks stuck up on end would not stop them."[8]

The exposed position on the frontier that troubled Austin's friends and enemies did not seem to deter Ward. From the moment he reached the nascent community, opportunity beckoned. Soon he determined to stay, committing his future to a political hub over a commercial hub. He had barely arrived in Austin when the House of Representatives elected him its chief clerk, a position he held for a year and for which he was paid some $3,000.[9] On the eve of his Independence Day accident, Lamar appointed him a notary public, one of two in newly formed Travis County, of which Austin was county seat. As he had done in Houston, he also acted as a lawyer and agent representing the interests of his clients in land claims, collection of money, and the like.[10] He may have even dabbled in construction and possibly had a hand in the design of the French Legation built by the French chargé d'affaires, Alphonse Dubois, thus accounting for its French Louisiana architectural features, such as a hipped roof.[11]

To these pursuits Ward added the duties of mayor in August 1840. "The city contains more inhabitants and better houses than Houston did, at the end of the first year from its settlement," crowed an Austin newspaper as he assumed the reins. Under his leadership the town took a number of steps to guard against the ever-present danger of fire and in other ways improve living conditions. Presiding over the mayor's court, he dispensed justice for minor crimes and forwarded more serious cases to the district court. But he was not in office long. Elected to serve the unexpired term of Austin's first mayor, who had resigned, Ward lost his bid for reelection in mid-December in a close race, 92 votes to 79. By then his term as chief clerk had also ended. Seemingly his career in government service had stalled. Ward, however, had friends in high places—this time David G. Burnet, a friend from his days in Green's Brigade and now vice president of the republic. When President Lamar fell ill in early December with an intestinal disorder—he later admitted he was "almost wasted to the grave"—Congress voted him a leave of absence and made Burnet acting president. Eleven days later Burnet nominated Ward to become the second commissioner of the General Land Office.[12]

Looking back years later on his seven-year tenure as land commissioner, Ward boasted that when he entered on duty "I found the business of the office conducted almost without system. When I went out of office in the year 1848, I had so far systematised the office as that the land system could easily be understood by all." The claim was by no means fanciful. Texas Governor Peter Bell, who took office soon after Ward's departure, praised the late commissioner for performing "the extraordinary task of reducing to order and system, a confused and complicated mass of valuable documents without aid derived from well digested land laws; enabling nearly every citizen to comprehend and establish his claims." The reputation for "superior executive ability" that Ward came to enjoy took root within months of his appointment.[13] "There are about a dozen clerks engaged in different duties of the office," observed an Austin newspaper editor in August 1841, "some in translating, others in map making, recording, comparing field notes, and filling up land patents. To walk through the ample apartments of this office, and see each of its officers, like clock work, pursuing his own special duty—it looks the very personification of industry, and reminds me, to use a homely similitude, much of the complicated yet orderly operations of a spinning factory." In other words, Ward ran a tight ship. His goal was to impose the same kind of order on the land system nationwide.[14]

Yet Ward's seven years as commissioner were, in other ways, far from orderly or harmonious; some of the time, they were tumultuous. Critics and adversaries abounded, especially in the ranks of Congress, which resisted many of his proposals to perfect the land system and then turned him out of office following an acrimonious investigation. The citizens of Austin, infuriated that President Houston had moved the government out of Austin in 1842, played havoc with Land Office operations when they took control of the office's records and refused for a year to release them. But what really put the commissioner in the hot seat was the pervasive and intense public involvement in the disposition of land. Land hunger was the driving force in the settlement of Texas—land to live on and farm, land for speculation—and the republic primed the pump of immigration by promising free land (a headright) to its white male settlers who immigrated before 1842.[15] It was the land commissioner's responsibility, as originally legislated in 1836 and as Ward understood it, to transform that promise into reality: "to secure to the honest hard-working-emigrant a title to the land donated to him as soon as possible," as Ward put it. But at the time he took office, not a single Texan out of the many thousands entitled to a head-right had managed to get legal title to his claim.[16] The problem was not a shortage of land. On achieving independence the republic laid claim to a public domain that was larger than France and Great Britain today combined. The problem was creating an effective system for transferring land from public to private ownership in the face of innumerable obstacles, from rampant fraud to defective records of what land was owned and thus of what land could be given away. Little wonder that an Austin newspaper called the Land Office the "most important" in the government but its duties "probably [the] most difficult to discharge to the entire satisfaction of the people." In a prophetic warning, the very first letter Ward handled as commissioner, from a prospective landowner frustrated in his efforts to patent his claim, cautioned that it "will require the patience of Job and an Ox combined to get along in your business."[17]

True to form, Ward found his job a political and managerial trial from the start. Texas's volatile political climate almost cost him the appointment before he began. When six of Texas's thirteen senators opposed his confirmation, the nomination was tabled. Nevertheless he squeaked through in a second vote and took office on January 5, 1841, only to have his clerks resign *en masse* a month later over "inadequate compensation."[18] They were soon mollified, but then, in an incident that exemplified the explosive emotions that land could generate, he locked horns with Samuel Luckie, an outspoken gentleman who accused him of partiality in patenting land. (Patent was the term used for the deed issued by the republic to convey legal title to land.) What set Luckie off was Ward's refusal to patent Luckie's claim because it was in an area disputed by two counties when, in fact, Ward had already issued patents to land in that area. Those patents, however, had been approved and prepared for signing by the president before Ward took office. Once in charge he directed his staff not to patent land in any disputed areas. Furious at the rebuff, Luckie not only poured his anger into a letter to President Lamar but pestered the Land Office clerks with questions until, in the words of an assistant clerk, "he became so inquisitive and consequently troublesome that one of the clerks of the office remarked that if he was not protected from insult while in the office that he should be constrained to leave it." So Ward asked Luckie to step into his office to discuss the issue, remarking that the work of the Land Office could hardly progress if the clerks were continually interrupted by the "Interrogatories of strangers." Not budging an inch, Luckie retorted that it was a public office and he had a perfect right to go into any part of it he thought proper, to which Ward—never one to back down—replied that he was the proper person to be the judge of that. Unfortunately for Ward, four months later Luckie was elected to Congress.[19]

Ward had barely won appointment when the Land Office moved three blocks up Congress Avenue to a building just to the east on what would become Hickory (Eighth) Street. Adjacent to the new quarters were two vacant rooms that he turned into his residence. Most days the "intense press of business" kept the commissioner and his clerks busy from eight in the morning until about five or six in the evening (with time out for a midday meal), trying to systematize the process for patenting land and get control over the thousands of pages of land records that threatened to inundate them.[20] Ward must have been reminded of the chaos he had witnessed in Houston when his predecessor, John Borden, first assembled the land records and they overflowed into the corridors and the basement of Ward's capitol. It was Borden (whose brother Gail gained much greater renown for inventing condensed milk and founding the Borden Company) who in 1837 took on the momentous task of organizing the Land Office and collecting the scattered records of several thousand Spanish and Mexican land titles issued in Texas before independence by land commissioners for various colonies, municipalities, and other jurisdictions. Though dismayed at learning some records were missing, others destroyed, and a good many plagued by a "loose manner of issuing titles," Borden and his tiny staff set about authenticating the surviving records to determine as best they could what land in Texas's vast domain was already owned. It eventually turned out (the Land Office continued to acquire records concerning Spanish and Mexican titles into the 1850s) that Spain and Mexico had granted some 26 million acres in Texas, an area five times the size of Massachusetts.[21]

Sorting through and translating a mass of Spanish language records commanded much of Borden's attention—he was first sent to San Antonio to learn Spanish—but it was hardly his only hurdle in getting the patenting process moving. The headright system, it became depressingly clear, was riddled with fraud. Texans seeking to establish eligibility for their headrights had to satisfy a county Board of Land Commissioners that they met the legal requirements, the very process Ward had participated in during 1838 as a member of the Harris County Board of Land Commissioners. Successful applicants—and few were turned away—received a certificate from the board specifying how much land they were entitled to. The recipient might then proceed to locate vacant land for patenting or he might sell his certificate to a speculator. If the latter, the certificate would circulate as a kind of currency—unlocated land paper—redeemable in land by anyone holding it. Once the original recipient or a subsequent holder decided he wanted to stake his claim to a vacant tract, or "locate" his certificate in the idiom of the day, he engaged an authorized surveyor, usually one of the deputy surveyors serving under the county surveyor in the county where the land was located.[22] The deputy's field notes (a legal description of the survey consisting of the metes and bounds of the tract) were then turned over, together with the certificate, to the county surveyor for approval. Those steps established one's claim to the land but did not give one title. That required forwarding the paperwork to the General Land Office for review to identify any errors, ambiguities, or conflicts, and it was only following the resolution of those complications and the fulfillment of any conditions of the grant, such as paying a fee and meeting a residency requirement, that the commissioner patented the claim. Mushrooming problems with certificates, however, brought the entire process to a standstill.

It was troublesome enough that boards sometimes ignored proper procedure or engaged in sloppy paperwork. It was calamitous that fraudulent certificates proliferated like locusts in a drought. Taking advantage of a cursory screening process—recall that the Harrisburg County board sometimes heard more than thirty cases at a single sitting—applicants indulged in false claims, perjured testimony, and double-dipping (obtaining certificates from more than one board). Forgers outdid perjurers, flooding Texas with fake certificates. For the first two years or so, clerks for each county board wrote the certificates by hand, a forger's dream but a land commissioner's nightmare. Counterfeiting declined when the boards began printing certificates, but they varied in appearance and some were plain, even primitive, thus still offering an inviting target. Handbooks for prospective settlers, like the *Emigrant's*

Guide to the New Republic published in 1840, cautioned readers not to buy certificates from strangers, especially before arriving in Texas. "Vast numbers of claims have been fraudulently obtained from the land commissioners, and still more numerous claims, offered for sale in the United States, are forgeries." Congress responded to the crisis in early 1840 by establishing a "travelling board of land commissioners" to reinvestigate the thousands of certificates already issued by county boards. A list of certificates deemed both genuine and deserved was to be forwarded to the commissioner of the General Land Office, who was directed to issue patents only on listed certificates and then only to the original grantees. Miscreants convicted of land fraud were to receive thirty-nine lashes on the bare back and jail terms.[23]

"I regret to inform you," Borden reported to Congress in October 1840, two months before resigning, "that so far as regards the issuing of patents to land for head-right claims, an event which the citizens of Texas have long been anxiously waiting for, nothing has been done in this office, and I fear but little of a permanent nature has been effected by the Examining [Traveling] Commissioners." Nor had Borden issued any patents on the many bounty and donation grants awarded for military service in the war for independence and barely any to holders of land scrip (land certificates issued to raise public funds or repay government loans). Ward thus took office in January 1841 facing a pent-up demand for patents but a patenting process that was dead in the water. By the time he left office in 1848 the Land Office had issued close to 12,000 patents on headrights, bounty and donation grants, and land scrip.[24]

Notwithstanding his "mutilation and severe suffering," opined the editor of the influential *Texas Sentinel* on Ward's appointment, the new commissioner enjoyed good health and was remarkably active. Moreover, his industry, steadiness, "excellent practical sense, and great honestty of purpose" made him a "first rate officer." Many Texans who had business with Ward during his first year in office found him gentlemanly and accommodating, but a number, such as Samuel Luckie, thought him obstinate and overbearing. So did some of his subordinates. Endeavoring to prevent fraud and forestall litigation over conflicting land claims, he became a stickler for proper procedure and precise detail. "The Autocrat of the Land Office has chosen in the plenitude of his power to require more evidence," one Land Office employee wrote a land agent concerning a headright certificate, "although that already deposited is doubtless all that any other man than Ward would have considered necessary."[25]

Ward was no sooner in office than he set about tightening up the land system, in some cases building on Borden's initiatives, in others putting his own stamp on things, but always keeping his eye on the law and interpreting it for officials and citizens as he thought proper. To county land boards he issued instructions to ensure uniformity in headright certificates. He insisted that county surveyors systematically plat all original surveys on county maps as required by an 1840 law, thus producing an up-to-date visual record that showed just what land was spoken for (claimed and surveyed or already patented) and how different claims were connected to each other; otherwise there would be overlaps and gaps in adjacent grants (see illustrations). No land would be patented in Victoria County, he told the county surveyor in typical fashion, until such a map was forthcoming. He directed county surveyors to settle boundary disputes among counties to avoid multiple claims to the same land. He pointed out procedural errors and pounced on faulty information.[26] One county surveyor who failed to correct several mistakes Ward had brought to his attention was admonished, "you seem to think there would be no impropriety in patenting on surveys whether they have their true position on the County map or not, you certainly know better than this." His scrupulous attention to detail, though irritating to many, was rewarded in September 1841 with plaudits for his "energy and foresight" when he uncovered a brazen attempt at land fraud in Jasper County. Someone intercepted, on its way to Austin, the traveling commissioners' report listing the holders of legitimate headright certificates from Jasper County. A forged substitute arrived at the Land Office that included seventy-five fraudulently inserted names, seventy-four of them supposedly entitled to 4,600 acres apiece. Ward attributed the chicanery to avaricious land speculators. "They dare do any thing that brings them gain."[27]

As reports from the traveling commissioners flowed into the Land Office during 1841, so, too, did demands from all parts of the republic for patents on those certificates deemed legal. "The whole country is anxious to obtain their final titles," an Austin newspaper observed, "which it is hoped will save endless and ruinous litigation." Austin may have been a "dull town" that summer, remarked the commissioner, but he had "plenty of business." Keeping up with it was no easy task. He hired three new clerks and did his best to accommodate impatient land seekers anxious to make good not only on headrights, but also on bounty and donation grants and land scrip.[28] It must have gratified him to hear from his good friend James Harper Starr, former secretary of the treasury in Lamar's administration and a burgeoning land baron, that citizens visiting the Land Office spoke of him "in the highest terms of praise." But the commissioner was fighting a tidal wave of requests. Notwithstanding his "unwearied attention" to his duties he could not get the job done without more assistance; too many people residing at a distance came to Austin for patents only to find they had to wait for days at considerable expense.[29] A changeover in administrations in December, with Sam Houston replacing Lamar as president, put the office even further behind. When the office ran out of the special paper used for patents in early 1842 (paper ordered a year earlier from the United States had never arrived), Ward breathed a sigh of relief, confessing to Houston that he was rather pleased to have a respite for a few weeks. The unrelenting demand for patents had prevented him from paying the attention necessary to the "well being and order of other business" in the office. Houston himself was unfazed by the pause, believing that the rapid patenting of land was conducive to fraud.[30]

Actually, some of the other business of the Land Office had fared tolerably well during 1841, in part thanks to John Borden. Prior to stepping down he had urged Congress, despite the republic's straightened circumstances, to come up with adequate funding for two crucial but lagging functions: translation of the voluminous Spanish language records and the preparation of county maps showing property boundaries, for which a skilled draftsman was needed in the Austin office since county surveyors were falling down on the task. Congress obliged in February 1841. Eight months later, in his first annual report to Congress as commissioner, Ward announced that the translating had progressed "with astonishing rapidity" while the office had derived "much benefit" from the draftsman (his surviving maps reveal him to have been careful and accurate). Most counties, however, still lacked reliable maps. Just think, Ward suggested, how much more benefit there would be if he had two draftsmen.[31]

Ward's report was hardly a self-congratulatory puff piece, but rather a comprehensive indictment of the land system, in particular its legal structure. There were, first of all, far too many different laws bearing on land policy. The numerous laws made his business very complex and tied him to his desk, he would complain to Sam Houston several months later. People were not satisfied with the opinions of his clerks however correct they might be unless he expounded upon them. But it was the many defects in the land laws that really troubled Ward, and he spelled them out in his report, subjecting one law after another to detailed criticism. The only solution lay in repealing them all and "embodying all their best provisions in one full and explanatory Law."[32]

The crux of his concern was an issue raised in the Constitution of 1836 but never resolved. Section 10 specified, with a view to simplifying the land system and protecting the citizenry and the government from litigation and fraud, that the "whole territory" of the republic be "sectionized." That single word had huge implications, referring as it did to the rectangular system of surveying public lands used in the United States and pioneered in the Northwest Territory. When U.S. public lands were surveyed, tiers of townships six miles square were laid out along lines running north-south and east-west. The townships were subdivided into thirty-six sections, each a mile square (640 acres), and each section was then subdivided into 160-acre quarter sections for sale to the public. This was a far cry from the "indiscriminate" method of surveying common in the southern United States and second nature to the many Texans who immigrated from that region. Their custom was to roam where they pleased, select a tract that took advantage of the best natural features of the land no matter what its shape, and designate its boundaries by trees, creeks, and stakes. The result was often a hodgepodge of irregular and imprecisely defined claims that sometimes infringed on each other—in other words an invitation to litigation. Selection of land in Texas under Mexican rule was similarly haphazard (empresarios like Stephen F. Austin let colonists choose their tracts from any unappropriated land within their colony), and surveying practices were inconsistent and inexact. The rectangular system, in contrast, was efficient and precise, minimized litigation, and facilitated the orderly transfer of public land to individuals.[33]

The first Congress took halting, halfway steps toward implementing the rectangular system. First, the legislators switched from using Spanish measurements (a league and a labor) for headrights to acres, in numbers compatible with 640-acre sections (320, 640, 1280). Then, in mid-1837, Congress mandated that the commissioner of the General Land

Office survey and sectionize, in tracts of 640 and 320 acres, enough vacant land to satisfy all claims for headrights, bounty and donation grants, and land scrip. Congress even directed that the entire republic be sectionized and that all new surveys for both individuals and the government be square if possible, though the surveys did not have to conform to sectional lines. But large-scale surveying projects were expensive, time consuming, cumbersome to implement in areas where some land was already titled, and sometimes dangerous. In 1838 all but six members of a twenty-five-man surveying party were killed when they were attacked by 300 Kickapoos. For financially strapped Texas the project was too much to stomach, and some legislators feared it would encourage land speculation. Nor did Texans seized with land fever relish the delays sectioning would involve. Texas officials may also have been aware of the headaches experienced by surveyors in nearby Louisiana as they extended the U.S. system over the entire state following its purchase from France in 1803, replacing land practices instituted under French and Spanish rule. Congress settled in December 1837 for declaring each county a section as a fulfillment of Section 10 of the Constitution. Each county surveyor was required to produce a map of his county on which plats of all deeded lands were recorded. It was a tactic that John H. Reagan, an experienced surveyor and soon to become one of Texas's best known politicians, would call "plainly a subterfuge and an evasion of the constitutional requirement" but one that "was from necessity sustained."[34]

In Ward's eyes it bordered on dereliction of duty, and he made no bones about it. The Constitution intended Texas to be sectionized in the U.S. manner, he insisted, and the failure to do so had already cost the republic nearly as much as rectangular surveying would have. Visitors familiar with the sectioned part of the United States "look upon our system with horror," he pointed out, for they see nothing in it but "law suits, trouble and litigation." Ward would soon concede that it was too late to implement the U.S. system, but he never backed off from the position that it should have been done in the first place. As for Congress's substitute, treating counties as sections, he admitted that it might satisfy the Constitution but only if Congress made sweeping reforms. The problems were legion. County boundaries were not defined precisely and many were in dispute. Few of the old titled lands had been platted on county maps with accuracy, and there was no provision made for paying surveyors for such work. Since county surveyors were elected by the voters, the most popular candidate, not the most competent or trustworthy, often gained offic e. "There are now men in offic e, who declare themselves incompetent to make a map of their County," he told Congress. Furthermore, county surveyors were not immediately responsible to any authority. That problem had concerned Borden, too, and he lobbied unsuccessfully for appointment of a surveyor-general in the Land Offic e. Ward simply proposed putting them under "one head," but anyone knowing the commissioner could not have doubted whom he had in mind for the job. In the United States, as Ward must have been aware, the surveyors in charge of each land district were appointed from above and were under the authority of the commissioner of the U.S. General Land Offic e. Whatever Congress did about reforming the land system, Ward concluded, it was imperative that "some plan [be] adopted by which the Country can be sectionized."[35]

James Harper Starr was impressed. "I have perused your 'Annual Report' with much satisfaction," he wrote Ward, "and am glad to see that you are laboring to remove the confusion & uncertainty in our land system, which . . . render individual claims to the soil of so little worth—If you succeed to the extent of your wishes a great work will have been accomplished." But Starr doubted Ward's recommendations would be adopted. There were too many Texans of the "genus speculator," who hold lands only for the purpose of selling them tomorrow and would resist the "present expenses" of "permanent advantages." For that reason, but also for several others, Ward would find it tough sledding getting action on his proposals in the years ahead. As historian Randolph Campbell has written, the infant republic was "plagued by factional politics and chaotic finances" throughout its ten years and "struggled constantly just to survive"—not exactly fertile ground for Ward's reforms.[36]

Reality set in for the commissioner not long after Sam Houston won election as president in September 1841, hell-bent on retrenchment. Within weeks Ward, like other government officials, found his staff pruned and his salary slashed, in his case from $3,000 to $1,200. Luckily, Congress had second thoughts, bumped his salary up to $1,500, and added four positions to the six already authorized, including the much-wanted second draftsman, but salaries were meager—too meager to attract qualified draftsmen to prepare the all-important county maps. H. L Upshur, the draftsman who had performed so admirably during 1841, left the office when his salary shrank from $3,000 a year to $700. Times were suddenly lean for government clerks. Congress "raked the boys down smart," one of them remarked.[37]

Houston had good reason for frugality. The republic was insolvent, its paper money worth but one-seventh of its face value, a crisis attributable to both reckless spending by the Lamar administration and a "terrible pecuniary depression" that had descended on Texas in 1840. Money was scarce, trade dull, land values stagnant, indebtedness everywhere. Houston himself was in financial trouble during 1841, reduced to asking a friend for a loan. So was Ward. In May he confessed to Andrew Briscoe in Houston that he was in urgent need of money and prodded him to get Augustus Allen to settle once and for all the judgments Ward had won against the Allens in 1837 and 1838, now amounting to more than $10,000. How could he, responded Briscoe, when the local sheriff, who was supposed to enforce the court's order, was himself insolvent and was "consequently in favor of no man's paying a debt except for a gaming consideration!"[38] "Poor Texas," Houstonian James Reily fretted in a letter to Ward that summer. "You who have fought & suffered so intensely & so much in her service have reason almost to despair. No one has money. Persons are destitute of even the comforts, some of the necessaries of life." In September Briscoe pried a settlement out of Allen and his associates for a small portion of the debt—not in currency, but in Houston-area land worth millions today, but then of scant value. Allen promptly wangled an injunction barring further sale of his property to satisfy the judgment. Still in a financial fix and convinced that Allen would "probably evade the payment of the debt for years to come," Ward broached with Briscoe the possibility of resorting to violence: "The present Congress will do nothing for us, but I fear will drive us to the use of the pistol or rifle." Briscoe himself was disgusted with the machinations of the Allen crowd—an alliance of swindlers and their tools, in his view. He replied ominously, "If Congress do nothing for you, I see no remedy but the pistol and Bowie knife. What I mean is cold premeditated murder in such a way as to avoid suspicion without ever acquainting me with your design."[39]

Dangerously frustrated by the protracted struggle with Allen, Ward also confronted a delicate political situation in Austin. When his good friend and patron David Burnet declared for the presidency in 1841,

Ward understandably backed him in his race against Sam Houston. But Houston crushed Burnet, and Ward found himself beholden to a man his friends had been vilifying for months in a campaign marked by a relentless spewing of invective on both sides. Burnet charged Houston with "beastly intemperance" and called him "Big Drunk." Houston called Burnet a "canting hypocrite" and "hog thief" and accused him of "foul unmitigated treason." Even Houston's victory failed to stem the flow of vitriol. "We have selected a President; oh, God and such a President!" an Austin newspaper whined, "a bloated and heretic blasphemer! a worn out and hopeless drunkard!"[40] Ward thus had political fences to mend as he approached the end of his first year in office. Appointed by Burnet to serve John Borden's unexpired term, at least he still had a year and a half before coming up for reappointment, time enough to placate his new chief.

Looking back on his first year as commissioner, Ward had much to be pleased about, despite his exasperation with the land system. Francis Moore Jr., longtime editor of the republic's most prominent newspaper, the *Telegraph and Texas Register*, certainly thought the commissioner merited kudos for his performance, as Moore made plain in a January 1842 issue: "He has by his urbane deportment and unwearied assiduity, secured the approbation of almost every person who has transacted business in that office. Under his direction a complete system of discipline has been established, which has resulted in the transaction of the whole business of the office with an expedition and accuracy that has never been excelled in any other department of the government." Above all in the eyes of many Texans, Ward had jump-started the patenting process, issuing more than 1,400 patents for headrights, bounty and donation grants, and land scrip and thereby taking a large step toward stabilizing property rights in the fragile and disorderly republic. Looking forward, he must have expected to forge ahead with reforms in the administration of Texas's vast public domain. Little did he know that he was about to become embroiled in a political brawl that would shut down his office for months and turn many of his fellow Austinites against him.[41]

CHAPTER 6

"Old Peg" and the Archive War

THOMAS WILLIAM WARD's thirty-fifth birthday celebration, on June 20, 1842, was one he undoubtedly remembered until his death—for the pleasure it afforded, and then the humiliation. In a private letter, one of Ward's bumptious clerks, James (Jim) Long, described what befell "Old Peg" (as his clerks called him behind his back).★ As the momentous day approached, Long related, Old Peg decided that "he like all other great men must need celebrate it." Some 200 residents were left in Austin at the time. Three months earlier Sam Houston had moved the government, except for the Land Office, back to his namesake city. Nevertheless the commissioner wanted a bash. The Land Office was "transmogrified and turned into a ball room at the expense of no little labor." Boughs of cedar trees decorated the room, and it was adorned with the furniture from the president's mansion. Invitations "in the finest style" were distributed to ladies and gentlemen in the area. On June 20 the company assembled for dinner and drank "a thousand healths" to the commissioner; "the scene closed with a dance."[1]

Peg Leg was so pleased by the event that he resolved to repeat it, this time with Austin's African-American residents in attendance. June 25 was set aside for a "hellsoaring frolic." Ward instructed his slave Clarissa to pass the word. The Land Office was again decorated for a ball, with large mirrors from the president's house suspended from the walls and the room ringed with sofas, side tables, and chairs. One table was spread with wines and sweet cakes. All was arranged "in a manner that would

★The 1842 correspondence of Ward's clerks provides the earliest surviving evidence of the use of the nicknames "Peg Leg" and "Old Peg." For more information on these nicknames, see the Appendix.

have done credit to the most aristocratic circles." On the afternoon of the 25th Austin's black community, along with some white residents, assembled at the Land Office. Old Shade, the shoemaker, struck up the tune of "Roaring River" and in no time the dance was "under full headway."[2]

But the commissioner had crossed a line that some white Austinites considered inviolate, Jim Long among them. "To think that one of the Public offices of the government, and that too in which all the papers and archives of the Govt had been stored for safe keeping together with the Presidents furniture—should be set apart and appropriated for a negro ball room!" Exasperated at Ward's conduct, they resolved to break up "Old Peg's negro ball." A large nail keg was filled with the contents of a privy together with a "sufficient quantity" of water, the hoops were loosened so that it would fall apart when hitting the floor, and the keg was lobbed through a back window into the middle of the ballroom, where it exploded and the foul mixture scattered all over the room. The partygoers fled, but Ward was "struck dumb and motionless" and stood for about five minutes in the midst of the fetid mess without speaking a word or even holding his nose. "At length recovering a little, he seized his gun, peged out into the yard, and challenged the town enmasse." This tactic failing to produce the culprit, he offered a reward of $200 in gold for anyone who would undertake his "apprehension and delivery." There were no takers. Ward retreated from the scene, and "the crowd went off victorious." For days afterwards the incident was the "whole topic of conversation" in town and "afforded much amusement to all." Wags mockingly threatened one another: better watch out or you'll get "a keg of shit" thrown in your window.[3]

For Ward the gross affront must have been mortifying. It "perfectly cooled the old Cock down," Long noted smugly. Cooling down was not what people had come to expect of Old Peg in such a situation. Years later when he told a friend, while in the midst of a diplomatic brouhaha in Panama, that he would never submit to any indignity let the consequences be what they may, his friend remarked to another, "he need not have told this to his old acquaintances." More in character was Ward's first response to the incident, grabbing his gun and threatening the townspeople gathered outside. But whom to challenge to a duel? How to redeem his honor? Somehow—extant sources shed no further light on the issue—Peg Leg coped with it and he moved on.

The episode, however, reflected and further embittered a deepening rift between the commissioner and the community. He soon found himself, in his own words, "almost totally excluded from such society as the place affords." The isolation was painful, but such was the price, he believed, of loyalty to his chief, Sam Houston, and of faithfulness to the duties of his office.[4]

The trouble had started the previous March. The month opened on a quiet note, with Austin "very dull" and "very sparse of population," Ward wrote Houston. Following Congress's adjournment on February 5, its members had dispersed and the president had headed by mule for Houston. Ward stayed put but announced that he would not issue any patents for at least two months due to running run out of blanks.[5] Austinites were no doubt relieved that no action had been taken to move the seat of government eastward. It was common knowledge that the president despised Austin and wanted to return the capital to Houston, a far more secure and convenient location in his view. Rumors circulated that if Congress did not act, the president might do so on his own authority. On the last day of the session Houston made clear to the legislators his dismay at how vulnerable the national archives were to enemy attack in Austin and how irreparable an injury their loss would be. Knowing the president was keen to make a move, Washington Miller, his twenty-seven-year-old private secretary and confidant, cautioned him in early March not to act precipitously: The "people of the West" were enamored with the idea of the capital being in Austin, he warned. "Under no circumstances will they consent to its removal so long as it may be practicable for them to prevent it—and under no circumstance will they consent to see the archives of the government removed (and this they are disposed to regard as paving the way to the final removal of the capitol)," except, Miller added, "in case of serious and actual invasion."[6]

Rumors of a Mexican invasion trickled in from San Antonio during late February and early March but were shrugged off. "We didn't believe such stuff," one resident, William Abell, admitted later. Thus the several hundred souls living in the remote community were stunned when on March 6 breathless messengers brought news, first that a large force was advancing on San Antonio, and then that evening that the town had fallen to some 500 Mexican troops believed to be the advance guard of a large invading army. Hours later came word that

Goliad had succumbed. Estimates in Austin of the invading force ranged from several hundred to 30,000. No one was sure just what the Mexican army was up to, but they thought they knew its next move.[7]

Officials and citizens in the capital, just eighty miles from San Antonio, scrambled to prepare for an attack. "It exceeded any excitement I ever saw," Abell remembered. Before the day was out Secretary of War George Hockley, a tested veteran who had commanded artillery at the Battle of San Jacinto, ordered the Texas militia in Travis and Bastrop Counties to rendezvous posthaste in the capital and instructed Ward to deploy artillery. Guards were posted and spies on horseback dispatched into the countryside south and west of town. Citizens formed a vigilance committee and called upon women and children to flee immediately to safer country. Government clerks hastened to box up and bury the national archives—land records, treaties and diplomatic correspondence, military service records, financial papers—the legal, administrative, and historical underpinning of Texas. "I will defend the archives to the Knife," Hockley assured Houston in a letter that evening. Less important papers were left in place on office desks to deceive the enemy.[8]

The following day (March 7) the women and children left town "in tears & in haste," the vigilance committee impressing teams of horses for the purpose. Men fled as well, including two members of the vigilance committee who skedaddled two days later with bag and baggage. Hockley declared martial law, closed all the saloons and grog shops, and prohibited men from leaving without permission from Ward or himself. Three infantry companies of Travis County men began "marching and counter marching—drilling and watching, and eating heartily and talking largely," reported Washington Miller, a Travis County militiaman. Two mounted companies from Bastrop County soon joined them, making a total force of some 225 citizen-soldiers, commanded by Colonel Henry Jones. To Miller's disgust a number of pretentious gentlemen, "very garrulous in prognosticating results," shunned the militia and chose instead to do "the windwork of the war."[9]

Put in charge of ordinance in addition to his responsibility for posting artillery, Peg Leg was on the go but no doubt undaunted, for he took readily to command. He placed two cannon on President's Hill east of Congress Avenue to command fords of the Colorado River immediately above and below town should enemy troops approach from the south, and another cannon on Capitol Hill west of Congress Avenue to guard against approaches from the west and the Hill Country. At the same time, he set about supplying the five militia companies with muskets, ammunition, and bayonets from the Austin arsenal. The size of the enemy remained in doubt, some crediting a report that the troops in San Antonio were not the vanguard of a larger force, others expecting the worst. Acting Quartermaster Jacob Snively expressed in a March 8 letter both the grittiness and apprehension of many defenders: "We will make a stand and defend the Archives to the last extremety, I have no doubt that western Texas will be over run and laid to waste."[10] But two more days passed with no sign of the enemy. On March 10 an express reported the Mexican army still in San Antonio. Another day or two of anxious waiting followed. Finally came deliverance—news that Mexican troops had evacuated San Antonio and retreated "Rio Grande-wards" loaded with plunder. It was a raid, not an invasion. The capital was safe. Hockley issued a proclamation urging the citizenry to stay home and no longer flee a phantom menace.[11]

And then the blow fell—not from the Mexican army to the south but from Sam Houston to the east. Late on March 15 a message arrived from the president ordering all government archives transferred forthwith to his namesake city. At an impromptu meeting that evening, Secretary of War Hockley conferred with Ward and Colonel Jones, the militia commander Hockley had placed in charge of the town when he declared martial law. A resident of the frontier and a veteran Indian fighter, Jones was a man of his own mind. Wary that he might balk at the order, Hockley, a longtime Houston partisan, made sure Jones understood he was required to obey it. He directed Ward to superintend the move. The conversation ended with Hockley under the impression both men were on board.[12] The secretary soon learned how mistaken he was about Jones. Ward, however, took Sam Houston's side and never looked back, true to his conception of his role as a government officer. As he later told James Harper Starr, his "sole ambition" as land commissioner was to know his duty and "perform it at all hazards." It was not his right to construe for himself the legality of the president's measures with a view to determining his official conduct, but to obey constituted authority or resign his office. Peg Leg's decision that day would earn him reappointment as land commissioner but almost cost him his life.[13]

The next morning Hockley and Ward got more than an inkling of what lay ahead. "Awful threats and terrific declarations have been uttered," Miller wrote Houston even before an aroused body of Austin and Travis County citizens assembled in protest at 10:00 a.m. When Samuel Whiting rose to chair the meeting he looked out an imposing group of leading property holders, armed militiamen, Colonel Jones, even Miller himself. Whiting had his own good reasons for challenging the president's order. A resident of Austin since 1839, he had seized on its opportunities, publishing its first and longest-lived newspaper, the *Austin City Gazette*, winning a contract as public printer, investing in buildings and other property in town, and speculating in land in the area. Convinced that Sam Houston "was predetermined to destroy Austin," he believed that removal of the archives meant relocation of the government and would spell his financial ruin, and eventually it did. "We are holding on to the Archivs like death to a dead negro," he wrote a friend three weeks later, "& are determined they shall not be taken from here 'till ordered by a higher power than Sam Houston."[14]

Despite the heightened emotions, the tone of the meeting that morning was restrained. Former Secretary of State James Mayfield gave voice to the anxieties of the gathering—that the capital would be abandoned to the "savage," the frontier desolated, and those who had dared to settle the west betrayed, many ruined. The participants signed a letter asking Hockley to suspend execution of Houston's order until they communicated with the president. He could not have been aware of the actual situation on the frontier, they argued, or he would never have issued it. The archives were safe, the enemy gone. The constitution authorized removal of the government only if Congress permitted it or if, in case of emergency in time of war, the public interest required it. But no such emergency existed any longer.[15]

Secretary Hockley responded swiftly and tersely. The president knew the true state of affairs on the frontier and had the authority to do what he did. His orders must be obeyed. At 4:00 p.m. Whiting convened the citizens' second meeting that day. Disappointed but undeterred, the group approved resolutions that escalated the conflict. If an attempt were made to remove the archives contrary to law (as they understood it), they would not stand idly by but instead would "return them to their proper places" and protect them from further attack—in other words use force. Colonel Jones held those cards and was prepared to play them. He ordered the Travis Guards to station a contingent on the outskirts of town to stop any wagons or horsemen from leaving unless in possession of his written permission.[16]

"The excitement still runs high," Miller advised Sam Houston the following day (March 17) and indeed it did. Hockley struck back quickly, Jones in his sights. He ended martial law, ordered Jones to send all his troops still in Austin home, furloughed the Travis Guards himself, and directed Ward to take charge of ordnance supplied to the militia. Ward commanded Jones to turn in all muskets, artillery, and other equipment. Hockley's hand was weak, however, and he knew it. He faced a rebellious citizenry with no military force to carry out Houston's wishes, and he was reluctant to use force, even had he had it. He rushed a "Private & Confidential" message to Houston's emissary, Colonel William Pettus, then on his way to Austin with whatever transportation he could muster for the archives, commanding him to halt "at some convenient place."[17]

While Hockley publicly counterattacked but privately retreated, his tormenters held more public meetings to advance their cause. They fired off a remonstrance to Sam Houston asking him to countermand his order—to no avail, they learned later—and pledged to sustain whatever vigorous measures Colonel Jones chose to pursue to retain the archives. As a first step they agreed to raise a company on their own in place of the troops Hockley had demobilized. Jones set up headquarters in an office adjacent to Bullock's Hotel, in the center of town, and posted orders anew requiring inspection of wagons leaving town. Hockley, who by then was understandably feeling out of sorts, decided it was time to tell Houston he could not pull off the removal and, moreover, that any attempt to do so would provoke violence and bloodshed. Jones's men soon made sure of that by seizing possession of the Austin arsenal with its cannon, small arms, and ammunition.[18] By then the "Archives war party," as opponents dubbed the insurgents, not only controlled Austin and Travis County, but also enjoyed widespread support beyond the capital, especially after James Webb, the area's most popular legislator, traveled through Bastrop, Fayette, and other nearby counties organizing the citizenry. A visitor from Houston reported that the people west of the Brazos River all the way to Austin declared "they would much rather take their rifles to prevent a removal than to fight Mexicans." [19]

It was a turn of events that had others gritting their teeth. "The town is guarded by a regular organized Company of disorganizers," an exasperated State Department clerk wrote a friend. Washington Miller railed against the "mob rule" and the "treason and open insurrection" of its leader, Colonel Jones.[20] Such sentiments were heard less and less in Austin, however, because many of those voicing them left town and left Peg Leg increasingly isolated. While Sam Houston grudgingly relented on moving the archives, if only for the moment, he ordered the government and all its officers to his namesake city. Anyone refusing was out of a job. Hockley and Miller departed at once. Clerks and other "Government boys" joined them by mid-April, but Peg Leg stayed behind. As he explained to the president, he knew no one in Austin he could trust with the Land Office archives, nor could a new office be opened in Houston without them. Were he ordered to move them to a place of greater safety, he suggested, he would willingly obey, even at the risk of his personal safety.[21]

On April 4 a messenger left the Bayou City for Austin with the order from the president that Ward had invited: "You are hereby invested with all proper and necessary authority to remove the archives of the government from the city of Austin to the city of Houston. . . . A force competent to effect this highly necessary object, will be furnished upon your requisition." Ward decided to see if he could pull if off without force, perhaps surreptitiously or perhaps thinking there was still a chance his fellow Austinites might be reluctant to carry through on their threats, especially since he had a letter from Houston for Jones stating that the Colonel would be punished for treason if he or anyone acting on his orders interfered. Ward arranged with local teamsters to provide three wagons, enough to transport the Land Office records, and set Monday, April 18, as the day of departure.[22]

The week leading up to April 18 gave Ward abundant reason for pause, and events that day stopped him almost literally dead in his tracks. Residents on the frontier, he learned, would go to almost any lengths to hold on to the archives, seeing them "as a kind of hostage for the return of the government," as one Austinite later put it.[23] The week started ominously with a mass meeting of 300 in the capital. Two days later, with word about Ward's intentions clearly getting around, the insurgents established a Committee of Vigilance and Safety to put more teeth into their surveillance. That evening Henry Jewett called on Ward in behalf of the citizens and offered him three wagons to remove the Land Office records to a safer place if and when they believed them to be in danger; otherwise the citizens would resist. Though weakened by a fever, Peg Leg had by no means lost his nerve. He turned Jewett down flat. Still feverish two days later, Peg Leg nevertheless went on the offensive and dispatched his deputy to Jones's home to deliver Houston's letter ordering the Colonel not to interfere. Like Jewett, Jones sought to mollify Ward by assuring him that wagons would be made available in a crisis but advised him otherwise to expect resistance, a message reiterated the next day by emissaries from the Committee of Vigilance and Safety. Ward did not budge. On Sunday, with just a day to go, his adversaries upped the pressure. Jones visited Ward at his rooms adjacent to the Land Office to announce he had sidestepped Houston's order by resigning his commission. Unarmed but leading a party he intended to prevent Ward from loading a single box, and should Peg Leg resort to arms—everyone knew he was no stranger to violence—he should prepare for bloodshed.[24]

Early Monday morning twenty armed men rode into Austin from Bastrop County vowing to stop the commissioner. A local resident tipped off Ward and warned him there might be an attempt on his life. One of the vigilantes, a fellow Ward had tangled with as commissioner over a land transaction, had threatened that if shooting started he would "pick his men," meaning Peg Leg and some of his clerks. Things heated up further at a midday rally of citizens. Apparently apprehensive the situation might get out of hand, Jones himself called on Ward later in the day and offered his services to protect him from assassination. Far too proud to accept the offer, Ward declined. Armed intimidation, however, was more than Ward's teamsters had bargained for. Ward suddenly found the three wagons unavailable—and that ended it. Years later an aged Austinite recalled that when Peg Leg realized he had been foiled, "there followed perhaps the most picturesque volley of profanity the world ever heard." Ward's advice to Houston that evening was more to the point: "I think it would be the best policy to make Austin the head quarters of one or two Brigades that could be relied upon and would protect the civil authorities of the Country in the discharge of their duties."[25]

Thwarted by determined opponents, the commissioner decided to await further instructions from President Houston. The threat of violence subsided and life went on, but the business of the Land Office came to a virtual stop. The office records had been boxed up and buried following the capture of San Antonio, then were dug up within a week and repacked in strong boxes for shipment, and they stayed that way. Ward wanted them ready at a moment's notice for removal to Houston or, in case of another sudden Mexican incursion, to any safe location. Few in Austin discounted Santa Anna's military meddlesomeness. In fact, just five weeks later, in mid-May, the town was shaken by rumors of another invasion. Ward warned officials in Houston that if true, Austin and its archives were "easy prey." The rumors proved false; but in September panic seized the town once more when Mexican troops captured San Antonio for a second time that year. Houston was convinced they intended to sack and burn the capital. Instead they retreated south after taking heavy casualties in a battle with Texas volunteers. The archives thus were seen to be in constant danger. Knowing how determined Houston was to remove them from Austin and how concerned he was for their safety in the meantime, Ward was not about to concede any hint of victory to Houston's enemies by conducting business as usual in Austin.[26]

The upshot was that while Ward stayed in Austin, his clerks had no ready access to the Land Office records they needed to do their job. The boxes were unpacked with some frequency to air the contents, especially after spells of wet weather; on occasion they may have been opened to examine certain items, as they were in one instance for a court case. Otherwise the records remained packed and stored for the rest of the year.[27] One incoming letter after another to the commissioner, many of them inquiries from county surveyors and aspiring patent holders, were marked "cannot be answered until the archives are had" or "to be answered when records are open for business." Outgoing correspondence ceased entirely. Issuing of patents, already suspended, did not recommence. "'Old Peg' will discharge most if not all of us," one clerk worried as the slow times dragged on. During the spring and summer months the office remained ostensibly open but conducted little business. Following the September incursion, the commissioner officially closed the General Land Office until further notice together with the operations of all county surveyors and boards of land commissioners, invoking an 1837 law that authorized him to do so if the republic was invaded and the president called out the militia. "Every man here speaks highly of the order," Ward explained to Houston in defense of his move. The commissioner believed that Congress's intent in passing the law was to prevent those remaining at home from selecting the best lands for themselves while the soldiers were away defending their country. Ward sympathized with that goal, but he may also have wanted to provide a legal basis for keeping the General Land Office records boxed up and business at a standstill. The order remained in effect for seven months, until May 1843. Texans could not even lay claim to lands by having them officially surveyed, much less get them patented.[28]

If business at the Land Office languished during 1842, so did Austin itself. By May the capital was a ghost-like town of scarcely 200 people, still beautiful, but forlorn. The cumulative impact of the first Mexican invasion and the departure of the government had depopulated the town, exposing it to Indian depredations that further desolated the once proud capital. "Little remains of its former greatness," lamented William Murrah, one of Ward's clerks. "The streets look lonely and deserted and the wind sighs mournfully around the Corners of vacant Houses."[29] The pace of life slackened. "We have nothing to do, and nobody to do it," Jim Long complained, "no money and no use for it— a plenty of good liquor and but few to drink it." Ward's clerks were restless. They not only had little work to do but few friends to party with now that the other government boys had moved on to Houston. "We kill time about as fast as we ever did," commented one of their chums, fishing, hunting, playing cards, and keeping their spirits up by pouring the spirits down. But even killing time could get tiresome. "*Glory to God*" declared Long when Ward left for Houston in late May to consult with the president, but when the commissioner returned and spoke of putting his staff back to work Long welcomed the idea: "I am worn out a loafing." Murrah, who had clerked for Ward more than a year by then, longed for the old days: "I really wish that things would come strait again, that the seat of Government would remain here, that all the same fellows would return, and that we could have some of our good old times again; for now we can do nothing but lounge about— and hope for better times."[30]

Romancing helped alleviate the boredom. There were at least twenty Austin women in search of beaus. Murrah's spirits were buoyed when one particular "little widdow" reappeared in town and took her place "among many other twinkling gems that illume our deserted village." At the Fourth of July celebration "all hands got pretty mellow," Long confided to a friend, and that night "*the ladies were assembled and what followed you know.*" Even Peg Leg got into the act, with dubious results. Joel Miner, Sam Whiting's printer, reported that "'Old Peg' has been paying his devours to Mrs. Barker for some time past, but a few nights since they had a blow up, and she came in to Haynie's to get a pistol to shoot him"—or at least that was what Miner was told. Later on his source denied the story. Whatever the case, Miner thought Peg Leg's intentions from the outset were "not of an honorable character."[31]

Despite the opportunities for courting, Ward's clerks obviously found living in Austin during 1842 a trial. They found Ward a trial, too, and he them. The commissioner had a reputation for quarreling with his clerks, reportedly going through three or four sets during his first year-and-a-half in office. He clearly was not in a forgiving mood during the spring and summer of 1842. Ward dismissed two clerks for siding with the "anti-removal party" and a third who threatened to join the army even if it meant leaving the commissioner in the lurch. Then he fired Jim Long following a confrontation and sacked his longest serving clerk, George Durham, for discourtesy, apparently in a huff over a trivial matter—he refused to lend the commissioner his fishing rod after Ward had refused to lend him a spur. Ward admitted he was finding his restive clerks difficult to manage but expected Durham's ouster to bring them to heel, at least the three who were left. His clerks learned that Ward was still not a man to cross, even though his opposition to the insurgency had marginalized his position in the community.[32]

If Ward was testy that summer he was also uneasy, with good reason. "Every man woman and child are daily pouring forth their curses against old Sam," Long reported; "between us and the gate post—I should not be surprised if he should meet an untimely fate." Peg Leg, old Sam's man in Austin, was a much more convenient target. When, in June, old Sam called a session of Congress to meet in Houston, not Austin, it "kicked up a h-ll of a dust in the west," according to Long. "This added to the archives question has doubly raised the Irish of these Colorado fellows." They all suspected Peg Leg of plotting to betray their interests, and he knew it. As he wrote his former deputy, Matthew Woodhouse, then acting secretary of the treasury, "They are aware that I rec[eive]d orders to remove the archives and have been suspicious that I would remove them secretly." But he would not explain it away for fear of creating distrust in Houston's mind. "In Texas a man's best intentions are misconstrued and oftentimes we are belied, so I thought of the old scriptural phrase 'thou canst not serve God & Mammon' and kept my instructions to myself and myself from the people." As a consequence, he told Woodhouse, his life was rendered more disagreeable than anyone could imagine. One evening in September, when feelings were running especially high in Austin following Houston's decision to move the government to Washington-on-the-Brazos, someone snatched Ward's musket from his hand and fired at him, but he managed to keep a finger on the muzzle and deflect the shot. "It was fired at me in consequence of my position here," he told Houston.[33]

By then the commissioner had come to believe that the people of Austin would never let the archives go "until the last family leaves," and so informed the president. The final straw was his clash with the Committee of Safety over removal of the archives to a more secure location after the fall of San Antonio in September. The committee refused to let Ward determine where they would be taken or how, an arrangement he felt he could hardly accept when he was acting as the president's agent for their safety.[34]

Sam Houston had had enough, too. The second Mexican foray into San Antonio was all the more proof in his eyes that Austin was unsafe for the seat of government. Furthermore it was aggravating trying to run the government without its records. "We are now going on as if we had begun in the Spring, *de novo*," Washington Miller grumbled, lacking "even the secret correspondence of the State Department or the ratified treaties." The session of Congress that met that summer in the Bayou City had gone back and forth over the issue of the capital—the most hotly debated of Houston's second term—without resolving it. Now that the president had settled on Washington-on-the-Brazos until Congress made up its mind, he wanted the archives moved there in short order. In October he directed Ward to requisition whatever means he needed to get it done and asked John Chenoweth, an anti-insurgent ally who lived near Austin, to lend Ward a hand. The situation was critical, Houston explained to Chenoweth, with the archives unsafe and the position of the commissioner far from pleasant.[35]

Austin, however, seemed as fixated as ever on regaining its former status. Not a day went by without people "cursing Old Sam," and their anger and frustration took many forms. They impaneled a grand jury, with Sam Whiting as foreman, that indicted Houston for "moral treason" for causing the "total ruin" of the once flourishing population of the upper Colorado.[36] When Houston dispatched Comptroller James Shaw to Austin to retrieve stationery and account books, they got wind of his mission and decided to make an example of him. He had ridden into Austin on a "fine blooded" mare, accompanied by a friend. That evening both horses' manes and tails were shaved and their ears cut off (an action for which Travis County was thereupon nicknamed "Shavetail county"). The Committee of Safety informed Shaw that if the president wanted stationery all he needed to do was to come back to Austin with his government. Shaw returned empty-handed and, according to a Houston newspaper, "exposed to the jokes and jeers of every wag on the road."[37] A few extremists went so far as to threaten to burn the archives if Congress ordered the president to remove them. Worried that they might actually carry through on their threats, Ward secretly moved the boxes of Land Office records into his private rooms.[38]

The defiance, however, masked a growing despair as Austin's population dwindled and its economy reverted to barter. Those remaining felt more vulnerable than ever to Indians in the area who occasionally preyed upon them. "We are God-forsaken and . . . given over to bats and Bollixes and bad liquor," Joel Miner quipped.[39] Sam Whiting admitted that he had lost all hope of the seat of government returning to Austin, not to speak of having personally "gone through troubles enough . . . to have put an end to almost any other mortal man living." His *Austin City Gazette* had ceased publication, and he was stuck with $7,000 worth of equipment and supplies that were no longer safe in Austin but which he could not afford to move. The majority of Austinites, Whiting included, had decided to sustain the authorities if Congress authorized a removal. Meanwhile Ward delayed carrying out Houston's instructions to organize a removal, in part due to complications occasioned by high water, too few horses, and too many Indians in the area.[40]

In an address to Congress on December 1 the president demanded that the archives be moved to Washington-on-the-Brazos and called on the legislators to support him. Before Congress had a chance to get bogged down in debate over the issue, Houston took matters into his own hands. In a December 10 letter he ordered two hard-bitten Indian fighters, Thomas I. Smith and Eli Chandler, to raise a sufficient force to spirit away the archives—all of them—together with any government supplies and hustle them to Washington-on-the-Brazos. For the archives alone Houston estimated that at least ten to fifteen wagons would be required. "Do not be thwarted in the undertaking," he exhorted, and "by no means let your object be known till you are ready to act. Threats have been made, that if the archives are ever removed, they will be in ashes." He advised that men be recruited on the pretense they were joining an Indian expedition. Upon arriving in Austin, Smith and Chandler were to report to Ward, whom Houston informed of the plot in a separate letter and then added, "Though I have not often written you, yet have I often thought of you, and your unpleasant position, surrounded as you are by so many difficulties and disagreeable circumstances. I hope that you will soon be relieved and placed in a community where you may be free from so many harassments." Finally, it appeared, there was going to be a resolution of the standoff that had crippled the work of the Land Office, set Austin against the commissioner, and tied the country in knots.[41]

In *The Raven,* his 1929 Pulitzer Prize-winning biography of Sam Houston, Marquis James provided an appealing if brief version of what befell Thomas Smith and his men when they entered Austin to steal away with the nation's archives:

> At midnight on December thirtieth Mrs. Angelina Ebberly, a boarding-house mistress whose table had been depleted by the turn of affairs, saw a wagon being loaded in an alley back of the land office. She repaired to Congress Avenue where a six-pound gun had been kept loaded with grape since the days of the Lamar Indian wars. Turning the muzzle toward the land office, she blazed away. The shot perforated the land office and aroused the town. Captain Smith departed with what records he had, but these were captured at daylight and brought back.

James's colorful and seemingly irresistible story has been oft-repeated in popular and scholarly writings but more recently called into question.[42] In fact, James's flair for the dramatic far outran the evidence. Eberly's actions are not mentioned in any reports or recollections of those who participated in the affair nor, indeed, in anything written about it until the 1870s, when she was tentatively given a lesser role, that of applying the torch to the powder of a cannon that an already aroused citizenry had loaded and brought to bear on Houston's men. "The citizens, finding out what was going on," wrote George Gray in 1875 in *A Texas Scrap-Book*, the first account to mention Eberly, "at once armed, and assembled in force. Great excitement prevailed. Cannon charged with grape and canister were brought out and planted. . . . As to who touched off the guns, it is not definitely settled, but it is generally conceded that it was done by Mrs. Eberly." Two years later a detailed history of Austin in the city directory was more circumspect. According to the account, several citizens confronted the intruders at the Land Office and warned them that the people of Austin were determined to retain the archives.

> The seven men then proceeded down the avenue to the place where the cannon was standing. During this time their numbers had been considerably increased, the gun was brought out . . . , charged with canister and sighted for the crowd around the Land Office. . . . As to who applied the fire to the cannon, it is not now definitely known, farther than that a lady previous to its discharge appeared on the ground with a firebrand in her hand, and it is admitted by some posted in regard to the affair that she touched it to the gun.[43]

So where did James get the story of the heroic figure who singlehandedly aroused a sleeping town and saved Austin from the disaster of losing the archives? Probably from an article containing much the same story that was published in 1910, almost seventy years after the affair, by eighty-three-year-old Alexander Terrell, a longtime Austin resident who had moved there from Missouri in 1852.[44]

The events in Austin and Travis County during the last two days of 1842 were truly striking, and Angelina Eberly was definitely a participant in the drama, but she was not its featured player. The best available evidence indicates that the climactic scenes of the Archive War unfolded as follows.

On Friday evening, December 29, Thomas Smith slipped into Austin and presented Ward with Sam Houston's December 10 letter. Welcome news though it was, the commissioner must have grimaced when Smith told him he and Chandler had only three wagons, not the ten to fifteen Houston wanted, and just twenty-six men. Many of their recruits, expecting an Indian expedition, had left for home when informed what the president was really up to.[45] The next morning Ward's clerks prepared the eleven boxes of Land Office archives for the jolting ride ahead (the commissioner decided against sending any other government archives). Soon the well-armed troopers and their three ox-drawn wagons pulled up at the Land Office, taking the town by surprise. But within minutes several stern-faced Austinites confronted them. Upon what authority were they removing public property from the seat of government, Houston's men were asked. Upon the president's, Smith answered. Joseph Robertson, John Nolan, and Charles King, speaking for the citizenry, bluntly informed Smith and Chandler that they respected the president's authority when sanctioned by law but any attempt to remove the archives on the president's authority alone would be resisted. Smith replied that they had better submit or face serious consequences. He was advised to prepare for a fight.[46]

Determined to stop the interlopers, several adamant residents decided that drastic action was called for. The means was right there before them, a howitzer that had been stationed in Congress Avenue near Pecan (Sixth) Street for defense against the Mexicans during the September invasion. They wheeled the gun into place and loaded it. One of their number—reputedly Angelina Eberly—readied a flame to touch off the powder. Two blocks away the objects of their fury prepared to leave, their wagons now loaded with the Land Office records. Just as they started up Congress Avenue, a thunderous boom filled the air. Grape shot rained on the men and wagons, and some pierced Ward's residence adjacent to the Land Office. Miraculously, no one was injured. Shrugging off the bombardment, Smith and company hastened north out of town toward Kenney's Fort, avoiding the more direct route to Washington-on-the-Brazos eastward through Bastrop County for fear of the havoc its citizens might wreak upon them.[47]

By then Austin was abuzz. Tensions were high, the townspeople angry, and Peg Leg suspicious that they were out to get him. He was sure that moments before the cannon was fired he heard the cry, "Blow the old house to pieces" (or "blow the damned old office and house into hell," as he put it in one retelling) and was convinced his residence was the target. Other sources indicate that the wagons and their escort, not Peg Leg, were the target, but his anxiety is understandable. He had, after all, already lost two limbs to cannon fire in traumatic events. Had the "mob" continued to fire, he told Sam Houston, "I could not have answered for the consequences, as I undoubtedly should have defended myself to the last." At a public meeting following the incident someone threatened him with a rifle.[48]

The townspeople were not only hot over the seizure of the archives but in a lather to get them back. Captain Mark Lewis, an experienced fighter, was put in charge of the posse that was forming. But the group was undermanned and short of horses and realized it was foolhardy to set right out in pursuit of Houston's henchmen, especially in light of the warning (spurious, it turned out) from Joseph Daniels, Ward's chief clerk, that Smith and Chandler expected to be reinforced by 100 men. To confront such a large force they needed to haul a cannon along, complicating preparations.[49] How desperate they were to get going was made plain in their near fatal treatment of Dr. Thomas Marston, a physician who resided in Austin with his pregnant wife and young son. John Nolan, one of the men who had challenged Captain Smith outside the Land Office, spotted Marston riding in town and asked him for his horse. When Marston refused, harsh words were exchanged. Nolan leveled his gun at Marston and ordered him to dismount. Nolan's fingers trembled nervously around the trigger of his gun, but before he could shoot, Captain Lewis wrenched the gun from his hands. Marston made his escape, but only for the moment. When an attempt to hitch mules to the cannon failed, an armed committee went after poor Marston's horse again. Suddenly he whipped by at top speed, and cries went up to "stop him," "shoot him," "kill him." Two men who had gone after another horse leveled their guns at him. One fired not intending to kill him, but the other, George Barrett, took dead aim, as he later admitted, only to have his gun misfire. In one of history's odd twists, Marston died a few months later of natural causes, and his widow married Thomas William Ward.[50]

As word of the seizure radiated out from Austin, volunteers rushed to join the posse. Soon a force of about fifty men and teenage boys (including at least one African American, Angelina Eberly's "black boy" Edmund) took off after the archives with the howitzer in tow, most of them on horseback but a few on foot. It was a wintry December afternoon, and the road was muddy from the almost incessant rains of previous days. The going was slow. Daylight began to fade.[51] After about ten miles, Lewis dispatched John Nolan and Joshua Holden with a small party of horsemen to "push on" and overtake Smith's party but not to open fire unless a request to halt was refused. The advance party caught up with the wagons about eighteen miles northeast of Austin, near Kenney's Fort on Brushy Creek.[52]

By then it was nighttime. Nolan and Holden shouted through the blackness that they had come for the archives, would not go back to Austin without them, and had a force of eighty men in a neighboring grove. If fighting erupted, the first to be shot would be the two clerks Ward had put in charge of the archives with instructions not to give them up to anyone for any reason. Smith and Chandler replied that they were acting under executive order to proceed with the archives to Washington-on-the-Brazos but intimated they were not eager for a fight. The two sides agreed to encamp for the night and settle it in the morning. Later that evening the balance of power shifted decisively in Austin's favor when the rest of Lewis's force arrived with the howitzer. At dawn Smith and Chandler found the gun commanding the ground over which their wagons had to pass. Lewis invited them to a powwow. They quickly yielded to his demands, surrendering the archives and, according to Lewis, acknowledging "the justice of our cause." That evening—New Year's Eve—the same wagons used to spirit the archives out of Austin brought them back to town, but not to the Land Office. They were stored in Angelina Eberly's home. Four days later an angry but defeated Sam Houston told Congress he was washing his hands of the matter and would leave it to the people and their representatives to determine what should be done with the archives. The Archive War was over so far as the president was concerned, but for the insurgents in the west the struggle was far from over.[53]

The Archive War is sometimes cast as an amusing episode in Texas history—a "farce." After all, the idea that anyone would go to war over archives is difficult to take seriously, and in this conflict no one died. But the issue was dead serious for the people of Austin and Travis County. They had everything to lose if Austin was permanently displaced as capital; temporary displacement was making that devastatingly clear. For much of 1842 they lived on the edge of violence, prepared to use force to hold on to the archives and directly threatening those who refused to cooperate, such as Ward and Thomas Marston. If violence rarely erupted, it was not because people were reluctant to turn violent if they felt circumstances warranted, as happened on

December 30 when several Austinites coldly fired a cannon at more than two dozen fellow Texans a short distance away. Given other circumstances (for instance, had Sam Houston been more aggressive in trying to regain control of the archives or had his men returned fire on December 30) the level of violence could have easily escalated. For four prominent figures that day—Mark Lewis, John Nolan, Joshua Holden, and George Barrett—the disposition to violence was clearly not far below the surface, as each soon demonstrated in vicious incidents. Hostility between John Nolan and Mark Lewis erupted in a shootout in downtown Austin in 1843 in which Lewis killed Nolan. Lewis gave himself up to the sheriff and was being escorted to the justice of the peace's office the next day when George Barrett and a second man rushed into the street with pistols drawn and killed Lewis in revenge. Four years later Joshua Holden got into a heated argument with a local newspaper editor and stabbed him to death.[54]

For Commissioner Ward and the General Land Office, and for innumerable aspiring Texas landholders, the Archive War was a disaster. The conflict for all intents and purposes closed the Land Office indefinitely. At year's end the situation deteriorated further. Ward's collusion with Houston, climaxing in the donnybrook on December 30, left his fellow Austinites more distrustful than ever. At a public meeting held three days later to determine what should be done with the Land Office records, the commissioner asked that they be placed in his charge, promising never again to turn them over to any party whatsoever. The citizens resolved to keep them. Four months later Senator James Webb of Austin gave voice to their unflinching defiance in a letter to Mirabeau Lamar: "We have now but a small population,—no business,—& are living under great privations—We have however, held onto the '*Archives,*' & will battle for them to the death." Not until 1844 would Peg Leg get his Land Office records back.[55]

CHAPTER 7

Recovery and Reform

IN A COUNTRY possessed by land hunger, few outdid James Harper Starr. By the beginning of the Civil War this pillar of Nacogdoches owned land in twenty-seven Texas counties. Years earlier, following his stint as secretary of the treasury under President Mirabeau Lamar, he had turned his passion for land into a profession, becoming a big-league land agent and an authority on Texas land laws. Impressed by his expertise and confident in his integrity, many a Texan, rich and poor alike, asked Starr to handle their land business. Among his clients he counted distinguished figures such as Mirabeau Lamar, Thomas Rusk, and General Albert Sydney Johnston. His extensive land interests soon proved so time consuming that he reluctantly abandoned his practice as physician to friends and neighbors in Nacogdoches, but his financial success did not alter the habits of frugality and abstemiousness that marked his lifestyle.[1]

Starr and Ward corresponded frequently on land matters and shared similar views about the deleterious consequences of the Archive War. In a July 1843 letter Starr deplored the latest turn of events. So long as the Land Office records were out of Ward's control and remained "'the bone of contention' between violent and conflicting parties," Starr wrote, the citizens of Texas would "feel with increasing anxiety that their rights to the soil they cultivate are in a most precarious condition." After all, he noted, "perhaps nine tenths of our citizens are personally interested directly or indirectly in the speedy completion of titles," yet patents to secure their claims were not to be had. Then there were the thousands who feared that "some accident" to the land records might either deprive them of their homes outright or make it too expensive and troublesome to perfect their claims. No wonder great numbers of Texans were "abandoning all claims and hopes in the country and its failing promises of protection."[2] Ward concurred, expressing dismay to Starr at his inability to provide "relief to the many whose sole wealth consists of land" and at "sending away from my office, daily and hourly, the many earnest applicants for patents, disappointed and dejected." Four months later, in his annual report to Congress, the commissioner warned that despairing Texans were selling their claims and their headright certificates to speculators for "trifling considerations." The situation, he insisted, was fraught with danger. The secret to Texas's past prosperity was its promise of free land and the industrious immigrants that policy drew to the infant republic. Whatever thwarted the fulfillment of that promise injured Texas's "welfare as a nation."[3] Several years later Texas Governor Peter Bell capsulized the issue nicely in a message to the legislature: "There is no subject which addresses itself more forcibly and directly to the mature consideration of the Legislature, than that of settling, upon a secure and permanent basis, the land titles of the country; because there is none other upon which its improvement and prosperity so materially depend." As historian Mark Carroll has pointed out, in a frontier society marked by stressful living conditions, social disorderliness, and institutional disarray, the inability to secure property rights had potentially grave implications.[4]

If the Archive War disrupted the land system, it also took a personal toll on the land commissioner. By January 1843 Peg Leg had been on the outs with his fellow Austinites for nine months and subjected to threats, humiliation, ostracism, and cannon fire. The Austinites who recaptured the archives at Brushy Creek even declared they would put him to death upon their return to town, or so Sam Houston told Congress. "Nothing but fear has saved him from assassination," Peg Leg's friend John Chenoweth wrote Houston in early 1843. "He has taken a bold and independant stand and has a few friends that would stand by him in any extremety," but he and his friends "are much abused by the ringleaders."[5] A man of Peg Leg's temperament—proud, imperious, contentious—was not about to back down before such treatment or entertain the slightest doubt that the Austinites were entirely at fault in the conflict. But for a survivor of two traumatic brushes with death there were undoubtedly more complex emotional consequences, especially given the threats to his life culminating in a bombardment of grape shot. Feelings of intense distress, anger, hostility, and an urge to

93

violence would make it all the more difficult for him to resolve his differences with the Austinites in the months ahead.

A week following the recapture of the archives word reached the commissioner that the insurgents contemplated returning his papers provided he resumed business at the Land Office. He responded with a message to Austin's Archives Committee stating that he now believed it his "imperative duty" to reopen the General Land Office and the county surveyors' offices and therefore requested return of his papers. But the message was loaded with combative, accusatory language, protesting seizure of his records and predicting their doom through rot and decay if not restored to his control.[6] The committee members took offense at the "high tone and insulting character" of his communication, but agreed to return the papers under conditions reflecting their own antipathy and distrust: the commissioner must pledge in writing that he was prepared to resume the duties of his office in Austin and would not permit clandestine removal of any portion of the archives even under orders from Sam Houston. Ward retorted that such a pledge was beyond his authority.[7]

And so it went during 1843. In March, Ward issued a proclamation putting the onus for the deadlock entirely on the shoulders of the Austinites, while defending himself from "slanders and misconceptions." The Archives Committee declared his proclamation "so repugnant to the facts" that its only purpose could have been to disseminate "erroneous impressions." Nevertheless the committee backed off its earlier position and promised to return the papers if Ward simply expressed his intention to open the Land Office in Austin and proceeded to discharge its duties. Ward rejected that proposal out of hand, too, insisting that he regain custody of his records before opening his office.[8]

With no resolution in sight the commissioner determined to go to the capital at Washington-on-the-Brazos without his archives and open his office there. He really wanted to stay in Austin to keep an eye on those holding his precious records, but the "extreme hostility" to government officers was wearing on him, a menacing atmosphere that had already cowed two of his clerks into resigning. In any case, he confessed, he was baffled as to who had his records and thus who warranted surveillance if he stayed (for most of 1843 they were hidden on the second floor of Angelina Eberly's house).[9] Even so, the ever-vigilant Austinites were not at all sure the commissioner departed for the capital empty-handed. Peg Leg and his deputy, Joseph Daniels, had barely set out on the morning of April 12 when the chairman of the Archives Committee dispatched an urgent communication to the people of Bastrop County asking them to intercept the commissioner. Evidence had just come to light indicating he may have secreted some government records in his wagon (State, War, and other department records were also still in Austin). Nothing seems to have come of the incident, but it exemplified the depth of the Austinites' distrust and their anxiety over further attempts to dispossess them of the archives.[10]

Washington-on the-Brazos was not much of a step up from deteriorating and depopulated Austin. Site of the convention that declared independence in 1836, it had then been abandoned by the politicians as they fled pell-mell before Santa Anna's army. They returned reluctantly in 1842. Situated on a high bluff overlooking the Brazos River, the village was home to just 250 residents, hardly more than in Austin at the time, and a cluster of leaky, weather-beaten houses, stores, and barrooms—"wooden shanties" one critic called them. Sam Houston described his new seat of government as "rather raw." One of the biggest buildings was Major Hatfield's saloon and gambling parlor, a favorite resort of the sporting crowd that frequented the town. First the Senate and later the House held some of their sessions in a loft on the second floor, but the saloon below remained conveniently open. A hundred miles or so to the east of Austin and a mere seventy northwest of Houston, Washington-on-the-Brazos was at least more centrally located than Austin and far less vulnerable to surprise attacks.[11]

For the beleaguered commissioner it must have been a relief to be out of harm's way and gratifying to be reunited with his political friends, Sam Houston above all. But he was probably taken aback upon his arrival to find the president decked out in a flaming red silk robe that was a gift of the Sultan of Turkey. Houston had donned the gown for a twelve-day parley and social get-together with the chiefs of six Indian tribes.[12] The chiefs were soon on their way, and Ward settled down to business. On April 25 he issued the proclamation for which so many Texans had been waiting. He directed all county surveyors and boards of land commissioners to resume their duties after May 1 and opened his own office for such business as "circumstances" (the absence of his records) permitted. Admitting that the militia, whose mobilization had justified his original closing order, had disbanded some time ago, he blamed the delay on "irresponsible" Austinites who refused to surrender his records.[13]

Once again Texans could obtain headright certificates and lay claim to land by having it surveyed. Patents, however, were another matter. "There have been numerous and urgent applications for patents from every part of the Republic," the commissioner informed one claimant five months later, "and I have in every instance, much to my regret, told the applicants that it was impossible for me to issue a patent until I obtained the records from Austin." He had no way of knowing, for instance, which headright certificates were valid and which were fraudulent or what lands in a county were already spoken for. The Austinites apparently even had the office seal he needed to authenticate patents and other documents.[14] "Confusion and embarrassment" were the order of the day, he told Congress. And patents were just the half of it. Often he could not respond to the simplest of requests, such as for a copy of instructions he had sent earlier to county surveyors. Without his letter-books he had no record of his previous correspondence. "It is to be hoped however that this state of anarchy will not last much longer," he remarked in a wistful moment.[15]

Adding to the commissioner's woes during 1843 was the decrepit house that passed for a General Land Office. In October when it rained for twenty straight days, water poured through the roof and drenched the tables at which his clerks worked, bringing business almost to a halt. Cold weather compounded the misery. When the shutters were opened to provide light by which to work, frigid air blew in through the glassless windows. "The houses in this place are to the last degree uncomfortable," Peg Leg complained. As winter approached he appealed for roof repairs, sashes and glass, and a Franklin stove.[16]

But all was not for naught. Among other things, Peg Leg provided much needed guidance to county surveyors and county land commissioners, many new to the job, explaining procedures, answering queries, and ruling on thorny points of law. Suppose, asked a county surveyor, that his predecessor had surveyed a piece a land for a claimant whose headright certificate he believed to be fraudulent. Could he now survey the same property for a new claimant? No, responded the commissioner, only the courts could annul a certificate issued by a county board, no matter how spurious it appeared to be. Concerned as ever that errors today would mean endless legal wrangles tomorrow,

Ward encouraged county surveyors to ask questions first and complemented those who did, expressing to one surveyor his "unqualified approbation of your prompt and efficient manner in seeking information rather than lead your people into error—as is too often, much too often done, in this country of speculation."[17] James Harper Starr, however, wanted Ward to broaden his focus and take a hand in resolving the legislative logjam over the archives by urging Sam Houston to hold the next session of Congress in Austin, a conciliatory gesture that Starr thought might do the trick. Ward was adamant in rejecting such a role for himself. Playing politics was outside the bounds of his duties as land commissioner, he informed Starr, which in any case were "sufficiently onerous and vexatious" without his "interfering with the prerogatives of others." Nor, he might have added, did he want to give an inch to the Austinites.[18]

Ward was hardly unmindful of the machinations of Congress, especially now that he was up for reappointment and the Senate had something to say about it. At first it seemed a simple matter. His good friend and former comrade-in-arms James Reily, Texas's late minister to the United States, was foursquare behind him and had President Houston's ear. Reily twice talked with Houston about it in March and both times was assured the president had no intention of changing land commissioners. Sure enough, when Ward's term expired in July 1843 Houston reappointed him, but with Congress in adjournment it was only a recess appointment. Houston would have to resubmit his nomination for Senate confirmation when the legislators reconvened in December.[19]

By November rumors were afloat of a move to replace Ward as commissioner. Reily soon determined that a "combination" had been formed against him. Houston insisted Ward was still his man, but some members of his cabinet had other plans. Ward later told his nephew, Charles Smyth, that they were anxious to replace him with "a favorite and talented son of South Carolina."[20] Their candidate probably was James Hamilton, a former governor of South Carolina who represented Texas's interests in Europe for several years, seeking loans and diplomatic recognition. His labors drained him financially and in 1842 he returned to South Carolina, but he remained interested in a government appointment in Texas and had highly placed friends. "Threats and entreaties were employed to change the mind of the President," according to the sometimes hyperbolic Smyth.[21] Had they succeeded in getting Hamilton appointed, it certainly would have put a man with a different cast of mind in charge of the public domain. Ward wanted above all to fulfill the promise of free land to those who had first settled and fought for Texas, and he attacked as the "greatest injustice" an 1841 law authorizing grants of large tracts to colonizers from which current residents were excluded. How shameful, he told Congress in 1843, to give prime land "to crowds of foreigners who never shared in our struggle for independence" and relegate "our own citizens" to "Comanche and Buffalo ranges" (an admonishment that Congress took to heart, soon repealing the 1841 law). Hamilton, on the other hand, wanted to use the public domain to raise funds to bolster Texas's credit abroad and finance the transportation and settlement of more immigrants from Europe.[22]

As December approached, Reily remained confident of Ward's success unless, as he warned the commissioner, "your enemies should attempt to injure you in the estimation of the Senators." That was a danger, given Ward's close identity with Sam Houston and his unpopular moves to deprive Austin of the archives, but anti-Houston sentiment was more muted in the Senate than in the House. When Houston finally put forward Ward's nomination it sailed through the Senate by a vote of twelve to two. How gratifying, Reily wrote Peg Leg, that the Senate had stood firm by a "meritorious officer in defiance of intrigue" and "all the efforts made to displace you." And what a relief for the commissioner. He now had three years to pursue his plans for reforming the land system, though first there was the heretofore intractable matter of his archives. Suddenly a resolution appeared imminent.[23]

On December 28, 1843, three days short of a year since the Land Office records had found their way to Angelina Eberly's home, Sam Houston instructed Ward to return to Austin and take charge of them —and stay there. While there were still many months of political pushing and shoving ahead before Austin would regain its status as capital, the clash over the Land Office records was resolved for the time being in Austin's favor. Even Ward took Houston's directive to mean that he should open for business in the former capital and start issuing patents, though the president did not explicitly say so. Judging by the commissioner's behavior during the following month it must have been a bitter pill to swallow. It certainly was once Congress got into the act. On

January 6 a committee of three representatives arrived in Austin, charged by the House with the task of examining the condition of the Land Office records and reporting back. Reassured by the presence of sympathetic House members and eager to take advantage of Houston's decision, the citizens of Austin turned over the Land Office archives to the commissioner. Then the fireworks started.[24]

In its report to the House two weeks later the committee set forth its acute displeasure with the commissioner. From the moment of its arrival, the committee asserted, he appeared "disposed to embarrass their proceedings; and, if possible, produce a collision with the committee"; his entire manner and conduct implied that "he regarded them as intruders upon his, imagined, peculiar privileges." What first put Ward off was the committee's brusque request that as soon as he obtained the archives he was to hand them over to the committee unopened together with a schedule of the contents. This after Peg Leg had been itching to regain control of "his" archives for a year. He complied, but was enraged when the committee proceeded to take testimony from several Austinites and three of his own clerks without informing him, much less allowing him to cross-examine the witnesses. The commissioner smelled a whitewash by a House committee in the Austinites' corner. At issue was whether the boxes had been opened and the records tampered with, perhaps some removed or lost, while in the possession of the insurgents. Ward seemed determined to establish that was the case and was dismissive of testimony to the contrary from Austinites taken by House members sympathetic to their cause. He proffered as evidence the fact that some papers were not in the boxes they were supposed to be according to a schedule prepared when the archives were packed for transfer to Houston in the spring of 1842. But his own staff undercut him. Two former clerks testified that during 1842 records removed for airing or consultation were not always returned to the same box. A third clerk, just rehired, swore that he had seen the boxes several times while they were in the hands of the Austinites and did not believe they were ever opened. Ward fired him the next day. Events went downhill from there.[25]

Few things stirred Peg Leg's ire more than challenges to his authority. Just as he believed it his duty to accept Sam Houston's authority and abide by his commands, so he believed it the duty of others to accept his authority over the Land Office, its records, and its staff. He did not take kindly to those who flouted his authority or simply went against his wishes, even over trivial matters, as a series of his clerks learned to their detriment. From the outset, Ward felt that the House committee—in particular John Grammont and Chairman Frederick Ogden—were meddling in his affairs. The tension came to a head, as is often the case in such situations, over a seemingly minor issue. Ward asked Grammont to return his schedule, and Grammont brought it to Ward's office but, while handing it to the commissioner, indicated he had not finished making a copy and wished to retain it until done. The commissioner said no, the schedule belonged to his office, and he needed it, whereupon Grammont pulled it back ("snatched it from me," Ward said), observing that it had been provided to the committee, not to him personally, and thus he would not return it without Chairman Ogden's consent. Furious at the rebuff, Ward threatened, "if you don't immediately deliver that schedule, I will have a warrant against you." And that is exactly what he did. He persuaded a town magistrate to issue a warrant for Grammont's arrest. When Ogden joined in the resistance, Ward had him arrested, too. That afternoon Austin was treated to the spectacle of two House members standing trial. The defendants were cleared, but not before the court was subjected to speeches by the commissioner and his chief clerk, James O'Hara, who insisted that the committee was "sent by a party in the House to sustain a mob" and would predictably report that the Land Office records were intact when in fact many were lost. No doubt Ward agreed, and he certainly did not entertain any thought that his cause might be unjust. "Their right to take and retain a record of this office [the schedule] I unqualifiedly deny," he told Sam Houston.[26]

The committee and the commissioner parted on what must have seemed at the time the sourest of terms, but in fact their enmity soon turned far more bitter. Ogden and Grammont held nothing back in reporting to the House what had transpired. Ward was castigated for "glaring outrages" and "gross insult" and accused of making contradictory statements and even of falsifying documents, but those allegations paled beside the charge of resorting to "deep, designing, and deliberate perjury."[27] A criminal charge against a high public official was most serious indeed, a charge of lying especially so. Men of honor never allowed anyone to call them liars, historian Kenneth Greenberg has written of the Old South. "The central insult that could turn a disagreement into a duel involved a direct or indirect attack on someone's word—the accusation that a man was a liar." Ward was apoplectic; his clerks "mad as March hares." One of them wanted to give Ogden a thrashing. The commissioner settled for challenging the House to either live up to its accusations or back down. The charges were of so grave a character, he declared, that the House should bring articles of impeachment against him so that he might have the proper opportunity to vindicate himself; otherwise the House should expunge the charges from its records. The representatives initially stood fast, but then voted to omit all charges and critical comments from the 250 printed copies of the committee report.[28]

And well they might have. The charge of perjury turned on the accusation that Ward first testified under oath that he willingly provided the schedule to the committee, but then swore out an affidavit accusing the committee of violently taking it. Conveniently ignored was the incident to which Ward referred in his affidavit, when Grammont handed the schedule to Ward but then pulled it or "snatched" it back. Denied his day in court, Ward still wanted the last word. He published a one-page "Card" accusing Ogden and Grammont of "a recklessness and malignity unrivalled by demons themselves" and, returning their egregious insult, called them "Liars and Scoundrels" (see illustrations). Though Peg Leg infrequently challenged his antagonists to duels any longer (in 1840 Congress had passed a tough law against the practice), he did not hesitate, as was the custom of the time, to abuse his political enemies with virulent language.[29] His enemies, however, had not finished with him. In March an attempt was made to prosecute him for the perjury charge in the Travis County District Court, but the grand jury failed to indict. "They were more than anxious to blast my reputation and sink me into a state of degradation equal to their own," Peg Leg exulted, "... but finding their pretence for a bill [of indictment] so frivolous, they for once felt shame," a dubious claim it must be said.[30]

Then, as though the fiery emotions of recent weeks had passed from the scene like a summer thunderstorm, Ward put the Archive War behind him. Eventually he would concede that "with one or two slight exceptions" no records were missing. The "slanderous" perjury charge continued to gall him, but he turned his attention to rescuing his newly recovered archives from their "state of confusion and derangement" in anticipation of once again issuing patents.[31] For the first time in two years he could envision the General Land Office operating under conditions that approached normal. He set up shop with his staff in the old Land Office building on Hickory (Eighth) Street, just east of Congress Avenue, and arranged to reside in the Moreland house next door, a log house on the Avenue a short distance north of the Quartermaster's Department.[32]

He could not, however, have found Austin an inviting place to live. Tensions with his neighbors aside, the town was "like a widow in her weeds, lonely, desolate, and forlorn," as one resident characterized it. To Peg Leg it was like living "upon the outer line of civilization." One day a large herd of buffalo, apparently unaware that the wilderness had been tamed, passed right through town.[33] How much Austin had regressed was captured best by a visitor the previous summer. "On entering the city of Austin, Lo! Dreariness and desolation presented themselves; few houses appeared inhabited and many falling to decay." The streets were "filled with grass and weeds," the president's house "falling to pieces," and the capitol "the abode of bats, lizards and stray cattle." Without prompt repair Austin's buildings would soon be "a heap of ruins." That prediction unfortunately applied to the Land Office. Among other problems the roof was so leaky that during heavy rains the clerks spent all their time moving papers, books, and maps from place to place to keep them dry. The former State Department building was so dilapidated, with its windows mostly broken, that on one occasion Ward found many boxes of department archives, still housed within, standing in two inches of water.[34] Austin's hardy residents endured the hardships and the monotony and held out hope for the return of the capital, encouraged by the opening of the Land Office and the upcoming expiration of Sam Houston's term as president. "Every friend of Austin doubtlessly hails the opening of the Land Office here . . . as the harbinger of returning prosperity," the surveyor of Travis County told Ward. In the meantime, with little else to do, everyone planted. Nearly every acre of enclosed land in Travis County was under cultivation during 1844. While buildings crumbled, crops of wheat and corn flourished.[35]

At the Land Office, Ward and his clerks struggled to get their records organized and surmount the vast amount of business that had accumulated since operations ceased in 1842. Like any good bureaucrat, the commissioner complained that he was short of staff. The fault lay with Congress, he told Sam Houston. The legislators had authorized additional positions but had not funded them. One explanation, Ward suggested with his usual bluntness, was their "unpardonable stupidity and ignorance of the laws." Additional staff were not immediately forthcoming, but after several delays the commissioner finally acquired the new office seal that he had been seeking ever since the previous seal went astray during the Archive War (see illustrations). Finally in June he resumed issuing patents.[36] Within two months the *Telegraph and Texas Register* reported the Land Office "in the full tide of successful operation" with its "complicated machinery" humming. Ward, however, was not in a celebratory mood as problems abounded. Hit-and-miss mail service to remote Austin made it difficult to conduct business "with any degree of regularity or promptitude." He still could not issue patents on bounty and donation grants awarded for military service. The secretary of war had to vouch for their authenticity but could not do so because he was in Washington-on-the-Brazos while most of his records were still in Austin. Many a veteran made the long trek to Austin seeking patents only to be turned away.[37]

What really troubled Ward, however, were more fundamental and long-standing problems of the kind he had raised with Congress during his first year in office. By now he had given up hope of imposing U.S.-style sectioning—rectangular surveying—on the public domain, but he still thought Congress's solution, designating counties as sections, was grossly defective. A far cry from the systematically surveyed mile-square sections in the Northwest Territory, Texas counties were slippery entities, ill defined and often changing. New counties were carved out of old ones, and the irregular boundaries of most were imprecise at best, imaginary at worst (running and marking county boundaries was just too expensive, a House committee maintained). Half the counties in existence in 1836 had different boundaries by 1845. Thus counties were moving targets, when what was needed for accurate and efficient surveying was sections that were fixed land areas. Otherwise how could reliable land maps be made, and what was to stop surveyors in adjacent counties from surveying the same land for different people, as happened far too often when boundary lines were so vague and transitory? To alleviate the confusion, Ward proposed making the counties as then constituted permanent sections (land districts) with well-defined and carefully surveyed boundaries and leaving those boundaries unchanged. Should Congress decide to alter county boundaries in the future to reflect changing population patterns, so be it. But the land district boundaries would stay the same, and thus counties and land districts would no longer necessarily be coterminous. County surveyors would henceforth be known as district surveyors.[38]

Counties, moreover, were ill served by their chief surveyors, Ward contended. Still elected by county residents rather than appointed by the commissioner, they often acted unprofessionally, as if, he told one official, they were subject "to no other control than the impulses of their own will which, I regret to say, has often been influenced by capricious self interest and, with those who are scrupulously honest[,] a mistaken apprehension of their legal duties." Some were incompetent, others careless, inattentive to their responsibilities, or uncooperative. It tried the commissioner's patience, for example, to receive a set of field notes that indicated neither the county in which the land was situated nor the quantity of land surveyed. Failure to heed his instructions placed a heavy burden on his office to detect errors and threatened to plunge the citizenry into "a vortex of contention and litigation."[39] Nor did Ward have kinder words for the land maps produced by county surveyors, as required by law. Intended to provide a visual record of legally valid claims, the maps were an indispensable tool in certifying that a new claim did not intrude on land already spoken for. Yet "almost every map now in the General Land Office is grossly incorrect," Ward informed Congress, with many of them missing lands titled prior to independence. The maps for Milam and Robertson counties, among others, were so glaringly deficient that he simply refused to patent land in those counties, a stance that did not endear him to property-hungry Texans. Some county surveyors saw themselves as victims of the situation, not its authors. They took office prepared to do the job justice only to inherit the deficiencies of their predecessors. "No county map and all the papers in perfect Confusion," one newly elected surveyor bemoaned; "I really believe it a moral impossibility to straiten them properly but I will endeavor to do the best I can." For Ward this kind of problem was all the more reason to reform the system.[40]

If incompetence and negligence exasperated the commissioner, corruption appalled him, believing as he did that the county surveyor system was rife with it. The cancer infecting the system was land speculation. Texas at the time was awash in land speculators, seen by many Texans as land sharks and "lynx-eyed land-grabbers." When it came to land,

Andrew Briscoe lamented in a letter to Ward, swindling was common-place.[41] Ward agreed, asserting that the "speculation tribe" was perpe-trating frauds daily and swindling naive immigrants out of their land. Many speculators, he insisted, had won office as county surveyors and used the position to carry out their "base schemes." He told one for-mer legislator, "I can now refer you to county surveyors who I doubt not will[,] if a fair price were offered, sell you locations & the field notes of land already surveyed [for others]." A few months earlier Peg Leg had been stunned to discover such skullduggery right in his own office, in the person of an obstreperous fellow named Hanson Catlett, one of his clerks. A former county surveyor of Brazos County, Catlett had made off with county land records when leaving office and was using them to plot vacant land in Brazos County and prepare field notes, which he backdated to his time as county surveyor and sold. Not about to condone such blatant fraud, Peg Leg sacked Catlett the moment he learned of it.[42]

The commissioner envisioned a district-based land system under his command that would operate with far more efficiency and integrity than the haphazard setup at the time. First, he wanted author-ity to appoint, supervise, and fire district surveyors. He was the best judge of their qualifications, he argued, and those he selected would be under his control rather than free agents accountable only to local vot-ers once every two years. Second, responsibility for county maps should be transferred to his office. Their preparation involved skills not commonly possessed by surveyors and was best done by professional draftsmen. He wanted four draftsmen under his direction to circulate among the districts compiling maps.[43]

In consultation with several legislators Ward incorporated these proposals into a bill that his political ally, Senator David Kaufman (for whom Kaufman County was later named), introduced in the Senate. The commissioner also apprised Congress of other reforms he thought necessary to correct the defects that tortuous history and bad legisla-tion had inflicted on the land system. Action was urgently needed, for instance, to facilitate surveying and patenting of claims by "assignees," holders of headright certificates who were not the original recipients but had purchased or otherwise acquired them, an increasingly press-ing problem because post-1841 immigrants were not entitled to head-rights and instead often purchased certificates from speculators. By mid-January 1845 Ward's reform bill appeared to be sailing through the Senate. "I have no doubt of its passage," Kaufman told him. But the next day the Senate changed course, acceding to a request from the House to cooperate in passing a House bill whose "whole, entire, and absorbing object," one representative declared on the House floor, was to legislate Peg Leg out of office.[44]

Ever since his appointment in 1841 Ward had kept his eye on the overall operation of the land system and the detrimental long-term consequences of its imperfections, not just on the day-to-day business of his office. While the low price of land at the time deterred litigation, he feared that eventually Texas would flounder in a sea of confusion, contention, and corruption if he did not proceed scrupulously while at the same time seeking to reform the system. James Harper Starr had warned him, however, that land mania made Texans impatient and short sighted. Their patience had already been sorely tried by the lengthy delays of the Archive War, and then the commissioner insisted on applying the strictest of standards, following the letter of every law and refusing altogether to patent claims in a number of counties until deficiencies were rectified. Responding to the discontent, newly elected President Anson Jones, in his December 1844 message to Congress, recommended measures to facilitate issuing of patents. Even Ward's firmest political allies were impatient with him, including Kaufman, whose request for several patents six months earlier Ward had ignored. "I trust you will be able to send us some Patents &c that will relieve our anxiety," the Senator wrote the commissioner in January on behalf of himself and two Ward supporters in the House. Nor, he emphasized, was their distress over patents just a personal matter. "There is no business in regard to which our Constituents demand a more rigid attention than their land business."[45]

Kaufman had leverage with Ward and did not hesitate to use it, making clear that his support of Ward's bill was not unconnected to his expectation of a prompt response regarding his patents. But how were others to combat Ward's stringency? Money did not seem to be the answer. As one representative declared in the commissioner's defense, he had a reputation as "a man beyond reproach: a man whom money cannot buy." On one occasion Starr had suggested that in exchange for a favor Ward would be "compensated in the usual way." The commissioner bristled at the insinuation and retorted that he never had and never would accept the slightest compensation of any kind for giving his attention to someone's business.[46] Bringing a man of the commissioner's determination and integrity to heel was no easy task. But some of those displeased with his policies and eager to get land surveyed and patented more quickly, less painfully, and perhaps fraudulently, thought they had found a way to circumvent him, especially now that his political patron, Sam Houston, had left office: abolish the position of land commissioner. They advocated legislation that called for dividing his responsibilities between two new positions, a surveyor general and a commissioner of patents, the latter to issue patents simply upon the presentation of proper field notes. The effect, Kaufman warned Ward, echoing comments made in the House, "will be to legislate you out of office." In Ward's view the General Land Office was to be dismembered, unleashing "mischief" that only those familiar with the intrigues of land speculators could fully appreciate.[47]

The commissioner had not, to the say the least, endeared himself to the House by his actions and his sympathies during the previous three years. Nonetheless several representatives rallied to his defense. They hailed him as "one of the best and worthiest" of officials—Texans never need fear for the legal validity of a patent issued by the Colonel—and scolded Congress for not passing the reforms he had urged for three years. A majority of House members, however, backed the legislation, and soon it was working its way through the Senate. His career in jeopardy, Ward faced up to political reality and decided to relax his standards; errors by surveyors would no longer necessarily sink a patent application. On January 27, the very day the Senate had set aside to debate the bill, the commissioner, presumably with an eye to affecting the outcome, instructed his deputy that henceforth patents would be issued on all field notes that qualified legally (as specified in sections 19 and 20 of the December 1837 General Land Office act) and could be plotted on a county map, regardless of any errors committed by surveyors; even in cases where there was a "manifest defect" that could render a patent worthless, the applicant would not be turned down out of hand but informed of the problem and given the option of still getting his patent. Later Ward assured a legislator from Milam County that he would not automatically refuse to issue patents in Milam and other counties with seriously flawed maps, reversing his public position of just a few months earlier. Instead, a genuine claim that was represented on a county map and did not conflict with "old titled land" or other surveys would be patented so long as the recipient signed a statement that he received the patent "with a full knowledge of all errors."[48]

Ward's retreat on January 27 notwithstanding, the Senate passed the ousting measure, and it was seemingly on the verge of becoming law, but when Congress adjourned five days later it had fallen short of enactment. Possibly Anson Jones, soon to become of one of Peg Leg's closest friends, vetoed it, but it is more likely that the legislature simply let it lapse, perhaps due to the concessions Ward made or perhaps due to a decision to hold off reorganizing the Land Office since annexation of Texas to the United States now appeared imminent (the U.S. House of Representatives approved annexation in late January). Even if the commissioner survived a formidable effort to depose him, his adversaries had little trouble thwarting his legislation. His reform bill died without ever coming to a vote. Ward believed that he was ultimately foiled by dishonest surveyors and land speculators who feared the consequences of his reforms and thus "resorted to every species of chicanery & falsehood to create an opposition to me."[49]

The commissioner's change of mind had immediate consequences for eager patent applicants. Congress made things easier for them, too, especially by passing the law that Ward had requested to expedite the patenting of claims by assignees. The Land Office was inundated by the "vast amount" of business that ensued. Issuing of patents, which had resumed in June 1844 after a hiatus of more than two years, suddenly accelerated. In just two months, from mid-February to mid-April 1845, the Land Office issued close to 600 patents on headrights, bounty and donation grants, and land scrip, almost three-quarters as many as had been issued during the entire three-year-presidency of Sam Houston.[50]

Anson Jones was undoubtedly gratified by this development, and he had further reason for confidence in his land commissioner. A friend Jones had asked to go to Austin and assess the situation reported that

> the business of the General Land Office proceeds with the utmost regularity and harmony; in fact, the system of order which prevails throughout all its details has rather surprised me, although a long acquaintance with Col. Ward had previously satisfied me of his capacity; yet the clamor which had become somewhat general had almost prepared me to find a somewhat

different state of things. Yet I am now perfectly satisfied that perhaps no other man in the Republic could supply his place, so perfectly acquainted is he with all that relates to the landed interest of the country as well as with the minutest details of the office.[51]

Recovering from the turmoil of the Archive War and getting the Land Office back on track had been difficult challenges for Ward; instituting major reforms in the land system had been an exasperating one. By early 1845 he could take substantial satisfaction in the former but scant in the latter. Ward, however, was strong minded and tenacious, attributes that had seen him through tough times before. Angered but not awed by Congress's flat rejection of his reforms, he was not about to give up.

While Peg Leg fought his losing battle during 1844 and 1845 to revamp the land system, it was his personal life that was transformed. At age thirty-seven he married a widow in her twenties with two toddlers; nine months later almost to the day she gave birth to their first child together. From the beginning, however, it was a troubled marriage, and for the rest of their lives both would live in the shadow of its failure.

Part Two

Peg Leg and Susan, 1844–1874

CHAPTER 8

Susan

L ITTLE IS KNOWN about Susan Ward's life in Texas before she married Thomas William Ward. Barely a trace of her survives in documents from those years. She and her first husband, Thomas Marston, had come to Texas from faraway New Hampshire in the late 1830s, when she was in her early twenties. Their first child, Robie, was born soon after, and by 1842 they resided in Austin, where Thomas practiced medicine. The Marston home was just a stone's throw from the temporary capitol. In April 1843 Susan gave birth to a second child, Mary. Three months later her husband died.[1]

At age twenty-six Susan found herself a widow with two young children and little means of support living in a desolated community "far from the home of my childhood and the friends who loved me." She felt "almost a stranger in a strange land." Her husband bequeathed her his modest estate of household furnishings, two cows, two calves, a horse, and some real estate. But in depressed Austin, where abandoned houses outnumbered occupied ones, his four town lots and home were worth only $150, little more than his horse. What is surprising is that Susan did not forsake Austin for the support and comfort of her family in the Northeast, as she did later when in desperate trouble. Instead she fell in love with Peg Leg.[2]

Susan Bean was born in 1817 in Candia, New Hampshire, a prosperous farming community of some 1,300 residents situated eighteen miles southeast of Concord. It was a setting so unlike the one Ward had known as a youth, surrounded as she was by fields and meadows, patches of woodlands, stone fences, and ponds. The Lamprey River (now known as the North Branch River), a good-sized mill stream dignified with the name "river" by locals, practically flowed through her front yard (see illustrations). The air was filled not with the din of the city, but with the noises of farm animals and frogs croaking and the distant tinkling of sheep bells. On Sunday mornings it was a different sound that permeated the air, a crescendo of voices as Elder Moses Bean, Susan's father and a Free Will Baptist minister, roused his audience with a fiery sermon and his listeners reciprocated with louder and louder shouts of "Amen!" and "Glory to God!" and some broke into tears.[3]

The sixth of Moses and Mary Bean's eight children to survive infancy, Susan grew up in a tightly knit family whose forebears had come to Candia in the mid-eighteenth century. Her father was a noted figure in the community, a spiritual leader who also engaged in milling and leather tanning and served Candia both as selectman and representative to the New Hampshire legislature.[4] His initiative and energy carried over to his children. Susan's brothers Aaron and Moses Dudley became well-to-do merchants in the highly competitive economy of mid-nineteenth century New York City, and her sister Mary headed the Female Department at the Mechanics' Society School in Manhattan and then ran her own private school in the city. The many extant letters of Susan and her siblings bespeak a level of literacy that reflects well on both the Candia schools and the educational environment at home. Somewhat shy and more comfortable in a small circle than a crowd, Susan shone among the talented Bean offspring. "Susan exceeds all this family in her variety and imagination," an admiring sister-in-law wrote. "I long to hear one of her well told stories."[5]

When Susan was a teenager Thomas Marston, a native of nearby Deerfield, began practicing medicine in Candia. Thomas had earned his physician's stripes through study at the Medical College of Maine and Vermont Medical College, receiving an M.D. degree from the latter. In 1835, when she was eighteen, Susan and Thomas married. The next year, much to her family's disappointment, they left Candia for Lowell, Massachusetts, and three years later set out for Texas. Susan would remember herself wistfully as "a pure minded and happy girl." Why the couple went to Texas is a mystery. What befell them there was a tragedy.[6]

At first, Susan's involvement with Thomas William Ward was a godsend. At the time of Marston's death Ward was living in Washington-on-the-Brazos, but in January 1844 he returned to Austin and soon reopened the Land Office. He soon took notice of the widow Marston as well, perhaps charmed by her pleasant manner, agreeable conversation, and comely appearance. She was a "fair specimen" according to one acquaintance. Whatever the allure, Ward showed Susan "a kindness and attention" that affected her deeply. Within weeks she was stopping by his house, and the commissioner was seen throwing her kisses.[7]

It is hardly surprising that Susan was smitten. Ward was thirty-six at the time (seven years younger than her late husband), highly intelligent and articulate, and a tall, handsome-faced fellow who made an imposing appearance even though missing two limbs. Susan's brother, Aaron, long remembered an evening party at his house in New York the following year when the Colonel stood in the parlor receiving guests, his arm resting on the mantelpiece and a white glove on his one hand. "Oh such a 'handsome man' they all exclaimed," Bean recalled. One guest later told Susan that upon entering the room he felt himself "in the presence of the handsomest noblest and most intellectual man I ever saw."[8]

If a man of dignified bearing, Ward also happened to be the most prominent and probably the wealthiest person in town, though in depopulated Austin that may not have been saying a lot. But for Susan, struggling to stay afloat as she was, being courted by a man of Ward's means must have been reassuring. That very year, in fact, he had finally settled his long-standing and acutely vexing suit against the Allens, winning control of the Long Row in Houston, a complex of stores that provided a hefty rental income. A few years later he would value all his real estate holdings at $40,000, a princely sum for Texas at the time.[9] What seems to have mattered most to her, however, was the attention and affection he bestowed on her at a time when she felt alone and lost. Little wonder she cast her suitor as the "ideal of her fancy and romance," according to her sister-in-law, or, as Susan herself expressed it, as "all that my imagination had ever made [of] the being I would worship and adore." She was not unaware, it should be said, that there was another side to the Colonel, a side to be wary of. Austin was too tiny a community for residents not to know of one another's faults. Several female friends tried to dissuade her from marrying him because of his fits of temper. Thus she may have had an inkling of what lay ahead and closed her eyes to it, understandably so given the situation.[10]

Susan and Peg Leg were married on June 20, 1844, his birthday. Susan was jubilant at the union. "Oh Col[onel]," she wrote her husband on their second wedding anniversary, "I shall never never forget the quiet unaloyed happiness I felt the evening of our marriage[.] Oh how ardently I loved you and I felt that I was loved and that I should never again be unhappy." With her two youngsters, Susan moved into the Moreland house, the Colonel's residence on Congress Avenue. Rough though the one story log house might appear to modern eyes, it was to her not only very comfortable but a "hallowed spot," for it was to there, she wrote her husband, that "you welcomed me a happy bride and under that roof that you then threw around me a protecting arm and became a father to my children." The Moreland house was connected to the Land Office, and later when Peg Leg was building a splendid new house three blocks away Susan voiced some regrets at the impending move, "for then I would not see you every hour as I can when I am in the old log house where I have spent the happiest hours of my life."[11]

For Peg Leg, a bachelor well into his thirties at the time he married, life at the Moreland house must have seemed hectic. Instant fatherhood descended upon him in the form of Robie and Mary—"frufru" they called him—and he did his part by fathering Dudley, born nine months later. Youngsters crying, running about the house, disobeying, getting sick, teething—these were not the stuff of bachelorhood. Two-year-old Mary was so ill at one point that the doctor virtually moved in, visiting her sixteen times in a week, night and day.[12] Helping out around the Ward house during the mid-1840s was an ever-changing cast of servants, all enslaved African Americans: Tom, Rosette, Bill, Ann, Gilbert, Clara, and Creecy. Tom, Rosette, and Bill were acquired as part of the settlement with the Allens, but the Colonel soon sold Tom (a jack-of-all-trades whom Susan thought "invaluable") so he could be reunited with his wife in Houston. Bill, a teenager who doubled as a porter in the Land Office, ran away at least twice and was eventually sold to an Austin neighbor. Clara, an older woman who attended Susan and was little Dudley's nurse, accompanied them on a trip to New York City in 1846 but fled one evening, never to be seen again. Susan's brother bought Creecy, a woman in her sixties, for Susan following Clara's disappearance, and Susan grew very fond of her. Sad to say, little is really known about any of the servants.[13]

Then there were the myriad guests. Since the near wholesale abandonment of the town in 1842 there had been few people of note to wine and dine, but that changed dramatically in 1845. The watchword that year was annexation as Texas moved headlong toward becoming part of the United States. When delegates convened in July to approve annexation and frame a constitution for the new state, they did so not in Washington-on-the-Brazos but in Austin, by order of President Anson Jones. The constitutional convention in turn named Austin the state capital until at least 1850. Austin suddenly abounded in potential dinner guests and politicians needing a place to stay. But a town described by one visitor in 1845 as the "picture of desolation" and by another as laying almost "in ruins" was hardly prepared to accommodate them. Some delegates camped under the stars. Even a year and a half later Austin had been upgraded merely to "a poor scattering little village."[14] The Wards responded by extending their hospitality to many a government official. "Dined to-day at Col. Wards," was a common refrain in letters back home. President Jones was just one of a number who stayed with the Wards, incurring many obligations, Jones later wrote the Colonel, "by your kind attentions to me while at Austin in 45 & 46," an experience out of which developed a long-lasting camaraderie between the two men. Susan, dubbed the "Lady of the hills" by her brother, entertained on her own while her husband was out of town, hosting a Christmas dinner for a distinguished gathering that included the Texas secretary of state and two prominent judges. Perhaps she was dressed in the fancy muslin that Ward's Houston agent had sent along for carriage tops or, failing that, for "a very pretty dress for the Madam."[15]

The Colonel was somewhat troubled by all the company and found it confining, and he antagonized Susan by calling upon her just days after Dudley was born to "arise from her sick bed" and play hostess to a large group. Nevertheless he no doubt found satisfaction in his many guests. They provided both relief from the "monotony of life" in the still sparsely populated town and reassuring testimony to the high regard in which he was held by his well-placed friends. The entertaining was by no means constant, it should be said. The pulse of Austin life once again beat to the legislative calendar, so the Wards experienced slower-paced periods between sessions. But what a remarkable change from those grim days in 1842 and early 1843 when Peg Leg was socially isolated and his life in danger.[16]

In early 1846 Peg Leg did some visiting of his own. While traveling to New York City on business he stayed with his new relatives, the Beans. By then Susan's mother and her four unmarried sisters lived with her brothers Dudley and Aaron and their wives and children near Washington Square in lower Manhattan.[17] The Colonel's visit set in motion a remarkable integration of the lives of the Wards and the Beans. Like Susan, the Beans were captivated by the Texas hero. His daguerreotype was placed on the mantelpiece in their front parlor where it was the first object to greet the eye. Aaron was so proud of his new brother-in-law that his boasting about Peg Leg's standing in Texas made Susan blush. Dudley's wife was swept away by one "so handsome, so refined and so intellectual," while the sisters wrote him gushy, fawning letters, one calling him "the hero of a hundred battles." Indeed, the sisters were so taken they probably did not blink an eye when their mother declared that she did not expect any of them ever to win a husband like Susan's.[18]

In the wake of Peg Leg's trip, family members began traveling between New York City and Texas like it was nothing more than a jaunt, sometimes for extended stays. When the Colonel returned to Texas in early 1846, Aaron accompanied him and then escorted Susan and two of her children, three-year-old Mary and one-year-old Dudley, back to Manhattan. Susan and Dudley lingered with the Beans for six months. Mary stayed for six years. Susan returned to Texas in the company of her twenty-three-year-old sister Joanna, who spent at least two months with the Wards and left with fond memories, of social evenings playing cards and drinking eggnog and brandy punch, of cantering with Susan over the prairie, and of a picnic at which Peg Leg displayed his unerring accuracy in a shooting match. To the Bean brothers the Colonel was more than an illustrious relative and good friend. He was a business connection. Soon he agreed to purchase stationery and other office supplies through Aaron in New York. Texas's first governor, J. Pinckney Henderson, was one of several government officials to follow his lead. Dudley Bean began advertising his services as a wholesale grocer and wine and spirit dealer in the Austin newspaper, with the Colonel named as a local contact.[19]

It did not take Ward long to realize that his one-story log house was not up to the demands of his new lifestyle as husband, father, and host to politicians and relatives. In the summer of 1846 he commenced work on a new home that would become by far the most imposing residence in Austin. It was undoubtedly of his own design and was built, as he later stated, "under his own personal superintendence," but given his disabilities and his demanding job he was hardly in a position to do the actual construction, so he hired his neighbor Abner Cook—a fortunate choice. It was Cook's largest undertaking to date, but he would soon become Austin's leading builder best known for his many outstanding Greek Revival houses, among them the Governor's Mansion, still the residence of the Texas chief of state.[20]

Susan, who was visiting her family in New York at the time Cook began construction, had mixed feelings about the project. "I fear it will be a pallace," she told her husband, "and then our neighbours will hate us for having so much better a house than they have." Yet she was delighted at the "comforts in the wilderness" planned for the house, like the luxury of water collected in two large cisterns running through the yard and into the bathroom behind the house. The site was familiar to her. She had lived at almost the same spot with her first husband, near the southwest corner of Hickory (Eighth) and Lavaca Streets. Susan and Peg Leg would eventually own ten lots in the same block. Their new home, out buildings, and grounds would soon cover seven of those lots, or a little more than half a city block.[21]

Spurred on by a report that William, as she sometimes called her husband, was building "the prettiest house in Austin," Susan scoured New York City for furnishings—a splendid easy chair expressly for William's use in the parlor, a "nice little dressing glass" for him to shave by, indeed "many useful things." She asked him for the dimensions of the central hall on the first floor (27 feet long and 14 feet wide) so she could buy oilcloth for the floors, though the Beans thought the cedar floors would be handsome without carpets. One week she and Joanna went shopping nearly every day, and Susan feared she might have been extravagant. When her many purchases reached Houston by schooner it took three wagons to get them to Austin.[22]

By fall 1847 the Wards had finally moved into their new mansion (see illustrations). Situated on a hill just two blocks west of Congress Avenue, the one-and-a-half-story frame house stood out dramatically in a town with few buildings of note. Facing east as it did, the eye of anyone in town looking west would have been caught by the three dormer windows on the second floor, below which was a lovely one-story gallery supported by six box columns. In all there were eleven rooms plus a kitchen and "dark Cellar," both underground. It was one of the coolest houses in town, a matter of no small moment during the long scorching summers, and the two stone cisterns, which could hold 60,000 gallons, provided a bounteous supply of clear water for drinking and bathing. Once completed, the grounds featured a carriage house and stable for five horses, a harness house, corn crib, smoke house, "all other necessary out houses," cow pens, vegetable garden, flowers and trees, an attractive white fence, and eventually a grape arbor. For Texas politicians, the house was finished just in time for the upcoming session of the legislature. Word spread that the Wards would accommodate some legislators. The house was finished, but life for the Colonel and his lady was soon busier than ever.[23]

By the time the Wards took up residence in their new abode they had been married three years, seemingly happy ones, certainly so in the eyes of Susan's family. "All feel sure that I am very very happy and say it is my own fault if I am not with such a husband as I claim for my own," she wrote Peg Leg while visiting New York in 1846. Yet Susan harbored doubts about her marriage that she could not bring herself to reveal to her family. Almost from the beginning she feared that her husband did not love her as she loved him, a fear that, by 1846, she was not hiding from him. "If I could feel that you love me with one half the devotion that I do you I would be the happiest of mortals," she wrote Peg Leg on her way to New York that summer. During her stay she was racked with anxiety at hearing from him so infrequently, "vexing herself to death with fears and conjectures," according to her sister. Shortly before leaving for Texas she again communicated her angst in a letter home: "I have but one fear in life . . . that you do not love me as your noble and generous soul is capable of loving."[24]

Her doubts and fears took root within days of her marriage when in a searing incident she first experienced the fierceness of his anger. The volley of harsh words shocked her, and his outbursts of threatening language in subsequent months and years devastated her. "From the first week of our marriage," she wrote her husband a decade later, "I felt[,] ah keenly too[,] that you believed your wife unworthy of you—and the bitter words you then uttered, (like a thorn planted deep in some vital part) corroded, and from that time have been consuming my very soul and being, and like any other slow poison will sometime destroy its victim."[25]

Other than that letter, what little we know of the initial incident and subsequent mistreatment during the first three years of the marriage comes from Susan's 8,000-word complaint to the New York court in

1859. What she remembered in that document was filtered through years of increasingly bitter feelings. Its purpose, moreover, was not to provide a faithful picture of her marriage but to establish a point of law—that her husband had been so cruel to her that she was entitled to a legal separation with alimony, cruelty being the only legal grounds upon which such a decision could be rendered in New York (adultery was the only grounds for a full divorce). As historian Norma Basch has written of such circumstances in *Framing American Divorce*, the grounds for winning a separation or divorce "provided the key to ordering the particular details of a failed marriage into a formal legal narrative." Thus Susan's complaint is a story of unremitting cruelty on Peg Leg's part. And committed as she was to securing a separation, she and her lawyers may have felt that the statutes gave them little choice but, in Basch's words again, to engage in "creative stretching of the truth." Yet, while her complaint is overstated and the details of his abuse while they lived in Austin uncorroborated and sometimes difficult or impossible to reconcile with other evidence—and virtually all her charges were denied under oath by the defendant—the fact that Peg Leg abused Susan verbally, psychologically, and even physically is not in doubt.[26]

While Susan was visiting her family in New York during 1846 she wrote her husband frequently. Seventeen of her letters survive. They are suffused with professions of her "all absorbing devotion." "You ever have and always will monopolise all the purest fondest and holiest love I ever knew," she wrote. Set against these avowals, it surprises and perplexes one to encounter her allegation that by then his mistreatment—verbal only up to that point, it appears—distressed her so much that before leaving for New York she had resolved not to return and told the Colonel so. That assertion, according to her 1859 complaint, touched off a sequence of events that has come to typify abusive relationships. He "expressed great penitence and sorrow for his conduct," beseeched her not to abandon him, and promised if she returned he would reform; and so she yielded to his entreaties; but later that year when he met her in Houston on her way home he resumed his verbal abuse even before they had reached Austin. Ward denied the truth of each and every detail of the allegation. A similar sequence of events occurred at least twice more in their relationship, according to Susan. Not so, swore Ward. But one instance, in 1856, is corroborated in detail by a private letter Susan wrote at the time to her confidant Lucadia Pease.[27]

What is striking is that Susan would raise the issue of separation with her husband in the first place, especially so early in their marriage. One would think that if she did indeed do so, it was with the intention not of ending her marriage but of saving it. In mid-nineteenth century America "marriages were meant to be permanent, for life," as Hendrik Hartog has written in *Man and Wife in America*; separation was perceived as a mark of failure and a reason for shame, divorce as an "occasional public remedy for a limited list of public wrongs," such as adultery or cruelty, "not a private right." Susan understood that. "I feel that it is my duty to endure unrevealed all the trials through which I have passed," she confessed to Lucadia Pease several years later. "I shrink with dread from bringing disgrace on my children." Susan understood, too, that as a wife she was subject to her husband's authority, that marriage was not a partnership of equals; her husband was in charge, legally as well as conceptually. The belief was not lost on the Colonel, who took his authority—public as well as private—to heart. He expected submissiveness from those dependent upon him, whether it be his wife, his children, or his Land Office clerks. But his wife, in return for her submissiveness, had every reason to expect him to love and care for her. In 1846, still very much in love with Peg Leg, she in all likelihood believed that the solution to his abuse lay in reformation rather than separation.[28]

In a breezy memoir of early Austin published in 1924, William C. Walsh, an Austin resident since 1840, told a story about Peg Leg that would have resonated with Susan. "Colonel T. W. Ward . . . was once chosen mayor. It is hard to tell what moved the people to the choice. He was known to be absolutely honest and fearless and he was also known to be a born tyrant. He did not make requests of his aldermen, he simply gave orders and walked off. . . . The people, regardless of sex, age or wealth, were his wards and he did not hesitate to halt them on the street or elsewhere and, in plain language, administer reproof." Reproof, harshly administered, was probably what Susan sustained early in her marriage. The mistreatment shocked and pained her, but it is entirely possible for her to have hated the abuse and still loved the abuser, especially if he promised to reform. What tormented her was the fear that his hurtful words bespoke a cold heart. "If you love me no longer and do not wish me to return for pitys sake do not hesitate to tell me," she wrote him from New York after going seven weeks without a letter from him, "for although it would be a death blow to my happiness yet if it is so I wish to know it at once."[29]

Sadly, according to Susan's 1859 complaint, Ward's mistreatment worsened after her return from New York. The Wards' impressive new residence may have imparted an air of well-being, but inside, family life deteriorated. A key factor in the escalation of abuse, Susan later told Lucadia Pease, was Ward's loss of his job as land commissioner and his conviction that the Beans had a role in it. Her husband's dealings with the Beans did indeed figure in his downfall, but it was his political enemies in the Texas legislature who did him in.[30]

CHAPTER 9

Downfall

THE ACRIMONY that eventually dominated the marriage of the Wards gave rise to mean comments and malicious charges by both spouses. According to Peg Leg, on one occasion not long before their final separation Susan declared while in the company of others that she had "sacrificed herself by marrying a man with one leg and one arm." However, for many Texans, and certainly the Colonel's political allies, his lost limbs were badges of courage. Wrote one friend at a time when ill political winds threatened his renomination as land commissioner, "May that mighty frame of yours (with an head yet erect) which has lost some of its limbs in the defence of your country, still defie the tempest, and breast the elements of the storm." What both statements had in common was an acute consciousness of his disabilities that was widely shared by those who knew him or knew of him. For Peg Leg, his disabilities were an ever-present factor in his life despite his remarkable success in surmounting them. Thus it was very important for him that the mid-nineteenth century brought significant technological advances in artificial legs available in the United States.[1]

For the Colonel the pivotal figure was William Selpho, an Englishman who came to the United States in 1839 and introduced the Anglesey leg, a breakthrough in the development of prostheses. Invented in England by limb maker James Potts and used most notably by the First Marquis of Anglesey, whose leg had been shattered by grape shot in the Battle of Waterloo, the prosthesis had knee and ankle joints and an articulated foot connected to the knee by artificial tendons. While the wearer of a peg walked with a stiff leg, the Anglesey leg came much closer to approximating a normal walking motion. It could be used with both above-knee and below-knee amputations.[2]

Selpho, who had worked for Potts, set up shop in New York and started manufacturing a modified version of the Anglesey leg, with a rubber sole added to reduce slippage and a rubber plate inserted at the ankle to reduce jarring. Peg Leg probably first made contact with Selpho while visiting the Beans in 1846. Selpho had a prosthesis ready that summer, but it took him several tries to fashion one that met the Colonel's expectations, a process that dragged on for almost two years as each leg had to be shipped back and forth between New York and Austin (or was transported by Aaron Bean, Peg Leg's intermediary with Selpho). "Your leg is now nearly or quite done," Bean wrote the Colonel in early 1848. "Selpho says he wishes he had commenced a new one for he would not have done so much work as on this. It looks first rate and I have no doubt you will be better pleased than with the one you have, or than with this when new." By then Bean was discussing with Selpho just how much he might charge "per annum for legs," presumably because complex artificial legs, unlike simple peg legs, not only could be noisy and required oiling but also succumbed fairly quickly to daily wear and tear, breaking or wearing out.[3] Within a few years, however, Peg Leg was getting prostheses from another innovative American limb maker—B. Frank Palmer (see illustrations). An amputee himself, Palmer bought a leg from Selpho in 1845 for his own use, experimented with improvements, patented them, and started manufacturing limbs. The Palmer leg was honored at the London World's Fair in 1851. According to one wearer, it was lighter than Selpho's and mimicked a natural leg more in appearance and movement. By 1860 Peg Leg seems to have accumulated quite a collection of prostheses from Selpho, Palmer, and probably other limb makers. After he moved back to Austin from New York that year his agent in New York wrote him, "Your trunk of Legs &c. will be duly shipped as directed." The cost for artificial legs was not insignificant. Selpho charged $125 for the first one, and Palmer's standard price was $150. But the Texas legislature helped out, appropriating $300 for the Colonel to assist him in replacing a leg he had lost fighting for Texan independence.[4]

Advances in prostheses improved the Colonel's mobility, lessened his discomfort, and enhanced his appearance, giving him a more normal look than did a peg leg whose wearers were often seen by strangers in a negative light, as "cripples." Yet Ward still faced every day the consequences of his limb loss. Getting around remained a fatiguing task that had implications for his career as well as his personal life. Shortly after he lost his job as land commissioner, the position became a statewide elective office. Eager to win the job back he ran in the first two contests, but it was an uphill battle from the start, and he found that the arduousness of campaigning in a state the size of Texas made victory all the more elusive for a candidate with his "personal infirmities." Nor did a more comfortable prosthesis mean the end of bouts of soreness and periodic acute pain in his residual (right) leg. Attacks of what was called rheumatism (probably osteomyelitis, an infection of bone and bone marrow) plagued him for the rest of his life. "Recently I suffered so much from my leg that life was burthensome," he wrote Susan from Panama in 1854, though in this case the situation unexpectedly improved without the dressings, surgical aid, or other medical attention that had been needed so many other times. On other occasions he complained that because his leg wound was open he could not wear his prosthesis, making it difficult getting about his house, not to speak of getting around the state. He does not appear to have experienced similar pain in his residual arm, but neither did he ever have the advantage of prostheses for his arm and hand, the development of above-elbow prostheses being in its infancy.[5]

If the stresses of living with one leg and one arm took their toll on Peg Leg, so did his three final years as land commissioner, climaxing in his downfall. "His Enemies tried all in their power to get him out of the office," House member Adolphus Sterne observed in 1848, "*right* or *wrong* all kind of low underhanded work was resorted to, and a determination not to give Ward a fair chance was clearly manifested." Colonel John D. McLeod concurred, after witnessing Ward's undoing from his vantage point as a Land Office clerk: "his opponents stooped to the lowest & basest means that men could possibly do to attain their object in his removal." Succumbing to one's enemies was a painful way for a proud, headstrong, hypersensitive person like the Colonel to end his career, but his final years as commissioner were nevertheless constructive as well as distressful. Moreover, he could take heart in surviving seven years in an administrative hot seat and, though often thwarted by uncooperative legislators, in leaving his imprint on the Land Office and the land system.[6]

Although political infighting ultimately sank Ward in 1848, four years earlier it had saved his job from elimination and given him opportunity anew to reshape the land system. In April 1844, representatives of Texas and the United States signed a treaty of annexation that stipulated Texas would cede its public lands to Washington and thus surrender responsibility for their management. But antislavery opposition and political gamesmanship during the U.S. presidential election campaign in 1844 doomed the treaty, and the U.S. Senate voted it down. Once the election was over, however, a renewed effort at annexation carried the day in Washington. Congress passed a joint resolution approving the historic step, and this time Texas got to keep its public lands (but also its sizable public debt as part of the deal). When delegates met in Austin in mid-1845 to write a constitution for the new state, management of Texas's still immense public domain was one of the subjects before the convention, in particular how the issuance of patents might be facilitated but the costs of running the land system reduced.[7]

Summer that year in Austin was typically sweltering—"hot enough out in the sun to roast eggs," one official wrote his wife. The delegates held forth at the rudimentary one-story capitol on a hill above Congress Avenue, the Stars and Stripes waving above it in anticipation of annexation. Across the Avenue at the Land Office Ward hammered out details of a plan to shift the patenting process into a higher gear. His solution should not have surprised the select committee of seven delegates chosen to review it. The problem, as the commissioner saw it, was not in Austin but in the field, and his answer was finally to give him some measure of real control over the field. As it was, he explained, he was forced to divert a third or more of his Austin staff to identifying and rectifying the many errors made in the field. If those clerks instead could devote their time to preparing patents, output would soar. The specifics differed from the reform proposal that Congress had nixed six months earlier. That bill had called for converting each of Texas's thirty-six counties into a permanent land district administered by a district surveyor selected by the commissioner. Now he proposed keeping counties as sections but grouping them into four or more land districts, in effect creating regional land offices, each of which, staffed by a Ward-appointed surveyor and draftsman, would oversee a number of counties, reviewing field notes for errors, compiling accurate maps, and otherwise putting things in order before patents were applied for. The result would be faster production of patents, which together with an increase in patent fees, would produce enough income to make the entire land operation self-supporting and thus relieve the financially depleted Texas government of the burden of funding his office.[8]

The select committee endorsed the proposal almost word for word and recommended that the constitution direct the first state legislature to reorganize the General Land Office to make it self-supporting and establish four to six regional land offices. That, however, was further than the convention as a whole was willing to go, not wanting to strait-jacket the legislature. In the end the new constitution directed estab-lishment of one General Land Office, located in the capital with exclu-sive authority to issue patents, and permitted establishment of such subordinate land offices as the legislature deemed necessary. Obviously management of the public domain in the new state was still open to debate, and heated debate it would get. As would the question of whether Peg Leg was the right man for the top job.[9]

The position of Land Office commissioner was widely conceded to be an exacting one with Texans so touchy and emotional about land. As one of Ward's defenders commented regarding his fall from power, "The multiplicity of fraudulent claims and conflicting titles in Texas, and the complicated and clashing interests of applicants, rendered his position as commissioner a peculiarly difficult and delicate one" Or as Ward himself put it, "I gained many enemies from the too numerous conflicting land claims, and diversified interests of the people, and so numerous were they [his enemies], and so much power had they, that for years I was assailed in the Congress of the Republic of Texas, and the Legislature of the State." His enemies, and those just frustrated or exasperated over some encounter with him, had any number of griev-ances. His passion for precision, for instance, struck some as whim or caprice or just plain obstructionism. His manner put people off. Tact was not in his arsenal of managerial tools, though it would have facili-tated his handling of the ticklish issues that were part and parcel of his job. He was accused by one especially hostile adversary of possessing "the bitterest tongue in Texas" and of treating hundreds with "coarse discourtesy." Many citizens resented the inconvenience and expense of traveling to distant Austin to get patents, especially if they then waited several days or returned empty-handed. Yet what ultimately mattered to Texans was the question of whose land claims prevailed; "the perfecting of land titles without infringing upon rights already acquired, is second to very few subjects engaging the attention of the State," pronounced an Austin newspaper. In August 1845, while the convention completed its work on the new constitution, Ward found himself in the midst of a firestorm over just such an issue.[10]

It erupted over a land map of Red River County in northeast Texas, where many residents were anxious to obtain patents. Months earlier Samuel Sims, county surveyor, had drafted such a map and journeyed some 300 miles to Austin only to have it rejected by the commissioner, rather unceremoniously, Sims later claimed. So Sims, concerned that county landholders would be denied patents until an acceptable map was forthcoming, arranged through Ward to have H. L. Upshur, an accomplished mapmaker and Land Office veteran, undertake the task. Sims was astonished, however, to receive a letter from Upshur indicating that the commissioner insisted the map include all the lands titled by Mexico prior to the War for Independence. "Those old surveys," Sims replied testily to Upshur, "have been looked on by us all the time as fraudulent and consequently they never have been respected by surveyors in this county." In other words since 1836 officials had been surveying claims to land that earlier had been titled by Mexico, in particular a number of huge eleven-league (48,712-acre) grants. If those grants were honored, Sims knew, many Red River County landholders faced a legal nightmare, if not dispossession. It was an explosive issue, and he was prepared to light the fuse. He published Upshur's letter in the *Clarksville Northern Standard*, the voice of northeast Texas and one of the most influential newspapers in the republic, together with his own commentary. He intimated that in rejecting his map without mentioning the question of old titled lands Ward was hiding something. Readers of the *Standard* undoubtedly grasped the unstated implication, that the commissioner was in league with land-greedy Texans who threatened to deprive county residents of their property. Sims ended with a challenge: "Are the citizens of Red River County to take these claims, or are the claims to take them?" Realizing he had stumbled into a hornet's next and abashed that Sims had published his private letter, Upshur backed off a bit in his reply, assuring Sims that Ward did not consider all the old claims in Red River County legal. As for the rejection of Sims's map ("if indeed that can be called a map," Upshur sniped), its numerous other flaws did it in, not the absence of the old claims. Readers of the *Standard*, however, were not apprised of

Upshur's response. Meanwhile, the issue poisoned county politicians, and those from neighboring counties with similar problems, against the commissioner.[11]

Few things made Texan hackles rise like the many immense and allegedly illegal grants made to individuals before independence from Mexico, unless, of course, one was a recipient. It was a matter of such moment that the framers of the constitution in 1836, rushing to complete the document as Mexican troops advanced and the Alamo fell, took time to debate what the constitution should say about it. The result was a paragraph intended to void many fraudulent claims, among them those to eleven-league grants within sixty miles of the border with the United States in violation of Mexican colonization laws.[12] But disagreement over specifics and constant litigation kept the issue alive and emotions on edge. In 1840 Ward's predecessor, John Borden, told a Senate committee that a great portion of northeast Texas, including Red River County, was covered with titles that, if not wholly spurious, were so uncertain as to their boundaries as to make it impossible to locate claims in the area without fear of being within the limits of one or more of those "false claims." The next year (1841) Congress addressed the specific problem of fraudulent claims within sixty miles of the U.S. border (including the Red River border) and directed the commissioner to issue patents on many recent surveys in the area even though the land may have been previously deeded by Mexican authorities.[13] Nevertheless the cloud of uncertainty over property rights cast by legally dubious Mexican grants troubled Texans for the rest of the decade. When queried at the annexation convention as to the extent of spurious grants, Ward responded that he could not provide an answer because he had no way of knowing how many disputed Mexican titles would be sustained by the courts. James Harper Starr worried that protracted litigation over the numerous large grants in the counties bordering the Red River, including those grants the framers of the 1836 constitution had intended to void, "would keep down the prosperity of that region for many years." In 1848 several anxious legislators from northeast Texas warned that "heartless minions of avarice" threatened to "swallow up" much of Texas through judicial enforcement of fraudulent Mexican titles. It was such a volatile issue that one could destroy a candidate for political office in northeast Texas simply by getting a rumor started that he was an owner or advocate of eleven-league claims.[14]

Against this background Samuel Sims's charges in the *Northern Stan-dard* understandably triggered an emotional storm in Red River County, and Sims, as Ward himself put it, assumed the "heroic character of a champion of the peoples' rights" waging war against the commissioner and his "unholy cause." Yet Sims's version of events rested on the "most shameful misstatements," Ward asserted, while his own position, though unpopular, was the legally proper one. He was not, he maintained, authorized to set aside titles issued by the Mexican government on his own. He could do so only if empowered by law. Thus he would require that all lands titled by Mexico be plotted on county maps except those affected by the 1841 legislation. It was the kind of forthrightness that led Sam Houston to write him following his downfall, "If you, colonel, had been less honest, you would have had fewer enemies." As for Sims's map, Ward insisted there was nothing unceremonious or suspect about its rejection. His draftsman gave it a thorough examination and found it "wholly erroneous"; the defects were explained to Sims, who apologized for his failings but declined an invitation to stay at the commissioner's home for a week or so while honing his map-making skills at the Land Office. Ward's trenchant rebuttal, however, did not appear in the *Northern Standard* (it was rejected, said Ward; not so, said the editor) but instead found a home in newspapers published in Marshall and San Augustine, towns that were distant from the Red River County audience he wanted to reach.[15]

The commissioner had long portrayed himself as the defender of the property rights of industrious immigrants against the schemes of speculators and colonizers. Now he found himself cast as the enemy of ordinary Texans. His policy on land titled by Mexico provoked the charge, but other factors may have helped make it credible. Ward was by no means immune to the appearance of impropriety. The land-greedy were certainly known to frequent the Land Office. "I have been visited by several Land mongers," Ward's deputy informed him on one occasion when the commissioner was out of town; one "bedeviled me for two days" and was put on notice that "I could neither be forced or coaxed into measures as easily as he immagined." Peg Leg, in fact, had extensive dealings with Texas's biggest land agents, two of whom, James Harper Starr and Jacob De Cordova, were personal friends. Starr at the time held 50,000 acres in land and land claims. It probably did not go unnoticed that Peg Leg accumulated substantial land holdings himself, but entirely by legal means it appears. And though it failed of passage, in early 1846 a bill was introduced into the legislature authorizing the commissioner to organize the Central Railway Company, and entitling it to occupy public land in a corridor up to 100 yards wide all along the route free of charge. Land was a passion for many Texans, including Peg Leg, and many were not above cheating to get it. So it is not surprising that people's suspicions were easily aroused when it came to land—with the machinations of those claiming large chunks of Texas especially giving rise to wariness and distrust. In such a climate it is also not surprising that allegations of impropriety might be believed, even when, as in Ward's case, there is no evidence to substantiate them.[16]

By the time the first legislature turned its attention to the Land Office it was late March 1846. Ward had just returned from New York City after wowing the Bean clan. Susan was about to depart for a lengthy visit with her family, her troubled marriage very much on her mind. The talk of Austin residents was not politics but the *Kate Ward*. For the first time a steamboat had made its way up the Colorado River as far as the capital, sending the town into a tizzy. "The productions of every country will be wafted to our doors," proclaimed a local newspaper, the "fertile valley of the Colorado" will be unlocked, and its rich harvest "poured into the lap of commerce." Little did they know that five years would pass before a second steamboat made it that far up the shallow and, near its mouth, driftwood-clogged Colorado. In 1846 the possibility that a "new era" was upon them beguiled people for days until the outbreak of the Mexican War in May grabbed their attention and held it for the rest of the year.[17] For the commissioner, patents were a bigger issue than ever. Annexation had generated keen interest in the new state, and many a Texan saw an opportunity to make a killing selling land. Given the uncertainty of titles, however, it was best to have a patent in hand. The commissioner reported that demand for patents had recently tripled.[18] That complicated his life, but utter confusion was potentially sown by the legislature's decision to create thirty-two new counties, all to be carved out of existing counties, a horrific prospect if counties were to be retained as sections. Ward wanted sections that were fixed land areas, but counties were about to start dividing like paramecia, each time necessitating redrawn boundaries, adjustments in the responsibilities of county surveyors, and revision of land maps—unless the commissioner got his way. He had draft legislation ready that converted the thirty-six existing counties into permanent land districts.[19]

The House took the first stab at fashioning Land Office legislation, taking its cue from the convention's select committee by introducing two bills: one to reorganize the General Land Office and a second to establish regional offices. There matters stood for two weeks when the Senate got into the act with a bill similar to the measure ultimately enacted. Drawing heavily on Ward's draft language, it converted Texas's thirty-six counties, as constituted before any division, into permanent land districts, each under charge of a district surveyor who was authorized to take custody of all surveys, maps, and other records in the county surveyor's office. The commissioner was about to get what he had long sought—but not everything he wanted. Where he envisioned authority flowing downward from the top, with the governor appointing the land commissioner who in turn appointed district surveyors, the Senate bill made both the commissioner and the district surveyors elected officials. Meanwhile the House bill to establish regional land offices disappeared into legislative oblivion.[20]

The legislators smiled on the idea of permanent land districts but took dead aim at provisions directly affecting the office of commissioner. The term was cut from four to two years, and a verbal brawl erupted over how he should gain office. Back and forth the senators went, one faction pushing for his appointment by the governor, another for a popular election, some opting for his election by the legislature. The Senate finally settled on a popular election, only to have the House reject that alternative in favor of an election by the legislature. Each side appealed to higher truths. Proponents of a statewide election invoked the principles of "true democracy." Opponents warned of the perils of rushing ahead with an "untried experiment"; the legislature could be counted on to select a commissioner with the managerial experience needed to do the job, but in the "present unsettled condition of the public mind" the voters might chose someone unqualified, with disastrous consequences. For some the rhetoric expressed deep-felt convictions, but for others it simply masked their views about whether Ward should remain as commissioner. Everyone knew that if Governor J. Pinckney Henderson did the choosing, Peg Leg was a shoo-in. He and Henderson were good friends, and when Henderson returned later that year from commanding Texas troops in the Mexican War, it was the Colonel who presided over the reception and dinner in his honor. The legislature was thought, on balance, to be in the commissioner's corner, too. But those seeking his removal believed he could be beaten in a statewide election. The impasse took several days and convoluted legislative maneuvering to resolve. Victory finally went to proponents of a legislative election. Three advocates of a popular election, representing Red River, Lamar, Bowie, and Fannin Counties, all bordering on the Red River, filed a strongly worded protest.[21]

Feuding over the bill delayed its enactment until May 12, the day before the legislature was to adjourn. That afternoon the two houses hurried to vote on a land commissioner before leaving Austin, but several senators broke quorum to prevent the senate's participation. The vote was not held, the legislature adjourned for a year and a half, and Ward was in limbo. Charles DeMorse, the thirty-year-old proprietor of the *Northern Standard*, later explained that the senators from the Red River region were provoked to break quorum by Ward's conniving with large land claimants. Gruff and sharp-tongued, DeMorse was admittedly "no admirer" of Ward's, not a surprise given the bitter hatred he harbored for the Colonel's patron, Sam Houston.[22] Taking up Ward's defense was his steadfast champion James Reily. The former Texas diplomat briefed the commissioner on what had transpired: "It gave me great pleasure to deny the charge, against you, upon which the Senators from Red River & Lamar & the Representatives, endeavored to defend their unmanly & unparliamentary conduct in breaking a quorum & thus prevent your election—You were charged as interested in eleven league grants. This I most unequivocally denied, in all those counties & took pains to circulate among the people its falsity." Ward does indeed appear to have been innocent of the charges, but Reily's defense did not sway his accusers.[23]

His tenure as land commissioner clouded, Ward also faced a staffing crisis. When the legislature, in another round of budget cuts, reduced the salaries of his clerks from $850 to $600, all but two resigned, temporarily crimping production of patents at a time when the commissioner was under pressure to accelerate it. Family men could hardly live on such a salary, one representative complained.[24] Peg Leg fretted about a "total change" in his clerks and then had to contend with myriad afflictions besetting the new ones. That summer, in fact, three died within a two-week period. "Our Office surely was not a health center," commented a survivor, Charles Pressler, whose own experience, however, suggests that life for the Land Office staff was by no means as dire as might appear. Peg Leg offered the highly trained young German $20 a month and free room and board (at the Ward home—Susan was in New York) for two months' work as a draftsman. "Here I lived very happy for a couple of months," Pressler wrote his family, enjoying a room with "a sofa, upholstered chairs[,] a mirror with a golden frame and a bed with mosquito-net," and three hot meals a day, "every one like a big german supper"—poultry of all kinds, ham, peaches, figs, and watermelon, with whole milk and freshly made buttermilk to drink. As for the work, it was "not hard at all, just drawing maps from 9–12 and 2–5 p.m."[25]

Despite his staffing problems the commissioner forged ahead and still managed to issue patents at a brisk pace during 1846 and 1847.[26] His own status remained murky, however. Sam Houston had appointed him to a three-year term in December 1843, so in the absence of a legislative election he filled out that term. On December 22, 1846, however, it ended, and Governor Henderson was in a quandary. With the property rights of so many Texans at stake he could hardly suspend Land Office operations for a year until the legislature reconvened. So he reluctantly exercised a "doubtful power" and gave Ward a recess appointment through the next session.[27]

While leaving him in the lurch, the legislature had at least granted the commissioner a major victory when it approved permanent land districts, a reform that benefited Texas for years to come as counties proliferated and the state expanded westward into unorganized territory. Texas's thirty-two new counties would not set in motion the administrative upheaval he had dreaded, nor would the additional eleven counties formed out of existing counties in early 1848. It must have dispirited him, however, not to be given authority to appoint and remove district surveyors, sentiments that James Harper Starr gave voice to when he wrote Ward condemning perpetuation of the "wretched system of electing County Surveyors & making them in a great degree independent of your control. Whilst the latter evil exists we may expect confusion & mischief from the fraud & incompetence of those officers." David Mitchell, district surveyor for the Robertson Land District, posed exactly the kind of problem that troubled Starr. In 1846 Mitchell and his deputies began "locating" land certificates—surveying claims—for individuals in territory that the republic had already granted to a group of investors to establish the Peters Colony, the empresario venture in North Texas. In other words, Mitchell and his colleagues were trespassing, ignoring a specific prohibition against locating certificates within the colony's boundaries. The colony's agent, not the commissioner, eventually halted the practice in 1848. There was little Ward could do to bring Mitchell to heel other than refuse to patent his surveys, and by then confusion reigned.[28]

Ward also grappled with another long-standing problem that the legislature had, from his perspective, once again shirked: preparation of the county (now district) land maps required by law and indispensable to preventing encroachment of new claims on old ones, a possibility that kept some Texans awake at night and prompted anxious letters to the commissioner. Over the years Ward floated a number of ideas and tried several tactics to rectify, in his view, the far-too-common negligence and ineptness of county surveyors' map-making efforts. These included centralization of map-making in the Land Office; circulation of Ward-appointed draftsmen among the counties; encouragement of counties to hire able draftsmen on their own, such as H. L. Upshur; prodding of county surveyors to take their drafting duties seriously; and furnishing surveyors with translations of Spanish language field notes dated prior to 1836 and other documentation needed to do the job properly. "It is to be hoped that neither time nor pains will be spared by you in compiling a correct and official map of your county" was an admonition that became familiar to many a county surveyor.[29] In 1846 Ward wanted the legislature to fund two draftsmen in Austin and another four who would circulate among the land districts. He was denied the latter, but the legislature at least authorized two permanent draftsman in Austin, tacit recognition of Ward's longstanding contention that the General Land Office had a significant role to play in map-making. The commissioner also hired temporary draftsmen, such as Charles Pressler, from time to time. A few years later Pressler would hire on full time and serve almost half a century in the Land Office, much of it as chief draftsman. In his final report to the legislature in December 1847, Ward threw up his hands at the error-filled maps produced by county and district surveyors and insisted that the "one correct course" was for professional draftsmen in the Land Office, like Pressler, to do the work. During the 1840s Ward set the stage, as one student of the subject has written, for the growth in the Land Office's drafting staff and the rapid increase in its map production that occurred during the 1850s.[30]

Though he was making headway, the commissioner found the never-ending struggle to win improvements in the land system wearing. The bruising legislative session of 1846 in particular took a toll, especially on top of earlier legislative rejections. By 1847 his reformist zeal was flagging. When James Harper Starr wrote him in mid-1847 recommending another push to make district surveyors appointive, he responded that he had but little influence with the legislature and thought his wisest strategy was to forego promoting new measures and instead concentrate on combating "such bad measures as the Legislature might get up." Whereas his annual reports in the early 1840s bristled with sweeping proposals and tough language, in his 1847 report he told the legislators he would not advise much change; reforms that had once been good policy would now bring more confusion than benefit to a citizenry that had learned to cope with a bad system.[31]

Instead, the commissioner urged replacement of the Land Office building. Several months earlier the President's House had burned to the ground and sparks from the fire almost took the Land Office with it, but wet blankets on the roof and then a fortuitous change in the wind—"a mere god send" in the words of one clerk—saved it. It was the danger of fire to a wooden structure that gave the problem such urgency, Ward stressed, especially since the dilapidated building adjoined several wooden houses. A new fireproof building, made of brick with stone or brick floors, a slate roof, and iron window frames and shutters, was imperative.[32] Three years later construction began on a stone building designed by Land Office draftsman Robert Creuzbaur. Located northwest of the present capitol, it was hailed by one observer as "a superb building, ample, and reared with rock neatly polished," with a "beautiful dome." But it quickly proved too small and was replaced in 1858 by a mock medieval, castle-like structure that housed the Land Office for almost sixty years. Known thereafter as the Old Land Office Building, it is now home to the Capitol Visitors Center and is situated on the southeast corner of the capitol grounds.[33]

With the approach of the 1847–1848 legislative session Peg Leg's friends and enemies steeled themselves for the anticipated strife over his future. Rumor had it that his adversaries planned to introduce a bill making land commissioner a statewide elective office. Colonel John McLeod thought the "old man" (he was all of forty) would beat them at that game since he had gained a great many friends of late. McLeod was close to the scene. A Land Office clerk for more than three years, he had known the commissioner for more than twelve—ever since that fateful evening in New Orleans when both enlisted in the Greys. McLeod was on the battlefield in San Antonio the morning a cannon shot shattered his friend's leg and was by his side on Texas Independence Day five years later when a prematurely firing cannon mangled Peg Leg's arm. He intended to stay by the Colonel's side during the upcoming legislative battle and would pay for his loyalty with his job. For now he was wary but hopeful. "Col Ward I think will have hard times of it but will I think weather the storm," he advised Thomas Rusk, then a U.S. senator from Texas. Whatever happened, Rusk could count on McLeod to keep him abreast of developments. McLeod expected six or seven legislators to board with him and would keep an ear cocked for their "*chit chat.*"[34]

By mid-December 1847 the state's second legislative session was under way. Riding into town to cover events for the *Northern Standard*, Charles DeMorse was struck by Austin's decay since his last visit several years earlier. The one-story log buildings housing government offices along upper Congress Avenue, rough to begin with, now made a "sorry appearance indeed," while the frame buildings further down showed the wear of time and weather. Yet, he was told, the town wore a much better look than it had when the Convention met in 1845 and "started the rabbits from the weeds."[35] Just as McLeod anticipated, within days of convening, Ward's opponents introduced a bill in the House making land commissioner a statewide elective office. It will "prove an abortion," McLeod predicted, and indeed it did encounter stiff opposition, first from a majority of the Land Office committee and then from the House as a whole. Ward's backers won the day, but before they prevailed, the issue engaged the members' attention for two weeks and generated heated speeches and much feeling on both sides. "The Red River delegation are exerting themselves to place the election with the people," DeMorse reported approvingly. Explaining the setback to the folks back home, a disappointed Red River County politician ascribed it to the fact that many House members from other parts of Texas came to Austin without a mandate on the question from their constituents.

They found the Land Office in "admirable order, well regulated, nothing out of place, but all like clock work" and the commissioner eager to accommodate them. "They do not feel disposed to turn him out of office, which they think they would do by giving the election to the people."[36]

Buoyed by their victory, the Colonel's supporters immediately called on the House to join the Senate in electing a commissioner. But his enemies were not about to capitulate. Defeated in the opening battle, they launched a second attack. That very day Representative William Bourland of Lamar County, in northeast Texas, (brother of Senator James Bourland, whose district included Lamar and adjacent Red River, Fannin, and Bowie counties), succeeded in pushing through the House a resolution calling for an investigation as to whether the commissioner had committed "malfeasance in office." The Land Office committee—"the committee raised to find Col Ward guilty," in Representative Adolphus Sterne's view—launched an inquiry: first into the manner in which the commissioner had spent funds appropriated for patents, stationery, salaries, and other expenses, and second into what fees he had charged for services and how he had disposed of the proceeds. The election was postponed.[37]

It was a nasty business from the outset. The committee called on Ward for detailed financial records and heard testimony from a number of witnesses, the most conspicuous among them Hanson Catlett, the former clerk Peg Leg had fired upon discovering he was selling forged field notes. Seizing an opportunity for revenge, Catlett promised the committee wonders if he was permitted to examine the commissioner's books, apparently expecting to put Ward on the spot when he refused to give Catlett access. Instead, when Catlett and the committee showed up at the Land Office, Ward produced every book and paper Catlett asked for and Catlett came up empty. But Peg Leg's victory would prove only momentary. "They are determined to beat Ward," McLeod told Rusk, "and no measure is left unturned in its accomplishment."[38]

Engineering the campaign that culminated in Ward's ouster were the Bourland brothers, William in the House and James in the Senate, "the best log rollers I have seen in Texas," McLeod declared. They were joined by a new force on the Texas political scene, John H. Reagan, the twenty-nine-year-old representative from Nacogdoches County and later a U.S. Congressman and postmaster general of the Confederacy. Reagan's vilification of the commissioner as a member of the investigative committee outraged Ward's friends. He "has sold himself soul & body to the Red River crowd," grumbled Sterne. McLeod, disgusted that Reagan had "fallen into the ranks of the Bourlands," called him "the poorest apology for a public man I ever became acquainted with." Ward loosed his own frustration at the unfolding of events in a letter to Starr: "So much corruption and intrigue I have never known as exists in a minority of the present legislature. I am almost sick of Texas."[39]

Five days later the investigative committee issued a majority report finding the commissioner guilty. Abuse upon abuse was charged: more than $5,000 in appropriated funds not accounted for, public funds spent for purposes not authorized or wasted on extravagant expenditures, clerks paid for services not rendered, unlawful fees collected, and so on. The committee's minority report, released earlier, had exonerated the commissioner, and now his friends in the House jumped to his defense, proposing that he be given an opportunity to respond to the charges. A dogfight ensued on the floor of the House. The words *"liar"* and *"skunk"* were "exchanged with some degree of liberality," Charles DeMorse reported. Representatives almost came to blows. In the streets of town the authors of the majority report were threatened with mobbing. In the end the proposal was tabled and Ward's right to rebut the charges denied.[40]

Looking back on these events three years later, DeMorse spelled out what many knew at the time but did not speak openly about on the floor of the House: "there was something else, having a bearing on the matter," something the committee investigating the commissioner did not say a word about because nothing that bore on it turned up in its investigation. The issue missing from the record but driving the investigation, according to DeMorse, was the belief "that the commissioner was in collusion with the large claimants of the Country, the gentlemen who hold claims for eleven to thirty leagues." It was this, he asserted in the *Northern Standard*, that "threw the members from this region *necessarily*, against his continuance in an office, where he might be so dangerous to their constituents and themselves." Emotions over Mexican titles ran so strong, in fact, that a bill was introduced that session, which, if passed, would have given private citizens a pretext for challenging the validity of many Mexican titles.[41]

Viewing the majority report's charges against Ward in the context illuminated by DeMorse helps explain why so many of them were open to question. The charges were not devoid of merit, but his accusers overreached, making more of the evidence than it warranted. They were determined the get him, and the charges provided the means. Much was made, for instance, of seemingly minor sins: paying a clerk $100 when he should have received only $50, and using funds appropriated for a clerk instead to pay a bookbinder to repair and bind more than 100 volumes of Mexican-era field notes, maps, and titles. True, the Land Office charged people fees not specifically authorized by law for making copies of titles, surveys, and the like, and Ward and his clerks kept the proceeds, but the practice was hardly as shady as might appear. The investigative committee itself admitted it dated from the opening of the Land Office in 1837 and was customary while John Borden was commissioner. Nor, Ward pointed out, had it ever been deemed illegal or improper, not even by the many legislators who obtained copies and paid fees. Similarly, the committee overreached in voicing its suspicions that two trips Ward took to New York, though made "ostensibly for the purchase of Patents," were "merely trips of pleasure at the expense of the State." While it was on one of those trips that Ward first met the Beans and was royally entertained, it is also true that he returned with a large quantity of urgently needed patent blanks. The most serious charge—that more than $5,000 in appropriated funds were not accounted for—appears to have been at best misleading. The commissioner had drawn on funds appropriated in 1846 and 1847 to purchase patent blanks and stationery, but due to extensive delays and other problems in acquiring them he had not yet filed vouchers for all the funds with the comptroller. The minority report made the point that until Ward received all the patents he could not be expected to close his accounts. Several months later, after another 5,300 patent blanks finally reached the capital, not only did the Texas comptroller certify that all the money had been properly accounted for, but also that there was a balance due Ward of $269 for patents and stationery he had paid for out of personal funds. The legislature, at its next session, saw to it that he was reimbursed.[42]

The irony of the indictment was that the Colonel, who so often had faulted others for not following the letter of the law, was tripped up himself time and again for doing the same thing. He collected and turned in $62,405 in patent fees, but, the committee noted, "in some instances" he patented land without charging the fees prescribed by law. And indeed he had, benefiting Anson Jones, Mirabeau Lamar, the secretary of the treasury, three Land Office clerks, and himself for a grand total of $65. A trivial amount but, said the committee, "a violation of the law." By weaving actions like this and more ominous appearing ones into a pattern of abuse, the majority report had its intended impact. "Fraud of a magnificent kind has been practiced in the land office," one House member concluded. McLeod lost almost all hope. The most energetic and efficient members of both houses were now in the opposition camp, "all well drilled under the Bourlands," he told Rusk, and so much feeling had been stirred up against the commissioner that unless there was a reversal of sentiment during the few days left before the election he would lose.[43]

On February 28, 1848, a joint session finally convened to determine the commissioner's fate. It was six weeks since his supporters, triumphant after derailing a bill establishing a statewide election, had called on the legislature to hold its election forthwith. Distraught at the antipathy generated toward him in the interim, Ward submitted an extended defense of his actions to both chambers, but it was too late. House members voted against him by a decisive margin, eclipsing his majority support in the Senate and giving the election to former representative George Smyth. "You never saw a tirant fall with such shouts," one representative rejoiced. "The struggle was great in his favour, but Justice had to be done." Two weeks later his opponents won another victory when the legislature made commissioner of the General Land Office henceforth a statewide elective office. Despondent at his undoing and the savaging of his reputation, the Colonel took comfort from the words of his patron and mentor Sam Houston, who assured him that he had served Texas well, saving her "millions of acres, and of money," whereas "had a Borden been in your situation, I am satisfied that Texas would have been a great loser and badly corrupted!"[44]

Peg Leg attributed his defeat to "knavery and falsehood" and, later, to bribery, but he was ultimately defeated by those who thought his policies as land commissioner, especially his support of claims in northeast Texas dating from before independence, threatened their interests. As time passed, though, he seized on another issue in his ouster, the role of his wife's family. The Beans figured in several charges brought against him. It was Aaron Bean's difficulties in filling his orders for patent forms that led to the charge of appropriated funds that were unaccounted for. It was a trip to New York during which he first met the Beans that helped spark allegations of unwarranted expenses. The clerk who was paid $100 rather than $50 was Aaron Bean's wife's brother, whom Peg Leg had encouraged to come to Texas to work at the Land Office and whom he had, in effect, credited with travel time in paying him. Whether the Colonel's accusers, who were undoubtedly aware of his tangled relationships with the Beans, had them in mind in framing their charges is unknown, but in Peg Leg's mind his involvement with them had played a role in his downfall. And thus it was that several years later Susan wrote plaintively to her confidant Lucadia Pease, "Oh my friend this defeat occasioned me hours, days, yes years, of agony—for strange as it may appear to you I have often been accused of being the cause of it through my relations." It was another grievance in a marriage about to be overwhelmed by them.[45]

CHAPTER 10

A Time of Troubles

O N A MAY MORNING in 1854 a horse-drawn carriage carrying
Susan Ward and her five children left Austin and headed east
for Galveston. She would not return for six years. Several months earlier her husband had departed the Texas capital for Panama City,
Panama, to serve as U.S. consul, and now Susan was on her way to New
York City to see her family. The trip across the sparsely settled prairie
was slow and uncomfortable. One day it rained torrents, and when they
crossed the rough Brazos River bottom a pain in Susan's side grew so
intense she feared she might die before they reached that night's
stopover. Four days later they arrived at last in Galveston, where her
brother Aaron waited to accompany them north. No longer under her
husband's roof, she sat down that afternoon and for the first time confessed the depth of her anguish to Lucadia Pease, whom she had
recently befriended and come to love dearly:

> The deeptoned sorrow and heartrending griefs of the last ten
> years of my life have subdued the highest and noblest aspirations
> of my soul and turned to bitterness and gaul allmost every feel-
> ing of my heart, and made me distrust nearly all mankind—I have
> tried to conseal my sorrows in the deepest recess of my heart,
> until they have well nigh consumed my very existence—for I
> would not endure the thought that this cold and cruel world
> should know my sufferings. . . . Read the Discarded Daughter
> and in the sufferings of Allice, Mrs Garnet, you will find but one
> tenth of the horrors of the last ten years of my life—[1]

If Lucadia Pease did indeed read E. D. E. N. Southworth's 1852
novel, *The Discarded Daughter*, she must have been stunned that Susan

thought her trials far worse than those of Alice Garnet. The sixth of more than forty novels written by one of nineteenth-century America's best-selling authors, *The Discarded Daughter* tells the story of a woman victimized and dispossessed by her husband during their "wedded life of tyranny on his side and sufferance on hers." Handsome, imposing, and dignified, General Garnet was also stern, unbendable, and when crossed, of violent temper. "He was a man who could unite the utmost inflexibility, and even cruelty of purpose, with the utmost graceful and gracious urbanity of manner." Under the General's rule Alice's life was endlessly painful. He tricked her out of her inheritance, disowned and banished her beloved daughter, and ultimately drove Alice to the depths of despair and nearly to death. A decade of "agony and intense suffering" at the Colonel's hands had likewise taken a heavy toll on Susan, she told Lucadia Pease. She felt "mentally and physically worn out" and hoped to find in heaven the quiet and rest that had not been hers for many years.[2]

By the time Susan set out for New York, six years had passed since her husband's defeat in the Texas legislature. That humiliating setback, in February 1848, had come at a time when the Ward family seemed to be thriving. The previous August they had moved into their new home. Two months later Susan gave birth to her second child with Peg Leg, James William, "the handsomest child I ever saw," declared his doting uncle. Predictably nicknamed Jim, he joined brothers Robie Marston, aged seven, and two-year-old Dudley Ward in the Ward "Castle," as Peg Leg called their spacious residence in jest.[3] The family lived in high style for Austin at the time, thanks to the Colonel's elevated position in the government and his success in accumulating an estate. He enjoyed an annual salary of $1,500 as land commissioner (among government officials only judges and the governor earned more), collected more than $1,000 a year in rents from the Long Row, and held real estate valued at $40,000 at a time when owning $20,000 in real property put one in the richest 2 percent of all urban heads of families in Texas.[4]

Yet 1847 and 1848 were troubled times for the Wards. Following his ouster, Ward was dispirited, restless, and bored. The capital city was not a stimulating place for a man of his intellect with time on his hands. He wrote Rusk, "I shall be miserable indeed in this lonely place without something to engage my mind." Now that the legislature had adjourned, Austin was reduced to its several hundred residents and a trickle of visitors. An "inconsiderable village" was how one visitor, future president Rutherford B. Hayes, characterized the town, while another frowned on its "muddy lanes, log huts, and drunken idlers."[5] Thankfully Rusk sent the Colonel some issues of the *Congressional Globe*, forerunner of the *Congressional Record*, and he whiled away some of the tedious hours perusing them. What Ward really wanted was "honorable employment." Without it, as he would write one of his sons years later, he simply could not be happy. Nor could he pay his debts. Short of cash, he sold one of his slaves and prodded the manager of the Long Row to come up with his rents. Finding employment commensurate with his skills and status was not easy. He sounded out Rusk about a government appointment, commencing a quest that would eventually take him to Panama.[6]

For Susan the years 1847 and 1848 were far more distressing, despite the joys of a new home and child. Peg Leg began to abuse her physically, or so she charged in her 1859 complaint to the New York court, the only surviving evidence of the abuse. The initial incident occurred early in 1847, not long after she returned home from her eight-month trip to New York and was reunited with her husband. It was about a year before the Colonel lost his job. Her sister Joanna was visiting them at the time. The incident was apparently triggered by Peg Leg's fury at Susan's brothers over an unknown grievance, perhaps a botched business deal or something to do with Aaron's exasperating delays in getting the Colonel his much-needed patent forms. This is how Susan described his abuse to the court. Peg Leg, while Joanna was in the room, called his wife a "damned liar" and said her brothers Aaron and Dudley were "damned liars also." When Susan objected to such language, her husband struck her "two violent blows upon her face with such force, as to cause the blood to flow freely therefrom, the marks of which blows were carried by plaintiff [Susan] many days thereafter." Upon Joanna's protesting, Peg Leg locked the door of the room, drew a pistol, cocked it, and threatened to shoot Joanna if she attempted to unlock the door or call for help. He then seized a horsewhip, doubled it up, approached Susan holding the whip over her in a menacing manner, and twice asked her whether she persisted in denying that her brothers were liars. When Susan finally replied that her brothers were not liars, Ward struck her two times with the whip.[7]

In his response to the court, the Colonel declared the allegations all "utterly untrue" and furthermore that the entire time he and Susan lived together he never said or did anything with the intention of wounding her feelings, a claim that is difficult to credit but may reflect his feeling that, her unhappiness notwithstanding, he had always genuinely cared for her. Casting more substantial doubt on Susan's allegations is Joanna's reaction. One would have thought that such an incident was traumatic for her and would turn her against her brother-in-law, but if that was the case she hid it, for there is no sign of it in comments she or her brother Aaron made after Ward took her to Galveston in May to join Aaron for the journey home. While *en route* to New York Aaron wrote Ward a very warm letter acknowledging the Colonel's "unbounded generosity and kindness" to his wife and remarking further, "I quite agree with [Jo]Anna, who was just saying she never met that man who was so capable of making one love him and who had such an influence over them as Brother Col Ward." No sooner was Joanna home than she penned an affectionate five-page missive to "mon cher frère," emoting that "the first object that attracted my attention on entering the parlour was the Col's picture looking—not half as well as the original when I saw him last—not half as well as on that glorious evening before we parted with the light of the moon resting on his brow, but still enough like the Col's self to be most valuable. How much I should like to see you all."[8]

It seems too much to believe that Susan made it all up, but it may well be that the incident was less traumatic than she would have it, that her memory of the episode was colored by the anguish of the intervening twelve years, or perhaps she or her lawyer deliberately exaggerated its viciousness for purposes of making a point in court. In either case, chances are she was not terribly exacting in recalling the details of incidents. She told the court, under oath, that in a confrontation a decade later her husband hit her in the face and she "bled at least two quarts."[9] Whatever the explanation, the Colonel's outsized reputation with the Beans remained intact despite his abuse, and Susan suffered alone, without emotional support from her family in New York, in whom she could not bring herself to confide.

Early the next year (1848) during the very months her husband was subjected to character assassination and forced retirement at the hands of his political enemies, Susan was subjected to further violence at the hands of her husband, according to her 1859 complaint. Twice that winter he knocked her to the floor, on one occasion knocking out a tooth. Another time, following his clamorous return home late one evening in the company of a drunken friend, he struck her with his clenched fist. Then, judging by Susan's allegations in 1859, Peg Leg's physical abuse seems to have abated for a time and their life went on. Susan was soon pregnant again and gave birth the next year to a daughter who lived only a short time. The Colonel set his sights on regaining his position as land commissioner, seeking not just employment but vindication. Victory in a popular election would, he felt, remove from his name the "unjust stigma" his enemies had branded it with and thus restore his honor.[10]

The first statewide election for land commissioner was scheduled for August 1849. As election day approached, a friend in Houston assured the Colonel that in Harris County "every appearance" was favorable to his winning, but prospects were not so bright in northeast Texas, where Charles DeMorse pointedly lavished praise on the incumbent, George Smyth, for his "unquestioned integrity" and "courtesy to applicants." Smyth declined to campaign, pleading the weighty duties of his office, and Ward mounted only a modest effort. He lost decisively to Smyth, taking a beating in Red River County and adjacent Lamar County by the whopping margin of 855 to 5. He obviously had some political fences still to mend. Not one to take defeat lying down, he convinced himself that had he canvassed the entire state he would have won, a dubious conclusion it would seem but one in which Anson Jones concurred. Ward resolved to make another run in 1851, and Jones stoked his combative fires by assuring him success was "CERTAIN."[11]

Though the voters had spurned him, he did not go wanting. Texas Governor Peter Bell gave him a temporary appointment during 1850 as a special land commissioner. His assignment: to mollify angry settlers in the Peters Colony in North Texas. The republic, in hopes of increasing its population, had granted large tracts of public land in North Texas to a group of investors, originally led by Englishman William Peters, on condition they recruit settlers. By 1850 the Peters Colony was home to some 1,400 families and single men attracted by promises of free land from the company running the colony, but the colonists were still without titles to their land. The company, moreover, insisted on retaining up to half the land granted each settler for services rendered, such as surveys, seed for planting, powder, and shot. The colonists fought back with petitions and mass meetings, convincing the legislature to step in and pass a law securing their claims. Ward's job was to travel through the colony issuing a certificate, much like a headright certificate, to each colonist for the amount of land due him. Since to establish a claim a colonist only needed two witnesses to swear that he had settled before July 1848, it seemed a simple matter, but the colonists were scattered over several remote counties. Ward set up temporary headquarters in five different towns. He was undoubtedly a sympathetic arbiter, having long seen himself as the defender of the rights of settlers against speculators and colonizers. Eventually he issued almost 1,300 certificates, and his efforts proved a fruitful, though by no means final, step in resolving the colonists' grievances. Grateful colonists in Johnson County honored him by naming their first county seat Wardville.[12]

Early in 1851, with the next election for land commissioner now just half a year away, the Colonel again threw his hat in the ring and this time followed it up with spirited words and action. He reminded voters of his former mastery of the office and defended himself against the malicious charges heaped upon him by his enemies. He professed how much he wanted to clear his name ("all that I have now to live for") and asked the voters to do him that justice by electing him. His campaign took him far afield, even into enemy country. In a speech at the Clarksville courthouse he laid into his nemesis, Charles DeMorse, sparking an angry exchange between the two in the *Northern Standard*. Ward polled much better in Red River and Lamar Counties than he had in 1849, but it was hardly enough. His former deputy, Stephen Crosby, defeated him 18,257 votes to 7,290.[13] Three straight defeats in races for land commissioner—the 1848 legislative election and two popular elections—were frustrating enough, but Ward's losing streak was not over. Six months later he was thwarted in an attempt to resuscitate his career as a builder. The state of Texas decided it was high time to construct a permanent capitol to replace the deteriorating temporary building dating from 1839. Ward, already a veteran of one capitol construction project, was nominated as superintendent, but at a joint legislative session convened to decide who should fill the position he lost by one vote.[14]

Four years after his downfall the Colonel still had not found himself. Then his luck changed. Perhaps it was a sign of better things to come when Austin voters elected him mayor in late 1852, but his big break came with the U.S. presidential election that year. Franklin Pierce, a Democrat, was chosen to succeed Millard Fillmore, a Whig. A Democrat himself, Ward had close ties to the two most powerful Texas Democrats in Washington, Senators Thomas Rusk and Sam Houston. A federal appointment suddenly loomed as a real possibility. In February 1853 he set out for Washington, armed with effusive letters of support from prominent Texas Democrats. By early March his backers, with Rusk in the lead, had targeted a specific position for him, U.S. consul to the port city of Panama on the Pacific side of the Panamanian Isthmus. The incumbent, Amos Corwine, a Whig, was a marked man under the spoils system. Rusk made clear to Secretary of State William Marcy that he took "special and strong interest" in the case and would regard Ward's appointment as a personal favor not soon to be forgotten. Marcy was besieged by office-seekers—befitting the man who coined the phrase, "to the victor belong the spoils"—but Senator Rusk was not a person to be trifled with.[15] The appointment came two months later. Ward was about to join a corps of some 130 men, based in ports and cities around the world, whose job it was to promote U.S. trade, monitor and assist U.S. shipping, protect but also discipline seamen on U.S. vessels, and come to the aid of U.S. citizens in trouble in their districts.[16]

The main question on everyone's mind at that point seemed to be how lucrative a position it was—how sizable were the fees it would generate for the Colonel. Before 1855 consuls were not paid salaries but instead kept the fees they charged for their services. Author Nathaniel Hawthorne had plucked the busiest consulate, Liverpool, but Panama City was a "money-making post," according the *New York Times*. Dudley Bean assured Ward that it was worth at least $10,000 a year and in two or three years would be the "second consulate in the world." The Isthmus was already a vital artery for Americans traveling between the East Coast and California, and Bean no doubt expected that, when completed, the railroad across the Isthmus then under construction would attract even greater numbers of people and goods in the absence of a transcontinental railroad in the United States. The *New York Herald*, however, called such claims "extravagant" and insisted that the post was worth only $3,000 to $3,500 a year, just enough to pay Amos Corwine's expenses. Whatever the case, Aaron Bean thought he and Ward could at least make a good deal of money on the side by establishing a business house in Panama City. Ward agreed.[17]

By June 1853 the Colonel was back in Austin making preparations for his venture, but troubles with his stump, brought on by a new prosthesis, kept him in bed and in pain, and improvement was slow. In the meantime it was decided that Susan and the children would stay in Austin for the time being, while Peg Leg went on to Panama alone.[18] In mid-August he resigned as mayor, expressing regret that his lengthy trip to Washington in the spring and his subsequent illness had prevented him discharging the duties of the office in the manner expected. In fact, he had not met with the city council since February. Before August was out he was on his way to New York, where he met New Yorkers with commercial interests in Panama and purchased a dozen books on subjects like international law, shipping, and Spanish. On October 7 he boarded the wooden side-wheel steamship *Ohio* for the voyage to Panama, his leg much improved but still not entirely well. His bosom friend Anson Jones was there to see him off.[19]

Peg Leg had been in Panama City but a few months when he received several disturbing letters from Susan. "I find very little in this cold world worth living for," she wrote. She spoke despairingly of her marriage. "I feel that I have lived in vain, that my life has been a perfect blank, for the only being that could have satisfied the romance of my girlhood or the more ardent and higher aspirations of my mature years never loved me, no no Col you deceived yourself when you believed that your poor Sue could make you happy." She went on to recall the feeling she had had from the first week of their marriage that he thought her unworthy of him and how the heartbreaking words he then uttered had been consuming her soul. "Dearest this is not the fancy of a diseased brain no no I ask heaven to witness that it is true." She thought a visit to her native state might restore both her spirits and her health; she was so thin he would be ashamed of her. So she planned to make a short visit to New Hampshire before joining him in Panama.[20]

The months since the Colonel's departure had been draining ones for Susan. The house was crowded with family, boarders, and guests, sometimes a dozen or more people besides the servants. Susan had five children now, thirteen-year-old Robie and ten-year-old Mary (home following her six year stay with the Beans), and her three children with Peg Leg, nine-year-old Dudley, six-year-old Jim, and two-year-old Anna, born in 1851. They were a handful, but it was the sad fate of her much beloved younger sister Joanna that took an emotional toll, the same Joanna who, according to Susan, had witnessed Peg Leg's abuse in 1847. Joanna had married a Galveston businessman who adored her— "the hope and stay of my life," he called her—and they had a child together, but Joanna was sickly, and by 1853 she was suffering from "consumption," probably tuberculosis. She came to the Wards in July 1853 to convalesce. Her husband arranged for their child to travel to New York with a nurse to live with the Beans, but the child died on the way. When Joanna's condition deteriorated despite all Susan's efforts and the care of a doctor, her husband came to Austin to be with her, but a month later, after several days' illness, he died of dysentery. By then it was mid-October and Peg Leg had been gone more than six weeks. Joanna lingered three more months, confined to her room and Susan confined to her house. "Mrs. Ward is nearly worn out with constant watching night & day," reported Anson Jones, who dined at the Ward home on both Christmas Day and New Year's Day. Joanna's suffering and her death in January 1854 left Susan devastated.[21]

In her sorrow during Joanna's final days Susan was comforted by the gentle words and tender sympathy of a new friend, and in the days that followed she came to appreciate more and more how blessed she was by that friendship. Eventually she would realize she had found a confidant to whom she could unburden herself about her marriage. Lucadia Pease, her husband Marshall, and their two little daughters had moved into the Ward residence a month prior to Joanna's death. They were boarders, living in one large room, though they received visitors in the family parlor. And visitors a plenty they had, for Marshall Pease was the new governor of Texas. In fact, he spent his very first night at the Wards' composing his inaugural address. Texas governors had been staying in hotels and boardinghouses since the capital returned to Austin. Construction of the Governor's Mansion did not begin until 1854 and was not completed until 1856, when the Peases became the first residents. Marshall had wanted to rent a house but could find nothing comfortable and so chose to board with the Wards, "a very pleasant family," Lucadia told her sister, with "a very good house for Texas."[22] Lucadia was thirty-nine at the time, Susan thirty-six. From the outset Lucadia found Susan "very agreeable," their like-mindedness fostered by their common New England origins. The Peases were from Connecticut. Lucadia, like Susan, had been well schooled and was a reader, and soon she was dipping into "Sue's novels." Unlike Susan, however,

Lucadia enjoyed a family life that was happy and loving and a bond with her husband that was strong and affectionate. She must have wondered why Susan barely spoke of her husband.[23]

Susan's new friendship did not rescue her from her melancholy. Grieving over Joanna's death, she also faced a crisis as great as any since the death of her first husband. Should she join her husband in Panama? He wanted her to, and she felt she should. His spirits, like hers, were depressed. He was lonely in Panama City and feeling deserted. His leg was troubling him, and his eyesight was so bad at the moment he could not read. To her intimation that she did not have sufficient means to meet her expenses, he responded that she need only make her wants known and he would provide. "I have no love for money, more than to use it for the comfort and happiness of those with whom I am connected, love and revere. . . . All I have is yours." He closed with "great assurances of untiring love." It was in reply to that letter that she told him she would go to him after a visit to her native state.[24]

Yet she did not want to. There were too many bitter memories, of his outbursts of anger, of the times he had threatened her, of the occasions when he had struck her. He did not love her, she was sure, thinking her unworthy of him. It was not only his abuse of her but of those close to her that pained Susan, in particular his two stepchildren, Robie and Mary, and her aged servant, Creecy, an affectionate and conscientious African-American woman. He insisted that he never inflicted violence on either of his stepchildren other than punishment, administered with her approval, that they deserved for disobedient conduct, but she remembered the times she had protested his mistreatment, in one instance two years earlier stepping between him and Mary and absorbing a rain of blows.[25]

She had thought often of leaving him, but there were so many things that held her back—the sacredness of marital relations and her duty to him as his wife, her lingering hope for his reformation, her dread of public scandal and the disgrace it would bring upon her children, her fear of his violent reaction to her leaving. When Susan finally confessed to Lucadia that her ten years of marriage had been full of "horrors" she felt guilty and anxious and asked Lucadia to destroy the letter, "for I would not have any eyes less generous than your own scan this proof of my weakness, yea almost unfaithfulness, to the father of my children."[26]

For years Susan had hidden her sorrows. "Let the veil of forgetfulness drop over the past," she wrote Lucadia. It was her duty to "endure unrevealed" all the trials through which she had passed. But she could not escape the emotional consequences of her unhappiness and her feeling of powerlessness in the face of it. She began to feel ill often and suffer pains in her back and side. She lost weight. She spoke frequently of the bitterness of life. She became irritated at her children, particularly her sons, who she feared were emulating their father. As she later wrote Marshall Pease, "when I saw my boys exhibit any conduct that I thought if unchecked would lead to what I shudder to see in men, I lost nearly all my patience. . . . For you well know that it is no easy task to make boys quiet gentle and good—when they are daily seeing imoral examples in adults which they consider manly and great."[27]

It was hard enough being hundreds of miles away from her relatives in New York, whom she looked upon as "her natural defenders and protectors" in the default of her husband, but in Panama she would be isolated from both her family and her Texas friends and alone with her husband. Brother Aaron, however, had other thoughts, which he first broached to the Colonel at the time of his appointment and elaborated on in a February 1854 letter. Aaron had come to Austin at the time of Joanna's death and stayed for several weeks. He had long thought Austin too confining for the Wards. "For a place of business give me New York—the great Emporium of the Western Hemisphere," he wrote Ward. The schools, moreover, were "ten times" better than in Austin. As for the Ward homestead, it was proving difficult to sell with money so scarce, but the Peases had offered to rent it for $900 a year. "I advise the letting of it, and by all means have the family go North." The Colonel could visit them in New York, and should he leave his consular post he could go into business in New York. If that did not work out, his house would be waiting for him in Austin.[28]

Much of what Aaron envisioned came to pass, not least because he did his best to make sure things worked out that way. He was a "take charge" kind of person, an attribute that did not endear him to Ward, who eventually came to feel that Susan's brother was intruding on his authority as Susan's husband. In fact, just two days after Aaron put his latest thoughts in a letter to the Colonel, Lucadia announced that they had rented the Ward house; Susan and her children would be going to New York. That same week Susan and Aaron took another telltale step.

Joanna, whose husband and only child preceded her in death, had left her sizable estate to Susan and another sister. Susan proceeded to give Aaron, who was executor of the estate, general power of attorney and thus not only control over her bequest from Joanna, but "unlimited control" over any property—money, real estate, personal items—that she either then owned in her "own individual right" or might acquire thereafter. Had the Colonel known, he would have been irate at the affront, for it was his legal right as her husband to control Susan's property during their marriage. Susan, however, did not tell him.[29]

Still feeling depleted by her ordeal with Joanna and terribly uneasy over her future with Peg Leg, Susan scrambled to get everything ready for her departure. The Peases waited expectantly, eager to get on with "putting the house in habitable order," as Lucadia unflatteringly put it. Finally in mid-May Susan and her five children left on their long journey north. She wrote Lucadia from New York that she felt much better than she had when leaving Austin, but she was sure her New York friends had noted "a fearful change" in her, and her doctor had prescribed weeks of rest and quiet. "In my next letter I will tell you all my plans—Oh I am very happy to be with my dear old mother and my kind brothers and sisters—But Alas how dark the future seems to me."[30]

CHAPTER 11

On the Isthmus

"**A**WFUL MASSACRE AT PANAMA" proclaimed the *New York Times* in its lead story on April 30, 1856. "Startling intelligence" had been received of a "terrible affray" between residents of Panama City and U.S. citizens passing through town on their way to and from California. Many Americans had been "slain outright," according to one source. Eyewitnesses reported that the U.S. consul had been untiring in his attempts to "suppress the fracas" but had met with little success. The *Times* worried that the riot would cut off communication between the eastern and western shores of the United States. "For all practical purposes, the union between the Atlantic and Pacific States is suspended, if not dissolved, by these outrages." With the route across Nicaragua already disrupted by violent conflict, one choice was left, the *Times* observed, between the "long and weary watery track round Cape Horn" or the "long and weary, but arid path, overland from Kansas to the Pacific." Either of those alternatives meant the dispiriting exchange of a three-and-a-half week trip for a tedious journey of several months.[1]

The "Panama Massacre," as the melee that took the lives of twenty-one people came to be known in U.S. circles, did not shut down transit across the Isthmus as the *Times* feared, but the newspaper had put its finger on just how crucial the Panamanian Isthmus was to the flow of people, mail, news, and gold between the country's east and west coasts. Between 1848, when gold was discovered in newly acquired California, and 1869, when the transcontinental railroad supplanted the Panama route, some 700,000 people crossed the Isthmus on their way to and from California and Oregon. More than 80,000 passed through Panama City while Ward was U.S. consul. Their problems and those of U.S. ships transporting them between Panama City and the port of San Francisco often became his problems. He took to heart President

Pierce's stirring words in his inaugural address that "upon every sea and on every soil" Americans citizens seeking the protection of the flag would be secure in their rights.[2]

Peg Leg was forty-six years old when he set out for Panama. It had been almost eighteen years since the storming of San Antonio and the amputation of his right leg. He had always been a heavy-set fellow and had added some pounds over the years. Getting around put a strain on his aging body, and the frequent trouble with his stump made walking all the more onerous. His vision had also weakened. He wore spectacles, at least to read, and could not read a word without them. Yet he approached his new job with all the fire and determination he had brought to his position as land commissioner. Before leaving New York he had a large number of prints made featuring his visage above his name and new title. Once in Panama City he put some of them in cheap gilt frames and hung them in American-run hotels and barrooms, thus announcing his presence and advertising his services (see illustrations).[3]

October 18, 1853, the day the Colonel first arrived in Panama City, was a typical sultry day, 88 degrees that afternoon. The rainy season still had two months to go. Three days earlier he and 800 fellow passengers on the steamship *Ohio* had debarked in Colón (called Aspinwall by Americans), the new, rickety-looking port town on the Caribbean coast and departure point for the trans-Isthmian railroad then under construction.[4] It was only fifty or sixty miles across the Isthmus to Panama City, depending on one's route. Once the railroad was completed the trip would take just three to four hours. Several years earlier, when gold-seekers first struggled to cross Panama in search of instant riches in California, it took almost five days—three-and-a-half ascending the Chagres River in primitive canoes poled by locals and another day by mule, two if by foot, crossing the Continental Divide and descending wretched trails through rocky defiles to the Pacific Coast. It was an arduous, uncomfortable, sometimes dangerous trip. Advised one early veteran to those "feverish to go to California. 1st. Stay at home. 2d. If you go there take any route but this." By the time Ward crossed the Isthmus the trip was far easier but still had rough stretches and hazards after the railroad tracks ended some twenty-three miles down the line at Barbacoas, where a bridge over the Chagres was under construction.[5]

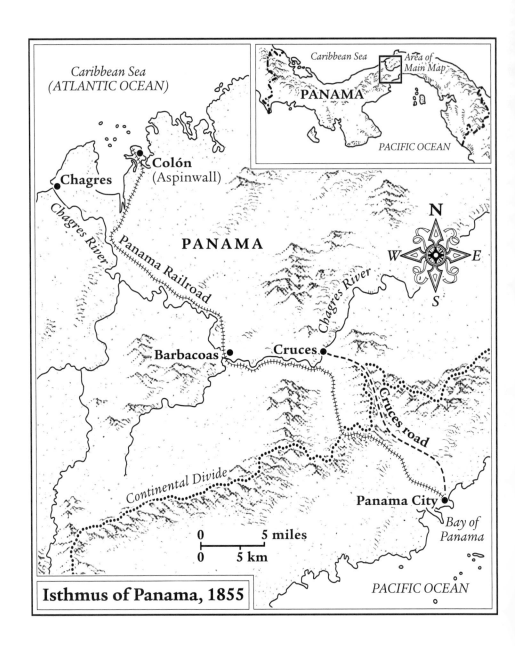

Caribbean Sea
(ATLANTIC OCEAN)

Caribbean Sea

Area of
Main Map

PANAMA

PACIFIC OCEAN

Chagres

Colón
(Aspinwall)

PANAMA

N

W   E

S

Chagres River

Panama Railroad

Chagres River

Barbacoas

Cruces

Cruces road

Continental Divide

Panama City

Bay of
Panama

0   5 miles

0   5 km

Isthmus of Panama, 1855

PACIFIC OCEAN

Soon Peg Leg was ensconced in his U.S. consulate, a whitewashed building on a narrow cobblestone street bounded by stone houses and darkened by the shadows of wooden balconies ranging one above another. He liked to sit on his balcony, relishing an occasional sea breeze and smoking a cigar, the American flag flying above him. Down the street he could see the twenty-foot-high wall that surrounded the city and through its arched gate the waters of the Pacific. Below him strolled local women in bright-ribboned panama hats, raucous Americans in red flannel shirts and boots, and padres in flowing black silk gowns. Across the street was the office of the *Panama Star*, one of the two English language newspapers in town, both run by Americans and read avidly by the several hundred English-speaking residents, mostly Americans, and by thousands of their countrymen pausing in town en route to California or back east. The next year the two English-language papers would merge to form the *Star and Herald* and become, for English-speaking residents and visitors, a fixture at breakfast tables for more than a century.[6]

The *Star* issued a hearty welcome to the new consul and trusted that he would find his new office as profitable and agreeable as he had been led to expect. But his first months were not happy ones, and not just because his work as consul got off to a slow start. Panama was a city that many Americans found wanting. Almost two centuries old, the once flourishing port had lost much of its importance with the decline of the Spanish Empire. Now its population of perhaps eight thousand was swollen by transients, sometimes as many two or three thousand waiting for ships to San Francisco or passage to Colón, a jumble of humanity ranging from upright men to downright thieves. "Our city is rammed, crammed, and jammed full of passengers for California," remarked a local newspaper on one occasion. Hotels squeezed six, seven, even ten or more guests to a room, sleeping on cots, while other travelers bedded down on plaza benches or camped in fields beyond the city walls.[7] Some Americans thought Panama a quaint town of ruined churches and convents, "decayed monuments of its ancient splendor," but in the minds of others it was blighted by "perpetual filthiness," exorbitant rents, bad government, and an indolent citizenry.[8] Americans viewed the majority of Panamanians with particular disdain. A U.S. diplomat reported in 1855 that in the Isthmus as a whole (the province of Panama plus three other provinces) whites composed just ten percent of the population, while 70 percent were *mestizos* (people of mixed European and native American ancestry) and another fifteen percent "various mixtures of the Negro race"—and "all exercise political privileges." In the Yankee Strip (the belt of land traversed by Americans crossing from one ocean to the other) and in Panama City in particular, the percentage of blacks was higher, including at least 2,000 and perhaps as many as 5,000 Jamaicans recruited to work on the railroad. In Ward's distorted view Panama's population was "mostly negroes." It was all the more jarring for slave owners like the Colonel to come to Panama City and find blacks on the police force.[9]

"I live here secluded in my office in a country of barbarism, idleness and vice," he wrote Susan a few weeks following his arrival. It did not help that the consulate was the target of thieves more than once. In one incident on a Sunday morning, Ward was entertaining some friends upstairs when a "native negro man" and two friends carried off a large table from his front hall and started up the street with it. Immediately Ward's servant discovered the theft, set out in pursuit, and somehow managed to get the culprits to bring it back. When Ward sought to arrest them, however, one thief tried to grab the pistol Ward customarily carried in his waistband. When that failed he fled and escaped after the Colonel, normally a dead shot, fired but only grazed his shirt. The other two men were turned over to authorities.[10]

Disenchanted though he was with his situation, Panama City's newest consul set about to make the best of it. At first he was somewhat limited in what he could do by not having his exequatur, official recognition as consul from the host country, the Republic of New Granada (now Colombia), of which Panama then was a part. Those duties he performed he found routine and monotonous—disposing of the effects of Americans who had died in his jurisdiction or at sea on the way there, arranging passage home for destitute U.S. seamen, authenticating documents in his role as a notary public, and coping daily, in his own words, with "the great confusion and noise of our citizens appealing to the Consul for redress of petty grievances." Official recognition finally came from distant Bogotá in January 1854, but initially it did little to cheer him up. Though he had managed to land a paying position as resident U.S. mail agent, his income as consul was disappointing. So were the profits from the store he had opened to sell wines, spirits, and other goods supplied by the Beans. And he was bored.[11]

Peg Leg's discontent with his consulship hardly surprised local observers. The *Star* had anticipated it in a light-hearted but astute piece written a few months prior to his arrival and entitled, tongue in cheek, "The Pleasures of a Consular Life in Panama":

> We presume there is no Consulate in the gift of any nation more filled with variety and vicissitudes than the United States Consulate is at Panama. . . . All the world coming through here, men, women and children, on their way to the promised land, look on the Consul as some grand Potentate, able to settle every difficulty. . . . If a riot takes place between the natives and foreigners, the first question is, where is the Consul? . . . If the taxes are thought to be too high, application is made to the Consulate to force the authorities to make a reduction. Should a transportation house fail to send the baggage or freight of the passengers in time for the sailing of the steamers, complaint is laid before the Consul . . . . Should a robbery take place, the Consul is sought after to aid in ferreting out the delinquents. . . . Every American . . . must have free access to the Consul—he must keep open his house for all. . . .[12]

A man of Peg Leg's strong self-image and aggressive personality was not about to settle for days devoted to petty grievances and other humdrum matters. He turned his attention increasingly to issues in which he felt the honor and dignity of his country were at stake, issues whose pursuit cast him more in the role of diplomat than consul and frequently pitted him against Panamanian authorities. Several years later the New Granadan minister to the United States would go so far as to declare that "Consul Ward was one of those, who influenced most the international relations of the two Republics." It was not meant as a compliment, however, but as reproof for what was felt to be the Colonel's antipathy to New Granada.[13]

Within days of receiving his exequatur Ward heard a rumor that an American passenger from California who set out for Colón had been murdered on the Cruces road, the rugged mule trail from Panama City up the Pacific slope and over the Continental Divide to the Chagres River (completion of the trans–Isthmian railroad was still a year away). Skeptical that Panamanian officials would investigate on their own, he decided to check out the rumored crime scene himself. He persuaded the governor of the province of Panama, José Maria Urrutia Añino, and the French consul to join him, and they were accompanied by Randolph "Ran" Runnels, an American whose express business between Panama City and Colón gave him a strong personal interest in the matter. Out the muddy trail the four men rode, occasionally passing the skeleton of a dead mule, until they reached the area of the alleged murder. In a ravine thirty feet from the trail they found a man with his head nearly severed from his body. Even though an eyewitness accused two men of the crime, several more days passed with no arrests. It was time, the Colonel decided, to put pressure on the governor. He dispatched a letter requesting a speedy trial of the suspects. The next day a second letter followed, signed by Ward together with the consuls from eight European and South American countries. Panamanian officials were taken to task for failing to bring to justice the perpetrators of a multitude of "outrages" inflicted upon passengers traversing the Isthmus, from insults to robberies to murders, a record of negligence, insisted the consuls, that further emboldened thieves and murderers. Urrutia Añino was incensed. The letter's "offensive expressions" were uncalled for, he replied; Panamanian authorities had taken many measures to prevent and punish such outrages. The *Panama Star*, however, dismissed that claim as "too notoriously *untrue* to be for one moment considered."[14]

With feelings on both sides heating up, the Colonel took a different tack. He had been tipped that a gang of robbers was hiding out in the hills near a village on the Cruces road. Could the governor issue him an order to arrest the bandits, a possibility they had discussed earlier? Perhaps Urrutia Añino might even provide some native citizens to assist in the undertaking. Failing that, would he sanction Ward's raising his own force to arrest the "lawless barbarians?" Fine, said the governor to the latter proposal; Ward should get his men together and hand them over to an army officer of the government's choosing, not exactly what the Colonel had in mind.[15] Eventually, the governor gave the job to Ran Runnels, and the crackdown urged by Ward took an ugly turn. Runnels formed a vigilante group of some forty men, known as the Isthmus Guard, and in August 1854 launched a seven-month campaign against banditry along the mule trails connecting Panama City with the rail line. Condoned by the governor and funded by the railroad, Runnels and his men browbeat, arrested, shot, and otherwise subdued dozens of "bad characters," Americans as well as Panamanians. Some were deported, among them fourteen Americans in the first month alone. Runnels's success at suppressing lawlessness won plaudits from the *Star and Herald* but not from the Colonel, who was put off by the violence and judicial corner cutting, at least when administered to Americans, some of whom, he advised Secretary of State William Marcy, were treated "harshly, unjustly, and illegally." Two Americans, he protested to Governor Urrutia Añino, were roughed up and arrested, convicted by a local court of vagrancy without being given an opportunity to defend themselves, and sentenced to work on a penal road gang 400 miles from Panama City. Ward was not squeamish about going after criminals, but when the very American citizens whose rights abroad he sought to protect were arbitrarily targeted, he drew the line. In this case, however, it was not Ward but the completion of the railroad in early 1855 that put an end to Runnels's excesses. With passengers no longer exposed to depredations on the mule trails, his Guard was disbanded.[16]

In March 1854, long before the Guard finished its work, the Colonel had seized on an even more troublesome issue: a law passed by Panama's provincial legislature taxing each ship arriving at or departing from Colón and Panama City one dollar per passenger, a modest amount it might seem, but U.S. steamship companies transporting thousands of passengers soon found themselves owing thousands of dollars. They were not happy about it. It was an American consul's job to protect and promote American shipping, and Ward stood diplomatically at the ready. He was soon exchanging strongly worded notes with Urrutia Añino. American residents of Colón were up in arms over the issue too, encouraged by Commander George Hollins, U.S. Navy, who parked his twenty-two gun sloop of war in their harbor and, in the company of the Colonel, informed Urrutia Añino he would resist payment of the tax until instructed otherwise by his government. The governor, however, was not easily intimidated, aware as he was of how crucial the tax was to the financially straitened provincial government.[17]

While not doubting for a moment that the passenger tax was "onerous and unjust," Ward found himself in something of a quandary after steamship companies balked at paying it. When an American vessel arrived in port, Ward, like U.S. consuls in other ports, was required to collect the ship's papers and retain them until all port fees, wages for discharged seamen, and other financial obligations had been met. Without its papers, a ship was not authorized to leave port for its next destination. It was a responsibility that put him in a bind. If a ship did not pay the passenger tax, should he refuse to return its papers? Though it was known that Marcy opposed the tax, believing that it violated an 1846 treaty between the United States and New Granada, the secretary had not issued instructions to Ward to surrender papers in such instances. Local pressure from Americans to do so was intense, however, especially after the U.S. consul in Colón started doing so. When word reached Colón that Ward had withheld the papers of the steamer *Yankee Blade* until the tax was paid, he was excoriated in the town's newspaper. On the other hand, when he returned papers to several ships that had refused to pay the tax he was censured by Urrutia Añino for violating New Granadan and international law and threatened with having Panamanian officials take control of U.S. ships' papers. He was damned either way. Far better to be damned by one's enemies than one's friends, especially with American interests and American honor at stake. He decided to defy the governor as a matter of course.[18]

With their heels dug in, Urrutia Añino and Ward were far from reaching any resolution of the problem. In any case it was not really theirs to resolve but Bogotá's and Washington's. But in Bogotá a coup d'état in April 1854 had disrupted the capital and triggered civil conflict. "There is no Government here to settle our difficulties on the Isthmus," reported the U.S. minister to New Granada. The issue dragged on, and Ward feared that turmoil in Bogotá would foment disorder on the Isthmus, a prospect with anti-American implications that seemed all the more grave when viewed through the lens of his racism. He wrote Marcy in May, "Should the colored population who are very ignorant and much opposed to the U.S. people, become excited, the consequences to the U.S. citizens who cross the Isthmus may be very serious." No less disturbing in his eyes was the reawakening of Panama's independence movement following the coup. Should it succeed, he wrote the secretary, "no respect will be paid to persons or property." Before long, he predicted, "some demonstration of a hostile nature" would be made against foreign residents of Panama City.[19]

The Colonel's solution to the many threats he envisioned during 1854 was simple: station a warship at Panama City. Panamanian authorities respected "nothing but absolute power," he declared, and only a warship anchored in the harbor would prevent the otherwise "inevitable" destruction of American life and property. It was a request Ward repeated many times to Marcy, until a warship was finally stationed there following the Watermelon War (as the Panama Massacre is now known). Ward had foreseen that calamity two years beforehand, yet often during 1854 the fears and warnings he communicated to Washington were inflated, fueled as they were by his contempt for Panama's leaders and citizens and his single-mindedness in serving American interests. Thus he was caught by surprise in October when Panama stopped collecting the passenger tax, a turn of events for which, however, he could take some credit.[20]

By then Peg Leg's mind was elsewhere—on his upcoming trip to New York to see Susan and the children. It had been more than a year since he said goodbye to them in Austin, a year filled with hours of loneliness. "Every evening I sit alone," he wrote Susan in February 1854, with "neither wife, child, relative or friend to converse, or associate with." Susan was still in Texas at that point, agonizing over her marriage, desperate to avoid joining him in Panama. Both were dispirited and both lost weight. "I am not sick, but I am so extremely weak that I cannot walk across the room without tottering," he wrote Susan. "I feel most sensibly, that great constitution which has borne me through so many misfortunes, is now giving way more suddenly than I anticipated."[21] Though his health improved and he made some friends, such as the French consul, Panama City remained for him a town with "no society," at least of the kind he would "care to mix with." As a former military officer, he seemed to enjoy most the company of U.S. naval officers whose ships were anchored temporarily in the harbor and whose captains now and then stayed with him. Sometimes it was small things that made his life difficult. On one occasion a friend accidentally broke Peg Leg's eyeglasses, and for six weeks, until Dudley Bean sent him another pair from New York, he could not read. Sometimes small things lifted his spirits, like the daguerreotypes that Susan sent him of the children and herself. On rare occasions his consulate was a joyous place, never more so than on his first Fourth of July in Panama, when, aided by funds subscribed by American residents, he entertained more than 200 people at a six-hour evening celebration featuring a band, great quantities of champagne, and fireworks displays. Already, however, he had decided he must return home, "to give some attention to his family," he explained to Marcy. He was disturbed by Susan's decision not to join him and knew that it was an ill omen. He requested a three months' leave of absence to begin once the political situation calmed down. In early November 1854, after thirteen months in Panama, he crossed the Isthmus to Colón and boarded a ship for New York.[22]

CHAPTER 12

In Jeopardy

"THE RESULT OF ELECTIONS, like marriages[,] are ever uncertain," Susan Ward wrote Lucadia Pease in 1855 upon hearing, after a long wait, that Marshall Pease had won his race for reelection as governor of Texas and thus the Peases would continue to reside in the Ward house. The fate of Susan's marriage, on the other hand, remained up in the air, but during 1854 she found that life without her husband was far more bearable than with him. "I have learned that I do not live wholly in ruin," she wrote Lucadia, "for I can make myself useful to my boys and girls, and they really love me." Living in New York with her mother, her three unmarried sisters, and her brothers Aaron and Dudley proved to her "that love and happiness still exist, for they are the same in kindness, and true devotion, as when I left them."[1]

Susan had come to New York City in June 1854 with her five children. They were welcomed into a bustling Bean household on West 14th Street that included eleven family members plus servants. Susan found comfort and reassurance in being once again with the family she grew up with. Her emotional healing was slow, however, and her profound pessimism about the future difficult to surmount. She also felt deeply the burden that the Colonel had placed upon her of seeing to the children's education, a longstanding concern of his that took on added urgency for him that year when it appeared his health might give out faster than he anticipated. "Col Ward throws the whole responsibility of our childrens education and behaviour upon me," Susan told Marshall Pease, "and I assure you that I really feel quite inadequate to the task of directing them right." Soon, however, she had enrolled Robie in a school in New Hampshire and was teaching eleven-year-old Mary, nine-year-old Dudley, and six-year-old Jim herself, dividing her time with them between the 14th Street house and the Beans' "country seat," as she jokingly called the cottage they owned in rural Westchester County north of Manhattan. A few months later she placed Mary in a local school but continued to teach her two boys. "Their improvement really delights me," she wrote Lucadia, a remarkably upbeat sentiment for a person who only months earlier had viewed life so darkly. By no means, however, had she escaped the pall that Peg Leg had cast over her life.[2]

In mid-November 1854 the Colonel arrived in New York and promptly moved in with Susan at the Bean home. He stayed three weeks and then was off to Washington to confer with government officials about the situation in Panama. By year's end he had returned to New York laden with Christmas presents for his wife. In early February he left for Panama.[3] Just how their relationship fared during the visit was debated in court documents four and a half years later and remains something of an enigma. In their depositions they agreed on nothing—no surprise there, given the gaping discrepancies between their versions of the relationship up to that point. Susan, for instance, claimed she consented to Peg Leg's staying with her only after he had apologized for his past misconduct and promised not to repeat it. "Utterly untrue," testified the Colonel; Susan welcomed him upon his arrival and seemed very pleased to see him.[4] Even at the time Susan and her husband had very different reactions to their two months together. For Susan their intimacy aroused fears that she was pregnant—a false alarm it turned out—but the experience undoubtedly made her all the more reluctant to join her husband in Panama. He dismissed the possibility of such a "mishap" befalling "old folks" like them (she was thirty-eight) and yearned to see her after his return to Panama, writing her passionately of his longing for "a thousand such embraces as none can give like you" and his desire to enjoy "the honeyed sweetness of my Sue's life."[5]

Though their claims and counterclaims muddy the truth about what happened during the visit, for Susan it was clearly a setback in her recovery from the despair that had gripped her earlier that year. "When Col Ward left New York last winter," she wrote Lucadia Pease several months after his departure, "he was not on speaking terms with my mother or one half of her family—although I assure you that every one of them did all in their power to make his visit pleasant—but he appeared dissatisfied with everyone even his youngest child—and this was the sole cause of my severe illness when he was in the city and for a long time after he returned to Panama." On the eve of his departure he told Susan that she was too intimate with her mother's family, that it offended him to see her so contented living with them—as well it might have, for he was a man of his times and believed that he was in charge of the marriage and his wife's place was by his side. Yet Susan chose instead to remain at a great distance in the happy embrace of her mother and siblings, unwilling even to visit him, while he endured a desperately lonely life in Panama without her. Peg Leg's vexation with the Bean family backfired, however. Some of the Bean women turned against him during the visit, and later that year, after he began pressing Susan once again to come to Panama and she resisted, the Beans closed ranks behind her.[6]

Oblivious to just how disaffected Susan was, Ward set out for Panama, but a different Panama from the one he had left three months before. Just days earlier the last rail had been laid in the Panama Railroad, and the first train crossed from the Atlantic to the Pacific, "beginning a new era in the history of the American continent," proclaimed a New York newspaper. In the United States it still took months to cross from one ocean to the other. In Panama it could be done in three hours. That was cause for celebration, and when Ward boarded the side-wheel steamer *George Law* in New York he was accompanied by a group of railroad representatives and well-wishers off to Panama to do just that, among them the new U.S. minister to Bogotá, James B. Bowlin. The two men had ten days together on shipboard, time to become well acquainted as they sat talking—wrapped at first in great-coats to protect them from the chilled February air and then sporting straw hats as the weather grew warmer—and time for Ward to warn Bowlin of the dangers he foresaw in Panama should the United States not make a show of force. During the months that followed they would correspond frequently, each expressing indignation at the "contemptible" actions of Panama's leaders. And how the two men must have thought back to those days on shipboard two years later when the *George Law,* on its regular run between New York and Colón, foundered in a severe gale with the loss of 423 lives.[7]

Ward and his shipboard compatriots, with the fireworks and banners they brought from New York, arrived in Colón in mid-February 1855 to join dozens of others in five days of celebration. A special train, decorated with flags, carried them along winding tracks over the Continental Divide and through floral arches at each way station to Panama City, where a brass band and a cheering crowd greeted them. At the Panama Railroad Company's sumptuous five-hour banquet Ward even put aside his grievances for the moment to express in a toast his high opinion of the people of New Granada. Unfortunately he burned his only hand seriously while setting off fireworks, and the burn troubled him for several weeks. To all those who participated in the festivities— railroad and steamship company officials, civil and ecclesiastical author- ities of New Granada and Panama, consular officers, newspaper edi- tors—the completion of the railroad was an epochal achievement. And so it was in the eyes of the tens of thousands of Americans who enjoyed the speed and ease with which they crossed the Isthmus for the next fourteen years. For stockholders the railroad produced consistently generous dividends, and for the government of New Granada, which shared in the railroad's profits and its income from mail contracts, it was the single most important source of revenue for a dozen years. But for many Panamanians and foreign residents the much-celebrated event was an economic kick in the stomach. Whereas once it had taken five days to cross the Isthmus followed by a sometimes lengthy wait in Panama City or Colón for passage on a ship, now steamship and rail- road schedules were coordinated to the extent that travelers debarked on one side of the Isthmus and embarked on the other in a matter of hours, spending barely any time or money on the way. For river boat- men and mule drivers, hotel proprietors and shopkeepers, transporta- tion agents and bankers, even for gamblers and thieves, business plum- meted. Many foreign residents left for greener pastures.[8]

Once the celebrations ended the Colonel slipped back into his rou- tine as consul. Some days that meant lending a helping hand to stranded passengers, such as the group from New Orleans, their travel schedule disrupted by the celebrations, that arrived in Panama City too late for the steamer to San Francisco but did not have funds enough to sustain themselves while waiting for the next ship. Ward persuaded the railroad company to cover the cost. Sometimes passengers lost their steamship tickets but were too poor to pay Ward's notarial fee for the affidavit needed as a substitute. He provided the affidavits anyway. Other days it meant rounding up deserters from a U.S. naval vessel or going aboard a cargo ship to investigate the complaints of a mutinous crew and putting some men in irons until willing to perform their duties. Every month, three or four U.S. commercial ships would arrive in port, most of them bringing people, mail, and gold from San Francisco, and each time the Colonel would have a flurry of business. On the side, he continued to sell the brandy and other spirits that Aaron Bean shipped him from time to time.[9]

Despite his three-month absence from Panama and the festive times upon his return from New York, Ward's mood once back at work was little changed from the previous year. He found Panama City dull, its commerce "almost null," and he was lonely. He spent many an evening by himself smoking cigars. He clearly missed Susan—to whom he professed "as much love as man possesses or can feel"—and his children; but, as he wrote her, prudence prevented his calling her to Panama City and thus "expose" a life he cherished. Besides, he acknowledged, their children needed the attention that a mother alone could give, and at their age it would be an act of madness to bring them to Panama, not only because of the dangers of the tropical climate but because they required an education. Two months later, more anxious than ever for Susan's companionship, he reconsidered. Ruling out another trip to New York for himself, he raised the possibility of Susan bringing four-year-old Anna and spending the next winter in the much warmer Panama climate, a change that might do Susan some good.[10]

Instead, Susan struck out on her own. During the summer of 1855 she left her mother, sisters, and brothers, with whom Peg Leg thought her too intimate, and rented a house for herself and her children twenty-five miles north of New York City in the village of Tarrytown, a picturesque community of 2,000 people on the Hudson River. Washington Irving lived nearby at Sunnyside, his home by the river. All the children but Anna began attending area schools, while Susan enjoyed her new independence and indulged in one of her favorite pastimes, riding horseback, sometimes "fast and hard," according to a disapproving neighbor. If New York City beckoned, it was an easy trip by steamship or rail. Much to Susan's consternation, her husband, upon learning of her move, pressed her even harder to come to Panama, unsettled more by her autonomy than by her absorption in her mother's family. Now he wanted his wife not just to visit but also to stay with him as long as he remained at his post. Already they had been living separately for two years. Distance from her husband had, to an extent, liberated Susan, and she was far from eager to surrender her independence. She responded that the long voyage would nearly kill her and that the children were still too young to be left in the care of strangers with both parents so far away. The Colonel, however, was not easily turned aside, undoubtedly feeling that he was in the right to want his wife with him. In reply, according to Susan, he threatened that if she would not obey his request he would "take all the children from me." Susan wrote Lucadia, "God only knows what will be the result, for all my relatives declare that I shall never again leave this state to join him – And I fear that the crisis which I have so long dreaded, and which I have more than once risked my wretched life to prevent is now at hand."[11]

It was not a crisis in his marriage that consumed Ward's attention during the next few months, however. He backed off his threat and tried again to coax Susan into visiting, still without success. Meanwhile he became absorbed in what the *New York Times* called a "grand consular smash-up." From the Colonel's perspective he was simply defending American honor in response to another in a procession of hostile actions toward Americans following the U.S. refusal to pay the passenger tax. The trouble started in April 1855, when Ward took umbrage at a Panamanian judge who seized control of the estate of an American who had died intestate in Ward's jurisdiction.[12] Then the Panamanians imposed another tax on U.S. shipping, even though the Supreme Court of New Granada had seemingly nixed such taxation by ruling the passenger tax unconstitutional. At least that was the understanding of the decision in Washington. Ward, ever suspicious, warned the State Department that the Panamanians, desperate for revenue, might pass a substitute measure, especially now that the Isthmus had assumed a new sovereignty. Responding to Panamanian aspirations for independence, New Granada had united the province of Panama with the three other provinces on the Isthmus and given the resulting federal State of Panama extensive legislative powers, though none in foreign relations. The Colonel's warning proved prophetic; the new state passed a law levying a tonnage duty on vessels entering Panama's harbors. A "mere attempt to insult our Government," James Bowlin called the law in a letter to Ward. "I must confess I see no end to these repeated harrassments, but in punishing these scoundrels." Similarly exasperated, Ward lodged an official protest with the Panamanian government and moved a step closer to overreacting to what he considered affronts to his country and himself. What pushed him over the edge—to the point that he would tell Marcy that no U.S. consulate had ever been "so harassed as this"—was a dispute over a procedural issue.[13]

By September 1855 Peg Leg had been suffering for weeks with soreness in his stump, and his hand and wrist were bothering him, perhaps still tender from the fireworks burn. It was the rainy season, and the humidity and warmth were wearing on him.[14] Susan had recently written him that she was not coming to Panama. What seemed to be most on his mind, however, was the welfare of an American named William Hunter, who resided in one of Panama City's prisons and was in ill health. Until recently the proprietor of a Colón hotel, Hunter had fallen on hard times after an overnight guest deposited three to four thousand dollars in his safe and the next morning the safe was open and the money gone. Hunter was arrested, but there was insufficient evidence to convict him of a criminal offense, so the case was arbitrated under the supervision of the U.S. consul in Colón. Hunter was held responsible for $3,000, which he covered with cash and notes. There the matter stood until a former lodger in Hunter's hotel, a fellow named Edwards, who had been present the night the money disappeared but then sailed to New York, returned to Colón and reported that Hunter had indeed taken the money and given him $1,200 of it, which he had frittered away in New York. When word of that development reached George Totten, chief engineer for the railroad and a bigwig in Colón, he ordered both men to leave Panama or face prosecution for theft. They chose the former, but later Totten ran into them on the streets of Panama City and saw to it that both were arrested and thrown in prison. Edwards escaped the next day. Hunter appealed to Ward for protection.[15]

The Colonel was not at all pleased to see Totten—with whom he had had an earlier run-in—throwing his weight around against Americans in his jurisdiction and engineering what had the earmarks of an illegal arrest against a person whose case had already been heard in Colón and officially settled. Nor did he think that Hunter, suffering from dropsy (edema) and intermittent fever, was likely to fare well if sent to prison in Colón and held there for trial, as was planned. Twice Ward wrote the state of Panama's top official, Superior Chief Justo Arosemena, inquiring about the arrest, and both times Arosemena responded cordially with information he had obtained from the governor of the province of Panama.[16]

So far, so good. But then Ward decided to write directly to the provincial governor. Until two months earlier the governor had been the top official and his contact in the Panamanian government, but now, with the incorporation of the province of Panama into the new State of Panama, he was a subordinate of Superior Chief Arosemena. In July 1855 the new state had specifically designated the superior chief as the sole recipient of communications from consuls. Even so, in late August the provincial governor and Ward were still corresponding, and Ward maintained that such contact with local officials was permissible, citing clauses in two treaties between New Granada and the United States stating that consuls could apply to "the authorities" of their consular districts. So in September he did not consider it inappropriate to send the provincial governor a note protesting the "illegal and uncalled for severity" of Hunter's arrest and asking that Hunter be allowed to stay in Panama City long enough to secure bail. The governor returned the note unanswered by way of a messenger who explained that the governor was not authorized to receive it. That was unacceptable to the Colonel, who had good reason to think a verbal explanation discourteous, but what really miffed him was not receiving a substantive reply in the first place. He wrote back requesting one and warning that he hated to think that the governor intended to insult him and his country by not responding. Back came the second communication, not even opened. At that point Ward's judgment succumbed to his fiery temper and his touchiness about honor. He issued an official protest against the provincial governor, the superior chief, even the government of New Granada, calling the governor's behavior a "gross and wanton outrage to the dignity of the United States." Then he struck the consulate's flag, signaling his suspension of all contact with officials of Panama and New Granada until, he declared, "proper and mete satisfaction [was] rendered by the aggressors." The suspension would last three months. He would not submit to any indignity, he wrote Aaron Bean; let the consequences be what they may. The protest was the talk of the town in Panama City. The *Panama Star and Herald*, the voice of the American community, backed his every move. A number of American residents, however, thought he had acted too hastily.[17]

It was Ward's misfortune that a special correspondent for the *New York Times* was on the scene looking for a story, and, lo and behold, the U.S. consul did him the favor of getting up "a little row." Francis W.

Rice was well versed in the issue of consular dignity, having endured imprisonment while serving as U.S. consul to Mexico. Rice clearly was not taken with the Colonel nor impressed by the gravity of the indignity he had suffered. In fact, Rice thought it self-inflicted, the consequence of applying to the wrong official and then acting rashly when the official rebuffed him. He wrote a melodramatic, snide account of the affair for the *Times* and appended texts of the various communications. Ward came off poorly but not as badly as in a scathing *Times* editorial the next day, which called him "a very especial and portentous dunce" who had "staked his dignity on a piece of needless, senseless impertinence—and lost it irretrievably." Secretary Marcy, predicted the *Times*, "will very likely inform Mr. Ward that his conduct has been, to the last degree, silly and ridiculous; and that, under the circumstances, he had better resign his post in favor of some aspirant more liberally endowed with common sense."[18]

It so happened that the New Granadan minister to the United States, Pedro A. Herrán, was in New York at the time and read Rice's article and the follow-up editorial. He immediately dispatched a trenchant communication to Marcy calling Ward's actions an insult to his government. Marcy thought the issue urgent enough that he went right to President Pierce with it. Suddenly, not only was the Colonel's marriage foundering, but now his job was in jeopardy. To Pierce it did not seem that the events justified the extreme measure of lowering the flag. He decided, however, to await further evidence. In the meantime he expected Ward to continue in office. In reporting back to Ward on the meeting in late October 1855 Marcy indicated that the Department of State thought he had acted inappropriately.[19]

Upon receiving Marcy's report the Colonel responded in characteristic fashion; he redoubled his efforts to convince the State Department that his interpretation of events, not Herrán's, was correct. In its response this time, the department was blunt: the provincial governor was not the proper channel of communication, and his decision not to respond was "sustainable," while Ward's reaction to that decision was not; thus the alleged indignity was not a basis for a "national grievance." Though still unpersuaded, by mid-January 1856 Ward had raised his flag.[20] For the New Granadan government that was hardly the end of the matter. Herrán requested Ward's recall, citing his disrespect for Panamanian authorities and his "ungovernable character." The secretary hesitated. While anxious to get along with the New Granadans he was not unsympathetic to the Colonel's difficulties in dealing with the Panamanians, especially over taxation of U.S. shipping. More to the point, he was reluctant to go against the wishes of Ward's patron, Senator Rusk, who interceded on his old friend's behalf. Rusk assured Marcy that Ward would control his temper and, though remaining firm in the discharge of his duties, would henceforth give New Granadan officials no just cause for complaint. Marcy agreed to stand by the Colonel, and Rusk made sure Ward understood exactly what the terms of the deal were.[21]

And what of William Hunter, the man whose misadventures had started it all? He was returned to Colón and found innocent of any crime. "How groundless were the charges upon which that unhappy man was so cruelly treated," Ward wrote Marcy. That outcome was by no means a trifling matter to the Colonel. Though he had acted unwisely as the affair unfolded, he felt deeply the responsibility that had prompted his involvement in the first place, to protect American citizens abroad against arbitrary treatment, the same commitment that had earlier impelled him to criticize the Runnels Guard. Nor would it be the last time that his dogged defense of the rights of American citizens would get him into trouble.[22]

By then more than two years had passed since Peg Leg first arrived in Panama. Susan remained in Tarrytown, as adamant as ever about not joining him. But now she paid a price. Peg Leg insisted that their oldest son, Dudley, a month shy of eleven, come to Panama instead. Susan's brother Aaron thought it a capital idea, an opportunity for the youngster to learn Spanish while providing good company for his father. In mid-February 1856 Susan and a reluctant Dudley boarded a train in Tarrytown for New York City, and she put him on a steamer bound for Panama. "I will not attempt to describe to you," she wrote Lucadia, "the suffering I have endured in being compelled to send one of my darling children from me." For days afterward she was sad. "We try not to speak often before ma about you," Dudley's older sister, Mary, wrote him, "for it makes her eyes fill with tears." Once again emotional stress took a toll on her health. She fell ill with a fever and head cold and occasional bouts of headaches and chest pains. Finally word came of Dudley's safe arrival and then letters from Dudley assuring his mother that he was happy living with his papa. Susan's spirits rallied and her health improved, but she was still uneasy, suspecting that Dudley's letters were "dictated by an older head than his."[23]

Dudley found himself in a city whose pace of life seemed to evoke one word, at least in the American community: dull. Business might be improving, the *Star and Herald* observed, but everything still looked dull. After Dudley returned to New York later that year, his father's secretary wrote him that the place looked duller, "if possible," than when he was there.[24] Yet a crisis loomed on the horizon, although not an unexpected one in Ward's eyes. More than a hint of what was to come appeared in late February in an article in the *Star and Herald* entitled, "Nuisance at the Railroad Station":

> There is not in or about the whole city so great a nuisance, or one which gives rise to so much mischief and disturbance, as that which arises from the privilege given to the very lowest grade of the negro population to hang around the station when passengers are there, ostensibly under pretence of selling fruit, but in reality to retail out the worse kind of rut-gut brandy, create rows and pick pockets when a chance offers. At every step, in every door-way, respectable people are insulted, jostled and frequently upset by these creatures; . . . but if any one attempts to retaliate or even to move them to one side, in order to pass bye, a whole troop of their darkey friends . . . step forward with the most abusive and threatening language, and, armed with machetes, stones and other weapons, are all ready to commence a fight at once.

It was a piece that bristled with hostility and oozed racism toward a group on the edge of violence, its anger inflamed by too many encounters with arrogant, insulting, inebriated Americans and by the evaporation of jobs that followed the completion of the railroad and the decision by the major steamship company to ferry passengers and goods to and from its ships—anchored in deep water two miles off-shore—exclusively on its own vessels rather than letting local boatmen continue to do the job. Two months later the volatile situation erupted in a murderous racial and cultural clash, and Ward found himself in the middle of the mayhem. For one terrifying day in April, no one thought Panama City dull.[25]

The Watermelon War and the Commodore

A PRIL 15, 1856, was a clear, sunny day in Panama City, and a peaceful one, so far, for the 1,000 or so people, many of them women and children, who arrived by three trains that afternoon. The railroad depot was near the beach and just three-eighths of a mile outside the city walls. Most of the passengers had disembarked in Colón that morning and expected to board a steamer for San Francisco late that evening, after the tide came in and the small steamer *Taboga*, then aground, could ferry them out to the larger ship. The passengers waited patiently, many for an hour or two, while clerks validated their steamship tickets. Then some boarded the *Taboga* while others waited on shore. Still others walked a short distance up a street adjacent to the depot to a handful of American-owned hotels, restaurants, and bars, in particular the Ocean House and the Pacific House, to imbibe, eat, or rest in rooms upstairs. The Golden Eagle saloon was the choice of a loudmouthed, bad-tempered American named Jack Oliver and his companions. Upon leaving the saloon several drinks later and clearly inebriated, Oliver snatched a slice of watermelon from the tray of a street vendor, José Luna, and walked away eating it, without paying. Luna followed, demanding a dime. "Don't bother me," barked Oliver, but Luna persisted. Luna drew a knife, Oliver a pistol. A friend of Luna's, Miguel Habrahan, grabbed Oliver's pistol, a scuffled ensued, the pistol discharged, and Habrahan fled with Oliver and his companions in pursuit. Habrahan disappeared into La Ciénega, a lower-class neighborhood of cane shanties and huts adjacent to the hotels and home to some of Panama City's poorest residents.[1]

For a few minutes that seemed to be the end of it, until a mob, angry and armed with knives, stones, and guns, suddenly swarmed the street by the hotels. As Americans scattered, some rushing into the hotels, the mob attacked the Pacific House, showering it with stones and making a shambles of the downstairs bar and dining room. Customers fled through doors and windows, some with rioters at their heels. Others were driven upstairs, and a few of them fired down on the rioters from the upper windows. "I heard the firing of Pistols and saw stones, bottles & clubs flying in every direction," testified one eyewitness. Then the rioters turned their anger on the Ocean House, breaking in through windows and doors and wreaking havoc on the first floor. People who escaped out the back door were pelted with stones and some knocked down. A wounded American fired at two Panamanians pursuing him and killed both. Shouts and screams and the frequent sound of gunfire pierced the air. At the railroad depot the three to four hundred people crowded inside grew alarmed. Those few who had pistols drew them. Others readied some twenty guns found in the building, the majority of them rusty old flintlock muskets. Four men began rushing out of the railroad compound, firing randomly into the huts of La Ciénega, then rushing back. It was close to 6:30 p.m.[2]

About this time Peg Leg was at his consulate in conversation with a U.S. mail agent when his secretary, Theodore de Sabla, interrupted to tell him he had just heard a rumor that there was a fight at the railroad station and that the cry, "Vamos á matar Yankees" ("We are going to kill Yankees") was in the air. De Sabla saddled up two horses, and he and Ward set out for the depot. Once through the city gate and on the beach they were accosted in Spanish by a band of men who threatened to shoot if they did not stop. De Sabla identified himself and Ward to the men, in Spanish, and even though they repeated their threat, de Sabla and the Colonel galloped off without drawing fire. Upon reaching the depot Ward was perturbed to find some armed passengers outside the fenced depot compound flashing pistols and rusty muskets in sight of the "native mob," a dangerously provocative action, he thought. Earlier, passengers had even dragged an old iron cannon to a position just outside the compound gate and loaded it with gunpowder and boiler rivets (lacking other ammunition). Two railroad officials, Alexander Center and William Nelson, and a steamship company agent, Allan McLane, were already on the scene calling for patience and quiet. Taking temporary command, the Colonel prevailed on the aroused passengers to at least keep their pistols and muskets out of sight and, together with Center and McLane, ordered them not to fire the cannon unless attacked. Aggressive moves by the passengers, gunfire in particular, it was feared, would precipitate the very assault they were trying to avert.[3]

Shortly after reaching the depot Peg Leg had dispatched de Sabla to find and bring Panamanian Governor Francisco de Fábrega to confer on means to quell the riot. De Sabla returned with word that Fábrega would be coming, but by then Ward had decided to ride up the street closer to La Ciénega and the hotels and meet the governor there, apparently intending to dissuade the rioters from firing on the railroad station. De Sabla hurried off to notify the governor. Stopping in the middle of street not far from the wrecked Pacific House, the Colonel sat on his horse waiting for the governor when first one and then another group of armed Panamanians entered the street from the cane huts. Ward called on them to back off, but they retreated no more than a step or two. Then a third, larger group appeared. There was a sudden exchange of gunfire, apparently between the Panamanians and some passengers. Ward's horse reared and jerked around, reacting to seven slight gunshot wounds. The Colonel regained control of his mount, no mean feat with one arm and one leg, only to see more armed Panamanians rushing into the street. A short distance away de Sabla and the governor had entered the street but were themselves caught in an exchange of gunfire. A bullet tore harmlessly through de Sabla's coat, but a second lodged deep in his thigh, a third put a hole in the governor's hat, understandably discomposing him, and another pierced the thigh of a man accompanying them. They all beat a hasty retreat, de Sabla to the U.S. consulate, Peg Leg back to the depot, and the governor to a meeting with his chief of police. Convinced that Americans at the depot had fired on him, the governor ordered the chief to "*march and occupy that house*," meaning the depot. "And if they fire on me?" asked the chief. "Do you so likewise," responded the governor.[4]

At the depot compound, gunfire from La Ciénega was now peppering the wooden buildings with a crackling noise, petrifying the already agitated passengers within. It was dark inside the depot as well as out. Ward, McLane, Nelson, and a fourth man, now virtually by themselves in the depot yard, sought shelter behind an old mess house. An assault seemed imminent, when suddenly the sound of a bugle was heard, signaling the approach of the police and "bringing relief to many an

NEW POST OFFICE, SACKVILLE STREET, DUBLIN.

Thomas Sautell Roberts, *The General Post Office, Sackville Street, Dublin*, 1818. Hand colored aquatint. Born in Dublin in 1807, Ward grew up on Moore Street, a block from this scene. Sackville Street (now O'Connell Street) was Dublin's premier street. To the right is the Nelson Pillar, erected in 1808 in honor of Admiral Horatio Nelson. Photo © The National Gallery of Ireland. *Courtesy The National Gallery of Ireland.*

Ward was six when his father, Henry Ward, a builder, began constructing these dormitories at Trinity College, Dublin. He was ten by the time they were finished. Little did Henry Ward realize at the start that he would be digging in reclaimed land and that beneath the surface lay an old mud-filled quarry. Almost two centuries later the buildings still provide accommodations for students. Photo by author.

In 1831, while working as a carpenter in New Orleans, Ward was hired to help construct a second story and garret for this home at 709-711 Royal Street in the French Quarter. More than a century later Truman Capote worked through the nights one of the upstairs rooms writing short stories and the early part of his first novel, *Other Voices, Other Rooms*. Photo by author.

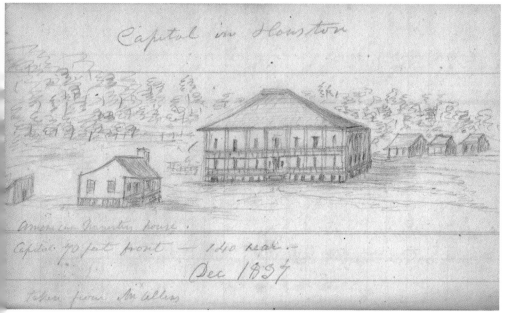

This 1837 sketch by Mary Austin Holley makes clear just how much the Texas capitol that Ward designed and built in Houston resembled a Louisiana plantation house, with its hipped roof sloping down on all four sides and its columned two-story gallery across the front. Holley apparently did the sketch from memory, for there are several errors, such as the nonexistent windows at ground level. *Courtesy The Dolph Briscoe Center for American History, The University of Texas at Austin (DI 04685)*

Ward's capitol is often depicted as it looked in this photograph of the Capitol Hotel taken about 1857, but then the building had long been converted into a hotel, its roof penetrated by chimneys and dormers, and a second story added to its wings. *Courtesy The Dolph Briscoe Center for American History, The University of Texas at Austin (DI 01345).*

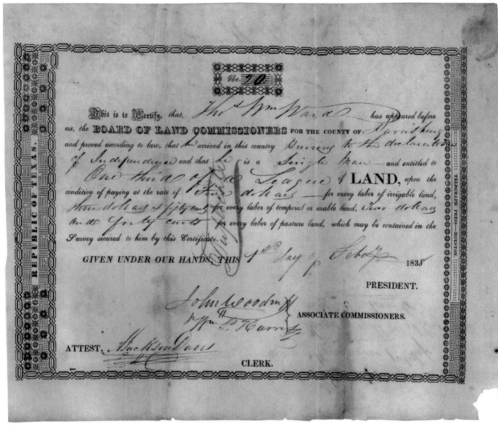

Adult males living in Texas on the day the republic declared its independence were entitled by the Texas constitution to a land grant known as a first-class headright. By this headright certificate, Ward was granted one-third of a league or 1,476 acres (heads of households received 4,605 acres). Texans found, however, that converting a certificate into titled land was a challenge, one that Ward sought to alleviate as land commissioner. *Courtesy Texas General Land Office.*

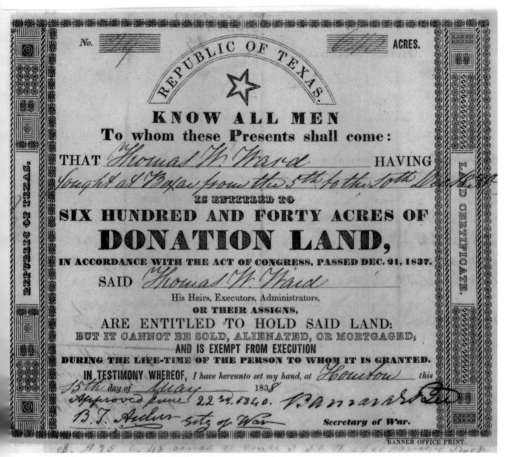

s a veteran of the storming of Bexar (San Antonio) in December 1835, Ward received a donation grant of ₄0 acres under legislation passed by the Texas Congress that rewarded participants in four battles of the ₁exas Revolution. *Courtesy Texas General Land Office.*

This hand colored lithograph of newly founded Austin was published in 1840. On the hill to the right is the President's house, while across the avenue on a smaller hill to the left is the temporary capitol. Government buildings line both sides of Congress Avenue. From *Texas in 1840, or, The Emigrant's Guide to the New Republic* (New York, 1840).

Drawn by Edward Hall   CITY OF AUSTIN THE NEW

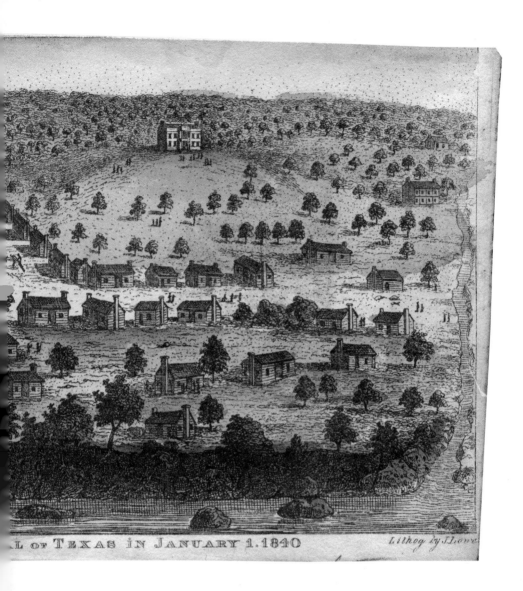

L OF TEXAS IN JANUARY 1.1840

Lithog by J. Lowe

Following the loss of his right arm to a prematurely firing cannon in 1840, Ward suddenly found himself, of necessity, left-handed and had to learn anew to write. His handwriting, and his signature in particular, changed markedly, as seen in these two examples, one from before the loss (at left), the other after. The closing at left reads, Yours Very Respt[ly] (Respectfully). From Author's Collection.

David G. Burnet, first president of the Republic of Texas and vice president under Mirabeau Lamar, was Ward's friend and advocate. In January 1841, with President Lamar ailing, Congress made Burnet acting president. Eleven days later he named Ward Commissioner of the General Land Office, a position he would hold for seven years. *Courtesy The Dolph Briscoe Center for American History, The University of Texas a Austin (DI 02290).*

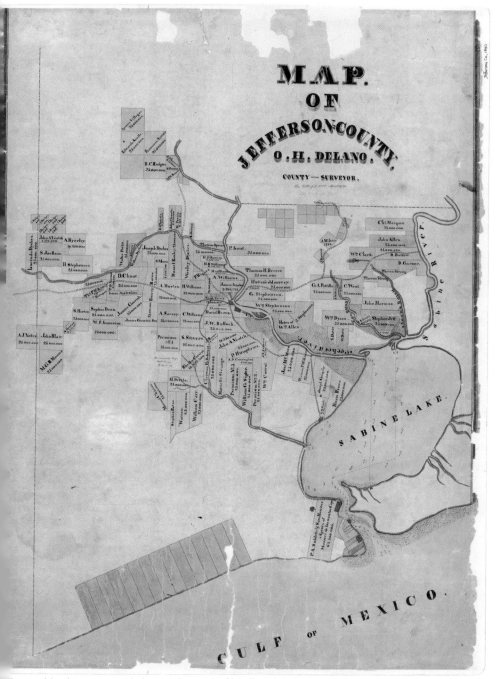

Detailed maps like this one provided a visual record of legally valid claims and thus were an indispensable tool for certifying that a new claim did not intrude on land already spoken for, but as land commissioner Ward often found county surveyors inept at making accurate maps. The different colors on this map denote the basis for each claim, e.g., first-, second-, or third class headright, military grant, land scrip, or old survey. Courtesy Texas General Land Office.

MRS. EBERLEY FIRING OFF CANNON.

To face p. 143.

In this iconic print of the Archive War, Angelina Eberly is seen "firing off" a cannon at Sam Houston's men. She may have put the torch to the powder, but otherwise she played a modest role in the affair, though she is credited by some with single-handedly rousing the town to action. In fact, it was other Austinites, not Eberly, who first confronted the interlopers and then charged the cannon. From D. W. C. Baker, *A Texas Scrap-Book* (New York, 1875).

Richardson. N.Y.

Anson Jones, last president of the Republic of Texas, was one of Ward's closest friends. Theirs was congenial relationship treasured by both men. It blossomed in 1845 while Jones was president and Ward land commissioner. Jones would often stay with the Wards while in Austin, and Ward would visit Jones at his Barrington plantation. From D. W. C. Baker, *A Texas Scrap-Book* (New York, 1875).

A CARD.

When men clothed with public authority, prostitute their character by rendering their high functions subservient to party feeling and party prejudice, to the injury and destruction of the private and public reputation of any individual, forbearance, under the infliction, ceases to be a virtue.

F. W. Ogden and J. J. H. Grammont, when clothed with authority by the House of Representatives, under a resolution of that House empowering them "to proceed to the City of Austin to examine into the condition of the Records and Archives of the General Land Office, and report the same to" said "House," passed January 1st, 1844, have not only insulted the dignity of the country, by transcending the authority vested in them by the resolution above referred to, but have set *law, truth, justice,* and even *decency* itself, at defiance; and, with a recklessness and malignity unrivalled by demons themselves, have taken advantage of the "little brief authority" with which they were "clothed," to include in their report to the House of Representatives, made in accordance with the above resolution, *one of the blackest falsehoods* in relation to my character, inasmuch as they have charged me with *perjury,* that ever enmity, aided by cunning, and stimulated by the *basest malice,* was capable of inventing. The cause of their making this charge was an attempt made by me at the City of Austin to recover, by legal means, a record belonging to the General Land Office of this Republic, which they feloniously and violently forced from my hands.

I therefore publish, for the information of the whole world, the fact that the aforesaid F. W. Ogden and J. J. H. Grammont, are LIARS and SCOUNDRELS, and unworthy of the confidence or notice of any honest man.

Washington, Feb. 3, 1844.   THOS. WM. WARD.

---

n an 1844 clash with Ward over the condition of Land Office records that had been held by the Austinites uring the Archive War, two members of the Texas House of Representatives accused him in an official port of "deep, designing, and deliberate perjury." Never one to flinch when his reputation was at stake, Vard responded with this venomous broadside. From Author's Collection.

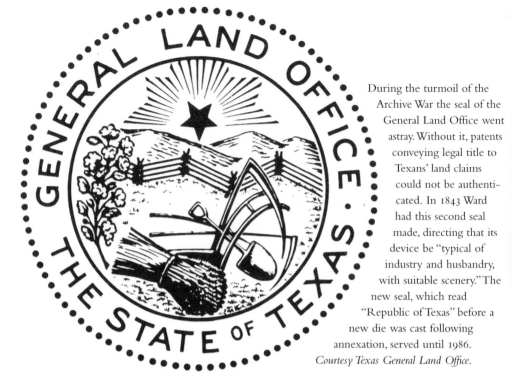

During the turmoil of the Archive War the seal of the General Land Office went astray. Without it, patents conveying legal title to Texans' land claims could not be authenticated. In 1843 Ward had this second seal made, directing that its device be "typical of industry and husbandry, with suitable scenery." The new seal, which read "Republic of Texas" before a new die was cast following annexation, served until 1986. *Courtesy Texas General Land Office.*

Susan Bean, who married Thomas William Ward in 1844, was a year old when this print was made of her family home in Candia, New Hampshire, a prosperous farming community of some 1,300 residents situated southeast of Concord. She grew up in a large but tightly knit family. From F. B. Eaton, *History of Candia* (Manchester, N.H., 1852).

Susan Ward's father, the Reverend Moses Bean, was a Free Will Baptist minister who moved many a worshipper to tears with his fiery sermons at this meeting house in Candia (at left). A noted figure in the community, Bean served Candia both as selectman and representative to the New Hampshire legislature. From F. B. Eaton, *History of Candia* (Manchester, N.H., 1852).

The Ward home can be seen to the right in the background in this view of Austin in the 1860s, looking west toward the Hill Country from near the corner of Colorado and Hickory (Eighth) Streets. By then Austin was a rapidly growing town, and the Ward house no longer stood out as it had in 1847 (see next page). Compare the dormers in the two images. *Courtesy Austin History Center, Austin Public Library* (J287).

Residence of Col.
Austin,

Sarah Ann Lillie Hardinge, *Residence of Col. Th⁵. W^m. Ward, Austin,—Texas*, 1852. Watercolor over graphite on paper. Designed by Ward himself and built by Abner Cook, the Ward family home was completed in 1847. Situated on a hill just two blocks west of Congress Avenue, it stood out dramatically in the sparsely populated capital and was easily Austin's most imposing residence at the time. *Courtesy Amon Carter Museum (1984.3.15).*

Lucadia Pease, pictured here, first met Susan Ward when Lucadia and her husband, newly-elected Texas governor Marshall Pease, boarded with the Wards in 1853. Soon Lucadia became Susan's confidant, to whom she revealed how desperately unhappy she was in her marriage, and later, how she had decided never to live with her husband again. *Courtesy Austin History Center, Austin Public Library.*

Mrs Susan S Ward
New York
To be left at the
Old Capitol
Houston

When Susan Ward wrote this note on the back of a calling card in 1854, she had lived in Austin a dozen years or more, but she identified her address as New York. Though she was still in Texas, she was headed for New York and planned to stay there—without her husband. *Courtesy Austin History Center, Austin Public Library (AF–Biography–Thomas William Ward).*

FROM VELPEAU'S FRENCH SURGERY.

PALMER'S PATENT

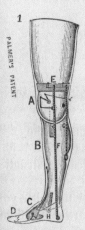
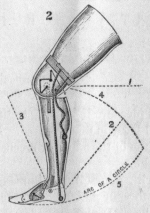
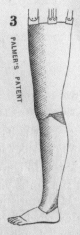

Internal view.   Internal view, semi-flexed.   External view.

" The articulations of knee, ankle, and toes, consist of detached ball and socket joints, A, B, C. The knee and ankle are articulated by means of the steel bolts, E, E, combining with plates of steel firmly riveted to the sides of the leg, D, D. To these side plates are immovably fastened the steel bolts, E, E. The bolts take bearings in solid wood (properly bushed) across the *entire diameter of the knee and ankle*, being stronger, more reliable and durable than those of the usual construction. All the joints are so constructed that *no two pieces of metal move against each other in the entire limb*. The contact of all broad surfaces is avoided, where motion is required, and thus friction is reduced to the *lowest degree possible*. These joints often perform for many months without need of oil or any attention,—a desideratum fully appreciated by the wearer.

" The tendo Achillis, or heel tendon, F, perfectly imitates the natural one. It is attached to the bridge, G, in the thigh, and passing down on the back side of the knee bolt, E, is firmly fastened to the heel. It acts through the knee bolt, *on a centre*, when the weight is on the leg, imparting security and firmness to the knee and ankle joints, thus obviating all necessity for *knee catches*. When the knee bends, in taking a step, this tendon vibrates from the knee bolt to the back side of the thigh, A. fig. 2. It descends through the leg, so as to allow the foot to rise above all obstructions, in flexion, and carries the foot down again, in extension of the leg for the next step, so as to take a firm support on the ball of the foot. Nature-like elasticity is thus attained, and all thumping sounds are avoided.

" Another tendon, H, of great strength and slight elasticity, arrests the motion of the knee, gently, in walking, thus preventing all disagreeable sound and jarring sensation, and giving requisite elasticity to the knee.

" A spring, lever, and tendon, I, J, K, combining with the knee bolt, give instant extension to the leg when it has been semi-flexed to take a step, and admit of perfect flexion in sitting.

" A spring and tendons in the foot, L, M, N, impart proper and reliable action to the ankle joint and toes. The sole of the foot is made soft, to insure *lightness and elasticity of step*.

" The stump receives no weight *on the end*, and is well covered and protected to avoid friction and excoriation.

" Fig. 3, is a view of Palmer's perfect model."

on after Thomas William Ward lost his right leg to cannon fire, in December 1835, he was fitted with a dimentary peg leg (thus earning a lifelong nickname). Later he wore complex prostheses like this leg vented by innovative limb maker B. Frank Palmer. From B. Frank Palmer, *The Patent Palmer Arm and Leg* hiladelphia, 1866).

COL. THOS. WM WARD,
U.S. Consul at Panama.

Appointed U.S. Consul to Panama in 1853, Ward put these prints in cheap gilt frames and posted them in American-run hotels and barrooms in Panama City, thus announcing his presence and advertising his services to the many thousands of Americans passing through the city on their way to and from Californi

Courtesy The Dolph Briscoe Center for American History, The University of Texas at Austin (DI 04687).

CROSSING THE ISTHMUS IN THE OLDEN TIME.

When Ward first went to Panama as U.S. Consul, the railroad across the Isthmus was unfinished, so, like thousands before him, he rode a mule over the Continental Divide and down wretched trails through rocky defiles to Panama City, a disagreeable experience made fun of in this 1855 cartoon. From Robert Tomes, *Panama in 1855* (New York, 1855).

1856 Ward was one of several officials who sought unsuccessfully to quell a violent clash in Panama City between local residents and Americans traveling to California. At least twenty-one people died, most of them Americans. In U.S. circles at the time, the melee was called the Panama Massacre, expressing a point of view also captured in this contemporary depiction. *Courtesy Joseph L. Schott.*

Upon receiving a presidential appointment in 1853 as U.S. Consul to Panama, Ward promptly expressed his gratitude to this old friend and former commander, U.S. Senator Thomas Jefferson Rusk, whose standing and influence, he recognized, had secured him the job. *Courtesy Library of Congress (DI 3a41933).*

Ward knew who was responsible when he was fired as Consul to Panama in 1856: this immensely influential shipping magnate, Cornelius Vanderbilt. Vanderbilt complained bitterly to the Secretary of State that Ward had refused to give two of his ships the papers they needed to leave port. Ward contended that their captains had mistreated their crews. *Courtesy Library of Congress (DI 3g04160).*

this unusual view of Austin in the 1860s from south of the Colorado River, the state capitol dominates town. Completed in 1853, it stood, like the capitol today, at the head of Congress Avenue. The tall lding to the right is the General Land Office building, now home to the Capitol Visitors Center. *urtesy Austin History Center, Austin Public Library (J-35).*

At the outbreak of the Civil War, Susan Ward was staying as a guest of Lucadia and Marshall Pease in this elegant Greek Revival mansion, known as Woodlawn, located in the country just west of Austin. Both Susan and her hosts initially expected her visit to be a relatively brief one while she secured a divorce, but she ended up staying four years. *Courtesy Austin History Center, Austin Public Library (PICA 02200).*

late 1865, while still awaiting resolution of her divorce suit, Susan Ward befriended Elizabeth Custer, ...n here with her husband, General George Armstrong Custer, who was stationed in Austin for several ...onths after the war. "I have not been as cordially received, and kindly treated, for many a day," Susan ...rd wrote upon first meeting Libby Custer. *Courtesy Library of Congress (DI 03130).*

LOST A LEG IN THE STORMING
OF BEXAR, 1835.
MAYOR OF AUSTIN 1840.
COMMISSIONER OF THE
GENERAL LAND OFFICE
OF THE REPUBLIC FROM 1840
TO STATEHOOD.
FIRST COMMISSIONER OF THE
LAND OFFICE OF THE STATE.
U.S. CONSUL TO PANAMA
IN 1853

Ward is buried in the Republic Hill section of the State Cemetery in Austin, nearby such notable Texans: Stephen F. Austin, Edward Burleson, Barbara Jordan, and John Connally. Photo by author.

aching heart," McLane recalled; "we congratulated each other, and in a moment more would have been outside of the inclosure to welcome our deliverers, when there was poured into the Station a heavy volley of musketry, accompanied with savage shouts for blood; this volley was quickly followed by others; the dreadful reality came upon us that the Police had joined the mob." The police chief and governor later insisted that the police acted in response to gunfire from Americans in the upper story of the depot; the Americans maintained that the attack was unprovoked. Whatever the case—the point was argued ad infinitum—the result was horrendous as passengers succumbed to gunfire, and the "infuriated and ungovernable mob"—the police chief's characterization—forced its way into the depot, looted and robbed, and left injured and dead in its wake.[5]

Meanwhile Ward and his three comrades had abandoned the depot yard for the beach, on foot, taking temporary cover under a large canoe. "I heard the screams of men, women, and children," Peg Leg recalled, "I heard the murderous musket fire of the police, I heard the cut of the machete, I heard the breaking of trunks." They determined to return to the city, find Governor Fábrega, and get him to stop the violence; but it was a perilous journey, and a fatiguing one for the hobbled Colonel. When they finally tracked the governor down, he balked at returning, reminding them he had gone to the area earlier and been fired on for his trouble, by the Americans, he declared. They implored him to go, even Ward, who was not normally given to pleading. Fábrega relented. McLane and Nelson escorted him to the riot area, and the three of them, together with the chief of police and others, finally brought the riot under control. By then it was past 10 p.m. Ward had returned to his consulate directly from the meeting with the governor, but his day was not done. He and his servant later went to the depot to do what they could for the wounded.[6]

The Watermelon War (a title, unlike Panama Massacre, that does not assume categorical Panamanian guilt for the affair) took the lives of eighteen foreigners, most of them Americans, and at least three Panamanians. Among the many wounded were more than a dozen Panamanians and an undetermined, but clearly greater, number of Americans. Theodore de Sabla, shot in the thigh, convalesced in bed for more than month, enduring great pain and a serious infection.[7] Property losses were substantial. Seven days after the riot a U.S. naval officer visited the site and reported that evidence of the "plunder and massacre" was everywhere. The ground was strewn with "trunks, carpet-bags, valices, and other specimens of baggage, which had been cut open and rifled of their contents. The buildings . . . which had been occupied by Americans as Hotels, Restaurants, and drinking Saloons, were wrecks, every fixture and article appertaining to them having been destroyed, or taken away; the doors and window-shutters lying in the street and the buildings perforated with bullets." The close of the riot opened an incredibly busy period for Peg Leg. "My labors have been incessant," he wrote Marcy. Right away he began taking depositions from English-speaking participants and eyewitnesses as to what they knew of the riot's inception and course and what they had personally seen. In early May he forwarded 365 pages of handwritten testimony to Marcy in Washington and Bowlin in Bogotá. Dozens of passengers (many from San Francisco) filed claims with the U.S. consul for lost baggage and items stolen from their persons, mainly gold, money, and watches. The Reverend John Smallwood, who suffered severe cuts to his head and a grievous wound from a musket ball that penetrated his chest and exited his side, added $10,000 to his claim for "damages done to his person" and time confined. The proprietor of the Pacific House put in a claim for an immense quantity of liquor and wine, 100 chickens, $3,000 in gold stolen from his safe, the safe itself, his kitchenware, thirty-six beds and forty-five cots, and the rest of his furnishings.[8]

Within a week of the riot Ward submitted a protest in behalf of the United States to Governor Fábrega in which he held the Government of Panama, its officers, and people entirely responsible for the violence and its consequences. His rhetoric, to say the least, was heated. "Life was lost," he wrote, "travellers baggage plundered, women violated and ravished, defenceless children and babes shot and mutilated, ministers of the Gospel wounded and plundered, and residents houses torn to pieces." Not one to take the blame lying down, Fábrega dispatched a communication to Bogotá the next day blaming the passengers for starting the riot and then for provoking the assault on the depot by firing on the police. Officials in Bogotá were themselves provoked by Ward's protest, calling it "insulting" and his claim of rapes a falsehood, for which, they later insisted, the United States justly owed New Granada a reparation.[9]

Ward, naturally enough, found a more sympathetic audience in

Washington. His reports to Marcy were no less impassioned. He maintained that there were "missing murdered" whose bodies may have been hurled into wells or buried in the sand. He declared that there would be no safety for Americans on the Isthmus unless the Panamanians were "punished for their past outrages and overawed by a strong and efficient force. . . . Nothing short of an absolute possession of this Isthmus by the United States, will be sufficient to protect and keep open this highway of Nations." Marcy agreed that the conduct of Panama's officials and people on April 15 was "to the last degree reprehensible," but he thought seizing the Isthmus too drastic a counter stroke. He assured the Colonel, nevertheless, that ships of war had been ordered to Panama City and Colón with instructions to intervene in any emergency imperiling the lives and property of Americans. The government of New Granada, moreover, would be held responsible for the riot and required to make adequate satisfaction. The president authorized an official investigation and selected Ward's predecessor as consul to Panama City, Amos Corwine, to conduct it. Corwine's assignment, Marcy told Ward, was to investigate "the outrages and injuries perpetrated against persons, property and rights of American citizens," language that made it clear just what kind of findings Marcy expected: New Granada guilty on all counts.[10]

For Peg Leg it must have seemed, at long last, vindication. For two years he had warned of a violent attack on American life and property and repeatedly called for stationing a warship at Panama City (heedless, at the same time, to the fact that cultural and racial attitudes like his were helping lay the groundwork for just such an explosion). Now Americans in Panama City were to be protected by a warship, though the riot had so unnerved them that even a naval vessel did not alleviate their considerable feeling of insecurity. Ward could also take heart, especially after absorbing a pounding for his role in the William Hunter affair, in winning plaudits from the president for his efforts on April 15. Pierce, through Marcy, expressed his approbation of Ward's conduct, marked as it was by "prudence, firmness and energy." The Colonel could not have helped but be pleased, too, with Corwine's report to Marcy—no coincidence, it would appear—as he had Corwine's ear during the investigation and was responsible for a significant portion of the testimony on which Corwine relied. Corwine concluded, debatably but predictably, that (1) the riot was premeditated, (2) the pivotal attack on the depot by the police was entirely unprovoked, and (3) Panamanian authorities were complicit in the affair. He recommended immediate occupation of the Isthmus from ocean to ocean—or what the *New York Herald*, in an editorial supporting the idea, called "a military occupation of the line of transit." Such a step, countered the *New York Times*, could undercut important negotiations then underway with the British over their involvement in Central America. The Pierce administration decided against permanent occupation but, besides demanding punishment of the guilty and compensation for losses, proposed a treaty with New Granada in which U.S. forces could intervene on the Isthmus whenever local police failed to provide adequate protection. Negotiations were protracted and bitter. For months New Granadan officials denied any responsibility for the riot, insisting that Jack Oliver had started it and American gunplay had inflamed it. The proposed treaty fell victim to the animosity. Finally, in 1857, New Granada acknowledged liability, but it still took years to settle all the claims for loss of life and property.[11]

If the Colonel was buoyed by the president's praise of his conduct on April 15, 1856, he had precious little time to enjoy it. Before May was out he learned from a friend that Ran Runnels, erstwhile leader of the Isthmus Guard, was in Washington "using every influence" to get his job. Runnels had planted an unflattering story about Peg Leg with an anonymous correspondent ("S") for the *New York Times* who, together with Francis Rice, had upbraided the Colonel during his "consular smash-up" the previous year for being peevish, arbitrary, and overbearing. This time "S" described at some length a supposed incident in which Ward treated a ship captain insolently. "Is it not a shame that Mr. Marcy keeps such a man as Consul at so important a point?" he asked rhetorically. "The Department has frequently been informed of his entire unfitness for the position, in consequence of his rudeness and his mania for a quarrel."[12] The Pierce administration undeniably had its doubts about the Colonel, but he had survived them despite a pointed request by New Granada for his recall. This latest pummeling was hardly enough by itself to dislodge him, but it was quickly followed by a far more lethal blow leveled by a formidable opponent. In June 1856, Marcy received a complaint against Ward from no less a figure than Cornelius Vanderbilt, the shipping magnate known widely as Commodore Vanderbilt, who at his death two decades later was the richest person in America. Two of his steamships, Vanderbilt explained to Marcy, had left San Francisco for Nicaragua but due to civil unrest in that country had gone on to Panama City instead, only to run up against an arbitrary U.S. consul who threw "every possible obstacle in their way, and subjected them to annoyances of the most grievous nature." Vanderbilt trusted that the government of which Consul Ward seemed "so unworthy a representative would not recognize such "unjust and unwarrantable" interference."[13]

A man of the Commodore's influence was not easily resisted, but Peg Leg did not blink. He intended to stand firm, he told Marcy, in support of "law and justice" and the poor seamen on Vanderbilt's ships who had applied to him for aid and protection—and squarely against the "powerful and wealthy Capitalists, whose monied interests would be promoted, by a defeat, of my Consular jurisdiction and decisions." It was an uneven fight, but Ward never shied from an encounter if he thought he was in the right, no matter who the adversary. The clash had its roots in the fiercely competitive Vanderbilt's decision several years earlier to initiate passenger service between New York and San Francisco by way of the Isthmus of Nicaragua. The distance between New York and San Francisco was 375 miles shorter by way of Nicaragua than by Panama, and although the Nicaraguan Isthmus was three times as wide as the Panamanian Isthmus, all but eighteen miles could be traversed by a water route. Vanderbilt began service in 1851. Within two years it appeared that Nicaragua's passenger traffic might catch up with, perhaps even surpass, Panama's.[14]

Prior to launching his bold venture, Vanderbilt had secured a charter from the Nicaraguan government giving the Accessory Transit Company, of which he was founder and first president, exclusive right to transport passengers across the Isthmus. While on an extended European cruise in 1853, however, the two men he had entrusted with management of the Transit Company in his absence, Charles Morgan and Cornelius K. Garrison, manipulated the company's stock and seized control. The Nicaraguan route was theirs. "I'll ruin you," Vanderbilt promised them upon his return. By December 1855 the Commodore and his friends had succeeded in buying up enough stock in the Accessory Transit Company to regain control. That turn of events, of course, did not sit well with Morgan and Garrison. By then Nicaragua was under the thumb of an American adventurer, William Walker. Earlier

Route of Transit Across Nicaragua, 1850s

that year Walker had invaded the country with a tiny private army of Americans and in four months managed to defeat opposing forces, set up a provisional government, and install a new Nicaraguan president— with help from Morgan and Garrison. So Walker returned the favor when the two men proposed that his puppet president annul the charter of the Transit Company, confiscate its wharves, stages, mules, and other property used in transporting passengers across the Isthmus, and grant it all to Garrison and Morgan in a new charter.[15]

Word of the charter annulment reached New York in mid-March 1856. Vanderbilt was taken completely by surprise—and livid about it. Four days later he retaliated by announcing that he was halting steamship service to Nicaragua from New York and San Francisco. His ships would "lay at their wharves" for now. But he had a problem. Two of his steamers, the *Cortes* and the *Uncle Sam*, were scheduled to depart San Francisco for the Nicaraguan port of San Juan del Sur before he could get word to them. So he dispatched his son-in-law to Panama to make sure the ships were intercepted on the high seas and diverted to Panama City. It was at that point, with Vanderbilt in a vengeful mood, that Peg Leg entered the scene and subjected the two ships and their captains to "annoyances of the most grievous nature." Meanwhile, the situation in Nicaragua deteriorated precipitately when Costa Rica invaded the country with the goal of ousting Walker. With transit across Nicaragua disrupted, passenger traffic soon dried up, not to resume for five years and then only in modest numbers.[16]

Diverting the *Uncle Sam* and the *Cortes* to Panama served the purpose of their owner but did not sit well with their crews. They had contracted for a voyage to Nicaragua and back to San Francisco. Now, without their consent, they found themselves in Panama, and the captains of the two vessels seemed in no hurry to leave. The *Cortes*, in fact, lingered four months. On board the *Cortes* there was first uneasiness and then open discontent over the uncertainty of the situation. The captain refused to inform the crew when their ship might depart, and he would not pay their wages. On board the *Uncle Sam* the crew, in the eyes of its captain and first officer, grew mutinous. When three seamen refused to follow an order, claiming that it was not work they had been engaged for, their hands were manacled behind their backs, and they were hoisted by their wrists and kept that way for hours, dislocating their shoulders.[17]

Protection of the rights of seamen had long been a duty of U.S. consuls—at least in theory if not always in practice. The United States was a seafaring nation, and at sea a captain had absolute authority over his crew, a situation that invited abuse. Thus some protection was afforded seamen under law. If a seaman complained that a ship was "out of voyage"—that its voyage was not the one the seaman had agreed to—and a consular officer found the complaint justified, he was required to discharge the seaman if he so desired and demand that the master of the vessel pay the seaman all wages due plus three months' additional pay. During May and June 1856, several groups of seamen from the *Uncle Sam* and the *Cortes* came to the American consulate, complained that their vessels were out of voyage, and asked Ward to discharge them with three months' extra pay. The Colonel investigated the complaints and eventually discharged all those who requested it, with extra pay, including forty-three of the eighty-seven seamen on the *Cortes*.[18]

Both captains were defiant, especially over the extra wages. Captain Robert Horner of the *Uncle Sam* accused the Colonel of fomenting mutiny on his ship and cited an extenuating circumstance for the midcourse change in destination; it was not until after the *Uncle Sam* left San Francisco that he learned that the transit route across Nicaragua "had been broken up by the wars of the country." Vanderbilt made the same point to Marcy: "the war between Costa Rica and Nicaragua was raging on the line of the Isthmus transit at the time when the *Cortes* & *Uncle Sam* would have arrived at San Juan del Sur—and it would have been madness to have attempted a passage through the country." The law did indeed provide for extenuating circumstances. If a vessel was out of voyage due to circumstances beyond the captain's control and without any design on his part to violate his contract with the ship's crew, the consul could, if he deemed it proper, discharge a seaman without exacting three months' additional pay. Ward was unaware of why Vanderbilt had rerouted his steamers, but he did not care why. He had no right, he insisted to Marcy, "to infringe upon the seamen's rights under their contract with the ships." On the contrary, he believed it his duty as consul "to protect the poor ignorant seaman by demanding for him his rights."[19]

The clash with Vanderbilt came to a head in June 1856, soon after Captain Horner decided to set out for San Francisco without paying the extra wages due his discharged seamen. Ward's demand was "unlawful and unjust," he insisted. It no doubt also involved a large sum of money—Horner had so few seamen left he had to require his waiters to double as deck hands. The Colonel, no slacker at holding his own in such a face-off, refused to give the *Uncle Sam* its papers and pressed Captain Theodore Bailey, commander of the sloop-of-war stationed in the harbor, to detain the *Uncle Sam* until Horner complied with U.S. law. But Bailey refused to cooperate, pleading that it was not U.S. Navy business. Just before sailing, Horner dispatched a message to Vanderbilt detailing what had transpired during his six weeks in Panama and how he felt about it.[20]

Armed with Horner's accusations against Ward, the Commodore

raised the issue with Marcy for the first time. Two days later the secretary took Ward to task. Vanderbilt's decision to divert its ships to Panama was entirely warranted, he wrote Ward, given the war in Nicaragua and the steps taken by the Nicaraguan government against the company. Vanderbilt had every reason to fear that if his vessels entered San Juan del Sur, Walker's army might seize them. Ward was directed to return the *Uncle Sam*'s papers and abide by Marcy's views in dealing with the *Cortes*.[21]

The Colonel responded to the secretary's rebuke aggressively and passionately, believing that his position was rooted firmly in U.S. law, but Marcy was not listening. There had been too many complaints and his patience was exhausted. Anyway, Vanderbilt carried far more weight with Marcy than Ward did. The Colonel did agree to give the *Cortes* its papers when it sailed, but oh so grudgingly, telling Marcy that to do so was "obnoxious" to his "sense of justice" given the "great wrongs" done its seamen. That attitude hardly placated the secretary, and then, at the last minute, when Captain Collins, without warning, demanded his papers immediately while Ward was ministering to a yellow fever victim who had contracted the disease on Collins's ship and been booted off, Ward told Collins he would have to wait at least until that evening. Collins threw up his hands and went to sea the next day without them.[22]

As soon as Vanderbilt got that news he complained to Marcy a second time. Once again, Marcy immediately called Ward to account, this time with finality. The president, he informed the Colonel in an August 1 letter, believed that the public interest would be served by a change in the U.S. consul at Panama City. "Dismissal," Peg Leg wrote on the letter. The *New York Times* did not forego its last opportunity to get in some sharp jabs. In a front page "Special Dispatch" from Washington, "S" reported that Ward had been removed as a result of "numerous complaints of his official conduct, as quarrelsome, overbearing, and in some cases grossly illegal" (the later presumably a reference to his charging Captain Horner fees in two instances that Marcy considered out of line).[23]

August 1856 thus brought an ignominious conclusion to Peg Leg's three years in Panama—or so it seemed, until the men in whose defense he had lost his job redeemed him. Upon finally getting back to San Francisco, the seamen discharged by Ward from the *Uncle Sam* sued Vanderbilt for their extra wages in U.S. District Court in San Francisco. On August 22 Judge Ogden Hoffman rendered his decision. He found for the seamen, without exception. The U.S. consul had acted properly in granting the seamen their discharges and their extra wages. "The allegation that, in doing what by law he was bound to do, he was animated by improper motives, is unreasonable in itself, and unsupported by proof." Not only had the seamen been brought to a port other than the one they contracted for, but they also had been detained thirty days by the time the consul discharged them, and it appeared the detention might be indefinitely protracted. Vanderbilt's case did not fare well. The extenuating circumstance pleaded at length by his lawyers was judged immaterial. Following the invasion of Nicaragua by Costa Rica, passengers would indeed have encountered dangers crossing the country, Judge Hoffman conceded, but that was not the reason Vanderbilt gave for diverting the two steamers in his directive to Captains Horner and Collins, nor could he have. Neither he nor his captains learned of the invasion until later. Furthermore, Vanderbilt was aware that a temporary arrangement had been made by Cornelius Garrison's son permitting the Commodore's passengers to transit the Isthmus. Vanderbilt decided nonetheless to withdraw his steamers from the Nicaragua route, and thus the company "incapacitated" itself, for by withdrawing the Atlantic steamers (which transported passengers from Nicaragua's Atlantic coast to New York) it could no longer land passengers on Nicaragua's Pacific coast without stranding them in Nicaragua. Vanderbilt directed Captains Horner and Collins to proceed to Panama instead, discharge their crews, and await further orders. Await they did, for days on end, but without discharging their crews. It was Peg Leg who finally did that.[24]

Vanderbilt's lawyers appealed the decision and lost again.[25]

Judge Hoffman's decision was reported in a New York newspaper in December 1856. By then Peg Leg was living in Tarrytown with Susan. He clipped the report from the newspaper and put it next to his dismissal letter—retribution perhaps, a means to reassure himself and convince others that, all along, he was right. That was exactly how his nephew, Charles Smyth, used Judge Hoffman's decision two years later in a biographical sketch of Peg Leg that appeared in Jacob De Cordova's *Texas: Her Resources and Her Public Men*: "It must be gratifying in no small degree to Colonel Ward and his friends to see that his course has been fully justified."[26] Not in the State Department's eyes, however; Judge Hoffman may have redeemed Ward's honor, but could not resurrect his consulship. He had antagonized too many people, from New Granadan Foreign Minister Herrán to Vanderbilt to Secretary Marcy himself. He had demonstrated too often that his was not the temperament of a diplomat. If he believed that American honor or his own was at stake or that American citizens, like William Hunter and Vanderbilt's seamen, had suffered injustices, he was unyielding in his determination to set the situation right as he saw fit. In Hunter's case he overreacted, with unfortunate results, but in his conflict with Vanderbilt, though he paid a heavy price, he could justifiably take pride in having the courage of his convictions.

CHAPTER 14

Reunion and Separation

THE DAY SUSAN WARD LEARNED that her husband had been dismissed as consul she became "allmost insane." After his contentious visit the previous year her friends all thought he would never return to New York, but she knew him better and feared, even expected, he would come. The prospect was all the more wrenching now that she had started a new life for herself and her children in Tarrytown. She relished living in a "quiet country settlement," away from the "fashion and bustle" of New York City. She lived "very plain," she told Lucadia Pease, with a cow in the yard providing fresh milk for the children, though not so plain that she could not entertain Lucadia and her relatives, for her house could accommodate "ten or twelve friends at a time" and she had domestic help. When Lucadia did pay a visit later that year she found Susan very pleasantly situated in a large, handsomely furnished home.[1] Susan's own relatives visited often, and the house reverberated with the sounds of youngsters playing and the barking of their dog, Moses. She was especially pleased to have enrolled her sons in a strict school nearby, just the place for "wild boys." Yet in her enthusiasm for Tarrytown she had not forgotten Texas. "Indeed," she wrote Marshall Pease, "no place but Texas will probably ever again seem like home to me." She even arranged to have an Austin newspaper sent to her year around and declared on one occasion, "I would give more at this time to see an old Texan than all the Kings, and Queens, in Christendom." Nevertheless she was averse to returning there if it meant living with her husband. "For you must know," she told Lucadia the day before the Colonel was dismissed, "that I have learned to act for myself since I left my home in Texas and I assure you that I am now beginning to have a little respect for myself."[2]

Ward arrived in New York on September 15, 1856. Susan herself tells best what happened next (in a letter written two weeks later):

> My relatives determined that I should never live with him again and my brother Dudley called on him before he left the city for Tarrytown and told him my fixed resolution—but he immediately came to my home but found I was in the city—where he forthwith directed his steps—when he called at my mothers all the family thought I had better see him on business—well it was a terrible struggle to meet him face to face—instead of meeting me with complaints as of old he commenced with regrets for his past conduct towards me—and begged me to forgive and forget his past offences—for he was an alterd man—and if I would again trust to his love and honor he would redeem the faults of the past by devoting his whole life to me &c &c—but all this did not move me—I refused to see him any more—and when he saw my dear old mother and listened to her recounting my wrongs and sufferings—he said "mother I blush and weep to think I have been guilty of all these outrages to your daughter, the best and truest of wives—but if you will try to forgive me I trust my God will[,] for [He] has forgiven the worst of siners"—
>
> My brothers and sisters also talked much with him—and feeling that he was really an alterd man thought that for his own salvation, and my childrens sake that I had better try him once more
>
> Before all my mothers family I told him I feared that years of devotion on his part could never obliterate from my memory my past wrongs—yet I would forgive and try to forget the past—
>
> I therefore came home with him last Tuesday one week tomorrow—and thus far he has been all kindness and devotion but God only knows how long it will be thus calm—Oh I forgot to mention that he has left off the use of all stimulating drinks—without this I should never have consented to a reunion—[3]

Thus the Colonel rejoined his family in Tarrytown, for the time being. In the weeks that followed he impressed people as an affectionate and attentive husband. Within the family circle he was known to take

Susan on his knee and press her to his chest. He bought her gifts—a second horse, a two-horse sleigh, an elegant four-wheeled carriage. Soon, perhaps even before September was out, she was pregnant again. Woe be to those who discomforted her. On one occasion when they were riding in a stage a fellow passenger lit up a cigar, and Susan found the smoke bothersome. Peg Leg asked the gentleman to desist. When he persisted, Peg Leg ripped the cigar out of his mouth and tossed it out the window. Lucadia Pease's judgment during an October visit was that if the Colonel continued to abstain from "spiritous liquors," he and Susan would "live pleasantly together." Susan, she noted, feared a relapse. And well she might have. Abstaining from "spiritous liquors"—distilled beverages like whiskey and brandy—did not mean abstaining from alcohol altogether, in particular fermented beverages like beer, ale, and wine. It was hardly out of the ordinary for the Wards and their guests to enjoy ale and wine with their meals, and once Ward started working, he routinely drank a glass of claret at lunch, though mixed with water. Sometimes the Wards served punch with a wine or brandy base.[4]

Within days of reuniting with his wife, Ward had another fateful get-together. His nephew Charles Smyth, son of his sister Caroline, paid a visit. It was Ward's first meeting with an Irish relative (other than his brother Henry in New Orleans, who had died in 1844) since sailing for Quebec twenty-eight years earlier. Even then the get-together was the result of a chance encounter between his brother Samuel, captain of a steamship operating off the Irish coast, and a Texan on board who mentioned knowing a fellow named Thomas William Ward. Amazed that the brother he had given up for dead was alive, Samuel wrote him, "I heard you lost your leg. I heard you lost an arm. I heard you lost an eye and died of your wounds. I heard you were shot in a duel. I heard you were stabbed with a Knife in New Orleans." From Samuel, Peg Leg learned that he had a nephew who was a Presbyterian minister in Delhi, New York, a small town some 110 miles (as the crow flies) northwest of New York City.[5] Though but one year old when his uncle emigrated, Charles had often heard his mother Caroline speak of him. It was Charles's understanding, however, that his uncle had succumbed in a duel in 1842. "I can scarcely believe that it is not all a dream," he replied upon hearing from Peg Leg. "I have read your letter with mingled feelings of awe and joy; it comes like an epistle from the invisible world." Eager to meet his uncle, he hurried to Tarrytown shortly after

Ward settled in. And so began a warm relationship between uncle and nephew—an intense one, in fact, on Charles's part. During the next four years he would visit the Ward home frequently, write his uncle 100 or so letters, and become embroiled in the Colonel's marital troubles as adviser and co-conspirator.[6]

It was in Texas, not Tarrytown, where Ward had intended to live upon his return from Panama, but Susan resisted. Aaron Bean helped resolve the impasse, with Susan's encouragement. He introduced the Colonel to a French-born businessman, Amedie Simonin, who was looking for a partner with cash to invest in a business venture—importing wine and liquor. It so happened that Ward had about five thousand dollars, primarily from his liquor business in Panama, that he was prepared to put into such a venture immediately. A partnership was struck, and on March 1, 1857, Ward & Simonin opened its doors at 37 South William Street in lower Manhattan. The decision, Ward told a delighted Charles Smyth, meant he would not return to Texas for five years.[7]

Eventually the two partners built up a fairly decent business selling a variety of imported spirits and other items: champagne, claret, sherry, gin, rum, brandy, cigars, and so on, a product line that was profitable but not the best thing for a man who had a drinking problem. Tasting wine and liquor was part of the job. Ward commuted daily from Tarrytown, a chore he put up with for more than a year before moving his family to West 30th Street in Manhattan. The biggest challenge early on was getting enough capital to keep the business growing. Ward put in at least $5,000 to start and then set about selling property in Houston and Austin to raise more capital. That process, he knew, would take time. Meanwhile, he told Simonin that Susan had promised to put $10,000 of her own money into the pot, money from her sister Joanna's bequest. About to depart on a buying trip to France, Simonin came out to Tarrytown to reassure himself about Susan's intentions. She put his mind at ease, according to Simonin. By then it was early May 1857. Ward had been back from Panama seven and a half months, and Susan was about seven months pregnant.[8]

The fissures in Peg Leg's marriage were papered over upon his reunion with Susan, but inexorably, like cracks in the walls of a house with a sinking foundation, they resurfaced as 1857 progressed. Susan found herself, once again, the target of periodic flashes of anger and verbal threats. He was a man of "very violent temper," she told a skeptical Charles Smyth. A few times he seemed about to strike her but held back. A continuing source of friction was Susan's bequest from Joanna, which Aaron Bean administered. Ward had reason under common law and custom to feel that, while it was legally her property, it was her husband's to manage, not her brother's. In late June, three days before she gave birth to their last child, Ward asked her about the money she had agreed to invest in his firm. When she refused to raise the issue with Aaron, he was furious and, according to Susan, remarked menacingly that her money would all be his when she was dead; then he took a pistol out of a drawer and, ominously, checked to see if it was loaded.[9]

Three months later Simonin returned from France to discover that Susan had not invested a cent. Why not, he asked. Because, she replied, she no longer trusted her husband or the firm with her money; and even if she wanted to, she could not withdraw the funds from her brother now, due to the financial panic gripping the city and the country since August (the Panic of 1857). Ward protested that Ward & Simonin had expanded its business on the strength of her promise and without her funds the firm would suffer greatly. No matter, she responded, she was not going to invest the money. That, at least, was Simonin's version of events that followed his return from France. At some point during 1857—just when is unclear—Susan did loan her husband some money, $500 according to him, $2,000 "or some other such Sum," according to Susan. In any case, he took offense at what he felt to be Susan's reluctance to support a venture he had undertaken solely to accommodate her desire to stay in New York, where he was "almost a Stranger." Aaron's meddling in Susan's finances compounded Ward's frustration, especially now that he had become aware that, while he was in Panama, she had given Aaron power of attorney over her bequest. He believed, moreover, that Aaron had invested a portion of the bequest in Galveston real estate under his own name (which he may have done). The Colonel would eventually sue his brother-in-law over the issue.[10]

Reading the testimony given in 1859 and 1860 in connection with the two lawsuits initiated by Susan against her husband, one comes away with the impression that the Ward household was a living hell by 1857. As a litigant, Susan sought to impose an identity on her husband as a relentlessly violent, abusive man. "I was waitress during this year," stated her longtime servant and ally, Jemima Rivington, "and I scarcely recollect a day when the defendant [Ward] did not speak cross and angry to some person. It was most generally to Mrs Ward, and when he spoke crossly he most always swore and cursed at her." Not so fast, responded Peg Leg and his friends. Susan was hardly the innocent victim. She had a temper, too. On one occasion, Peg Leg charged, when they were on a steamboat on the Hudson, she flew into a rage and called him a fool, an idiot, and "other abusive epithets" in front of all the passengers, scandalizing him. A neighbor testified that from his home across the street he "often heard Mrs Ward's voice sounding loud, as if scolding some person." One evening in 1857 he was in the Wards' parlor while Susan and her husband were playing backgammon, and Susan "lost her temper, became very much excited because the Defendant won a game, used harsh and abusive language towards him," and "called him a cheat." What emerges from the pages of these depositions, therefore, are caricatures that dwell on the issues of anger and verbal and physical abuse that were at the heart of the lawsuits.[11]

That Ward had an anger management problem is beyond dispute, but his personal relationships were hardly as one-dimensional as they were later made out to be. He was, for example, a caring father. In the spring of 1857, after Dudley began attending an academy in Delhi and living under his cousin Charles Smyth's charge, his father wrote him affectionate, chatty letters full of news about family members, even the dog. He often inquired about Dudley's studies and complimented him on his letter writing while diplomatically noting areas for improvement. Once Ward & Simonin was on its feet, the Colonel arranged for his sixteen-year-old step son, Robie, to help out in the business and paid him $20 a week, far too much in Simonin's eyes for someone learning the ropes. Years later his daughter Anna, born in 1851, recalled how as a child she was loved fondly by her father.[12] His Dublin relatives, after contact was reestablished, saw another side of Peg Leg, his generosity. More than once he helped Charles Smyth through financial squeezes by lending him money. Peg Leg encouraged his sister Caroline and her family to come to New York and live at the Ward home in Tarrytown. "Oh how like my generous Brother even when a Boy," Caroline responded. Then he insisted on paying for their passage. In September 1857 Caroline, her husband, George, and their twenty-five-year-old daughter, Carrie, bid farewell to Dublin and came to Tarrytown, where they enriched an already lively Ward household. Uncle George, Robie discovered to his delight, was a "jolly old man" who danced and sang and told stories about their Irish relatives. Caroline and Carrie entertained family members on the Wards' piano.[13]

The family joy, however, was short lived. Shortly after the new year, Caroline Smyth fell gravely ill. Ward had gone to Texas in hopes of selling the Austin homestead and other property. Charles Smyth came to Tarrytown to be with his mother. In February, Caroline lapsed into a "dreamy state." Within a week she was dead. The Wards and the Smyths were overcome with sorrow.[14] His older sister Caroline's death was the third such tragedy in the past half year to befall someone close to Ward. First was the shocking death of his longtime comrade and patron, Thomas Rusk. Despondent over the death of his wife, Rusk committed suicide. Then, while Ward was in Texas, so did his treasured friend, Anson Jones. "I assure you my Dear Colonel," Jones had written him a few weeks earlier, "I have no friend whom it would give me more pleasure to take by the hand again, than yourself."[15] Ward no doubt responded to that sentiment, stopping by Jones's plantation on his way from Houston to Austin in late December, just two weeks before Jones killed himself. The three deaths must have taken a toll on the Colonel's psyche, and perhaps they help explain why, on his return home in March 1858, his disposition was more volatile than ever.

The very day Peg Leg arrived in Tarrytown he was conversing with Susan at the dining table when he erupted in anger, accusing her of encouraging Robie and Mary to use her first husband's name, Marston, rather than his. It was insulting, he declared, and he was damned if he would allow it. Periodic outbursts of anger marked the next few weeks. He would curse Susan, and on two or three occasions he threatened her with a pistol. One evening an altercation between the two escalated into a horrific family scene, with Peg Leg threatening to shoot both Susan and himself, George Smyth trying to hold him back, Carrie Smyth in tears, and Susan pacing the floor and yelling, "Let him alone—he wont do it."[16]

Men who abuse their spouses are often abusers of alcohol. Recent studies, for instance, indicate that one-fourth to one-half of the men who commit acts of domestic violence in the United States have problems with alcohol and other drugs. By reducing inhibitions, distorting perceptions, and becoming itself an excuse for violence, alcohol increases the likelihood of abusive acts.[17] If Jemima Rivington is to be believed, alcohol figured significantly in Peg Leg's abuse of Susan. Irish-born and in her mid- to late-twenties, Rivington was a servant and res-ident in the Ward home for all but four of the twenty-two months Peg Leg and Susan lived together in Tarrytown and New York City. Her sympathies were clearly with Susan, undoubtedly coloring her recol-lections when she gave a deposition in 1860, but her testimony still sheds light on the deterioration of the Ward marriage in 1858. The Colonel drank "very freely" after his return from Texas, Rivington stated, including the spirituous liquors from which he had abstained on first coming to New York. "My daily orders were to have the quart decanter filled with brandy to be ready for him when he came home [from work]. I was also in the habit of carrying liquor to his room at night." She went so far as to claim, in fact, that the Colonel "was very frequently so intoxicated at night as to be very boisterous, and disturb the whole house by the noise." Susan, too, accused him of frequent intoxication in the months before she left him. Ward, defiant on the issue, denied that he ever drank to excess. His nephew, Charles Smyth, who stayed with the Wards many times, backed him up. Here, as so often in dealing with testimony generated by Ward versus Ward, it is difficult to know exactly where the truth lies. It seems reasonable to conclude, however, that Peg Leg had an alcohol problem that affected his behavior at home and was a destabilizing factor in his marriage.[18]

The unfolding crisis in Peg Leg and Susan's marriage reached a turning point in June 1858. By then the Wards had been living for a month on West 30th Street in Manhattan. Susan later testified that on the evening of June 9 she noticed that a memorandum from her brother, apparently concerning money he had paid her from her bequest, was missing from her writing desk. When she asked her hus-band if he had taken it, he angrily denied it. Once both had retired to their bedroom he began railing at her, threatened her with a pistol, and then he "struck her a violent blow upon her face" either with the pis-tol or his fist, knocking her to the floor. Jemima Rivington recalled the episode and its aftermath vividly:

> That night after he and Mrs Ward went up to their room, I went
> up to my room to go to bed. As I passed by the door of their
> room on my way up, I heard him cursing and swearing at Mrs
> Ward. . . . My room was on the fourth story. After I got to my

room I heard a loud and violent scream from Mrs Ward's room.
I knew her voice. I also heard a noise as of something falling. I
was very much startled. It was the worst thing I had ever heard
in the house, and I immediately went down stairs into the nursery adjoining Mrs Ward's room. I stayed there all that night. I
heard Mrs Ward groaning for a long time; the next morning I
went to Mrs Wards room to take up some ice-water to him. I
was always required to do this; and I was always admitted into
the room on every other occasion but this. This time the defendant [Ward] would not let me in. He came to the door and
opened it a very short space, only large enough to put his arm
through. The defendant then ordered me to give Robie his
breakfast, and send him downtown [to his job at Ward &
Simonin]. Mrs Ward came down stairs very late to breakfast.
Miss Carrie Smyth was at the table when she came down.
When I saw Mrs Ward, I was greatly shocked by her appearance.
Her nose was swollen and out of shape. Her face black and blue,
and her eyes swelled. I was so much affected by her appearance
that I could not help crying. Miss Carrie said to her[,] O Aun-
tie! what has happened to you? Col. Ward said that she had
knocked her head against the door. Mrs Ward did not say anything. But I saw her put up both her hands to her face as if to
cover it. Mrs Ward ate nothing at breakfast. After I breakfasted,
I went up stairs and in the closet adjoining Mrs Ward's room, I
saw her night clothing all wet with blood.

Later it was determined that the Colonel had broken Susan's nose.[19]
Susan knew at that point that she could not take it any longer—the
fits of temper, the verbal abuse, the attempts to intimidate and control
her, and now physical abuse. She had lived apart from him for three
years and knew that life was better without him. But it was one thing
not to join him while he was in Panama and quite another to walk out
on him in New York. Leaving was fraught with risks and difficulties for
herself and her children. To begin with, he had made plain his hostility
to the idea of a separation, and she feared a violent reaction. So she told
him she was thinking of going to New Hampshire that summer with
their two youngest children, Anna and one-year-old Thomas William
Ward Jr., to spend several weeks with relatives. It was two months later,

on August 13, when they finally departed. Susan "took a kind and affectionate leave" of him, Ward testified later. Not until he came home from work that evening and found a note from her did he realize that she had left him for good.[20]

At first Peg Leg and his son Jim lived alone, not counting servants, yet the Colonel thought they managed to "pass over the time quite agreeably." Then Peg Leg decided he also wanted his son Dudley, still in Delhi, at home. Joining them was Carrie Smyth, Charles Smyth's sister. For the next few months the four of them lived together on West 30th Street—Ward, now fifty-one, sons Dudley and Jim, age thirteen and eleven, and their cousin Carrie, who was twenty-eight and single.[21] Susan and her two youngest children spent the next several months in New Hampshire; Robie and Mary stayed with Bean family members in Manhattan. Ostensibly planning just a summer trip, Susan had not taken warm clothes for the children or herself. When the weather turned chilly, she wrote her husband asking him to send them along, but he refused to do so and urged her to return home. The response only highlighted what she already knew too well—she had found temporary refuge from him, but she was still his dependent. She had no separate legal identity, no source of income other than her bequest from Joanna, no lawful control of her children. He had possession of even her most personal items, her clothes, her private papers, her keepsakes, her writing desk. Wifely subservience was what the law—and the Colonel—still expected of her, but she was through with wifely subservience. How, then, to proceed? Because her husband resided in New York, and legally, as his wife, she did too, a legal solution would have to be pursued in the New York courts. That meant returning to New York City, and there she would discover, if she did not already know, that the only ground for a full divorce was adultery. The courts viewed dissolution of a marriage not as a right but as a public remedy for a public wrong inflicted by one spouse upon the other, or, put another way, as a violation of the marital contract to which both had consented and whose terms were set by the state. New York courts did, however, grant what was known as a divorce from bed and board—a legal separation from one's spouse—if extreme cruelty was proven. If successful, Susan would gain the right to live apart from her husband and quite possibly custody of her children and alimony for their support and her own.[22]

On March 22, 1859, Susan filed suit against her husband in the

Supreme Court for the City and County of New York. A prominent New York law firm represented her, no doubt thanks in part to the deep pockets her brothers, Aaron and Dudley, who believed that Ward had put their sister through hell. "God only knows how this poor woman has suffered for the last fifteen years," Aaron wrote Marshall Pease; what "dreadful tortures and misery she has endured for the sake of her children and family." Susan asked for a legal separation, custody of all the children, alimony, and a restraining order. In her eight thousand word complaint she described, in chilling detail, what she claimed was fourteen years of "grossly abusive cruel and inhuman" treatment, culminating in a "brutal assault" on June 9 that had permanently impaired her health. She also sought to cast her husband as an unfit father, alleging that he had encouraged their sons to drink alcohol and visit prostitutes and had often used profane language in the presence of the children. Since, she asserted, she had reason to believe he would harass or harm her and use force to reclaim his two youngest children, she requested a restraining order. Four days later the court complied, ordering the Colonel, his agents, and his servants to refrain from taking custody of the children and from interfering with Susan in any way. At the outset of her case, Susan had gained the recognition and protection of the court.[23]

In early May Ward counterattacked. Susan's allegations were fabrications, he told the court in his answer to her complaint, each and every one of them, and they masked her own sins. It was she who had the violent temper, to which she repeatedly gave vent, following him about the house when he tried to escape her fury. It was she, moreover, who was in the habit of beating the children. And she was such an extravagant woman that she often put him in an embarrassing financial position. For none of these claims, however, did he offer any specific examples, unlike Susan's painstakingly detailed complaint. His request that her complaint be dismissed fell on deaf ears.[24]

For Ward, that was just the beginning of a campaign to discredit his wife. By suing for legal separation and publicly charging him with "the most unheard of cruelty" she had not only challenged his identity as a husband and head of his household but had impugned his honor and put his reputation at risk. Susan was "at war" with him, he insisted. So he responded accordingly. He went to Texas that summer, and there, lo and behold, discovered, as he later stated, that Susan was not the "chaste and pure" person he had thought her to be. His information came, he said, from individuals who were aware that Susan was suing him and so were now willing to speak out about her transgressions. At the time she married Ward, he was told, she was having an affair with Thomas Wood Ward (a twenty-year-old Austin resident who, though no relation, was no stranger to Peg Leg; several months later he had begun working as a clerk in the Land Office). The Colonel would later maintain that there was reason to believe the affair continued after their marriage, and, worse still, that from the time they married, in 1844, until Susan left Austin in 1854, she had "illicit intercourse" with other men.[25] Before returning to New York, he talked up Susan's infidelity in conversations with Austin friends, even with Marshall Pease. Once back in New York City he reported his "discoveries" to Charles Smyth, who replied that he was not surprised. "I have had suspicions of Aunt's fidelity for a long time." Smyth explained that in 1857, while Ward was in Texas and his mother, Caroline, then living at the Ward home in Tarrytown, became deathly ill, he had come to Tarrytown to help care for her. During his month-long stay he could not help but notice Susan behaving indiscreetly with Isaac Trowbridge, the doctor treating Caroline. She would shut herself up with him in different rooms in the house, sometimes in the parlor and reception rooms but most frequently in the nursery, with the door locked, and in that room, he noted pointedly, there was a bed. The Colonel added Trowbridge to his list of Susan's adulterous affairs. It was one thing, however, for Ward to talk informally about Susan's alleged indiscretions and another to swear to them in court. Husbands who were sued for divorce commonly responded with charges of infidelity, so commonly, in fact, that in Texas the Supreme Court held that baseless charges of adultery were actionable cruelty and therefore potentially grounds for divorce. It was a measure of Ward's determination to discredit Susan that, nonetheless, he eventually introduced those charges in a Texas court and was about to introduce them in a New York court when the case was resolved.[26]

Susan's lawsuit and Ward's reaction to it irretrievably ruptured their marriage—and split their family, too. While her husband was in Texas, Susan visited Dudley and Jim several times, both at their school and at their home on 30th Street, but the meetings were awkward and, on the boys' part, cool. On one occasion Susan invited the boys to their brother Tom's second birthday party. "We of course replied in the negative," Dudley wrote his father. Both boys made it clear that they sided with their father, not their mother, whom Dudley cheekily referred to in another letter as "the former personage."[27]

The rift in the family became an unbridgeable chasm in January 1860 after the Supreme Court issued an interim decision in Susan's lawsuit. The Colonel was ordered to pay his wife $800 to defray the costs of carrying on her suit against him plus $35 a week, calculated from the previous August, to cover living expenses for herself, Anna, and Tom. The lawsuit was thus to go forward at Ward's expense. She was still his wife, and it was his obligation to support her even though they were opponents in court. That, however, was an arrangement Ward could not stomach.[28]

Two days later, without Susan's knowledge, the Colonel sold all the furnishings in their 30th Street home to a relative who lived in New York—every last chair and table, all the rugs, curtains, and bedding, the china and kitchenware, the piano, even the baby carriage, everything that made their house a home. Then he sold his interest in Ward & Simonin to his partner for $30,000 in promissory notes (but ultimately realized less, perhaps substantially less, than that sum). He was liquidating his assets in New York with an eye to putting them beyond Susan's legal reach, and he was preparing to go to Texas. It was hardly a propitious time for him to travel. His stump troubled him so much that he had barely left his bedroom for several weeks. But he was intent on going. Susan had won a court order that he was determined to evade, to say nothing of more draconian court orders that he suspected lay ahead. In February 1860, together with Dudley and Jim, Ward left for Texas, never to set foot in New York again.[29]

One day in March, after he had taken up residence in the family's Austin homestead, he was astonished to learn that Susan was in town, accompanied by her oldest son, Robie. The very next day he found out why. She had filed suit against him in the Travis County District Court, once again charging cruelty; but this time, under more liberal Texas law, asking for a full divorce, equitable division of their community property, restoration of her separate property, custody of Anna and Tom, occupancy of the homestead, and an allowance (alimony) while the suit was litigated. A "bold and remarkable step," marveled her brother Aaron. Without parallel, grumbled a stunned Peg Leg. He had intended to file his own suit for divorce, but she beat him to the punch. Patrick

Rooney, his friend and agent who had agreed to look after his interests in New York City and assist in his defense there, was aghast at the news. "I cannot understand how Mrs. W could leave here some 2 weeks after you & arrive in Austin before you had commenced your proposed suit. . . . I fear you have committed a fatal error in delaying your proceedings." Three days later, to top it off, the Travis County Court ordered Peg Leg to pay Susan $100 a month in alimony while the suit was pending. He had not avoided paying alimony after all, not unless he abandoned Texas, so he gave in and made the first payment of $100, only to receive a communication from Susan asking him to pay the court costs and alimony now due under the New York court order, some $2,000 (less, she conceded, the $100 he had just paid). "I am ready to respond to and defend either one of Mrs Ward's suits," he wrote the sheriff of Travis County, "but think she is entitled to but one, for the same purpose." That may have made sense to Peg Leg, but not to Susan nor to the courts in New York and Texas. He had two lawsuits on his hands and an uphill fight ahead of him in both. In Texas, attorneys for both sides dispatched a blizzard of interrogatories to people in New York with personal knowledge of the couple—relatives, domestic help, neighbors. It was the New York case, however, that would be decided before the year was out.[30]

Susan and her lawyers knew that the Colonel's flight to Texas did not sit well with the New York court, and his absence further hampered his defense. How advantageous it would be to go to battle in Texas with a favorable decision in New York already in hand. The possibility certainly worried Patrick Rooney. "Can she succeed in this double game?" he wondered. Certainly not if he had his way. Rooney, an outspoken, combative fellow, despised Susan; he thought her a dangerous woman of "*low* cunning" and "sharp practice." Suspicious of her every move, he even had her shadowed after she returned to New York. In the end, when Ward had lost, he blamed it partly on her unscrupulousness: "With the usual cunning of the 'Yankee' this Woman has Bribed the Bench with either money—Prejudice—or some more convenient commodity always available with woman."[31] Charles Smyth, his uncle's adviser throughout the litigation, matched Rooney's spitefulness. He called Susan "demented," a "mad-woman," the "very D–l incarnate." He warned his uncle that if she was allowed to bring "her perjured minions" into court and perjure herself she would ruin him. Given to conspiratorial thinking—he saw "deep and black" motives at work—he was convinced that Susan had tried to poison her husband while they were in Texas and feared she might try again. He even suspected her of having had designs on the lives of both his parents at the time his mother, Caroline, died. "Murder was part of her plan," he told Peg Leg, "getting rid of an important witness." When he learned in early 1860 that Jim and Dudley had both become indisposed while Susan was still in Austin, he wrote his uncle, "Does their mother visit them at school? They ought not to eat anything out of her hands."[32]

To Rooney, Susan's behavior, so utterly shameless in his eyes, reflected just how much the North had been corrupted by "Woman's rights," and indeed Susan may well have been energized by the women's rights movement that bloomed in the Northeast and Midwest during the 1850s. How repugnant, Rooney thought, for a woman not only to turn her back on wifely conduct by taking her husband to court but then also to pursue the case against him with unwomanly aggressiveness. She "seemed ferociously to pursue her prey," Rooney commented after she appeared on the Manhattan doorstep of the man who had possession of the family furniture and demanded entry. To Smyth, Susan was "all energy." She will "stir heaven and earth," he warned his uncle. On one occasion, much to his disgust, she spent two hours in Amedie Simonin's office urging him to answer her attorney's interrogatories, and when he still balked, she got a court order forcing him to. On another occasion, when Smyth was in Tarrytown hunting people to testify for Ward, Susan "got on our track in some way . . . ," he told his uncle, "and though yesterday was a very stormy day, she went round in the wind and rain to see a number of persons out of whom she thought to make capital."[33] What a dramatic change for a woman who had believed for so long that she must "endure unrevealed" all the trials through which she had passed. "Forbearance [had] ceased to be a virtue," she declared. Seizing the opportunity to escape her past and shape her future, she was tireless. Time and again she and her lawyers stole a march on their opponents. For his part in mounting Ward's defense, Rooney decided to try his hand at turning some of the servants who had taken Susan's side. "The nurse Sarah Foley will be the most difficult job," he wrote the Colonel, "as she is under Mrs W's eye at present—but there is a *way* to do anything." His "way" included dispensing money, leaning hard on people, and playing on their Catholicism ("all of them that are Catholic I can make tell the truth," he claimed). Rooney kept at it for a while but finally gave up, declaring that "Mrs W has every servant fixed in her interest." Charles Smyth found that his conspiratorial rumor mongering did not go unheeded by the plaintiff. Susan's lawyers got a warrant issued for his arrest on a charge of slander. What really provoked the two men, of course, was the realization that they were losing the New York case—and to a woman. How could it be, other than by artifice?[34]

Rooney was determined to get Susan's lawsuit dismissed at the court's session in June 1860, but had to settle for a continuance to October. It was a measure of how poorly Ward's case was faring that Thomas Nelson, his lead attorney, decided to withdraw. A strategic retreat, Rooney called it in a letter to Ward. "I believe he considers the case as *lost by you & won by Mrs. W.*" Few tears were shed at Nelson's exit. Instead, he became the fall guy, accused of ruining Ward's case either by his neglect or stupidity (Charles Smyth was not sure which), in particular by not seeking out witnesses in the New York area—servants, visitors, and neighbors not already in Susan's camp—who would testify in Ward's behalf, a not unjustified charge. There was even a suggestion of treachery on his part, of collusion with Susan, based not on evidence, but on the assumption that there must be a nefarious explanation for Susan's success. When Peg Leg slipped out of New York, for instance, and Susan appeared in Austin on his heels and filed her lawsuit first, who tipped her off? Nelson?[35]

When the Supreme Court of New York City and County convened in October 1860 for a special term and a trial date was set for Susan's lawsuit, Ward's only hope was to get another continuance. Not only was he still in Austin, but his stump had flared up again, and whatever attention he could give to his legal problems was focused on the Texas lawsuit, leaving Rooney and Hooper Van Vorst, who had taken over for Nelson, in the dark as to how he wanted them to proceed. "Pray why is it that you don't write to me or Vanvorst at all?" asked Rooney. The Colonel's sons Dudley and Jim, potentially crucial witnesses given their inside knowledge of family relations and their implacable loyalty to their father, were in Texas, too. Having failed either to turn any of Susan's witnesses or ferret out significant new ones, the Colonel's defense team had just three witnesses ready to testify, none of them immediate family members or house servants. Susan had thirteen, including Robie and Mary, three Bean siblings, two doctors, five house servants, and Susan herself. It had been anticipated on Ward's side that, at the least, affectionate family relations, especially between husband and wife, would be documented in court through reading some of the family correspondence Ward had saved, including quite a number of ardent letters Susan had written him over the course of their marriage, but her counsel succeeded in blocking that strategy. "So here we are high & dry," Rooney summed it up.[36]

In a last ditch effort, Van Vorst filed a motion for a "perpetual stay of proceedings." A stay was granted for an indefinite period, but with an unpalatable condition: Ward must pay, forthwith and in cash, the court costs and alimony awarded Susan in January, a sizable amount that neither Van Vorst nor Rooney was prepared to hand over without the Colonel's go-ahead, and time did not permit contacting him. With certain defeat staring them in the face and the trial less than a day away, Rooney, Charles Smyth, Van Vorst, and a trial lawyer hired at the last minute, Charles Tracey, debated whether to put forward a defense at all. Desperate though they were, they rejected an offer by Susan's attorney to settle the case for $1,500, concerned that accepting it would give ground to Susan in the Texas case and arm her with the funds she needed to win it. Instead, seeking to lay the foundation for an appeal or new trial, Van Vorst and Tracey asked the judge for a postponement on the grounds that the defendant was not present, indeed not even aware that the New York case was about to be tried. Justice Benjamin W. Bonney denied the request. Tracey protested the decision, and then the Colonel's lawyers and witnesses withdrew. The trial proceeded without them. Van Vorst explained to Ward that they withdrew because they feared that by taking part in the trial when they had no testimony, their presence "might give the Judgment a higher sanction in the Texas tribunals."[37]

In early December, Justice Bonney issued his decision. In the absence of a defense it was not exactly a bolt from the blue that his findings mirrored Susan's allegations. He found the defendant to be a man of "violent temper" whose treatment of his wife during their marriage had been "cruel and inhuman." At the time his wife left him he had "become addicted to the excessive use of intoxicating drinks." On one occasion, the night of June 9, 1858, he struck her a violent blow across the nose and face and "knocked her senseless upon the floor." On other occasions he "used profane and abusive language" toward her and "threatened her with violence and with deadly weapons." All these acts he committed "without cause or provocation." Based on these and other findings, Justice Bonney granted Susan a divorce from bed and board (a legal separation), custody of Anna and Thomas, and $3,000 per year in support calculated from the day Susan filed her lawsuit (meaning Ward already owed her $5,041). The restraining order was extended indefinitely. Is it any surprise, Rooney remarked bitterly, that a Southern man contending against a New England woman failed to get justice from a Northern judge?[38]

For Susan, Justice Bonney's ruling meant legal vindication. She had not abandoned her husband. She had left him with good cause. It was he who had violated his marital responsibilities. She had, moreover, gained legal standing as a separated wife along with custody of her two youngest children. Yet, she had known all along that only by winning in Texas would justice be fully hers. As it was, her husband was beyond the reach of Justice Bonney's decision. Peg Leg was hardly about to pay Susan thousands of dollars in alimony after fleeing New York to avoid just such an obligation—unless compelled to do so by the Texas court. What is more, the Texas court could grant her a full divorce and with it the autonomy she hungered for, and she would be entitled to half the couple's community property in addition to her own separate property. In mid-December Susan left for Austin with a copy of the New York court proceedings in hand. Robie, Mary, Anna, and Thomas all stayed behind. By early January 1861 she was staying with Marshall and Lucadia Pease at their stately home west of town. By then her lawyer had already added Justice Bonney's findings to the allegations against Ward under consideration by the Travis County District Court and had petitioned the court to enforce the New York judgment, in particular payment of the $5,041 already due her. She hoped for an early decision.[39]

Susan could not have helped but notice, however, that all Austin was consumed by another issue: should Texas secede from the federal union? In December, six weeks following Abraham Lincoln's election as president, South Carolina had seceded, the first state to do so. By January 11, Mississippi, Florida, and Alabama had followed suit. In Austin hundreds of supporters of secession paraded through the principal streets—state and local officials, a blaring band, women on horseback carrying the flags of the Southern states.[40] Yet it would have been impossible for Susan to foresee just how devastating an impact secession, and the Civil War it triggered, was about to have on her life— impossible to know that she would still be in Austin when the war ended, that a son would be dead, that her lawsuit would be stalemated, and that she would not have talked to her children, save Robie, for four years.

CHAPTER 15

Civil Wars

DURING JANUARY AND FEBRUARY 1861, while Texas marched steadily toward secession, Peg Leg was confined to his home by a painful attack of osteomyelitis, an infection in his stump. Some days he was bedridden, and even on his better days he felt out of sorts and often dispirited. A man of passionate convictions about the future of his country, it frustrated him not to be in the middle of the fiery debate that erupted in Austin over secession. Yet, still a hero in his hometown, he was by no means ignored. His cause was the cause of many Austinites—the Union. Though the fire-eaters, as the secessionists were dubbed, mounted colorful processions and delivered rousing speeches, other townspeople vigorously opposed them or at least hesitated to join them. They formed the "Austin Association for Maintaining Our Rights in the Union." They called for a convention of slaveholding states to seek a settlement with the nonslave states. They conducted "serenades," parades around town, usually accompanied by a band, during which they stopped at the homes of prominent Unionists to serenade them and were rewarded with stirring speeches. On several occasions it was to Peg Leg's home they marched. Ignoring the pain in his residual leg, he would come out on his porch and exhort them to stand firm by their principles and uphold the Union. On February 23 the question of Texas's secession was put to a popular vote. The Colonel was flat on his back that morning. Determined to cast his ballot, he had himself carried from his bed to his carriage and was driven to the polls, where an election judge came out and took his vote. He was one of 704 Austin and Travis County residents to vote against secession; 450 voted in favor. But in Texas as a whole, more than 46,000 votes were cast for secession and fewer than 15,000 against it. Seven weeks later Fort Sumter was fired on, and the Civil War began.[1]

Austin at the opening of the Civil War was a far different place from the town Peg Leg had known before leaving for Panama. Finally, it had a look of permanence (see illustrations). Gone were the dilapidated log and plank lumber structures thrown up in a rush in 1839 to house the government. At the head of Congress Avenue stood the first permanent capitol, a soft cream limestone building that dominated the town. Nearby were the recently constructed Treasury and General Land Office buildings and the handsome Governor's Mansion, its front graced by a Greek portico with six Ionic columns. Brick and stone commercial establishments lined upper Congress Avenue, and a block west of lower Congress Avenue, on Cedar (Fourth) Street, stood the five-year-old Travis County courthouse, a two-story stone building that was soon to become the scene of renewed legal strife between the Wards. Beyond the Avenue were many new homes, ranging from salt-box frame cottages to Greek Revival mansions built by master builder Abner Cook for members of the town's elite. No longer did the Ward home capture the eye as it had upon its completion in 1847, when Austin was a ramshackle village of a few hundred hardy souls. Now it was home to thirty-five hundred people. Yet the capital was far from a residential mecca, especially for its one thousand enslaved blacks. Most Austin whites believed slavery to be a legitimate and worthy institution, and at least one-third of white families owned slaves. Austin, moreover, was a town of its times, with no paved streets, no running water, no sewers, and no municipal garbage collection, but lots of animal life, with chickens, dogs, hogs, and, of course, horses in yards and in the streets. Its location was still distant from many settled parts of Texas and frustratingly remote from the military conflict about to grip the North and the South for four long years. In Austin the war was "the all absorbing topic," remarked one resident to a friend in Arkansas, yet "its events become history with you before rumors of them reach us." Situated on the periphery of the Confederacy, Austin was beyond the reach of railroad or telegraph.[2]

Living just two blocks west of Congress Avenue, Peg Leg and his two sons could hardly fail to take notice of the war fever that seized the town following the attack on Fort Sumter. "Companies are passing through our city every day," one observer reported, "and the roll of the drums arouses the spirit of our people." The outbreak of war put Austin's still reluctant Unionists on the spot. Peg Leg never doubted that secession was misguided, but once the die was cast he yielded his allegiance "to the demands of the *de facto* Confederate government," as he put it, and supported it faithfully. So did the majority of Austin Unionists. By early 1862 there were probably fewer than sixty Unionists left in the area, and they were no longer seen as political adversaries but as "public enemies" and "traitors." By then, too, more than six hundred Austin and Travis County men and boys had volunteered to fight for the Confederacy. Later that year Dudley, now seventeen, enlisted in a Texas unit serving on the Gulf coast. By spring 1863 he was in Mississippi with the Second Texas Infantry fighting in the defense of Vicksburg.[3]

Meanwhile, a mile and a half northwest of the Ward home, in the country, Susan lived quietly with the Peases at Woodlawn, their Greek Revival mansion, hoping against hope she could win her suit and return home to her children in New York. Though the circumstances that brought Susan to Austin were trying, she at least had the opportunity to stay in one of the capital city's most elegant and comfortable homes, probably the largest and costliest home Abner Cook ever built (see illustrations), and there she enjoyed the company of the woman who had been her confidant since 1854.[4] Little did the Peases realize, of course, that their guest would end up staying more than four years!

Unlike the Colonel, Susan probably never made peace with secession and the Confederacy. It was not only that she was New England–born and bred and a resident of New York. Her hosts, the Peases, were unrepentant Unionists. Susan's misgivings about the Confederate cause troubled her far less, however, than her fears that the fighting might take the lives of her sons. No sooner did Fort Sumter fall than Susan began agonizing over the possibility that Robie, then twenty-one and living in New York, would be drafted. Lucadia worried that such an eventuality, on top of Susan's legal struggles, would, like the proverbial straw that broke the camel's back, "crush her."[5] Robie, however, managed to avoid service and even came to Austin for a time early in the war. When Dudley decided to enlist, Susan was terribly anxious to see him before he left. She had not spoken with him for three years; he had rebuffed her entreaties. Yet here they both were, living a mile and a half apart in a community small enough to ensure that their paths would cross occasionally. "I have just learned that it is your intention to leave Austin very soon to enter the Army," she wrote Dudley in August 1862 in her comma-laden writing style.

Oh my own, precious child, as you hope for success, in this, world, and peace hereafter, I pray and entreat of you to see your poor, unhappy mother before you leave town. . . .

Dear Dudley, I feel that if I could once again, press you to my aching, heart, and give you a mothers, blessing, it would be the greatest comfort, I have known for many a long and weary day.

You can never know how my heart has longed for you, and dear little Jimmy, since our separation—

And when you last refused to speak to me, the grief it caused, wellnigh exhausted, both my mental, and physical, strength. My son, I know you have a heart, therefore consider that it is a mother, who makes this, perhaps her last request, of a child to whom she gave life . . . , and grant me an interview at any time, or place, you may name.

Dudley left town, however, before Susan had sent off the letter, so she held on to it and two years later enclosed it in another letter she wrote Dudley. Realizing that the missive was from his mother, Dudley balked at reading it before his father had and instead forwarded it to him unopened (with the enclosure), together with the following comment: "The writer evidently begins to feel the remorse consequent on her bad deeds, and the pangs of an evil conscience, are having their influence and she doubtless realizes the extent of her crime in destroying the unity of a family; but I assure you that she is sadly mistaken if she expects to receive any aid or comfort from me." Justice Bonney's decision may have exonerated Susan in the eyes of the law but not in Dudley's eyes, and his bitterness only deepened once the setting for his parents' legal battles shifted from New York to Austin. It was there a few months later, in June 1861, that his mother had his father arrested and held in the Travis County jail. The Colonel was every bit as sour about it as his son. Susan was out to ruin him, he was sure. What probably did not occur to him was another explanation for his troubles: that he had brought them on himself.[6]

When Susan sued her husband for divorce in Travis County, in March 1860, she had put him in a bind. Texas had an unusually liberal standard for determining cruelty in a marriage, a standard that Ward's abuse, as set forth by Susan, far exceeded. And in Texas, too, progressive marital property law, based on Spanish law rather than the customary British common law, gave women property rights not enjoyed in the more settled Southern states. Not only could a married woman own property in her own name, she retained ownership of any "separate property"—property she owned at the time of her marriage or acquired thereafter by gift or inheritance. Susan's bequest from Joanna, for instance, was her separate property. Ward, of course, could claim as his own separate property the extensive land holdings and other property that he owned before his marriage, like the Long Row and the rental income it had generated. On the other hand, any real and personal property acquired by a couple during their marriage that did not qualify as separate property was deemed community property. Texas courts routinely awarded a divorcing woman half the couple's community property in addition to all her separate property. Faced with the likelihood of Susan's winning her case if it went to trial, Ward also faced the possibility of losing control of property he thought of as his own.[7] It did not help that Susan had retained as her lead attorney an acknowledged leader of the Texas bar and a successful divorce lawyer, George W. Paschal, who later gained renown for several legal works. An unwavering Unionist, he was a man of passionate conviction. Susan's suit became for him a cause as well as a case. Joining Paschal in representing Susan was no less a figure than Nathan George Shelley, an Austin lawyer and steadfast Confederate who served as Texas attorney general from 1862 to 1864.[8]

How, then, was Ward to stop his wife? Stall, counseled Patrick Rooney. "I would certainly try & prolong this case according to the usual course of all such cases," he wrote the Colonel. Rooney had in mind one of the nineteenth century's most notorious divorce cases, starring Edwin Forrest, the leading American actor of his time. Forrest accused his wife, Catherine Sinclair Forrest, of adultery and sued for divorce. She countersued, charging him with adultery. The six-week trial that began in late 1851 captivated the public. Every detail was reported in the press. Catherine Forrest was acquitted and awarded $3,000 a year in alimony. Edwin Forrest kept appealing the decision. Years went by without her getting a penny. "If Mrs Forrest can be *held 10 years* in court without Rec[ei]v[in]g 1 Dollar why cant you litigate [the] Pl[ain]t[i]ff in like manner?" Rooney asked Ward. Charles Smyth put the issue to Ward a little differently, but just as bluntly: "*I would not leave it in her power* in any case, whether she gained her suit or not[,] *to gain one cent* by it—you understand what I mean." What he meant was that his uncle should put his property beyond Susan's, and the court's, reach. Delay and do not pay—that was the crux of Rooney's and Smyth's advice. Of course, there were limits to stonewalling. Edwin Forrest found that out, eventually. In 1868, after five appeals had failed, he gave up the fight and paid his former wife more than $60,000.[9]

At the urging of his attorney, the Colonel gave some thought to settling with Susan, but it was Rooney's and Smyth's advice he followed. The strategy of delaying and not paying was not, however, the be-all and end-all of his defense in the Texas case. In his answer to Susan's complaint, he once again denied Susan's allegations of cruelty and responded with cruelty charges of his own, this time with specific examples of her abuse. His version was a mirror image of hers. During occasional "violent exhibitions of temper," she would "heap epithets and abuse" upon him and beat the children, often compelling him to intervene for their protection. Then she would win him back with a show of her "captivating grace and wily manner." What must have troubled Susan far more, however, were the allegations of infidelity that he spelled out for the court. She "had been guilty of the most gross violations of her duty to him," he declared. He named names, one Texan and one New Yorker, and intimated there were other men. He lodged those charges confident that at least two allies, Charles Smyth and Henry L. Kinney, the founder of Corpus Christi and an old crony, would back him up under oath.[10] Intending to further taint Susan's reputation, Ward sought out evidence that she had deliberately tried to abort their last child, alleging that, among other things, she had "set on hot water" during her pregnancy. Some consideration was even given to introducing testimony (hearsay at best, it would appear) that Susan had contracted a venereal disease, an affliction Charles Smyth felt would be "much against her" in court, that she could not prove had been contracted from her husband. It was primarily the charge of adultery, however, that Ward relied on to put Susan in such a bad moral light that the court would dismiss her suit or at the least deem her unworthy of a judgment in her favor. The Colonel was not necessarily opposed to a divorce, but he could not abide one on Susan's terms. Property and custody issues aside (he insisted on custody of all four children), he was determined not to end up the guilty party and risk public censure and disgrace. The court, however, refused to dismiss Susan's case or set aside its March 1860 order awarding her a monthly allowance ($100 at first, lowered to $50 in July when the court learned that the children in Susan's custody were in New York, raised back to $100 in January 1861 at Susan's urging, and fixed at $75 six months later).[11]

In the meantime, Peg Leg maneuvered to put his property out of Susan's reach. Secreting assets, it is called, and in today's world it is a time-honored tactic in divorce suits. Were Susan not suspicious of her husband's machinations, she would have had every reason to think he was flush with funds. In addition to selling his interest in Ward & Simonin that January for $30,000, he had sold the Long Row the previous year for $12,000 (an unwittingly shrewd move—fourteen months later it was devastated by fire). Ward, however, sought to steer clear of holding funds that a court could readily put its hands on. He wanted to be in a position to plead an inability to pay whatever the Texas court ordered rather than appear unwilling to do so. Given his extensive assets it was no easy matter, but he was remarkably successful at it. According to Lucadia Pease, by the time Susan came to Austin to carry on her Texas suit, in January 1861, Ward had already managed to dispose of his property in such a way that the court had "not been able to get it for her."[12]

To say the least, Peg Leg was devious in hiding his assets. Here is how he explained to the court the status of the promissory notes Amedie Simonin had given him in payment for his interest in their partnership: "The notes taken from this sale were for different amounts due at different times[.] I have not a memorandum of them. . . . [They] were transferred . . . to a third person by me—they are not in my possession or under my control and I do not know where they now are." Accessibility to another $10,000 evaporated in the spring of 1860 when Ward hurriedly worked out a deal with Henry Kinney. An adventurer and land speculator who had virtually bankrupted himself with his filibustering ventures in Nicaragua during the 1850s, Kinney desperately needed money to avoid a forced sale of his land holdings in Texas. Ward had funds in hand that he desperately wanted to tie up. They struck a bargain. Ward would let Kinney have $10,000 at 12 percent annual interest, to be secured by a mortgage on Kinney's land holdings in Texas. Right in the middle of their negotiations, however, Susan appeared in Austin to file for divorce. Caught off guard, Ward urged

Kinney to seal the deal "without delay of *even one moment*," fearing that Susan would learn of their scheme through her "spies" and would get the court to intervene. She did get wind of it, but too late.[13]

By the time Susan came to Texas in December 1860, Peg Leg had already made it clear that in Texas, unlike New York, he was going to fight her tooth and nail. Alimony became the battleground. In fact, the allowance granted by the district court led to so much legal wrangling that the court simply put aside the issue of enforcing the New York court's much larger award. After paying Susan for six months, the Colonel suddenly stopped, about the time he realized the New York suit was lost. By January 1861 he had missed three payments in a row and had made it clear, in writing, that he refused to make any more payments. Susan asked the court to cite him for contempt. Peg Leg responded that he was "wholly unable" to pay $50 a month and provided a brief explanation that Susan's attorneys scoffed at as "wholly insufficient." The court demanded a full accounting, in the form of answers, under oath, to probing interrogatories about his finances submitted by Susan's attorneys.[14]

This time details poured forth from Ward about his investments and expenditures. He even acknowledged that he had reacquired the family furniture, supposedly sold to a relative in New York in what now was transparently a ruse. To say that Ward was forthcoming, however, is not to imply that his response was a model of candor. He denied out of hand that he had ever sought to dispose of his assets in a way that would defeat the court. Instead, he attributed his delinquency entirely to the secession crisis and the widespread economic disruption it had wrought. Were times normal, he assured the judge, he would have had "abundant means" to pay the alimony. And, indeed, early 1861 really was a difficult time in the Texas capital, with many Austinites hard-pressed financially. "Dead flat" was how one resident characterized the business climate.[15] The judge, however, was unmoved. He found Ward guilty of contempt and ordered his arrest. Jolted into action, the Colonel came up with the overdue $150 in a matter of hours (after scrambling to borrow it, he later said) and was released.[16]

Ward's invoking of civil disruption in his defense, though unsuccessful this time, foreshadowed a serious problem for Susan. As Charles Smyth wrote his uncle in early 1861, "Secession is advancing rapidly. So much the better for your suit." The unfolding national crisis promised many opportunities and excuses for bringing the case to a standstill. Following Fort Sumter in April, Smyth highlighted two such possibilities—enactment of a stay law (suspending legal action to collect debts, perhaps including alimony) and a shutdown of civil courts. Ward himself was aware that, with war at hand and men rushing off to enlist, public pressure had reportedly led to the suspension of district court proceedings in an adjacent county. And a new, but limited, stay law was already on the books. It was not a leap of imagination to conclude that the best strategy was delay. Indeed, the Colonel's lead attorney, John A. Green, a former Travis County district attorney and a member of a prominent Austin law firm, Hancock and West, thought he could probably postpone the court case from term to term indefinitely. Should that strategy fail and the case go to trial and result in a divorce decree, the Colonel had a fallback position (one hotly contested by Susan): there was virtually no community property to divide. True, he conceded, he had earned lots of money during their marriage in salaries and fees, but, down to the last penny, the family's living expenses had swallowed it up. Nearly all the remaining assets, not counting Susan's bequest from Joanna, were his separate property—property that he had either owned at the time of their marriage or that could be traced to it, including even his interest in Ward & Simonin. The ever venomous Charles Smyth had a different take on how Susan would fare in a trial in Confederate Texas: "What chance . . . will a Yankee strumpet have before a Southern Court & Jury in a suit against a true Texan hero?"[17]

Actually, the true Texan hero was not faring so well with the district court. Shortly after squaring accounts with Susan, he balked anew at paying. Soon he was called on the carpet again. Ward explained that his finances had been squeezed by debt payments and the costs of repairing and painting his house. Money was simply too tight for him also to come up with Susan's alimony. By June 1861, Judge Alexander W. Terrell had heard enough. He cited Ward for contempt and ordered him confined to the county jail. Located within the brick walls of the courthouse, the jail was a wretched place known as "the dungeon." Constructed so that it afforded no ventilation, it was judged by Austin's medical community to pose a threat to the health—and life—of anyone confined there for "any length of time."[18] Hardly about to put up with such treatment, Ward petitioned the Texas Supreme Court for a writ of habeas corpus. His arrest, he declared, was without authority in statute and violated the Texas constitution. After two days, the Colonel was brought before Supreme Court Associate Justice James H. Bell. The opposing attorneys argued the case. Three days later, on June 21, Judge Bell issued his decision. The Texas constitution stipulated that no one be imprisoned for debt, he explained. Alimony awarded by a court becomes a debt. Were a husband imprisoned merely because he refused to pay alimony, that would be imprisonment for debt. To imprison him for contempt, the court must show that, in his refusal to pay, he was willfully contemptuous of the court. Yet no evidence was offered that countered the Colonel's explanation, under oath, for not paying. Furthermore, it was Bell's opinion that a court should never imprison a person to compel him to pay alimony until all milder means had failed. The court had not, for instance, issued an execution against Ward's property. A portion of his estate could be placed in the hands of a receiver and rented or sold to produce the necessary funds. Bell ordered Ward released.[19]

Naturally enough, George Paschal immediately asked Judge Terrell to appoint a receiver, but Ward's attorney objected on nine different grounds, and that was the end of that. Ward once again refused to pay alimony, protesting anew that he had "no money." Three months later, however, in October 1861, he finally came around. He transferred a promissory note to Susan worth $500 and followed that up with regular monthly payments of $75. For Susan it was a victory that promised far more than it delivered. Every last dollar was paid not in hard currency (specie) but in depreciating Confederate treasury notes at face value. At first, following eight months with no alimony, it probably seemed a far better bargain than nothing at all, but as Confederate paper money steadily lost value during 1862 and 1863 she found herself increasingly hard-pressed to defray her expenses. Her quest for a divorce, moreover, languished as the war consumed everyone's attention. By mid-1862, the judge who had jailed Ward, Alexander Terrell, though still serving his judicial term, was an aide-de-camp with the Confederate army in Arkansas. Ward's attorney, John A. Green, departed to serve as an aide to his celebrated brother, Brigadier General Thomas Green. More than two years passed without the district court taking any action on Susan's suit. In fact, during all of 1863 the court met in Travis County for a mere two days and transacted very little business of any sort.[20]

Stalled litigation was hardly the only impact that the fighting had on the Wards. By 1862 the "pinch of war" had touched most everyone in town as the goods on store shelves thinned out and prices spiraled. It became difficult, and sometimes impossible, to find everyday items such as coffee and tea, paper and ink, pins and needles, and candles. Eventually people turned to dried yaupon leaves for tea, sumac berries for ink, and mesquite thorns for pins. Peg Leg gained some renown for his inventiveness in the face of the stringency, in particular for his homemade sulphur matches and the smoking pipes he fashioned out of common clay.[21] Yet life for both the Colonel and Susan was far from austere. Peg Leg and his sons enjoyed the ministrations of three servants for much of the war, enslaved African Americans who cooked, did household chores, tended the garden and animals, and farmed. The Ward garden in town produced a variety of fruit and vegetables for meals. On his out lots (beyond the city limits—official Austin was only one square mile) the Colonel grew corn and other crops for his table and for forage. The family acquired flocks of sheep and goats and raised pigs for pork and bacon.[22]

The war, though never close at hand, was never out of mind with so many Austin sons and husbands in uniform and the threat of a Union invasion forever hanging over the state. June and July 1863 were especially difficult months for the Wards as conflicting reports trickled in about the fate of General Ulysses S. Grant's siege of Vicksburg, Mississippi. So much was at stake, for the Wards as parents, with Dudley fighting in Vicksburg's defense, and for the Southern cause. Everyone feared, with good reason, that a defeat would give the Federals control of the entire Mississippi River, split the Confederacy in two, and leave Texas more vulnerable than ever to invasion. One by one rumors and erroneous reports would flourish and then fizzle. One day the town was despondent over rumors that Vicksburg had capitulated. Two days later dawn broke with bells ringing and cannons firing at news—false, it turned out—that Grant had been repulsed with thirty thousand dead. For weeks nothing was heard from Dudley, though earlier in the year he had written home at least once or twice a month. Finally, on July 16, Dudley's parents learned the awful truth. Vicksburg had fallen on July 4, and Confederate forces had surrendered. Susan was beside herself with anxiety, as she wrote Dudley months later (in another letter he received but never read): "My child, you can form no idea of the terrible agony, I endured during the siege of Vicksburg—for I knew, that my brave boy was there; and on the day we heard of its fall, my heart was so lacerated, that all physical, strength failed me" Stress and anxiety often felled Susan, and so it did this time. "I was compelled to take [to] my bed," she told Dudley, "and for several weeks, my friends feared I would not recover." Days passed with no news of Dudley's fate. Finally, word came that he had been captured. He was released under parole and arrived home in mid-August on furlough. He stayed three months and then left to rejoin his unit, on the Texas coast south of Houston, without ever having spoken with his mother.[23]

By the fall of 1864 war-weariness had settled over Austin. The fighting was obviously going badly. Even Atlanta had fallen. Peg Leg was morose. "Austin is a dull place, it seems like the grave," he wrote Colonel Ashbel Smith, commander of Dudley's regiment, then stationed in Galveston. He asked Smith to grant Dudley a furlough. "My health is very precarious," he pleaded. "I am at present quite alone & feel the want of one of my children very much." It was mid-September, and in Galveston an epidemic of yellow fever had broken out. Dudley assured his father that he was "doing remarkably well" and had "no fears of the disease." Five days later "Yellow Jack" took his life.[24]

The pain and sadness that befell the Wards upon the death of their oldest child must have been intense, but neither spouse was in a mood to console the other. The bitterness between them was too deep. That summer they had clashed again over alimony, a storm that had been brewing since early 1863, when Ward stopped making monthly payments. The impasse dragged on fifteen months before a district judge addressed the issue, in June 1864. By then Susan's debts for her maintenance were mounting. To pay her laundress, she testified, she had sold some of the few remaining pieces of her jewelry. Ward again offered Confederate treasury notes, but by 1864 a dollar in paper money was worth less than a dime in coins. Susan took heart, however, when the court came down emphatically on her side. The sheriff of Travis County was ordered to take possession of the Austin homestead and the couple's four farm lots (132 acres) on the edge of town and rent or sell enough property to come up with the alimony that Ward owed her, in hard currency, amounting to about $1,200 including interest.[25]

In this instance, as so often in the protracted legal fistfight known as

Ward versus Ward, nothing was won without a struggle. The Colonel lodged numerous objections and, when those failed, got a temporary injunction enjoining the Travis County sheriff from executing the court order. He reiterated that his failure to pay the alimony was due not to a "want of the will" but a "want of cash" at a time when his income was depressed by wartime conditions. As an alternative to alimony he offered Susan exclusive use of the homestead, but only if she brought Anna and Tom to Austin and placed them under his care.[26] True to form, the Colonel thus refused to budge from a position he had staked out earlier, but the renewed fighting with his wife and the prospect of dispossession upset him. Dudley advised backing off in a letter to his father written shortly before he succumbed to yellow fever: "Knowing the infernal disposition of the woman you have to deal with and the continual annoyance of mind which the matter causes you, I would[,] were I placed in your position, have the matter brought to termination at once, no matter what the consequences may be, and rest assured you will be the gainer by it." But the Colonel was not prepared to compromise. Nor was Susan. Though often enervated by stress, she was tough as nails in her legal encounters with her husband, her resilience fortified by attorneys Paschal and Shelley. After five months of arguing and maneuvering, she won out, for the moment. The sheriff took possession of the couple's four farm lots and auctioned them off at a hotel on Congress Avenue. Susan's financial situation was eased by $560 in hard currency, but that was less than half the sum sought by the court and far less than the lots were worth. The new owner, moreover, was Susan's lawyer, N. G. Shelley. Ward was not about to stand for it. A few weeks later he and his helpers started cutting down trees on the lots, removing fences, and otherwise harassing Shelley, who sued, further complicating what was now becoming a Byzantine legal battle. Eventually, through legal action of his own, Ward regained title to the lots, but, as will be seen, they still wound up in Susan's hands![27]

In the meantime, the court's order to sell the lots in the first place so encouraged Susan that she filed a motion, in December 1864, to proceed to trial on the original issue of the lawsuit—a divorce. Once again Ward countered with a barrage of objections, all of which were overruled. The case was ordered to trial. For the first time since she filed suit it appeared that Susan was about to get a full hearing and a decision.

But her hopes were dashed later that very same day. Responding to a motion by Ward's attorney, the court instead granted a postponement. The reason given: Ward's regular attorneys were serving in the military and his present attorney, Marmion Henry Bowers, had not had an opportunity to familiarize himself with the voluminous records generated by the case.[28]

As 1865 opened, whatever chance Susan still had for prompt action was preempted by the confusion and disorder that marked the closing weeks of the Civil War and its immediate aftermath. A dominant figure in Austin during that topsy-turvy period was none other than the target of her litigation—the Colonel himself. Indeed, an Austin newspaper went so far as to claim that when confronted with the violence that accompanied the breakup of the Confederate army in Texas, "he exerted an influence no other man could have commanded, to stay the storm that threatened the whole town." Perhaps so, but Austin by no means escaped the turmoil.[29]

Peg Leg's return to center stage had started innocently enough in November 1864. Although subjected to the embarrassment of having his property seized and auctioned off to satisfy a suit by his wife, his public standing seems not to have suffered, at least among the men of Austin. Three weeks later they voted him mayor. He took office on December 3. Though as mayor he was both chief administrative officer and chief magistrate, his duties at the time were routine. Austin was quiet. City council meetings were perfunctory. Hundreds of miles to the east, in Georgia, Tennessee, and Virginia, the fighting thundered on, but in Austin the war was a distant rumble difficult to follow and reported sporadically by a press cut off from Confederate sources of information. By early spring 1865, however, the mood in town had changed. The unthinkable, a Confederate collapse, now seemed possible, even likely. "Every one is gloomy," noted Amelia Barr, a cultivated Austin homemaker who kept a diary (she would later distinguish herself in New York literary circles by publishing some fifty novels). And everyone was on edge. Uneasiness about the town's security had been growing for several weeks. In February there were fears of a slave insurrection, in March of banditry by "jayhawkers"—roving gangs of desperadoes and disgruntled Confederate soldiers preying on people in nearby counties. Members of one band were believed to have scouted out Austin with a raid in mind. Another, about twenty-five strong, was spotted just twelve miles from town.[30] Austin, like other Texas cities, had no standing police force. Neither did the county or state governments, nor were there troops available in central Texas for local defense. On March 23, 1865, Mayor Ward summoned the city council for the first of four meetings that week on measures to protect the city. Then the mayor chaired a citywide "mass meeting" on the state of affairs. The city marshal was authorized to hire two deputies, and steps were taken to enroll citizens in a temporary special police force and to acquire arms from Texas governor Pendleton Murrah.[31]

The immediate threat of violence from jayhawkers soon passed without serious incident, to Ward's credit, only to be supplanted by more foreboding developments. On April 26 disastrous news reached the capital city: two weeks earlier, General Robert E. Lee had surrendered at Appomattox. By mid-May all but the most die-hard Austinites knew the cause was lost. During the following days many thousands of Texans in the Confederate trans-Mississippi army, demoralized by defeat and angry at having gone months without pay, deserted their units and headed home. On the way they raided and plundered, rationalizing their depredations as just compensation for their service. Why, they asked, should government stores of clothing, leather, food, ordnance, horses, and mules be left to fall into the hands of their conquerors when those who had fought in defense of the Confederacy were in need and many had not been paid.[32]

Outbursts of looting struck cities and small towns alike in late May. In many communities the local citizenry joined in, and the pillaging quickly spilled over into private property. Town by town the tidal wave of looting swept across Texas toward Austin. On Saturday, May 20, the town of Hempstead, 110 miles east of the capital city, was "utterly sacked," one eyewitness testified. Two days later in La Grange, 65 miles east of Austin, soldiers pilfered wagons, mules, leather, and wool, and plundered the local hat factory.[33] Austin's turn came on Thursday, May 25. Amelia Barr was dismayed at the tumult that descended on the community. "Confederate soldiers, without officers or order, are coming in every hour, and there is nothing but plunder and sack going on—and the citizens are as bad as the soldiers." Looting was indeed widespread and continued off and on for two more days, but to Austinite De Witt Clinton Baker, who was there at the time, it bore more resemblance to "holiday sport" than heinous lawbreaking:

Crowds of soldiers collected in front of every government building in town, demanding the keys, and when these were not forthcoming at once, the doors were broken in, and the grab game commenced. . . . Numbers of men who had never taken any part in the war, together with women, children, and negroes, assembled around the places where coffee, flour, sugar, salt, bacon, cloth, rope, leather, cotton, medicines, etc., etc., were dealt out with unsparing hands. Individuals might be seen going away from these places, loaded in the most grotesque manner. Here a man with a bale of rope in his hands, and a string of tin cups around his neck; then another with two or three saddles on his back. . . .

To Amelia Barr it seemed "as if every one had a claim against the Confederacy, and were paying themselves."[34]

To Mayor Ward looting was still a crime, no matter whether committed in a spirit of holiday sport or by soldiers with legitimate grievances. What had befallen Texas, he believed, was a "reign of terror" that was turning the law into a "dead letter." It was the duty of authorities to see that the laws were strictly enforced and the duty of citizens to assist them in bringing lawbreakers to justice. He again called on Austinites to volunteer as special police and to pledge themselves to support the mayor in the discharge of his responsibilities. Almost immediately, however, he met with resistance and became involved in a battle over both turf and principle.[35]

Late afternoon on Friday, May 26, the second day of rioting, a group of returned soldiers met at the capitol. With Willis Robards, state comptroller and a Confederate veteran himself, in the chair, they reached an agreement on the looting: a military company would be organized to restore order; civilians and private property would be protected; public stores, whether in government or private hands, would be collected and distributed equitably among soldiers and their families. Two prominent Austinites were among the leaders: Colonel Edward Clark, former Texas governor, and Colonel George Flournoy, former Texas attorney general. When presented by Ward that same day with a tender for their services in his special police, both signed up but stipulated, in writing on the tender, that it was with an understanding that nothing would be done in conflict with the meeting's decision to apportion public stores among soldiers and their families. The next day Ward was informed that it was the sense of the meeting that the citizens and city authorities of Austin should all abide by such a policy.[36]

It was a sign of how angry the mayor was that on the back of his tender he wrote, "Opposed and defaced by Clark & Flournoy." In his view the soldiers' actions smacked of vigilantism. Without legal sanction, without even consulting city authorities, plans had been made for a military force to exercise police powers and confiscate public property, while turning a blind eye to the criminal acts that had been perpetrated by the looters. The mayor, however, faced a dilemma. Decisive action was needed right away to stem the rioting. His own efforts to recruit special police had encountered strong headwinds, while a small company of returned Confederate soldiers, under the command of Captain George R. Freeman, was ready to act. Though he loathed having Austin policed by "self constituted military forces" composed in part of nonresidents, Ward decided not to stand in their way. In deference to Comptroller Robards, he suspended efforts to recruit his own special police. Later he would let Robards know just how offended he was.[37]

Captain Freeman and his men put a stop to the unbridled looting fairly quickly and then disbanded, probably without doing much to redistribute public stores, certainly without any cooperation from Mayor Ward. On May 29 he called on citizens to deposit looted public property in his office, to "be returned to where it belongs." Several days later he conducted a citywide search, though not primarily with domestic booty in mind. At issue, he told the city council, was gunpowder, and it posed a serious threat to public safety. A huge amount (some 60,000 pounds) had been stolen and much of it taken to homes and other buildings around town. Ward knew that people were handling it carelessly, "as if it had been so much sand," a resident commented. At least six people were killed or seriously injured. One man living a few miles outside of Austin spread thirty or forty pounds out on a table to dry and accidentally ignited it with his pipe, setting fire to his clothes and fatally burning himself. With city council approval, the mayor instituted a house-to-house search for the gunpowder and "other State property." The owner of every building was asked to consent to the search but could opt out. All gunpowder found was transported out of town. How much other property was recovered is not known.[38]

By the beginning of June the orgy of looting across Texas had pretty much dissipated. But fear and uncertainty prevailed, and bands of jay-hawkers roamed the countryside. In Austin, Mayor Ward shared with city council members his concerns about the town's vulnerability and the danger of "lawless persons" in their midst. It was, to say the least, a challenging time to be mayor. The Confederate national government had ceased to exist. The state government was disintegrating. Governor Murrah and several other top Texas officials, anticipating retribution by the victors, were about to flee to Mexico. White residents eyed black residents uneasily, wary of impending emancipation. Amelia Barr's anxiety, as expressed in her diary, is palpable: "Everything in confusion. Everyone suspicious and watchful, and there is no law." Yet Union troops, so recently the enemy but now looked to for deliverance from insecurity, would not reach the capital city for another seven weeks, on July 25.[39]

The vulnerability of the capital city, and the state government in particular, was laid bare on Sunday evening, June 11, when a gang of thirty or forty bandits set upon the state treasury. The noise of hammering on safes could be heard all about the surrounding neighborhood. Informed of the brazen assault, Captain Freeman quickly rounded up nineteen volunteers. At their approach, the robbers fled, taking with them about $17,000 in specie (more than half the gold and silver in the treasury), but not before an exchange of gunfire mortally wounded one of the robbers. Determined to prevent another such disaster, Comptroller Robards and Treasurer Cyrus Randolph, the state government's executive rump, hired a company of thirty men, raised by the indefatigable Freeman, to protect state property. "The Mayor of the City with all his efforts," Robards told a friend, "has so far failed to furnish sufficient protection and I fear he will not be able to do so." Known as the Treasury Guards, Freeman's company served a little more than a month and won some praise for its efforts, but not from the mayor.[40] Ward was no more persuaded this time than last that Freeman's quasi-military organization was sanctioned by law. Furthermore, the Guards made life doubly difficult for the city marshal and his two deputies and unnerved the citizenry with their false alarms. Ringing bells and discharging firearms at every insubstantial rumor was hardly the way to combat real danger, the mayor lectured Freeman. Contrary to Robards, he believed that "legally constituted authorities"—the mayor and his city council—were up to the job of maintaining law and order. To prove his point, he called anew for the organization of a volunteer police force.

By then, however, his most pressing concern was different from that of Robards, who feared another treasury raid by desperadoes. What worried Peg Leg by late June was the threat to life and property posed not so much by "desperate white men" as by the "large number of Negroes turned loose by their owners."[41]

When Union General Gordon Granger, newly appointed commander of the Department of Texas, landed at Galveston on June 19, he immediately announced the Emancipation Proclamation and officially freed all slaves in Texas. Blacks in the Austin area relished the revolution in their status, but whites feared a new wave of lawlessness and took an especially dim view of those blacks who left their former owners, "squads" of whom, they complained, could "be seen loafing around the streets at all hours of the day, without home or master, and without any visible employment." Conventional wisdom assumed that if left alone they would resort to thievery to support themselves. Even General Granger publicly urged freedmen to remain with their former masters for the time being, as wage earners, both for their own good and to provide vitally needed labor. Idleness, he warned, was "sure to be productive of vice."[42]

Mayor Ward and the city council responded quickly with a muscular two-part program. First, they established a volunteer police force of up to fifty men to guard the town at night for three months, under the Colonel's overall command. Second, a tough vagrancy ordinance was enacted to keep freedmen at work and off the streets.[43] The ordinance's definition of vagrancy was broad but also to the point, including as it did, in addition to able-bodied people found begging or trespassing or "lodging in the open air," all able-bodied former slaves who had abandoned their masters "for the purpose of idleness." Violators were to be brought before the mayor's court and, if found guilty (they could request a jury trial), fined from $3 to $100 or, if a freedman, punished either by fining or by whipping. Persons of color who did not pay their fines promptly were to be hired out to the highest bidder (who was empowered to "inflict such chastisement as may be necessary") or else put to work for the city at fifty cents per day until the fine was paid. In such cases, the city marshal could, if necessary, shackle the defendant with a ball and chain.[44]

Though the law was stringent, Ward was something less than draconian in handing out punishment to black violators, judging by his rulings the first week the law was in effect. The mayor did sentence "Tom" and "Lawrence" to receive fifty lashes each on the bare back and to be returned to their former owners but then cancelled the whipping because neither had been in trouble before. "Jo" and "Jim," who waived a jury trial, were reprimanded and released on good behavior. Two others were fined, one of whom was condemned to work on the streets in default of payment. Later, it appears, the mayor did carry through with a sentence of whipping. Whether he did so frequently is not known.[45] What the law accomplished, in the eyes of Austin's newspapers, was to rid the streets of "idle" freedmen and propel many of them "back to their former quarters." Austin whites could breathe more easily; it was still their city, the *Gazette* commented wryly on the overheated reaction to emancipation.[46]

On the morning of July 25, 1865, Major General Wesley Merritt, his staff, and the 18th New York Cavalry rode into Austin. The Stars and Stripes were hoisted atop the dome of the capitol, and the air reverberated with booms of a thirty-six-gun salute. A week later Peg Leg headed an escort welcoming Andrew Jackson Hamilton, President Andrew Johnson's appointee as provisional governor of Texas, to the capital city.[47] For Austin and Mayor Ward, the Civil War and the vicissitudes of its immediate aftermath were finally behind them after four difficult years. For Peg Leg and Susan, however, their civil war was far from over, though it had been seven years since Susan walked out on her husband and five years since she had filed suit against him in Texas. The Ward family remained divided, with most of the children in New York but seventeen-year-old James in Austin, living with his father and estranged from his mother. At war's end both parents resided where they had at its beginning, a mile and a half apart but with an emotional ocean between them. Susan was eager, desperate really, to go home to New York and to her children. Peg Leg soon faced a new set of problems as mayor and the following year would take on a very different challenge in a different city as a federal official overseeing a huge new customs district. Each looked to a future without the other, yet both were locked in a legal struggle that seemed to have no end.

CHAPTER 16

Final Years

I N NOVEMBER 1865 General George Armstrong Custer, who had fought unexpectedly well in the Civil War but would suffer an ignominious death at the Battle of Little Bighorn eleven years later, rode into Austin with 4,000 Federal cavalrymen and his spirited wife, Elizabeth. The Custers took up residence at the unoccupied Blind Asylum, a luxuriously roomy place to a couple who had been living in a tent. An intelligent, socially astute person, Libby Custer fell in easily with members of Austin's upper crust. "Refined, agreeable and well-dressed women came to see us," she recounted in her colorful memoir, *Tenting on the Plains*. One of those women was Susan Ward. For Susan, the get-together three days before Christmas was a joy. "I have not been as cordially received, and kindly treated, for many a day," she exulted. Upon saying their goodbyes, a friend accompanying Susan remarked that after such a warm reception, she should certainly be in high spirits for some time to come. Yet, no sooner had Susan returned to her room than her spirits plummeted. "I felt sadder than before my visit, for I then realized my lone condition, far, far, from all who love or really care for me." By the next day the debilitating pain in her side that often accompanied distress had returned.[1]

Christmas that year was an especially trying time for Susan, separated as she was not only from her children and her beloved siblings, but also from her closest friends in Austin, Lucadia and Marshall Pease, who were on extended trips north now that the war was over. On top of that, Susan had just endured yet another disappointment in her lawsuit. Earlier in December, George Paschal had thought they might be on the verge of a settlement or a trial, but Peg Leg's attorney balked, and the case was continued to the spring 1866 term. Nor was she amused by her husband's involvement with a Mrs. Sterne, who, Susan observed tartly, was "now occupying my house, with the delectable Col, and my still dear, little Jimmy, for boarders."[2]

With the war over and her court case seemingly deadlocked after five frustrating years, one might have thought Susan would throw up her hands and go back to New York and her children. As it was, their letters constituted her "chief pleasure." Life seemed cheerless when she did not hear from them. Her perilous financial situation, however, and thus her determination to get at least a financial settlement out of Peg Leg presumably overcame her longing for home. Unfortunately the next session of the district court was more than four months away, so she decided to take a long-delayed trip to Hempstead, Texas, to visit old friends. The Custers invited her to join them in their private carriage as they, too, journeyed the 110 miles to Hempstead, the start of a long trip east for them (George Custer had been mustered out of the volunteer service). Libby Custer remembered how quickly the trip to Hempstead went as relays of horses carried them swiftly over good roads, their pace unencumbered by a column of soldiers. Susan was smitten by how "agreeable, courteous, and kind" the Custers were to her. "I assure you," she wrote a friend, "that I enjoyed the journey, more especially, their society, exceedingly." Not until May 1866 did she return to Austin, just in time for the spring session of the district court.[3]

While Susan was hobnobbing with the Custers and steeling herself for the next round of legal combat, her husband was facing a new set of challenges as Austin's mayor. At first, following the arrival of federal troops, he was shunted to the wings. Provisional Governor Hamilton and the military took center stage. The mayor's court became the provost marshal's court. On September 11, however, Hamilton reinstated Ward as mayor and restored his council. In Ward, the governor had found an ally who had opposed secession in 1861 and now openly advocated the policy of presidential reconstruction Hamilton had been commissioned to implement.[4]

Ward's appointment came at a difficult time for many city residents. The war had taken a toll—in lives devastated, expectations shattered, livelihoods lost. At war's end it was estimated that some five hundred families of soldiers in Travis County were indigent. According to a local newspaper, the war had "reduced many [Austinites] to comparative poverty who were previously in independent circumstances." The conflict so impoverished George Paschal that in 1866 he left for greener pastures in the Northeast. Emancipation and its implications—that black men might be given the vote, for instance—compounded the edginess of many whites. These were problems largely out of the hands of town government, but they perhaps help explain why Ward, as a symbol, may have had a special appeal for townspeople at that moment, for he was a living reminder of better days—glorious days, indeed—a sentiment given voice on more than one occasion following the war by the Austin *Southern Intelligencer* to generate support for the Colonel: "The name and fame of Col Ward are the common property of Texas. He is one of the few remaining survivors of that heroic band of patriots and stalwart sons of Mars who, with trenchant blades hewed the 'Lone Star' from the bleeding side of Mexico." Upon Ward's appointment, the *Intelligencer* retold the heroic story of the battle for San Antonio in 1835 and how Ward's leg and Ben Milam's body were buried in the same grave. "If such men as Ward had not fought and conquered, Texas would still be a vast cow pasture for the half savage Mexicans." As for the Colonel's qualifications for the job, the *Intelligencer* was no less impassioned: "He is thoroughly informed in politics and general affairs; is industrious and prompt in business habits; writes well with his left hand; and by his weight of character, commanding personal appearance, agreeable manners and many genial and attractive personal qualities, carries more influence into the mayoralty, than any other person whom Governor Hamilton could have appointed to the position."[5]

In early October Mayor Ward convened a council meeting and laid out his program for the city. There were myriad, if relatively modest, problems that demanded attention. Texas and its capital city had escaped the physical destruction sustained by much of the Confederacy, but wartime stringency had left Austin's infrastructure, such as it was, in poor shape. The public wells, used by those too poor to afford wells and cisterns of their own, had deteriorated badly. The streets were in wretched condition, riven with gullies and washes. Broken-down footbridges over the open sewers running down both sides of Congress Avenue made crossing the Avenue an ordeal for pedestrians. In addition, the mayor stressed, the city ordinances needed revamping, given the "change in the position of colored people," the voiding of all ordinances passed during the war, and the meager revenue available to city authorities.[6]

Under Ward's guiding hand, the council launched a street repair program and approved a series of new ordinances. Earlier ordinances regulating enslaved and free people of color were repealed. Whipping and shackling were eliminated as punishments for vagrancy. Offenders who could not pay their fines were now to be committed to a workhouse and compelled to labor on city projects for up to fifteen days. To raise funds for civic improvements, the council imposed a sales tax on most merchandise and expanded the range of businesses required to purchase a license, even mandating payment of a license fee for every exhibition of puppets, wild animals, wax figures, tightrope walking, and "tricks of legerdemain."[7]

Though given a fair amount of leeway by federal authorities, Mayor Ward and his council hardly had a free hand when it came to maintaining public order. At the time of his appointment, policing the city was entirely in military hands. Just as he had during the chaotic days at the close of the Civil War, the mayor thought civil authorities, with roots in the community, better suited to keeping the peace. The military, and the provost marshal in particular, saw it differently. When a fight broke on Congress Avenue in late October the city marshal arrested the two antagonists and started for the mayor's office. The military officer of the day forcibly took custody of the two prisoners and ordered the city marshal not to interfere in the future with military business. The matter was laid before Governor Hamilton, and in this instance he came down on the side of the civil authorities. At a city council meeting a few days later he assured members that he would "not meddle with or interfere in any way with them as City officers." The mayor's court resumed adjudicating violations of city ordinances, at least those by civilians. But city officials soon learned there were significant limits to their oversight of public safety. In December several suspicious fires broke out, at a time when the city was already experiencing an unusual number of burglaries. A committee headed by the mayor asked Governor Hamilton for permission to organize a voluntary citizen police force. Hamilton turned them down flat. Military police would take care of the problem, he stated. The military instituted a nightly patrol and imposed a 9 p.m. curfew, and soon the threat of incendiarism faded along with public anxiety.[8]

In January 1866 a sizable group of voters petitioned Governor Hamilton for an election of city officials, the first for mayor since Ward won office in November 1864. Hamilton agreed, and the election was scheduled for early February. Whether the Colonel was fed up with the job and bowed out or the voters were fed up with him and wanted him out is not clear, but he garnered only 19 votes compared with 109 for the victor and 69 for the runner-up. Chances are he already had his eye on the election coming in June for land commissioner, a job that, unlike mayor, paid a salary, no small matter to a man whose financial resources, though hardly negligible, were not what they had once been and who was under financial pressure from his wife. For more than five years he had not had gainful employment. Because of the turmoil of the war, promissory notes he held were now worthless. The $10,000 he had loaned Henry L. Kinney in 1860 to keep it out of Susan's hands was gone. In 1862 Kinney had died in a gunfight, bankrupt, and so far the Colonel had nothing to show for his mortgage on Kinney's land. In May he declared his candidacy for land commissioner. Perhaps haunted by memories of his father's financial collapse at a similar age, he implored voters in an uncharacteristically disheartened tone, "I need the office. . . . I am now an old man, reduced in means and maimed of a limb, given to my country." On a less plaintive note, he touted his experience in office under three Texas presidents and two governors during the 1840s. His main opponent, however, Stephen Crosby, his former deputy, had served nine years as land commissioner during the 1850s and 1860s. Ward's day as land commissioner was past, but he soldiered on, only to lose the election badly.[9]

The same week in mid-May 1866 that Ward announced his candidacy, the district court for Travis County began its spring term and Susan arrived by stage. She took up residence at the home of her attorney, N. G. Shelley, and his wife. In New York, Susan's brother Aaron conveyed his impatience for a resolution. "My poor dear sister is yet struggling for something like justice," he wrote Marshall Pease. "Cant she obtain it some way? Her children here are suffering on account of her absence and for proper means of support."[10] Suddenly, or so it must have seemed after six years, there was a breakthrough in the bitter litigation over alimony. Both sides were weary of it. Susan yearned to go home but had made it clear by staying so long that she was not going home empty handed. The court again made it clear to Peg Leg that, unless he settled, more property would be sold to satisfy his arrears, and he would still owe Susan $75 a month. Peg Leg's attorney, M. H. Bowers, a bulldog of a negotiator, drove a hard bargain. It was agreed that

Susan was to have a judgment against her husband for $5,000 and costs. In part payment of that amount she was given exclusive title to the four farm lots, now valued at $3,000, that had been sold in 1864 at court order. It was further agreed that the settlement satisfied Judge Bonney's award of $5,041 in alimony in the New York case.[11]

Susan would eventually realize $3,750 from the sale of the lots, but Peg Leg had not given up a great deal for what he got, relief from alimony awards in two lawsuits potentially amounting to many thousands of dollars. From his perspective, of course, compromising at all with a wife who had publicly vilified him was a major concession. What the settlement did not address was the issue of a divorce, Susan's ultimate goal from the beginning. With the alimony issue finally out of the way, she must have anticipated moving on to a trial, but Ward and Bowers—and the court—treated the settlement as though it brought Susan's lawsuit to a close. The prediction of the Colonel's first lawyer, John A. Green, that her suit could probably be postponed from term to term indefinitely, proved correct. At its next session, in November 1866, the court disposed of a considerable number of civil cases, but several others, as a local paper noted, were "passed to the heel of the docket; among them, as a matter of course, the case of Ward vs. Ward." Susan went to stay for a while with a cousin in nearby La Grange, apparently holding out for a divorce at the court's next session. At its spring 1867 session, however, the court was unresponsive, again moving her case to the end of the docket. Susan's ever-fragile health deteriorated. Her daughter Anna, who was just nine years old when Susan came to Texas in 1860, was now sixteen and feared she might never see her mother again. Within a couple of months Susan returned to New York.[12]

Several months later, Lucadia Pease visited Susan and found her "lame, sick, and in trouble." While Anna and ten-year-old Tom were fine, she had lost contact with her oldest son, Robie Marston, who had been in prison while she was in Texas and then had married a "servant girl." What probably concerned her most, however, was how she would support herself and her family now that it was clear her husband had succeeded in withholding from her the lion's share of the financial resources she had counted on. Even so, she had not given up her legal struggle entirely. Four years later, in 1871, she again urged the court to grant her a divorce and appealed for "general relief." Nothing came of it.[13]

By the time Susan left Austin for New York City, Ward had already left Austin for Corpus Christi, the small but fast-growing seaport on the gulf coast 200 miles to the south. What took him there was a second presidential appointment, this time as a regional customs official, a reward for his opposition to secession and support for presidential reconstruction. President Johnson granted the appointment in October 1866 but with a hitch. The Senate was in adjournment, so it was a recess appointment contingent on Senate approval before its next session ended in early March 1867.[14] Paying little heed to mounting Senate opposition to the president over reconstruction, the Colonel leapt at the opportunity. The annual salary of $1,500, plus fees of up to $1,000 a year, was compelling. The job eased his financial worries and placed him exactly where he needed to be to pursue foreclosure of his mortgage on Henry Kinney's vast land holdings in Nueces County, including 1,165 town lots in Corpus Christi. Kinney's debt, with interest at 12 percent a year, amounted to more than $17,000. But another creditor, Lucien Birdseye (whose grandson invented and developed frozen foods), held what appeared to be a trump card—a mortgage on Kinney's lands dated six years earlier than Ward's, also for a $10,000 loan on which Kinney had defaulted. The question of title to Kinney's lands was, in fact, ensnarled in a web of competing claims. Ward seethed at the possibility of losing out. In January 1867 he leased his Austin homestead and, together with his nineteen-year-old son James, relocated in the "city by the sea." By the beginning of February he was on the job as customs collector for the District of Corpus Christi.[15]

Every April 15 Americans are reminded, though few have forgotten, that income taxes are the backbone of the federal budget. During the nineteenth century, in contrast, the primary source of federal revenue was the tariff—duties levied on most imported goods. Collecting import duties, the responsibility of the U.S. Customs Service, a division of the Department of the Treasury, was thus serious business. In Texas it was also a difficult business. The porous Rio Grande boundary with Mexico in particular posed a managerial challenge, especially for a manager stationed more than 140 miles away, in Corpus Christi.[16] Created by act of the U.S. Congress in July 1866 and carved out of two other customs districts, the district under Ward's purview embraced an enormous area; while it included much of South Texas, what mattered were its boundaries on the Gulf of Mexico and the Rio Grande. Along the Gulf Coast, the district stretched about 100 miles southwest from

San Antonio Bay, opposite Matagorda Island, to Baffin Bay, opposite northern Padre Island. Corpus Christi was the port of entry. Along the Rio Grande, the district stretched about 180 miles northwest from a point more than 100 miles upstream from the river's mouth (and about twenty-five miles west of McAllen). Deputy collectors were stationed in the river communities of Rio Grande City, Roma, Carrizo (in Zapata County), and Laredo. Port Isabel, Brownsville, and the first 100 or so miles of the Rio Grande upstream from the gulf were in a separate customs district, Brazos Santiago.[17]

Two-and-a-half years later, upon Ward's leaving office, a local newspaper praised him as probably the "most efficient" federal official in Texas. The "order and system" that prevailed at his customs house at Corpus Christi were "not surpassed, if equalled, in any other Customhouse on the Gulf coast." Business was dispatched so quietly "you could hear a pin drop." Those comments are reminiscent of the ones made about Ward's Land Office in Austin. Once again, he ran a tight ship at his headquarters. Once again, however, he had trouble imposing the same kind of order on operations in the field, and he found those government officials to whom he was beholden a stumbling block. As land commissioner it was the Texas Congress with whom he butted heads. As customs collector it was administrators and politicians in Washington who tested his patience.[18]

As soon as he arrived in Corpus Christi, Ward set about organizing his customs house, but smuggling also commanded his attention from the outset, especially along the Rio Grande, where hides, lead, live stock, wool, mescal, and other goods were smuggled into the United States with impunity. One of Ward's deputy collectors put the problem this way: he was responsible for thirty miles above and below his post and "at every mile there is a crossing and a boat." The Rio Grande border, in other words, was a sieve. The Colonel dashed off a letter to the secretary of the treasury urging the appointment of mounted guards to patrol the border and new deputy collectors for two busy but unmanned crossing points.[19] On the Gulf Coast smuggling was not so flagrant but was by no means negligible. Ward was particularly troubled by the opportunities created by lightering. Corpus Christi was not a deep-water port (and would not be until 1926), so ships lay over in deep water and offloaded some or all of their cargo onto shallow draft vessels (lighters). Ward had good reason to believe not all the lighters ended up in Corpus Christi harbor. He mandated that ships offloading cargo get lightering permits from his deputy collector at Aransas Pass—after an examination of their cargo. As backup, he appointed his son James an inspector with responsibility for keeping an eye on the lighters.[20]

The Colonel's superiors in Washington were themselves troubled by smuggling, but naturally took a broader view of the problem as they sought to reestablish an effective customs service in the former Confederate states. The entire Gulf Coast from Key West to Port Isabel and the Rio Grande concerned them, not just a 100-mile stretch in Texas. Along the Rio Grande they focused initially on the Brazos Santiago district. It was there, they decided, that mounted patrols were needed immediately for the "protection of revenue." Ward's turn would come later. Nor did they see fit to put additional deputy collectors in his district. The Colonel believed that running an efficient organization required appropriate personnel in adequate numbers, but his superiors in Washington wanted to keep expenses for a district "in proportion to the revenue collected." On that basis Ward's needs did not seem to them so urgent as those of other districts.[21]

About three months after Ward began functioning as collector, in early May 1867, official letters started arriving from Washington addressed to "Daniel C. McIntyre, Collector of Customs, Corpus Christi, Texas." The Colonel could not have helped but think the Senate had probably failed to confirm his appointment and he had been replaced, but during the next six weeks no one notified him nor did McIntyre appear. He dismissed the thought of stepping aside for his deputy, David Layman, since he had appointed Layman on March 7, three days after the Senate session ended, and thus if his own authority had expired by then, his deputy had none to begin with. So he continued to perform his duties and kept his mouth shut until late June, when he finally asked the secretary of the treasury about it. Six weeks later he received a brusque reply. The secretary informed him of the Senate's rejection (he was just one of thirty-three presidential nominees for customs collector to be turned down), ordered him to cease functioning as collector, and advised him that, under a law enacted five months earlier, he was liable to heavy fines and imprisonment for performing official duties after his term expired. The law was news to Ward. Known as the Tenure of Office Act, it was devised by Congressional Republicans to handcuff President Johnson. Six months later, the House of Representatives would impeach Johnson based primarily on his alleged violations of the law. Just how its murky language applied to Ward is unclear.[22]

The Colonel was in a tight spot, but it was hardly just of his own making. He had fallen victim to a bureaucratic process that was, to say the least, muddled. The Treasury Department had failed to notify him of his rejection and then, despite receiving periodic communications from him through the spring and summer, professed ignorance of his remaining in office. A replacement, Daniel McIntyre, had been appointed and confirmed by the Senate, but he soon resigned without setting foot in Corpus Christi. The Treasury Department lost McIntyre's letter of resignation, requested another, waited weeks for a response, and when none was forthcoming, suspended him (actually, he had died). There was still no replacement on the scene when, in August, Ward received the order to step down, so he was compelled to turn over his duties to a deputy who had no more legal authority to perform them than he did. To top it off, because of bureaucratic red tape, the department had failed to pay either Ward or his subordinates for six of the seven months he was on the job.[23]

Peg Leg had sought a presidential appointment to relieve his financial worries. Now he was out of a job and under a cloud. Disgusted at his treatment by the Treasury Department and, at age sixty, wearied by the burden of his infirmities, he was anxious to return to Austin. But first of all he wanted to settle things with Secretary of the Treasury Hugh McCulloch. The problem was how to go about it. Fifteen years earlier, when the Colonel was seeking an appointment as U.S. consul to Panama, Thomas Rusk had introduced him to William Seward, then a U.S. senator. Seward lent his influence to Peg Leg's candidacy. Now Seward was in his seventh year as secretary of state, first Lincoln's and then Johnson's. Though many years had passed since their meeting, Peg Leg doubted it would be difficult to jog Seward's memory; how often did he encounter a person with just one leg and one arm? In fact, Seward had asked for the introduction out of curiosity about Ward's looks. In a lengthy letter, Ward laid out the unhappy history of his dealings with the Treasury Department and asked if Seward would intervene on his behalf with McCulloch.[24]

It was a start, even if all Seward did was "respectfully" refer Ward's letter to the secretary. That winter the Colonel went to Washington himself. Just how he pulled it off is unknown, but his success was stunning, testimony to his determination and skill in looking after his own interests. In early 1868 the Treasury Department reversed its position and admitted fault for not informing him of the Senate's rejection. The commissioner of customs drafted a bill, enacted in July 1868, that authorized six months' back pay. President Johnson capped his comeback by reappointing him, with Senate approval. Ward reassumed command of the Corpus Christi district in August, a year after he had stepped down. He must have wondered, however, whether he would fare any better this time than last, after yet another letter arrived from the Treasury Department addressed to Daniel C. McIntyre, Collector of Customs, Corpus Christi.[25]

The Colonel probably was not taken by surprise to find "business in arrears" at his customs house and in the district generally. For almost a year his deputy, David Layman, had tried to run things despite having no official sanction, a point not lost on those he was supposed to regulate and supervise. Two deputy collectors even refused to turn over the duties they levied. The Treasury Department retained Layman but did not fund him—he was not authorized to receive funds. So no one was paid. The commissioner of customs, putting a better light on the situation than it merited, called it an "anomalous condition of affairs."[26]

By August 1868 both the Treasury Department and the Colonel had initiated steps to set things right. People were paid. Recalcitrant deputy collectors were brought to heel or dropped. Nonetheless, five months later Ward's skeletal staff was still catching up with old business and working long hours to do it. Even while bedridden for several weeks with typhoid fever, Ward got up periodically to sign official papers and keep things moving forward. Predictably but justifiably, he wanted more staff, especially given the increasing volume of goods passing through his port, but the Customs Service was trying to reduce expenses. Reports of revenue lost through smuggling, however, still touched a nerve in Washington. When the Colonel requested a deputy collector for the new town of Rockport, on Aransas Bay, he got his wish by explaining how easy it was for cargo bound for Corpus Christi to be smuggled through Rockport. He was given two additional mounted inspectors on the Rio Grande after a State Department official reported that smuggling was rife, though actually it appears to have been at a low ebb.[27]

By spring 1869, Ward had his district back on course and his customs house running smoothly. But he found, once again, that in politically volatile times, especially in the age of the spoils system, the life of a government official could be precarious. Newly elected President Ulysses S. Grant, a Republican who stood far apart on the issues from his Democratic predecessor, replaced Ward upon taking office in March 1869. His second stint had lasted nine months, two months longer than his first. There was some grumbling in Corpus Christi. Why remove a good Union man, able administrator, and Texas hero, puzzled one newspaper editor. Ward, however, had finally reached the end of his long career in public service, as soldier, military officer, mayor, land commissioner, consul, and customs collector.[28]

In January 1869, following his recovery from typhoid fever, the Colonel decided to make out his will. He directed that his estate be divided equally among his three surviving children by Susan: James, Anna, and Tom. Yet he had not seen either Tom or Anna in more than a decade, had not even written them, and certainly had not been charitable when it came to financial support. In September 1870, Anna, a well-educated, strikingly attractive nineteen-year-old who would soon marry into one of New York City's prominent families, conveyed her bitter feelings in a letter to her father:

> During my childhood and since I have been grown I have often wished to hear from the father who once seemed to love me so fondly . . . ; and as you have never during our long separation either by letter or message appeared to remember you had a daughter, once your 'idol', it seemed out of the order of things for me to open a correspondence— But my desire to learn if you still retain a spark of affection for me, is one incentive to write. . . . I cannot help feeling the wide difference in your treatment towards your children and mother's treatment of us—for I believe everyone knows that since Mother left Dudley and Jimmy she has constantly written and sent kind messages to them; And if a parent loved his child I cannot see how he could refrain from acting in like manner.

On the back of the letter Peg Leg wrote, "an offensive epistle."[29]

Yet, a thaw in family relationships soon followed. In December, James, bearing Christmas presents from Peg Leg, went to New York to spend Christmas with Susan, Anna, Tom, and Mary. To Anna her father's gift was the reassurance she sought that he still loved her. For Susan, it was the reunion with James that made Christmas that year so memorable. After agonizing for years over what kind of man her husband might make of him, she was exhilarated to find him "so pure, good & noble." Susan by then had found her bearings in New York. With the proceeds from selling three of the four lots the Colonel signed over to her, she had acquired a home on East 21st Street in Manhattan and had started taking in boarders at $50 per week.[30] In January 1871 Anna accompanied James on his return trip to Corpus Christi and was reunited, after thirteen years, with her father, but it must have been a shock. She found him in pain and immobile. His leg wound was open again, and he could not wear his prosthesis. He was suffering as well from the effects of a bizarre accident. His favorite dog had run into him while he was walking from one room to another and had knocked him violently against a door, cutting a deep gash in his head and shaking him up badly. It was an accident from which, it was reported at his death almost two years later, he never fully recovered.[31]

By summer the Colonel's leg had improved enough for him to walk about his home, but a major setback in his acquisition of Henry Kinney's property had left him smoldering. Two years earlier he had seemingly gained control of a huge amount of Kinney's property as payoff of his mortgage. But now the district court unexpectedly upheld an earlier court judgment that Lucien Birdseye had won giving him a prior claim on Kinney's property. The court gave Kinney's executors six months to pay off Birdseye's $10,000 mortgage, plus interest, in land, some of the very land the Colonel thought to be his. He was so angry he wanted to file articles of impeachment against the judge but was dissuaded by a lawyer. Kinney's executors, who were on Ward's side, appealed the decision to the Texas Supreme Court.[32]

Late that summer Ward decided to return to the town that three times had elected him mayor and looked upon him proudly as one of its leading citizens. It was a homecoming motivated in part by his belief that he might secure a special pension from the state legislature. The Austin *Statesman* greeted the "old hero" warmly, recalling how he had lost his leg in the Texas Revolution and gained his sobriquet, "Old Peg Leg." He settled into the Avenue Hotel and renewed friendships with his many well-wishers, but the change in scene neither restored his health nor brightened his mood. It did not help that the Kinney case dragged on with no sign of a resolution. In early November he poured his frustrations into a letter to his niece in New York, who reported afterwards that he was in "low spirits, unwell, and broken." But later that month, the legislature came through. Expressing official gratitude for his gallantry and sacrifice in 1835 and recognizing that he was "now old and in need," the lawmakers granted him a special annual stipend of $700.[33] It was paid just once. In late 1872 he was felled by a second bout with typhoid fever. He died in Austin at 4 a.m. on November 25, at age sixty-five. He was buried the next day in the presence of "a large civic attendance." Five more years passed before the feud over Kinney's lands was settled. Lucien Birdseye got the largest share, but the Colonel's heirs benefited very nicely, thanks in no small part to their father's characteristic tenacity in pursuing what he felt to be his due.[34]

Within a few months of Peg Leg's death, in March 1873, Susan and Anna came to Austin. Susan's lawsuit against her husband, filed thirteen years earlier, was still pending. At her attorney's request, the court granted her permission to withdraw from the records of the case "all pleadings and depositions" she wished, whether filed by her side or her husband's. The court records were thus cleansed of details about her alleged infidelity. Four months later the case was dismissed.[35]

It was land business, however, that occupied much of Susan's time in Austin. By law, the "use and benefit" of the homestead fell to Susan upon her husband's death and, while in Austin, she resided there. In fact, she had long owned several of the lots, no small matter given that the homestead included most of a city block in addition to the Ward home and out buildings on the property. Though aware that her husband was legally entitled to manage her property, it had galled Susan for years that he had treated the homestead as his possession and, after their separation, had collected rent on it for his own use when not living there. The three lots on which the Ward house was situated had actually been purchased by her first husband, Thomas Marston. After his death, she owned them jointly with Robie and Mary.[36] In 1854, moreover, while Peg Leg was in Panama, she had bought four adjacent lots in the same block in her own name with her own money, for about $150. Peg

Leg, on the other hand, had good reason to think that his own interest in the homestead was substantial. It was he who had paid off the installments still due on the property Thomas Marston purchased and who funded the improvements on the homestead property, in particular the house and out buildings. He also acquired sole title to three other lots in the same block. Upon his death, however, James, as executor, treated those three as community property (and thus now under Susan's control) and made no further claim on the homestead for his father's estate. The homestead was thus in Susan's hands, and she turned it into a source of income.[37] Just four months following Peg Leg's death, she sold three of the lots she had purchased while he was in Panama, for $4,250, and rented the rest of the property.[38]

Before leaving for New York City, Susan made out her will. It was testimony to the trials she had endured living on her own after her separation. She left what "little property" she had to her two daughters—her silver, jewelry, watch, portrait, her interest in the homestead, her money, everything she owned. She did so, she explained, "not for any lack of affection for my sons" but because "women have not the same advantages for making a living that men have."[39]

Susan returned to New York City and sometime the following year went to New Hampshire. She was fifty-seven years old and had suffered ill health for much of her adult life, though nothing that can be identified as life threatening. By late 1874, however, she was gravely ill with a lung disease and was being cared for at her niece's home in Manchester. She died at 12:30 a.m. on December 30, 1874.[40]

Retrospect

For almost thirty-seven years, from that traumatic morning in 1835 when a cannon ball shattered his right leg until his death in 1872, Thomas William Ward lived with the consequences of his horrific injury. Though he surmounted his suicidal feelings, mobility was an unending challenge, and he was periodically tormented by pain in his stump. His disfigurement, magnified by the subsequent loss of his right arm, played a significant role in how people perceived him. To the Masonic Order he was an incomplete man. To William Seward he was a curiosity. To Sam Houston he was an object of pity. To his Land Office clerks in 1842 he was an object of derision; Old Peg's humiliation at his birthday party afforded them much amusement. Early Houstonians were amused by the spectacle (or the tale) of his adversary in a duel shooting him in his wooden leg.

The Colonel, however, did not readily fit the image of an oddity. His mutilation, incurred in the war for Texan independence, was seen by many as testimony to his bravery and selflessness. He embellished his heroic stature with claims, widely accepted, that he had organized and led the New Orleans Greys and that his leg had been buried with Milam's body. He was physically imposing despite his missing limbs, taller than most men of his day and big-shouldered. A military officer during his first year in Texas, he still made a commanding personal appearance thirty years later.[1] He was self-confident and assertive and could wow people with his intellect. Over the course of his career he established a well-deserved reputation in Texas for competence and effectiveness in his roles as Land Office commissioner, mayor, and customs official. His circle of friends came to include some of Texas's foremost citizens.

Ward thus overcame both appalling physical injuries and the social biases they sometimes engendered, and he enjoyed a decidedly favorable public standing. That achievement, however, made him all the more incensed when his wife portrayed him publicly in an entirely different light, as an abusive, violent, blasphemous, often inebriated husband and father. To the extent that Susan Ward was believed, it was an unmasking of him; he was not the person others thought him to be or that he portrayed himself to be. He was not, in other words, an honorable man but a shameful one. The Colonel, however, was not about to stand by and let his wife defame him and then strip him of his husbandly identity and control over his dependents. So he responded maliciously. He invented an impure past for Susan, the purpose of which was not merely to defeat her lawsuit, but also to preserve his reputation by besmirching hers. The fact that she stretched the truth stoked his anger. His blindness to how much he had wounded her emotionally over the years made it easier for him to give full vent to his ire.

Undoubtedly many a Texan was not struck dumb by Susan's accusations, not that they necessarily thought of the Colonel as an abusive husband, but that they were aware he was headstrong and had a volatile temper. The fierceness of his emotions was captured by Peg Leg himself in a letter to Susan, written from Panama, in response to her comments about an Austin friend with whom they both had had a falling out: "Since I have been alone and reflected upon things past, I have learned to abhor him. So pray, never let me hear of his ever entering our house, or even his daughter. I detest them with such an intensity, that I can hardly believe myself sane."[2] To what extent his traumatic injuries gave rise to his hostile feelings and fits of rage is difficult to say without knowing more about his upbringing, but a connection appears likely. As the Colonel aged and the practice of dueling waned, his displays of anger became less flamboyant. Dramatic confrontations, like his assault on Francis Lubbock and his periodic demands for satisfaction in a duel, became things of the past. Yet he remained a contentious person, prone to clashing verbally with a neighbor, filing a lawsuit at the drop of a hat, and, in the privacy of his home, abusing his wife with angry words, threatening gestures and, on far rarer but more devastating occasions, physical blows. Though his mistreatment of Susan stopped and started and she was free of it while he was in Panama, it did not stop for good until she left him in the fifteenth year of their marriage.

Combative, thin-skinned, and stubborn as Ward was, it is not surprising that these traits influenced how he went about his work, not just his personal life, and sometimes they impaired his judgment. During the Archive War he became indignant over the refusal by the Austinites to permit transfer of the Land Office records to East Texas. As long as the records stayed in Austin he was determined not to give an inch to his adversaries, certainly not by conducting business as usual. He ended up closing the Land Office and kept it closed for seven months. When he finally opened it, he did so not in Austin but in Washington-on-the-Brazos, even though his records were still in Austin. He returned to Austin only after instructed to do so by President Houston. In much the same fashion thirteen years later, in Panama, he became indignant over the supposed insult inflicted on him by the provincial governor. He was determined that the Panamanians make amends for it. So he closed his consulate to any dealings with Panamanian officials and kept the consulate closed more than three months, dead set as he was against giving in. He reopened it only after ordered to do so by the secretary of state.

Yet Ward was, nonetheless, an unusually able public servant who attacked demanding jobs with dedication and resourcefulness. Observers were constantly impressed with his executive ability—a "master business mind," he was called—and with how conversant his was with the entire range of his responsibilities. He had a head for detail, for the nuts and bolts of an organization, and was a stickler for procedure. Proper procedure, he believed, could save Texans from mountains of litigation over land, and though such litigation did plague Texans as the century wore on, his efforts undoubtedly kept it from becoming far worse. His offices ran like clockwork, and he did a first-rate job of record keeping, not just at the Land Office, but wherever he served. He found the records of the Panama consulate in a sorry state upon succeeding Amos Corwine, but Corwine found them in "admirable condition" upon succeeding Ward. "I do not think any Consulate can boast of a more perfect set of books," Corwine wrote him. A reputation for "close application to detail in its minutest form," as one businessman put it, did not mean, however, that he lost sight of the big picture—far from it. If he peppered county surveyors with demands for accuracy and precision, he pressed the Texas Congress with one proposal after another for reforming a defective land system.

What Texas needed, he urged, was a rational, efficient method for fulfilling its promises of free land and securing the property rights of all its citizens, and though Congress often proved uncooperative, he succeeded in turning the Land Office into an effective servant of those goals. If he spent many a day in Panama City redressing petty grievances and dealing with ships' papers, he was ever vigilant about the larger issue of U.S.-Panamanian relations and what he could do to protect and advance U.S. interests. In both jobs he thought of himself, with good reason, as defender of the rights of ordinary citizens—not speculators and colonizers but everyday immigrants and the soldiers who had fought for Texan independence; not moneyed men like Cornelius Vanderbilt or Panamanian officials working hand-in-glove with Americans of an arbitrary bent, like Ran Runnels and George Totten; but their victims, people like William Hunter and the seamen aboard Vanderbilt's ships. His unflinching defense of the seamen ended up costing him his job as consul, but in a bitterly ironic twist of fate, he was ousted as land commissioner when he became identified, unjustly, as an ally of those claiming huge swaths of Texas at the expense of common settlers.[3]

The Colonel also prided himself on his command of, and commitment to, the law. "The law must be strictly observed," it was said of his management of the customs house in Corpus Christi.[4] Indeed, adherence to the law was a guiding principle of his public life, sometimes with a stringency that alienated those whom he served or who were subject to his oversight. In the case of land policy lawfulness was vital, he believed, to achieving his goals, but he was also known to insist on fidelity to the law even though it jeopardized attainment of his goals. As mayor at the close of the Civil War he faced serious outbreaks of violence without the means to curb them but stubbornly resisted the formation of self-constituted military forces, even though their objective, like his, was the restoration and maintenance of order. If Peg Leg extolled the law in his public life, however, he flouted it in his private life once his wife sued him for divorce. The law became a threat—to his reputation, his roles as husband and father, and his property. In the years that followed he fled the law, ignored it, manipulated it, and violated it. He did not, of course, think of it that way. It was she who had destroyed the unity of the family, he maintained, by abandoning him and publicly lodging outrageous charges against him, in particular that he had brutalized his wife and stepchildren and was an unfit father to all his children. He was damned if he would capitulate to slander.

The same legal proceedings that put the Colonel on the spot gave his anguished wife a new lease on life. Driven to litigation in New York by his renewed abuse, Susan Ward won the protection of a restraining order and the right to live apart from him with their two youngest children. No longer was her autonomy dependent on keeping at a distance from him, as had been the case when he was in Panama. Whether or not she ever won a divorce, she knew she would never live with him again and he could neither persuade nor compel her to.

It was a tragic ending for a wife who had fallen so deeply in love with her husband and thought him the fulfillment of her dreams. Though shocked when, within days of their marriage, he lashed out at her, and though disheartened to realize over time that those harsh words were not an anomaly but an omen, her feelings for him remained ardent. Eventually, however, certainly by the time he went to Panama, the burden of his abuse had sapped her affection. His stressful visit to New York in late 1854 and early 1855, after a tranquil period apart from him, bore out what she had reluctantly come to believe: the emotional and physical cost of living with him—anxiety, depression, recurring illness—was too high. She was certain, she told Lucadia Pease, that he was the sole cause of the severe illness that befell her during his visit.[5]

If Thomas William Ward struggled for much of his adult life with the burden of his injuries, Susan Ward struggled for much of hers with the burden of frequent ill health. "Mrs. Ward is as usual some what ailing," Lucadia Pease once commented after a visit with her good friend. Susan's letters and those of her family and friends reveal a woman beset with physical and emotional woes: pains in her back, side, head, and chest, mental and physical exhaustion, melancholy, and other, unspecified, maladies. Following one lengthy sickness, at age thirty-eight, she feared that she would "never again feel well and strong."[6] Ill health, however, especially ill health involving psychological problems, was by no means unusual for a woman of her era. During the nineteenth century, American women suffered debilitating illnesses like nervousness, hysteria, backaches, and headaches with uncommon frequency—or at the least they thought of themselves as often sick. Why that was the case has been a subject of some discussion and debate among historians.[7]

For Susan, as for many married women of the time, the demands of childbearing and domesticity must have sometimes seemed overwhelming. Susan gave birth to seven children and oversaw a very busy household of children, servants, visiting relatives, guests, and boarders (like the Peases), not to speak of caring for a dying sister for months on end and dealing with many other such crises. Yet, it seems clear that the many pressures of running a large household and raising several children were not a major factor in Susan's recurring sickness. Rather, what mainly seems to have affected her was the emotional turmoil of her relationship with her husband. As historian Nancy Tomes has written, "In a culture where the meaning of women's lives was closely bound up with personal relationships, disruptions of those relations . . . could become an enormous source of suffering." Time and again when Susan's relationship with Peg Leg reached an especially stressful point, she fell ill—when she faced the wrenching question of whether to join him in Panama, or when he returned to New York City in late 1854 for what turned out to be a nerve-racking visit, or in early 1856 when he ordered her to send ten-year-old Dudley to Panama to live with him. Once Susan resumed living with her husband, in September 1856, her spirits and her health were profoundly affected, according to the deposition given in 1860 by Jemima Rivington, Susan's servant in Tarrytown from 1855 to 1858. Though undoubtedly overstated, Rivington's testimony is nonetheless striking:

> The effect of all the violent conduct [during 1857 and 1858] . . . was very destructive of Mrs Ward's health, happiness, and spirits, and affected her nervous condition. I know this because I saw it myself. Before the defendant came [back from Panama] . . . , Mrs Ward was strong and healthy. I don't think she was ever sick on more than one occasion, during the whole time before he came to Tarrytown, & that was, when she had a cold. She also seemed uniformly cheerful, and in good spirits until the time when she heard he returned from Panama. After the defendant returned Mrs Ward [was] almost all the time more or less unhappy. She seemed low spirited and melancholy. She suffered a great deal from pain in the head, and she was sick more or less a greater a portion of the time. The only time I knew her to seem like herself was when he was gone to Texas in the winter of 1857 and 1858.[8]

It was not just Susan's troubled relationship with her husband, it should be noted, that affected her health. So did emotional distress involving her son Dudley, who took his father's side in the marital breakup and shunned her. On one occasion his refusal to speak with her hurt her so terribly that, as she put it, her mental and physical strength were exhausted. Later, in 1863, when she learned that Vicksburg, where Dudley was fighting, had fallen to Union forces, she was prostrated by her anxiety over his fate and took to her bed for several weeks.

For Susan, psychological distress plainly could have debilitating consequences. Whereas her husband was known to react to stress with anger, even violence, Susan had learned to bear her burdens like a stalwart Southern woman of her day—in silence. It did not help that her family in New York made it clear to her, when she began to question Ward's love for her, that if she were unhappy with such a husband as Ward, it was her own fault. Early on she did broach with him the subject of her unhappiness and may have protested his mistreatment, only to grow increasingly heavy-hearted at his insensitivity to her distress. Feeling trapped as she did by social conventions and expectations, she could not abide the thought of speaking of her "sorrows" with others but instead buried them in the "deepest recess" of her heart. It was a situation that invited depression and psychosomatic illness.

Susan eventually turned her back on forbearance with a burst of energy as she sought to take control of her future through the courts, but freeing herself from the constraints of her marriage was a lengthy, frustrating process. Her initial decision never to live with Peg Leg again, made while he was in Panama, fell victim to his entreaties upon his return. Her Texas suit was impeded by his defiance and the disruptions of the Civil War. She endured humiliating charges of infidelity, a dispiriting separation from her children, and losing battles for a just financial settlement and legal dissolution of her marriage. Given these strains and the challenge of becoming self-supporting, it is not surprising that she appears to have continued to suffer some from recurring illness. She did, nonetheless, succeed in gaining what she had long sought, a life of her own.

When Susan Ward died in 1874 she was buried in Manchester, New Hampshire, her grave marked, at her direction, by a plain slab.[9] Though she was fond of Texas and had resided there and in New York virtually all her adult life, she lay in death just twelve miles from her birthplace.

She had always loved New Hampshire and had returned on several occasions to restore her health and her spirits. It was there she had fled when she left her husband for good in 1858. New Hampshire was a haven, and now a final resting place.

When Thomas William Ward died he was buried, fittingly, in the State Cemetery in Austin. His grave is marked by a granite headstone that pays tribute to the loss of his leg in the storming of San Antonio and to his roles as mayor, land commissioner, and consul (see illustrations). Peg Leg never returned to his birthplace nor, for many years, gave much thought to his Irish family and relatives. It was Texas, not Ireland, where he made his mark and where he was held in high esteem. He went to Panama for financial reasons and then to New York to accommodate his wife, but he hardly thought of either place as home. He returned to the Lone Star State in 1860 and never left again. He died, in the words of an Austin newspaper, a Texas "patriot and hero."[10]

Appendix

A. Note on the Nickname "Peg Leg"

DURING HIS LIFE and for many years following his death, Thomas William Ward was known in Texas by the nickname he acquired following the amputation of his right leg in 1835, Peg Leg, or variations of it, Old Peg Leg in particular but also Old Peg. Though the nickname was probably in use prior to 1842, it does not turn up in any surviving record until that year, when it appears in the private letters written by three of Ward's Land Office clerks to a common friend, Matthew Woodhouse. "Tom ('Peg-leg') Ward" was how one of the clerks referred to the Colonel, but their favorite nickname was "Old Peg." Later on, the nickname is found in newspapers. Following Ward's decision in 1869 to run once again for commissioner of the General Land Office, a Corpus Christi newspaper published a letter from a veteran of the Texas Revolution hailing his candidacy: "His old comrades are pleased to know that 'Old Peg-leg' is on the 'stump,' and they will support him." Ward, incidentally, thought enough of the item that he cut it out and kept it in his papers. Two years later, when Ward returned to Austin from Corpus Christi, the local newspaper announced his arrival thus: "Col. Thos. Wm. Ward, formerly Commissioner of the Land Office and one of the heroes of San Antonio, where he lost a leg and gained his sobriquet 'Old Peg Leg,' is now in the city."[1]

For decades after his death people remembered that in life Ward had been known publicly by his nickname. In 1879, upon the untimely death of Ward's youngest son, Thomas William Ward Jr., the *Galveston News* wrote a piece on his father, speculating that the younger generation might want to know more of "'Old Peg Leg,' as the deceased veteran was called." Dictating his memoirs in 1899 at age ninety-two, Noah Smithwick, who had lived in Texas since 1827, devoted a paragraph to the Colonel, noting that he was "otherwise known as Peg Leg Ward, he having given his right leg for the freedom of Texas." A few years later Frank Brown, a resident of Austin from the 1850s until his death in 1913 and a man well acquainted with Ward, said of the Colonel in his "Annals of Travis County and the City of Austin" that "a wooden leg gave him the name 'peg leg.'"[2]

There is much, however, that these bits and pieces of information do not reveal. For instance, did people ever call Ward by his nickname to his face or in a letter? It seems highly unlikely. There is not a single example of such a letter in his voluminous papers. Yet, given the temperament of the man and the conventions of the age, this is not really a surprise. No one, other than family members, is known to have addressed him in a letter even by his first name. It is all the more unlikely that Ward himself ever used his nickname; and as to what he thought of it, he left no record.

These days the nickname "Peg Leg" is seen as having a pejorative connotation, and calling someone Peg Leg is eschewed as "politically incorrect" and as offensive to a person with a disability. For some nineteenth-century Texans, like Ward's youthful Land Office clerks in 1842, several of whom had hard feelings about their taskmaster, the nickname may well have been a means of mocking him. That certainly seems have been the case with James Long in his letter discussed at the beginning of Chapter 6. But Ward was clearly not an object of ridicule to many veterans of the Texas Revolution, like those who cheered his candidacy in 1869, nor to thousands of other Texans who thought of him as a hero. On his return to Austin in 1871, the *Statesman* would hardly have greeted the three-time mayor and distinguished longtime citizen by noting his nickname if it were thought to be a pejorative term. Publicly, it was his friends who used the nickname, not those who were contemptuous of him.

B. Note on the Thomas William Ward Papers

The author initially conducted research in the Ward Papers during the 1990s in a photocopy set that the Center for American History at the University of Texas at Austin made available for research in 1991.

However, that set, copied from originals owned by Rebekah Connally of Houston, Ward's great great-granddaughter, was by no means complete; on the other hand, it included copies of a number of originals (including letters from Sam Houston and the Civil War correspondence of Thomas William Ward's son, Dudley) that had been sold. Later Ms. Connally gave the author full access to all the original Ward Papers in her possession. A relatively small portion of her collection had been loaned to another of Ward's great-great granddaughters, Sara May Meriwether of Austin, and Ms. Meriwether gave the author full access to those papers. In 2008 Ms. Connally formally agreed to donate the entire collection, including the portion that had been in Ms. Meriwether's possession, to the University of Texas over a three-year period.

Footnotes in the book to documents from the Ward Papers identify them, in the absence of folder titles, by the file numbers found on a great many of the documents, a numbering system that Ward himself started. His numbers run from 1 to 750, but documents 151–200 have not been found. Ms. Connally numbered a good many of the unnumbered documents. Her numbers are preceded by "U" and run from U1 to U299. In both cases decimal points are occasionally used (641.1, 641.2; U27.1, U27.2). The Center for American History has a list of the documents in the photocopy collection that, arranged by file number, briefly identifies each document. Ms. Connally prepared transcripts of a good many of the documents in her collection, which are very helpful. At the time research was conducted in the Ward Papers, the papers in Ms. Meriwether's possession included photocopies of some documents concerning Ward that she had found while doing research on Ward at the Texas State Archives, and a few of those photocopies are cited in this book.

Notes

ABBREVIATIONS

AHC: Austin History Center, Austin Public Library

CAH: Dolph Briscoe Center for American History, University of Texas at Austin

ConDis, Panama: Consular Dispatches from Panama City, Panama, Microfilm Publication M139, General Records of the Department of State, Record Group 59, National Archives

DCTC: Records of the District Court for Travis County, Microfilm, Travis County Courthouse, Austin

MP: Microfilm Publication

NA: National Archives

NHT: New Handbook of Texas

NYCC: Index #GA 625 of 1860 (Susan L. Ward versus Thomas W. Ward), Division of Old Records, New York County Clerk, New York City

OST: Office of the Secretary of the Treasury

RG: Record Group

SHQ: Southwestern Historical Quarterly

SLW: Susan L. Ward

TGLO: Archives and Records Division, Texas General Land Office, Austin

TSA: Texas State Archives (Archives and Information Services Division, Texas State Library and Archives Commission), Austin

TWW: Thomas William Ward

Ward Papers: Thomas William Ward Papers, Dolph Briscoe Center for American History, University of Texas at Austin

NOTES TO INTRODUCTION

1. *Democratic Statesman* (Austin), Nov. 26, 1872 (1st quotation); *Houston Courier*, Nov. 29, 1872 (2nd quotation).

2. Peter Bell to Franklin Pierce, Jan. 18, 1853, roll 46, MP M967 (Letters of Application and Recommendation During the Administrations of Franklin Pierce and James Buchanan, 1853–1861), RG 59: General Records of the Department of State (NA).

3. *Houston Courier*, Nov. 29, 1872 (1st quotation); TWW to William H. Seward, Aug. 23, 1867, Records re Custom House Nominations, box 440, Appointments Division, RG 56:

General Records of the Department of the Treasury (NA) (2nd quotation); News clipping, September 1869, #U159, Ward Papers (3rd quotation).

4. SLW to Lucadia Pease, May 14, 1854, FP. A. 1, S. 1, Niles-Graham-Pease Papers (AHC).

5. *Houston Courier*, Nov. 29, 1872 (1st quotation); *Democratic Statesman* (Austin), Nov. 26, 1872 (2nd quotation).

NOTES TO CHAPTER 1

1. Caroline Smyth to TWW, June 24, 1832, #357 (2nd and 3rd quotations), Mar. 19, 1857, #535 (1st quotation), Ward Papers. Ward's birth date of June 20 is revealed in a letter from James M. Long to Matthew P. Woodhouse, July 5, 1842, 2-22L/10, Matthew Woodhouse Papers (TSA).

2. John Gamble, *Sketches of History, Politics, and Manners, in Dublin, and the North of Ireland, in 1810* (London: Baldwin, Cradock, and Joy, 1826), 22 (quotation); Jacqueline Hill, *From Patriots to Unionists: Dublin Civic Politics and Irish Protestant Patriotism, 1660–1840* (Oxford: Clarendon Press, 1997), 197–198.

3. Baptism Register, St. Mary's Parish, 1807 (Representative Church Body Library, Dublin).

4. G. N. Wright, *An Historical Guide to the City of Dublin* (2nd ed.; London: Baldwin, Cradock, and Joy, 1825), 71; James Collins, *Life in Old Dublin* (Dublin: James Duffy & Co., 1913), 32; Henry A. Wheeler and M. J. Craig, *The Dublin City Churches of The Church of Ireland: An Illustrated Handbook* (Dublin: A. P. C. K., 1948), 26.

5. Jacob De Cordova, *Texas: Her Resources and Her Public Men* (Philadelphia: J. B. Lippincott, 1858), 160; J. C. Beckett, *The Anglo-Irish Tradition* (London: Faber and Faber, 1976), 10. The biographical sketch of Ward in De Cordova's volume states that on his mother's side Ward was a relative of the Marquis of Hastings while on his father's side he was a descendant of the Earls of Dudley. Charles Smyth, Ward's nephew, who drafted the sketch based on information his uncle provided, wrote a short time later (*New York Herald*, Mar. 3, 1858), in an obituary for his mother, Ward's sister, that on her father's side she was a member of the noble family of the Dudley Wards and on her mother's side a relative of the Marquis of Hastings and of Lady Hutchinson. Since neither Ward's father's family nor his mother's family has been identified, it has not been possible to trace his lineage and verify these statements.

6. Baptism Register, St. Mary's Parish, 1792–1815; Vestry Book, St. Mary's Parish, June 17, 1818, Oct. 21, Dec. 17, 1823 (Representative Church Body Library, Dublin).

7. Hill, *From Patriots to Unionists*, 270, 293–296; "An Alphabetical List of the Freemen of the City of Dublin, 1774–1824" *The Irish Ancestor*, 15 (Nos. 1 and 2, 1983), 132; Fergus D'Arcy, "An Age of Distress and Reform: 1800–1860," in *Dublin Through the Ages*, ed. Art Cosgrove (Dublin: College Press, 1988), 105–106; John J. Webb, *The Guilds of Dublin* (London: Ernest Benn, 1929), 242; Sir Jonah Barrington, *Personal Sketches and Recollections of His Own Times* (Dublin: Ashfield Press, 1997), 113. Ward was admitted not by right of birth or by apprenticeship to be a guild member, but by special grace, a decision of the guild to admit him upon payment of a fee.

8. J. Warburton et al., *History of the City of Dublin; From the Earliest Accounts to the Present Time* (2 vols.; London: T. Cadell and W. Davies, 1818), II, Appendix No. I, table facing vii,

Appendix No. II, xxiii; *The Dublin Almanac and General Register of Ireland for the Year of Our Lord 1835* (Dublin: Pettigrew and Oulton, n.d.), 287. The 1835 city directory was the first to list names and occupations by street.

9. Baptism Register, St. Mary's Parish, 1792–1815; Samuel Ward to TWW, Nov. 15, 1855, #628, Ward Papers (quotation). The two boys born just after Thomas did not live to adulthood.

10. Charles Smyth to TWW, Nov. 16, 1855, #U1.1, Caroline Smyth to TWW, Dec. 18, 1856, #538 (1st quotation), Mar. 19, 1857, #535, Samuel Ward to Jacob De Cordova, Aug. 17, 1855, #626.2 (2nd quotation), and Samuel Ward to TWW, Nov. 15, 1855, #628, Ward Papers; De Cordova, *Texas*, 160 (3rd and 4th quotations).

11. Max Caulfied, *The Easter Rebellion* (Boulder, Colo.: Roberts Rinehart Publishers, 1995), 256–259.

12. Eamon Walsh, "Sackville Mall: The First One Hundred Years," in *The Gorgeous Mask: Dublin, 1700–1850,* ed. David Dickson (Dublin: Trinity History Workshop, 1987), 30, 33, 42–43; Peter Somerville-Large, *Dublin* (London: Granada, 1981), 222.

13. De Cordova, *Texas*, 160.

14. Ibid.

15. J. V. Luce, *Trinity College Dublin: The First 400 Years* (Dublin: Trinity College Dublin Press, 1992), 72–73; *The Architecture of Richard Morrison (1767–1849) and William Vitruvius Morrison (1794–1838)* (Dublin: Irish Architectural Archive, 1989), 84–85; Warburton et al., *History of the City of Dublin,* II, 1149–1150, 1150n; Documents concerning Botany Bay, MUN/P/2/119, and Registry of Trinity College Board Minutes, 1813–1817, MUN/V/5/6 (Manuscripts Department, Trinity College Library, Dublin).

16. Memorial #722-326-493761, Dec. 3, 1817, #753-305-512122, May 1, 1820, #760-592-516527, Jan. 30, 1821, and #798-536-539-272, Jan. 8, 1825 (quotation), Memorials (Registry of Deeds, Dublin); Somerville-Large, *Dublin,* 224.

17. Hill, *From Patriots to Unionists,* 285–287; D'Arcy, "Age of Distress and Reform," 99–101; Author's conversation with Professor David Dickson, Department of History, Trinity College, Dublin, on June 2, 2000.

18. Minute Book of the Commissioners for the Making Wide and Convenient Streets in the City of Dublin, Nov. 29, 1822 (1st quotation), June 20, 1823 (2nd quotation) (Dublin City Archives); Memorial #798-536-539-272, Jan. 8, 1825, #830-346-558281, Dec. 11, 1827, #842-347-564847, Jan. 1, 1828, and #1833-12-241, Apr. 11, 1833, Memorials.

19. Caroline Smyth to TWW, June 24, 1832, #357 (1st quotation), Mar. 19, 1857, #535, Samuel Ward to TWW, Nov. 15, 1855, #628 (2nd quotation), Ward Papers.

20. TWW to SLW, Feb. 28, 1855, #U198, Ward Papers (1st quotation); Warburton et al., *History of the City of Dublin,* II, 882–883; *Freeman's Journal* (Dublin), Jan. 4, 1819 (4th quotation), Jan. 4, 1822 (2nd quotation), Jan. 4, 1825 (3rd quotation).

21. De Cordova, *Texas*, 160. It has been stated in some sources that Ward actually became a cadet in the East India's service, but Ward himself indicated that this was not the case, and a careful search of the British Library's East India Office Collections concerning cadets turned up no evidence to support that contention.

22. Memorial #842-347-564847, Jan. 1, 1828, Memorials; Charles Smyth to TWW, July 9, 1868, #1.105, Ward Papers; *New York Herald,* Mar. 3, 1858; Jimmy O'Toole, *The Carlow*

Gentry: What Will The Neighbours Say! (Carlow: Jimmy O'Toole, 1993), 85–88. Richard Corrigan, a longtime resident of Garrettstown House, near Beechy Park, provided the information about Beechy Park Cottage in letters to the author of Sept. 14 and Oct. 23, 2000.

23. Caroline Smyth to TWW, June 24, 1832, #357, and Samuel Ward to TWW, Nov. 15, 1855, #628 (quotation), Ward Papers; De Cordova, *Texas*, 160.

24. Kerby A. Miller, *Emigrants and Exiles: Ireland and the Irish Exodus to North America* (New York: Oxford University Press, 1985), 193–197, 202–206, 252–261; De Cordova, *Texas*, 160; Passenger lists for Dublin Packet, arriving May 23 and Oct. 13, 1828, rolls 11–12, MP M237A (Passenger Lists of Vessels Arriving at New York, New York, 1820–1897), RG 36: Records of the U.S. Customs Service (NA); *Carlow Morning Post*, Feb. 25, 1828 (quotation); *Dublin Evening Post*, Apr. 26, 1828; *Dublin Mercantile Advertiser*, Apr. 7, 28, 1828.

25. De Cordova, *Texas*, 160; *Democratic Statesman* (Austin), Nov. 26, 1872 (1st quotation); Noah Smithwick, *The Evolution of a State or Recollections of Old Texas Days* (Austin: University of Texas Press, 1983), 195 (2nd quotation).

26. Earl F. Niehaus, *The Irish in New Orleans, 1800–1860* (1965; reprint, North Stratford, N.H.: Ayer Company Publishers, 1998), 35, 57; Merl Reed, "Boom or Bust—Louisiana's Economy During The 1830's," *Louisiana History*, 4 (Winter, 1963), 35, 43–44; Liliane Crété, *Daily Life in Louisiana, 1815–1830* (Baton Rouge: Louisiana State University Press, 1981), 50–51.

27. Contract between Joseph Martin and James Loughrea, Apr. 23, 1831, Acts of L. Feraud, No. 3, and Release from Thomas Ward and James Loughrea to Joseph Martin, Jan. 16, 1832, Acts of Carlile Pollock, No. 38A (New Orleans Notarial Archives); "709–11 Royal Street," Vieux Carré Survey (Williams Research Center, New Orleans).

28. Caroline Smyth to TWW, June 24, 1832, #357 (quotation), and Samuel Ward to TWW, Nov. 15, 1855, #628, Ward Papers; Mark M. Carroll, *Homestead Ungovernable: Families, Sex, Race, and the Law in Frontier Texas, 1823–1860* (Austin: University of Texas Press, 2001), 85. Henry was still living in New Orleans at his death in 1844, which was reported in the *New Orleans Daily Picayune*, July 24, 1844.

29. Caroline Smyth to TWW, June 24, 1832, #357, Ward Papers (1st quotation); SLW, Complaint to the Supreme Court of the City and County of New York, Mar., 22, 1859, p. 35 [87], NYCC (2nd quotation); Walter Johnson, *Soul by Soul: Life Inside the Antebellum Slave Market* (Cambridge, Mass.: Harvard University Press, 1999), 2 (3rd quotation); Mary Cable, *Lost New Orleans* (1980; reprint, New York: American Legacy Press, 1984), 184; Harriet Martineau, *Society in America* (3 vols., 1837; reprint, New York: AMS Press, 1966), III, 55–56; Samuel Ward to TWW, Nov. 15, 1855, #628, Ward Papers.

NOTES TO CHAPTER 2

1. James E. Winston, "New Orleans and the Texas Revolution," *Louisiana Historical Quarterly*, 10 (July, 1927), 321, 323–324; *Bee* (New Orleans), Aug. 8, 1835.

2. Paul D. Lack, *The Texas Revolutionary Experience: A Political and Social History, 1835–1836* (College Station: Texas A&M University Press, 1992), 3–34; Arnoldo De León, "Mexican Texas," in Ron Tyler, Douglas E. Barnett, Roy R. Barkley, Penelope C. Anderson, and Mark F. Odintz (eds.), *NHT* (6 vols.; Austin: Texas State Historical Association, 1996), IV,

692; *Bee* (New Orleans), Oct.12, 1835 (quotation).

3. *Bee* (New Orleans), Oct.13, 14, 1835; *Louisiana Courier* (New Orleans), Oct. 12, 1835 (quotation).

4. Herman Ehrenberg, *The Fight for Freedom in Texas in the Year 1836*, in Natalie Ornish, *Ehrenberg: Goliad Survivor, Old West Explorer: A Biography* (Dallas: Texas Historical Press, 1997), 85–87 (1st and 2nd quotations); Edward L. Miller, *New Orleans and the Texas Revolution* (College Station: Texas A&M University Press, 2004), 58–59; *Bee* (New Orleans), Oct. 14, 1835 (3rd quotation); *Louisiana Courier* (New Orleans), Oct. 14, 1835; *Telegraph and Texas Register* (San Felipe de Austin), Nov. 14, 1835.

5. *Texas State Gazette* (Austin), Nov. 23, 1850 (quotation); Orazio Santangelo, "Petition to the Honorable Congress of the Republic of Texas," Charles A. Gulick, Jr., et al. (eds.), *The Papers of Mirabeau Buonaparte Lamar* (6 vols.; Austin: Texas State Library, 1921–1927, II, 144; Luciano, G. Rusich, "Santangelo, Orazio de Attellis," *NHT*, V, 889.

6. William Cooke to James Cooke, Aug. 7, 1839, in Harry Warren, "Col. William G. Cooke," *Quarterly of the Texas State Historical Association*, 9 (Jan., 1906), 212 (1st quotation); *Louisiana Courier* (New Orleans), Oct. 13, 1835 (2nd quotation); *Bee* (New Orleans), Oct. 14, 1835.

7. Miller, *New Orleans and the Texas Revolution*, 78; *Bee* (New Orleans), Oct. 19, 1835. The *Ouachita* departed on the 17th but its main shaft broke that evening and it was towed back to New Orleans on the 18th, where it remained two days or so for repairs.

8. *Telegraph and Texas Register* (San Felipe de Austin), Oct. 31, Nov. 7, 14, 1835; Warren, "Col. William G. Cooke," 212; M. L. Crimmins (ed.), "The Storming of San Antonio de Bexar in 1835," *West Texas Historical Association Year Book*, 22 (Oct., 1946), 96–98 (quotation). Crimmins's article contains Bannister's memoir. Bannister states that the Greys landed at Velasco on October 22, but I have used the date October 25, which was published in the *Telegraph and Texas Register* on Nov. 7, 1835, and was presumably provided by Edward Hall, who led the expedition.

9. Crimmins (ed.), "Storming of San Antonio," 98–101 (quotations); Austin's Register of Families, vol. 2, pp. 85, 89 (TGLO); Endorsement for document #U3 ("Tho⁵. Wᵐ. Ward Certificate of Citizenship Oct. 28th, 1835"), Ward Papers; Gary Brown, *Volunteers in the Texas Revolution: The New Orleans Greys* (Plano, Tex.: Republic of Texas Press, 1999), 37–46, 291–309.

10. Crimmins (ed.), "Storming of San Antonio," 101–103 (1st quotation); Moses Albert Levy to his sister, Dec. 20, 1835, Saul Viener, "Surgeon Moses Levy: Letters of a Texas Patriot," *Publications of the American Jewish Historical Society*, 46 (Dec., 1956), 107 (2nd quotation). Evidence regarding the date the Greys arrived at San Antonio is conflicting. Gary Brown believes it was in early November, based in part on the statement, made a year later by Thomas R. Stiff, a member of Ward's company, that he arrived at the Texan camp on November 8. See Brown, *Volunteers in the Texas Revolution*, 46, 74; and John H. Jenkins (ed.), *The Papers of the Texas Revolution, 1835–1836* (10 vols.; Austin: Presidial Press, 1973), III, 388. However, there is far weightier evidence indicating that the arrival date was about November 21. In fact, on November 22 Commander Stephen F. Austin issued an order stating that "the company of volunteers from New Orleans commanded by Capt. Morris joined the Army on the 21st in the afternoon and the Capt. reported his company ready

for duty, this day." Three days earlier, November 18, Austin had reported that he was in favor of storming San Antonio "so soon as the orleans Greys get up from Goliad." Moses Austin Bryan reported from camp the same day that "we will have 100 men from La Bahia or Goliad in a day or two." It was Morris's company of Greys that came by way of Goliad, passing through town sometime in mid-November. The company of Greys that came by way of the Red River (Breece's) was never in or near Goliad. On November 18 they were in Washington-on-the-Brazos, from which they proceeded to Bastrop and then took about six more days to get from Bastrop to San Antonio. See Jenkins (ed.), *Papers of the Texas Revolution*, II, 447, 455, 489, III, 80–81; *Telegraph and Texas Register* (San Felipe de Austin), Nov. 21, 1835; and Ehrenberg, *Fight for Freedom*, 113–129.

11. It is stated in some accounts from the 1840s and afterwards that Ward was captain of artillery by December 5, the day San Antonio was attacked. This may have been the case, but the evidence is by no means decisive. In a communication to Ward dated Nov. 23, 1838, Charles Mason, Acting Secretary of War for Texas, certified that Ward had held the rank of captain from December 10, 1835, the day following the battle. See Republic Claims, Audited Claims, TWW, Claim #8342 (microfilm; TSA). No documentation on the battle from 1835 identifies Ward as a captain, though other captains are identified. Frank Johnson's battle report, December 11, and the injury list submitted by Samuel Stivers and Amos Pollard on December 17 both list only one captain, not Ward, as injured during the battle. See Jenkins (ed.), *Papers of the Texas Revolution*, III, 160–164, 240. On the other hand, it appears that Ward may have been at least a lieutenant by December 5. In a document dated December 31, 1835, William Cooke, who was then captain of the company of Greys to which Ward had belonged, and J. C. Neill, then commander of the Béxar garrison, stated that Ward had become a member of the Greys in October 1835 and "continued as such until appointed to a Lieutenancy in the Artilery." Ward clearly entered battle on December 5 with an artillery company, not with the Greys. See Thomas W. Ward, Army of the Republic, #401-12, Texas Adjutant General Service Records, 1836–1935 (TSA).

12. Ehrenberg, *Fight for Freedom*, 131; Alwyn Barr, *Texans in Revolt: The Battle for San Antonio, 1835* (Austin: University of Texas Press, 1990), 16–17, 26, 29, 33–35, 67–69; Stephen L. Hardin, *Texian Iliad: A Military History of the Texas Revolution* (Austin: University of Texas Press, 1994), 53–59, 63; Albert A. Nofi, *The Alamo and the Texas War of Independence, September 30, 1835 to April 21, 1836: Heroes, Myths, and History* (New York: Da Capo Press, 1994), 28; Brown, *Volunteers in the Texas Revolution*, 73. Here and elsewhere in this chapter I have used Barr's figures on number of troops.

13. Rena Maverick Green (ed.), *Samuel Maverick, Texan, 1803–1870: A Collection of Letters, Journals, and Memoirs* (San Antonio: privately printed, 1952), 39–43; Dudley, G. Wooten (ed.), *A Comprehensive History of Texas, 1685 to 1897* (2 vols.; 1898; reprint, Austin: Texas State Historical Association, 1986), I, 555–556 (1st quotation); Austin's Order, Nov. 21, 1835, and Austin to James Perry, Nov. 22, 1835, Jenkins (ed.), *Papers of the Texas Revolution*, II, 479, 487–488; Joseph E. Field, *Three Years in Texas* (1836; reprint, Tarrytown, N.Y.: William Abbatt, 1925), 17 (177); Ehrenberg, *Fight for Freedom*, 134–135 (2nd quotation); Brown, *Volunteers in the Texas Revolution*, 75.

14. Green, *Samuel Maverick*, 39 (quotations); Paula Mitchell Marks, *Turn Your Eyes Toward*

Texas: Pioneers Sam and Mary Maverick (College Station: Texas A&M University Press, 1989), 36–37.

15. Green, *Samuel Maverick*, 43–44 (quotations, other than Milam's challenge); Barr, *Texans in Revolt*, 42, 44 (Milam's challenge); Warren, "Col. William G. Cooke," 213; *Texas Sentinel* (Austin), Sept. 26, 1840; Ehrenberg, *Fight for Freedom*, 140–144.

16. Barr, *Texans in Revolt*, 45, 71.

17. Ehrenberg, *Fight for Freedom*, 146, 154–156; Henry Dance to the Editor, Apr. 25 [?], 1836, Jenkins (ed.), Papers of the Texas Revolution, VI, 57–58 (quotation); Bill Groneman, "Carey, William R.," and Beryl B. Bowen, "Langenheim, William," *NHT*, I, 974, IV, 67.

18. Ehrenberg, *Fight for Freedom*, 147 (1st quotation); Barr, *Texans in Revolt*, 46; Frank W. Johnson to Edward Burleson, Dec. 11, 1835, Jenkins (ed.), *Papers of the Texas Revolution*, III, 161 (2nd quotation).

19. Henry Dance to Editor, Apr. 25 [?], 1836, and William R. Carey to his brother and sister, Jan. 12, 1836, Jenkins (ed.), *Papers of the Texas Revolution*, III, 492 (Carey's quotation), VI, 57–58 (Dance's quotations); Hardin, *Texian Iliad*, 80–81(other quotations).

20. Samuel Maverick to Sammy Maverick, Jan. 30, 1852, General Correspondence, 1852–1853, Maverick Family Papers (CAH); Report by Albert Levy and John Wood, Dec. 29, 1835, Republic Claims, Audited Claims, TWW, Claim #184 (1st quotation); Statement by William Cooke and J. C. Neill, Dec. 31, 1835, Thomas W. Ward, Army of the Republic, #401-12, Texas Adjutant General Service Records (2nd quotation); Frank W. Johnson, *A History of Texas and Texans* (5 vols.; Chicago: American Historical Society, 1914), I, 354–355; Samuel Stivers and Amos Pollard to the Provisional Government of Texas, Dec. 17, 1835, William C. Binkley (ed.), *Official Correspondence of the Texan Revolution, 1835–1836* (2 vols.; New York: D. Appleton-Century Co., 1936) , I, 212, 213n; Ehrenberg, *Fight for Freedom*, 154–156; *Southern Intelligencer* (Austin), Sept. 22, 1865. In his memoir Herman Ehrenberg states that it was the third day of the battle when the artillerymen "suffered severely," with all but one of them "heavily wounded" and Cook "killed." But other evidence indicates clearly that it was the first day. Ehrenberg also states that the twelve-pounder was not put into action until the second day, but Frank Johnson's battle report indicates it was dismounted the first day.

21. Henry Dance to the Editor, Apr. 25 [?], 1836, and Stiff Notes, n.d., Jenkins (ed.), *Papers of the Texas Revolution* III, 390, VI, 58; Moses Albert Levy to his sister, Dec. 20, 1835, Viener, "Surgeon Moses Levy," 109

22. Hardin, *Texian Iliad*, 59 (quotation); Frederick F. Cartwright, *The Development of Modern Surgery* (London: Arthur Barker Limited, 1967), 13. Among the physicians and surgeons who participated in the storming were Thomas R. Erwin, Joseph E. Field, James Grant, William Howell, Albert Levy, E. F. Mitchison, Samuel Stivers, and possibly Amos Pollard, surgeon of the regiment. However, Grant and possibly others did not act in a medical capacity. See Pat Ireland Nixon, *The Medical Story of Early Texas: 1528–1853* (Lancaster, Pa.: Lancaster Press, 1946), 168–180; Field, *Three Years in Texas*, 18; Brown, *Volunteers in the Texas Revolution*, 299–301; Pat Ireland Nixon, "Field, Joseph E.," Robert Bruce Blake, "Grant, James," Diana J. Kleiner, "Levy, Albert Moses," and Bill Groneman, "Pollard, Amos," *NHT*, II, 990–991, III, 282, IV, 178, V, 259.

23. Green, *Samuel Maverick,* 23 (quotation), 23n; Cartwright, *Development of Modern Surgery,* 13–14, 25–27; Mark J. Schaadt, *Civil War Medicine: An Illustrated History* (Quincy, Ill.: Clearwood Publishing, 1998), 50; C. Keith Wilbur, *Civil War Medicine, 1861–1865* (Old Saybrook, Conn.: Globe Pequot Press, 1998), 51–54. The available evidence does not indicate whether the amputation was above or below the knee.

24. *Texas Sentinel* (Austin), Sept. 26, 1840.

25. *Texas State Gazette* (Austin), Sept. 8, 1849.

26. Moses Albert Levy to his sister, Dec. 20, 1835, Viener, "Surgeon Moses Levy," 109 (quotations); Cartwright, *Development of Modern Surgery,* 45–47; Schaadt, *Civil War Medicine,* 70–71; Marvin P. Rozear and Joseph C. Greenfield, Jr., "'Let Us Cross Over the River': The Final Illness of Stonewall Jackson," *Virginia Magazine of History and Biography,* 103 (Jan., 1995), 38–39.

27. Ellen Winchell, *Coping with Limb Loss* (Garden City Park, N.Y.: Avery Pub. Group, 1995), 20, 49–50, 79–82, 103–111, 122–132, 138–140; Lawrence W. Friedmann, *The Psychological Rehabilitation of the Amputee* (Springfield, Ill.: Charles C. Thomas, 1978), 17–19; Report by Albert Levy and John Wood, Dec. 29, 1835, Republic Claims, Audited Claims, TWW, Claim #184; Samuel Maverick to Sammy Maverick, Jan. 30, 1852, General Correspondence, 1852–1853, Maverick Family Papers.

Notes to Chapter 3

1. Barr, *Texans in Revolt,* 50, 62; *Texas State Gazette* (Austin), Dec. 13, 1851; *Democratic Statesman* (Austin), Nov. 26, 1872; "Ward, Thomas William," in Walter Prescott Webb and H. Bailey Carroll (eds.), *The Handbook of Texas* (2 vols.; Austin: Texas State Historical Association, 1952), II, 861; Sara May Meriwether, "Ward, Thomas William," *NHT,* VI, 820.

2. De Cordova, *Texas,* 161; Smyth to Ward, Feb. 2, 1857, #U1.4, and Mar. 3, 1857, #U1.5 (quotation), Ward Papers; Pension application and accompanying affidavit, Nov. 30, 1870, Republic Claims, Republic Pensions, TWW, roll 244, frames 402–403 (microfilm; TSA).

3. *Texas Sentinel* (Austin), Sept. 26, 1840; *Southern Intelligencer* (Austin), Sept. 22, 1865 (quotation); *Democratic Statesman* (Austin), Nov. 26, 1872 (quotation).

4. Charles F. Stansbury, *Argument on Behalf of the Applicant: in the Matter of the Application of B. Franklin Palmer, for the Extension of Letters Patent, Granted to Him 4th November, 1846, for the Improvement in Artificial Legs* ([Washington, D.C.?, 1860]), 6.

5. My thinking about the relevance of posttraumatic stress disorder (PTSD) to Ward's life was influenced by discussion in February 2002 with John Riskind, Ph.D., a cognitive psychologist and Professor of Psychology at George Mason University. Based on what I told Riskind about Ward's life and personality and about what befell him in December 1835 (the intense combat, the devastation of his leg by a cannon shot, the gruesome amputation that followed, and the emotional and physical impact of the amputation), it was Riskind's view that Ward was permanently affected by that experience and that studies of PTSD in Vietnam veterans were very relevant. Furthermore, as will be seen, Ward experienced two additional encounters with cannon fire, in 1840 and 1842, the first of which severely injured him and necessitated amputation of his right arm. The relevant literature on PTSD and Vietnam veterans is extensive, but see, for example, Jean C. Beckham et al., "Interpersonal Hostility and Violence in Vietnam Combat Veterans with Chronic Post-

traumatic Stress Disorder: A Review of Theoretical Models and Empirical Evidence," *Aggression and Violent Behavior*, 5 (Sept.–Oct., 2000), 451–454; Claude M. Chemtob et al., "Anger, Impulsivity, and Anger Control in Combat-Related Posttraumatic Stress Disorder," *Journal of Consulting and Clinical Psychology*, 62 (No. 4, 1994), 827–832; B. Kathleen Jordan et al., "Problems in Families of Male Vietnam Veterans With Posttraumatic Stress Disorder," *Journal of Consulting and Clinical Psychology*, 60 (No. 6, 1992), 916–926; and, for a different approach to the issue, Eric T. Dean Jr., *Shook Over Hell: Post-Traumatic Stress, Vietnam, and the Civil War* (Cambridge, Mass.: Harvard University Press, 1997).

6. John H. Bowker and John W. Michael (eds.), *Atlas of Limb Prosthetics: Surgical, Prosthetic, and Rehabilitation Principles* (2nd ed.; St. Louis: Mosby Year Book, 1992), 665, 709 (quotation); *Telegraph and Texas Register* (San Felipe de Austin), Feb. 20, 1836.

7. J. C. Neill to the Governor and Council, Jan. 6, 14, 1836, J. C. Neill to Sam Houston, Jan. 14, 1836, and G. B. Jameson to Sam Houston, Jan. 18, 1836, Jenkins (ed.), *Papers of the Texas Revolution*, III, 425, IV, 14–15 (quotation), 58–60; *Houston Courier*, Nov. 29, 1872; Brown, *Volunteers in the Texas Revolution*, 130, 308.

8. John Duffy (ed.), *The Rudolph Matas History of Medicine in Louisiana* (2 vols.; Baton Rouge: Louisiana State University Press, 1958–1962), II, 43–46; *True American* (New Orleans), May 2, 1836; Randolph B. Campbell, *Sam Houston and the American Southwest* (New York: HarperCollins College Publishers, 1993), 71–72.

9. De Cordova, *Texas*, 161; John Smith to D. C. Barrett, Jan. 23, 1836, Jenkins (ed.), *Papers of the Texas Revolution*, IV, 130 (1st quotation); Dudley Bean to TWW, Oct. 22, 1846, #203, Ward Papers; Advisory Committee to the Acting Governor, Feb. 1, 1836, Committee Reports, Folder 57b, Record Group 307, Legislative and Executive Bodies Prior to the Republic Series, Texas Secretary of State (TSA) (2nd quotation); Report of the Committee on Finance, Feb. 6, 1836, Republic Claims, Audited Claims, TWW, Claim #184 (3rd quotation); *Telegraph and Texas Register* (San Felipe de Austin), Feb. 20, 1836; William F. Gray, *From Virginia to Texas, 1835: Diary of Col. Wm. F. Gray* (1909; reprint, Houston: Fletcher Young Pub. Co., 1965), 119. David Gerber discusses the issue of government assistance to disabled veterans as repayment for a personal sacrifice in "Introduction: Finding Disabled Veterans in History," *Disabled Veterans in History*, ed. David A. Gerber (Ann Arbor: University of Michigan Press, 2000), 12.

10. De Cordova, *Texas*, 161; Friedmann, *Psychological Rehabilitation of the Amputee*, 69–70, 74; Bowker and Michael (eds.), *Atlas of Limb Prosthetics*, 667–668, 675–677, 681–682.

11. Marilyn McAdams Sibley, "Thomas Jefferson Green: Recruiter for the Texas Army, 1836," *Texas Military History*, 3 (Fall, 1963), 129–136 (quotations); Thomas J. Green to David Burnet, Apr. 8, 1836, Binkley (ed.), *Official Correspondence*, II, 607.

12. *Bee* (New Orleans), Mar. 28 (2nd quotation), Apr. 4 (1st quotation), 5, 6, 11, 12, May 18, 1836; Henry Stuart Foote, *Texas and the Texans* (2 vols., 1841; reprint, Austin: Steck Co., 1935), II, 341n; William Bryan to David Burnet, Apr. 30, 1836, Binkley (ed.), *Official Correspondence*, II, 648 (3rd quotation); Thomas J. Green to TWW, May 2, 1836, Thomas Jefferson Green Papers (microfilm; Southern Historical Collection, Wilson Library, University of North Carolina at Chapel Hill); Sibley, "Thomas Jefferson Green," 135–136, 138–144. It is difficult to be very precise about the number of men who sailed with Green. The *Bee* (New Orleans) reported in its May 18 issue that Green had 400 to 500 on board. Sibley

states that muster rolls in the General Land Office at Austin credit him with about 400, but she believes the number was actually much closer to the 230 cited by Henderson Yoakum in his *History of Texas: From Its First Settlement in 1685 to Its Annexation to the United States in 1846* (2 vols.; New York: Redfield, 1856) II, 171. However, 230 was actually the number of men that Green took with him to Velasco after arriving at Galveston with a larger force and dispatching part of it (at least three companies, it appears) to Lavaca Bay. See Thomas J. Green, *Journal of the Texian Expedition Against Mier* (1845; reprint, New York: Arno Press, 1973), 484.

13. Thomas J. Green to TWW, May 2, 1836 (1st quotation), and "Texas Movers," May 10, 1836, Green Papers; *Bee* (New Orleans), May 14, 18, 1836; *True American* (New Orleans), May 16, 1836 (2nd quotation); *Commercial Bulletin* (New Orleans), May 25, 1836; De Cordova, *Texas*, 161.

14. Green, *Journal of the Texian Expedition*, 484–487 (1st quotation); M. B. Lamar, Relation of Scenes and Events Concerning Santa Anna, Gulick et al (eds.), *Papers of Mirabeau Lamar*, I, 525–527; General Order No. 5, June 4, 1836, Green Papers (2nd quotation). Although Green states in his journal that Ward was in command of the men he dispatched to Lavaca Bay, other evidence indicates clearly that Ward first went to Velasco with Green and then was ordered by Green to Lavaca Bay on June 7. See General Order No. 11, June 7, 1836, #U10, Ward Papers. Evidence concerning the seizure of Santa Anna at Velasco is contradictory in details. For a version of events that varies from the one presented here, see Captain H. A. Hubbbell's letter of June 4, 1836, in Jenkins (ed.), *Papers of the Texas Revolution*, VII, 16.

15. General Order No. 11, June 7, 1836, #U10, Ward Papers; General Order No. 10, June 6, 1836, Green Papers; Green, *Journal of the Texian Expedition*, 487.

16. Cleburne Huston, *Towering Texan: A Biography of Thomas J. Rusk* (Waco: Texian Press, 1971), 1–3, 20; Priscilla Myers Benham, "Rusk, Thomas Jefferson," *NHT*, V, 721; Lack, *Texas Revolutionary Experience*, 134 (quotation).

17. William C. Binkley, "The Activities of the Texan Revolutionary Army after San Jacinto," *Journal of Southern History*, 6 (Aug., 1940), 333, 342, 345–346; Thomas Rusk to TWW, June 20, 1836, Thomas J. Green to Thomas Rusk, Aug. 1, 1836, and Thomas Rusk to Alexander Somervell, Aug. 7, 1836, Jenkins (ed.), *Papers of the Texas Revolution*, VII, 217, VIII, 95 (2nd quotation), 152 (1st quotation); Thomas Rusk to TWW, June 17, 1836, #U8 (3rd quotation), and F. A. Sawyer to TWW, Sept. 3, 1836, #U16, Ward Papers; Joseph Milton Nance, *After San Jacinto: The Texas-Mexican Frontier, 1836–1841* (Austin: University of Texas Press, 1963), 22–23.

18. Binkley, "Activities of the Texan Revolutionary Army," 340–341, 344–346 (1st quotation); Nance, *After San Jacinto*, 17–23 (2nd quotation); Hiram Taylor to Thomas J. Green, June 28, 1836 (3rd quotation), TWW to Thomas J. Green, June 27, 1836 (4th quotation), and General Brigade Order No. 26, July 13, 1836, Green Papers; J. W. Bunton, Proceedings of a Court Martial, July 14–15, 1836, Jenkins (ed.), *Papers of the Texas Revolution*, VII, 459–460.

19. *Muster Rolls of the Texas Revolution* (Austin: Daughters of the Republic of Texas, 1986), 204; Marilyn McAdams Sibley (ed.), "Letters From the Texas Army, Autumn, 1836: Leon Dyer to Thomas J. Green," *SHQ*, 72 (Jan., 1969), 378n; Resolutions Offered by the

Officers on the 10th of August, 1836 (quotation), and TWW to Thomas J. Green, Aug. 11, 1836, Green Papers; James Milroy to TWW, Aug. 22, 1836, #U25, Ward Papers.

20. Thomas J. Green to Thomas Rusk, Aug. 23, 1836, and H. Moscross to Thomas J. Green, Aug. 25, 1836, Green Papers; Thomas Rusk to TWW, Aug. 23, 1836, General Correspondence, Rusk Papers; James Milroy to TWW, Aug. 22, 1836, #U25 (quotation) and #U26, Ward Papers.

21. Thomas J. Green to Thomas Rusk, Aug. 23, 1836, Green Papers (quotation); Thomas Rusk to TWW, Aug. 23, 1836, General Correspondence, Rusk Papers; David Burnet, Commission of TWW as Major in the Regular Texas Army, Sept. 1, 1836, #531, F. A. Sawyer to TWW, Sept. 3, 1836, #U16, and Thomas J. Green to TWW, Sept. 13, 1836, #U6, Ward Papers; Charles Mason to TWW, Nov. 23, 1838, Republic Claims, Audited Claims, TWW, Claim #8342; Mary Starr Barkley, *History of Travis County and Austin 1839–1899* (3rd ed.; Austin: Austin Printing Co., 1981), 44–45.

22. James M. Denham, "New Orleans, Maritime Commerce, and the Texas War for Independence, 1836," *SHQ*, 97 (Jan., 1994), 529–534; *Louisiana Courier* (New Orleans), Sept. 20, 1836 (1st quotation); David Burnet to Thomas Toby and Brother, Sept. 3, 1836, and Thomas Toby and Brother to David Burnet, Sept. 22, 1836, Binkley (ed.), *Official Correspondence*, II, 978 (3rd quotation), 1032 (2nd quotation).

23. C. P. Green to Thomas J. Green, Oct. 6, 1836, and Thomas J. Green to Felix Huston, Oct. 25, 1836, Green Papers; Thomas J. Green to TWW, Sept. 10, 1836, #U14, Ward Papers (quotation).

24. Nance, *After San Jacinto*, 24 (1st quotation); Binkley, "Activities of the Texan Revolutionary Army," 346; *Louisiana Courier* (New Orleans), Oct. 28, 1836 (2nd quotation); TWW, Receipt for $460, Sept. 2, 1836, Republic Claims, Audited Claims, TWW, Claim #825.

NOTES TO CHAPTER 4

1. *Telegraph and Texas Register* (Houston), May 16, 1837.

2. Andrew Forest Muir (ed.), *Texas in 1837: An Anonymous, Contemporary Narrative* (Austin: University of Texas Press, 1958), 38–39 (1st, 2nd, and 3rd quotations); Andrew Forest Muir (ed.), "Diary of A Young Man in Houston, 1838," *SHQ*, 53 (Jan., 1950), 301, 301n; *Telegraph and Texas Register* (Houston), Mar. 3, 1838 (4th quotation).

3. *Telegraph and Texas Register* (Houston), May 16, 1837 (1st quotation); Ernest W. Winkler, "The Seat of Government of Texas: I. Temporary Location of the Seat of Government," *Quarterly of the Texas State Historical Association*, 10 (Oct., 1906), 165–170 (2nd quotation). A total of fifteen sites, including Houston, were nominated for the new capital. One of them was a joint entry, Velasco and Quintana, and thus it is commonly stated that Houston won out over fifteen competitors rather than fourteen.

4. *History of Texas, Together with a Biographical History of the Cities of Houston and Galveston* (Chicago: Lewis Pub. Co., 1895), 262 (quotation); *First Congress—First Session. An Accurate and Authentic Report of the Proceedings of the House of Representatives* (Columbia, Tex.: G & T. H. Borden, 1836), 157, 161, 182–183, 226; *Telegraph and Texas Register* (Columbia), Dec. 27, 1836.

5. Augustus Allen to Thomas J. Green, May 6, 1836 (Green Papers). Allen chose not to return to Texas with the brigade, however.

6. Kenneth Hafertepe, *Abner Cook: Master Builder on the Texas Frontier* (Austin: Texas State Historical Association, 1992), xviii; William Christy to TWW, Jan. 21, 1837, #240, Ward Papers; *Telegraph and Texas Register* (Columbia), Feb. 10, 14, 21, 28, 1837; Agreement between Nicholas Hansen and TWW, Feb. 16, 1837, Accession No. 16304c (L-493), Tod Collection (Herzstein Library, San Jacinto Museum of History).

7. Contract between TWW and Augustus Allen, Feb. 18, 1837, Acts of William Christy, vol. 28, No. 377 (New Orleans Notarial Archives) (2nd and 3rd quotations); Ernest W. Winkler, "The Seat of Government of Texas: II. The Permanent Location of the Seat of Government," *Quarterly of the Texas State Historical Association*, 10 (Jan., 1907), 186 (1st quotation).

8. Petition from Doswell & Adams to the District Court, May 31, 1838, File No. 7, vol. 2, Records Library, Civil Records, District Clerk's Office, Harris County Courthouse; Francis R. Lubbock, *Six Decades in Texas* (Austin: B. C. Jones, 1900), 48–49, 54.

9. Lubbock, *Six Decades in Texas*, 49 (1st quotation); Winkler, "Seat of Government: Temporary Location," 171; *Journal of the House of Representatives of the Republic of Texas at the Second Session of the First Congress* (Houston: Telegraph Office, 1838), 20 (2nd quotation), 51; Samuel Wood Geiser, *Naturalists of the Frontier* (2nd ed.; Dallas: Southern Methodist University Press, 1948), 127 (3rd quotation).

10. *Telegraph and Texas Register* (Houston), Mar. 17, 1838; Winkler, "Seat of Government: Permanent Location," 186 (quotation).

11. Muir, "Diary of A Young Man," 290–291, 303; *Houston: A Nation's Capital, 1837–1839* (Houston: Harris County Historical Society, 1985), 106–110. For the dating of the 1857 photograph, see A. Pat Daniels, *Texas Avenue at Main Street* (Houston: Allen Press, [1964]), 31.

12. Mary Austin Holley to Mrs. William M. Brand, Dec. 30, 1837, Mary Austin Holley Papers (CAH) (1st quotation); J. P. Bryan (ed.), *Mary Austin Holley: The Texas Diary, 1835–1838* (Austin: University of Texas Press, 1965), 36–37 (2nd quotation and sketch); Ernest Beerstecher, Jr., "An Early Likeness of the Capitol at Houston," *Texana*, V (Fall, 1967), 232–237. Holley wrote on her sketch that the capitol was "70 feet front," exactly the width specified in the contract, and "140 rear." The total depth front-to-rear called for in the contract was 114 feet, including the galleries and wings. An 1844 illustration of the "Old Capitol" hotel in a newspaper advertisement, discussed by Beerstecher, indicates that the wings were indeed one-story to begin with but did not have a gallery running along the outside, as called for in the contract.

13. Lubbock, *Six Decades in Texas*, 75 (quotation); H. B. Cenas to TWW, May 23, June 17, and June 17, 1837, # 241.2, #241.3, #241.1, Ward Papers.

14. Harrisburg County Court Minutes, Oct. 27–28, 1837, Jan. 24, 26–30, 1838, Feb. 11, 1839, vol. "4/2/37–7/7/40," pp. 29, 31, 51, 53–54, 57, 60, 61, 256 (County Clerk's Office, Harris County Courthouse); *Telegraph and Texas Register* (Houston), Feb. 17, 24, 1838 (1st quotation); District Court Minutes (Civil), Harris County, June 13, 1839, vol. B., p. 220 (microfilm; Houston Public Library); James Wilmer Dallam, *A Digest of the Laws of Texas* (Baltimore: John D. Toy, 1845), 371–373 (2nd quotation); *Morning Star* (Houston) Apr. 11, May 7, Aug. 5, Sept. 4, Oct. 4, 1839.

15. Lubbock, *Six Decades in Texas*, 65, 75–77 (Lubbock quotations); Muir, "Diary of A Young Man," 305–306; *Journals of the Senate of the Republic of Texas, Adjourned Session—Sec-*

ond Congress (Houston: [Telegraph Power Press], 1838), 9–10 (last quotation); William S. Red (ed.), "Extracts from the Diary of W.Y. Allen, 1838–1839," *SHQ*, 17 (July, 1913), 45.

16. William Ransom Hogan, *The Texas Republic: A Social and Economic History* (Norman: University of Oklahoma Press, 1969), 267–290; James David Carter, *Masonry in Texas: Background, History, and Influence to 1846* (Waco: Committee on Masonic Education and Service for the Grand Lodge of Texas, 1955), 272–273, 289, 299–301, 306; Lubbock, *Six Decades in Texas*, 65–66 (1st quotation); *Proceedings of the Grand Lodge of Texas* (2 vols.; Galveston: Richardson & Co., 1857), I, 27, 31–32 (2nd quotation); Albert G. Mackey, *A Lexicon of Freemasonry* (Philadelphia: Moss & Brother, 1855), 17–18 (3rd quotation). Carter mistakenly identifies Thomas William Ward as a Mason, confusing him with Thomas Ward, a prominent Mason who lived in Austin from the 1840s until his death in 1859.

17. Kenneth S. Greenberg, *Honor & Slavery: Lies, Duels, Noses, Masks, Dressing as a Woman, Gifts, Strangers, Humanitarianism, Death, Slave Rebellions, the Proslavery Argument, Baseball, Hunting, and Gambling in the Old South* (Princeton, N.J.: Princeton University Press, 1996), 15 (1st quotation); Bertram Wyatt-Brown, *Honor and Violence in the Old South* (New York: Oxford University Press, 1986), 33 (2nd quotation), 146–152; *Telegraph and Texas Register* (Houston), May 2, 1838.

18. Lubbock, *Six Decades in Texas*, 64, 67–68; *Telegraph and Texas Register* (Houston), June 24, Nov. 18, 1837; David G. McComb, *Houston: A History* (Austin: University of Texas Press, 1981), 50–51.

19. Account with TWW, Apr. 10, 1838, Republic Claims, Audited Claims, TWW, Claim #685 (quotation); Marguerite Johnston, *Houston: The Unknown City, 1836–1946* (College Station: Texas A&M University Press, 1991), 22; Deeds dated Nov. 4, Nov. 28, 1838, Harris County Deed Record, Book A, pp. 158, 169 (microfilm; Houston Public Library). The property that Ward sold to Briscoe, block 44, lot 1, was donated to Ward by the Allens. See the Houston Town Lot Book, Vertical Files (Houston Public Library).

20. License to practice law, Jan. 2, 1838, #401, Ward Papers; *Telegraph and Texas Register* (Houston), Mar. 3, 1838.

21. Land Grants to TWW: Fannin Co., B-11, bounty grant, warrant dated Jan. 5, 1838; Washington Co., 1-7, grant for permanent disability, certificate dated Feb. 1, 1838; Fannin Co., 1-29, 1st class headright, certificate dated Feb. 2, 1838; Goliad Co., B-8, donation grant, certificate dated May 15, 1838, Headright Grants and Military Land Grants (TGLO).

22. H. P. N. Gammel, *The Laws of Texas, 1822–1897* (10 vols.; Austin: Gammel Book Co., 1898), I, 1407–1410; Minutes of the Board of Land Commissioners, Harris [Harrisburg] County, Texas (TSA; 2 vols.; typescript; transcribed from the records of the Texas General Land Office for the Chambers County Historical Commission, 1980), I, 4, 55. Ward was appointed to replace a member who had resigned by the remaining two members. Congress officially elected him to the position in May.

23. Minutes of the Board of Land Commissioners, Harris County, I, 55–115, II, 1–70; Lost Book of Harris County, Box G629 (TGLO); Curtis Bishop, *Lots of Land* (Austin: Steck Co., 1949), 119 (1st quotation); Gammel, *Laws of Texas*, I, 1407, (2nd quotation); Report of the Commissioner of the General Land Office, Oct. 23, 1839, Harriet Smither (ed.), *Journals of the Fourth Congress of the Republic of Texas, 1839–1840* (3 vols.; Austin: Von-Boeckmann-Jones Co., [1931?], III, 163–164, 168. On Sam Houston, see Minutes of the

Board of Land Commissioners, Harris County, vol. 1, p. 113 (3rd quotation). Houston lived with Tiana in the Cherokee nation in Oklahoma. While running for president in 1841 Houston was accused by the *Centinel*, a virulently hostile Austin newspaper, of having fraudulently used his Cherokee wife to obtain a headright grant of a league of land in Austin's colony in 1833. "He was only entitled to one-fourth of a league," contended the *Centinel* in its issue of July 22, 1841, "having no family in the country—unless it was that he claimed his Cherokee wife and her children—which according to the ritual of the church and the law of the land, he had no right to claim."

24. TWW to S. A. Cook, Oct. 19, 1872, Ward Papers. Ward ran in statewide elections for land commissioner in 1849, 1851, 1866, and 1869 and lost all four. He also lost a legislative election for land commissioner in 1848.

25. *Telegraph and Texas Register* (Houston), July 7, 16, Sept. 8, 1838, Jan. 2, 1839; Thomas Bryson to TWW, Oct. 13, 1838, #232, Ward Papers (quotations); Patsy McDonald Spaw (ed.), *The Texas Senate: Volume 1, Republic to Civil War, 1836–1861* (College Station: Texas A&M University Press, 1990), 331n.

26. Commission as Postmaster of the City of Houston, Apr. 12, 1839, #532, Ward Papers; *Morning Star* (Houston), Apr. 12, 13, 1839; Ala May Newell, "The Postal System of the Republic of Texas" (M.A. thesis, St. Mary's University of San Antonio, 1940), 63–67. Ward's successor was appointed on Jan. 13, 1840, but by then he had been in Austin for several weeks.

27. Gustav Dresel, *Houston Journal: Adventures in North America and Texas, 1837–1841*, ed. Max Freund (Austin: University of Texas Press, 1954), 78 (1st quotation), 131; Edward Stiff, *The Texan Emigrant* (1840; reprint, Waco: Texian Press, 1968), 68–69 (2nd quotation).

28. Dresel, *Houston Journal*, 102–103 (1st quotation); Johnston, *Houston*, 30 (2nd quotation).

29. Winkler, "Seat of Government: Permanent Location," 221–222 (1st quotation); S. A. Roberts to Mirabeau Lamar, July 9, 1839, Gulick et al (eds.), *Papers of Mirabeau Lamar*, III, 38 (2nd quotation).

30. *Telegraph and Texas Register* (Houston), Sept. 4, 1839; Republic Claims, Audited Claims, TWW, Claim #2699; Jackson Smith to James Harper Starr, Sept. 13, 1839, Seymour V. Connor (ed.), *Texas Treasury Papers: Letters Received in the Treasury Department of the Republic of Texas, 1836–1846* (4 vols.; Austin: Texas State Library, 1955), I, 269; Winkler, "Seat of Government: Permanent Location," 234.

31. *Morning Star* (Houston), Nov. 6, 12, 1839; William S. Red (ed.), "Extracts from the Diary of W. Y. Allen, 1838–1839," *SHQ*, 17 (July, 1913), 60.

32. Peter Bell to Franklin Pierce, Jan. 18, 1853, roll 46, MP M967, RG 59; Republic Claims, Audited Claims, TWW, Claims #184 (i.d. 97330) and #8754.

33. William C. Walsh, "Austin in the Making" (a series of newspaper articles published in the *Austin Statesman*, February–March 1924), 9th installment, Vertical File: Austin History (CAH) (1st quotation); Sam Houston to Washington D. Miller, Sept. 13, 1853, Amelia W. Williams and Eugene C. Barker (eds.), *The Writings of Sam Houston, 1813–1863* (8 vols.; Austin: University of Texas Press, 1938–1943), V, 457 (2nd quotation); Friedmann, *Psychological Rehabilitation of the Amputee*, 66.

NOTES TO CHAPTER 5

1. *Texas Sentinel* (Austin), Feb. 26, Mar. 4 (1st and 3rd quotations), 1840; Barkley, *History of Travis County and Austin*, 44 (2nd quotation); *Austin City Gazette*, Mar. 4, 1840; *Morning Star* (Houston), Mar. 10, 1840. A similar accident occurred at the Texas Independence Day celebration in Galveston on Mar. 2, 1845, when, as William Hogan notes in *The Texas Republic*, p. 114, "one of the persons engaged in firing a salute at Galveston had an arm blown off."

2. *Austin City Gazette*, Mar. 11, 1840; Miroslaw Vitali et al., *Amputation and Prostheses* (London: Balière Tindall, 1978), 5–6; John Culbert Faries, *Limbs for the Limbless: A Handbook on Artificial Limbs for Layman and Surgeon* (New York: Institute for the Crippled and Disabled, 1934), 38–39; Jennifer Davis McDaid, "'How a One-Legged Rebel Lives': Confederate Veterans and Artificial Limbs in Virginia," in *Artificial Parts, Practical Lives: Modern Histories of Prosthetics*, ed. Katherine Ott et al. (New York: New York University Press, 2002), 126.

3. TWW, Account, Apr. 20, 1840, Republic Claims, Audited Claims, TWW, Claim #3900; *Austin City Gazette*, Aug. 19, 1840; *Southern Intelligencer* (Austin), Mar. 22, 1866.

4. John Salmon Ford, *Rip Ford's Texas*, ed. Stephen B. Oates (Austin: University of Texas Press, 1963) 213n (1st and 3rd quotations); William G. Cooke to TWW, Oct. 2, 1842, #226.6, Ward Papers (2nd quotation).

5. *Southern Intelligencer* (Austin), Sept. 22, 1865 (2nd and 3rd quotations), Mar. 22, 1866; TWW to William H. Seward, Records re Custom House Nominations, Box 440, Appointments Division, RG 56 (1st quotation).

6. Dubois de Saligny to Dalmatia, Mar. 17, 1840, Nancy Nichols Barker (ed.), *The French Legation in Texas* (2 vols.; Austin: Texas State Historical Association, 1971–1973), I, 130–131; Sam Houston to Anna Raguet, Dec. 10, 1839, Williams and Barker (eds.), *Writings of Sam Houston*, II, 322 (quotation); Winkler, "Seat of Government: Permanent Location," 242–244.

7. Robert Potter to friend, Feb. 11, 1840 (1st, 2nd, and 3rd quotations), and William Adams to his wife, Dec. 21, 1845 (4th quotation), AF-A 8250 (AHC).

8. Maurice Garland Fulton (ed.), *Diary & Letters of Josiah Gregg* (2 vols.; Norman: University of Oklahoma Press, 1941–1944), I, 106; *Appendix to the Journals of the House of Representatives: Fifth Congress* (Austin: Gazette Office, n.d.), 264; Dubois de Saligny to Thiers, July 26, 1840, Barker, *French Legation in Texas*, I, 158–159; *Austin City Gazette*, Apr. 22, 1840 (quotations).

9. Republic Claims, Audited Claims, TWW, Claims # 2913, 3048, 3380, 3493, 3497, 3625, 3842, 3913, 4154, 4426, 4566, 4753, 4900, 5154.

10. Ernest Winkler (ed.), *Secret Journals of the Senate, Republic of Texas, 1836–1845* (Austin: Austin Printing Co., 1911), 184; *Austin City Gazette*, Aug. 26, 1840; *Telegraph and Texas Register* (Houston), Oct. 21, 1840; William Carper to TWW, Sept. 14, 1840, #144, and Charles Bigelow, Power of Attorney, Dec. 4, 1840, #87.1, Ward Papers.

11. *Daily Bulletin* (Austin), Dec. 10, 1841; Kenneth Hafertepe, *A History of The French Legation in Texas: Alphonse Dubois de Saligny and His House* (Austin: Texas State Historical Association, 1989), 15–16.

12. *Texas Sentinel*, Sept. 5, 1840 (1st quotation); *Austin City Gazette*, Sept. 16, 30, Oct. 7,

21, 28, Dec. 16, 1840; Mirabeau Lamar to Charles DeMorse and others, Mar. 9, 1841, Gulick et al. (eds.), *Papers of Mirabeau Lamar*, V, 460 (2nd quotation).

13. *Southern Intelligencer* (Austin), Sept. 22, 1865 (3rd quotation), May 17, 1866 (1st quotation); Peter Bell to Franklin Pierce, Jan. 18, 1853, roll 46, MP M967, RG 59 (2nd quotation).

14. *Texas Centinel* (Austin), July 22, 1841.

15. Unlike first-class headrights (granted to heads of families and single men who were in Texas on March 2, 1836), second-, third-, and fourth-class headrights (granted to those who arrived after March 2, 1836, and prior to January 1, 1842) included residence and other requirements and thus were conditional upon the recipients fulfilling the requirements. Second- and third-class headrights, for instance, were conditional upon the grantees residing in the republic for three years, performing all the duties of citizenship, and paying the requisite surveying and other fees.

16. TWW, Report to the President and Congress, Nov. 15, 1843, ESA (Early Letters Sent), roll 1, part 2, vol. 3, p. 288 (microfilm; TGLO) (quotation); *The Land Commissioners of Texas: 150 Years of the General Land Office* (Austin: Texas General Land Office, 1986), 104. According to *The Land Commissioners of Texas*, 104, one Texan did receive a patent on a headright prior to 1841 (on January 25, 1838) but it was hardly a normal headright. The patent, for land that became the town of Galveston, was issued to Michel B. Menard after he and his associates paid the republic $50,000 to clear the title. Through a complicated process, Menard had gained control of the land after it had been granted as a headright to Juan Seguin by Mexico prior to Texas's independence. See Margaret Swett Henson, "Menard, Michel Branamour," *NHT*, IV, 613; and David G. McComb, *Galveston: A History* (Austin: University of Texas Press, 1986), 42–43.

17. *Texas State Gazette* (Austin), May 7, 1853 (1st quotation); Joel Panton to Henry Raglin, Jan. 5, 1841, #1327, Box 2-10/3, General Land Office Correspondence (TSA) (2nd quotation).

18. Winkler (ed.), *Secret Journals*, 190–192; Samuel Cranwill to TWW, Feb. 4, 1841, #1637 (quotation), and letters from W. P. Lewis, Nathan Mitchell, George Durham, and M. P. Woodhouse to TWW, all dated Feb. 3, 1841, Box 2-10/4, General Land Office Correspondence.

19. Nathan Mitchell to TWW, May 7, 1841, Box 2-23/961, Swante Palm Collection (TSA).

20. Aloise W. Hardy, "A History of Travis County, 1832–1865" (M.A. thesis, University of Texas at Austin, 1938), 67; *Texas Sentinel* (Austin), Feb. 25, 1841; TWW to Mirabeau Lamar, [Sept. 1841], #271.4, Ward Papers; TWW to Andrew Briscoe, June 21, 1841, Box 92, Andrew Briscoe Papers (Herzstein Library, San Jacinto Museum of History) (quotation); TWW, Report to the President and Congress, Oct. 7, 1841, Harriet Smither (ed.), *Journals of the Sixth Congress of the Republic of Congress, 1841–1842* (3 vols.; Austin: Von Boeckmann-Jones Co., 1940–1945), III, 449. The Land Office was in block 97.

21. Bishop, *Lots of Land*, 118; *Land Commissioners of Texas*, 3–8, 13; John Borden, Report to the President and Congress, Apr. 10, 1838, ESA (Early Letters Sent), roll 1, part 2, vol. 1, p. 95 (quotation); Thomas Lloyd Miller, *The Public Lands of Texas, 1519–1970* (Norman: University of Oklahoma Press, 1971), 12; John G. Johnson, "General Land Office," *NHT*, III, 124.

22. Sometimes county surveyors did the surveying themselves. For informative accounts of surveying by deputy and county surveyors during the period 1838–1842, see Lucy A. Erath, "Memoirs of Major George Bernard Erath," in *One League To Each Wind: Accounts of Early Surveying in Texas*, ed. Sue Watkins (Austin:Von-Boeckmann-Jones, 1964), 204–211; John H. Reagan, *Memoirs, With Special Reference to Secession and the Civil War* (1906; reprint, Austin: Pemberton Press, 1968), 37–43; and Susanne Starling, *Land Is the Cry! Warren Angus Ferris, Pioneer Texas Surveyor and Founder of Dallas County* (Austin:Texas State Historical Association, 1998), 75–124.

23. Bishop, *Lots of Land*, 119–122; "Texas Land Grants: A History of the Texas General Land Office and the Public Lands of Texas" (typescript, Apr. 22, 1998), 11, 13–16 (TGLO); *Texas in 1840, or the Emigrant's Guide to the New Republic* (1840; reprint, New York: Arno Press, 1973), 268 (1st quotation); Miller, *Public Lands of Texas*, 32–34 (2nd quotation).

24. John Borden, Report to the President and Congress, Oct. 17, 1840, *Appendix to the Journals of the House of Representatives: Fifth Congress*, 250 (quotation); *Land Commissioners of Texas*, 104–107. It should be noted that the data on patents in *Land Commissioners of Texas* "has the possibility of a small fraction of error," according to the author on page 133. While certificates for headrights were issued by county boards of land commissioners, land certificates for military service were issued by the secretary of war while Texas was a republic. From February 1846 to October 1855 they were issued by the adjutant general. See Miller, *Public Lands of Texas*, 50.

25. *Texas Sentinel* (Austin), Feb. 25, 1841 (1st quotation); D. P. Barhydt to James Harper Starr, June 23, 1841, #751, James Harper Starr Papers (CAH) (2nd quotation).

26. ESA (Early Letters Sent), roll 1, part 2, vol. 3, pp. 122–226. Legislation enacted February 5, 1840, required each county surveyor to prepare and maintain in his office "a map on which all the surveys made in his county shall be laid down and properly 'connected,' which map shall be corrected at the end of each month." Legislation enacted January 19, 1841, specified that no patent should be issued upon any claim unless a map of the county in which the claim was situated had been returned to the General Land Office by the county surveyor. See Gammel, *Laws of Texas*, II, 366, 528.

27. TWW to James Howlet, July 15, 1841, ESA (Early Letters Sent), roll 1, part 2, vol. 3, pp. 179–180 (1st quotation); *Texas Centinel* (Austin), Sept. 9, 1841 (2nd quotation); TWW, Report to the President and Congress, Oct. 7, 1841, Smither (ed.), *Journals of the Sixth Congress*, III, 447 (3rd quotation), 454–460.

28. *Texas Centinel* (Austin), July 22, 1841 (1st quotation); TWW to Andrew Briscoe, June 21, 1841, Box 92, Briscoe Papers (2nd quotation); TWW, Report to the President and Congress, Oct. 7, 1841, Smither (ed.), *Journals of the Sixth Congress*, III, 449–451.

29. James Harper Starr to TWW, Oct. 6, 1841, #88, Ward Papers (1st quotation); *Daily Texian* (Austin), Nov. 23, 1841 (2nd quotation).

30. M. P. Woodhouse to Henry Austin, Jan. 19, 1842, Box 2-10/6, General Land Office Correspondence; Harriet Smither (ed.), "Diary of Adolphus Sterne," *SHQ*, 33 (July, 1929), 76; TWW to Sam Houston, Feb. 23, 1842, Houston Letters, Box 2-23/891, Hearne Collection (TSA) (quotation); Spaw (ed.), *Texas Senate*, I, 111.

31. Borden, Report to the President and Congress, Oct. 17, 1840, *Appendix to the Journals of the House of Representatives: Fifth Congress*, 254, 256–257; Gammel, *Laws of Texas*, II,

614–615; TWW, Report to the President and Congress, Oct. 7, 1841, Smither (ed.), *Journals of the Sixth Congress*, III, 449 (quotations); Michael T. Moore, "Mapping Texas Public Lands, 1824–1900" (typescript), 6 (TGLO).

32. TWW to Sam Houston, Feb. 23, 1842, Houston Letters, Box 2-23/891, Hearne Collection; TWW, Report to the President and Congress, Oct. 7, 1841, Smither (ed.), *Journals of the Sixth Congress*, III, 448 (quotation).

33. Harry Lewis Coles, *History of the Administration of Federal Land Policies and Land Tenure in Louisiana, 1803–1860* (New York: Arno Press, 1979), 1–8, 77–78, 82; Everett Dick, *The Lure of the Land: A Social History of the Public Lands from the Articles of Confederation to the New Deal* (Lincoln: University of Nebraska Press, 1970), 19–20 (quotation); Virginia H. Taylor Houston, "Surveying in Texas," in Watkins (ed.), *One League To Each Wind*, 23, 28, 30.

34. Gammel, *Laws of Texas*, I, 1283, 1323, 1326, 1417–1418, II, 358–359; Spaw (ed.), *Texas Senate*, I, 35–36, 78–79; Reagan, *Memoirs*, 54 (quotation); Starling, *Land Is the Cry*, 95–96; Bishop, *Lots of Land*, 119n; Coles, *History of the Administration of Federal Land Policies*, 158–162. The idea of sectioning was briefly revived in 1840 following expulsion of the Cherokees, when Congress mandated that their lands be divided into six-mile square townships and subdivided into thirty-six one-mile square sections. Again, however, Congress balked at the cost.

35. TWW, Report to the President and Congress, Oct. 7, 1841, Smither (ed.), *Journals of the Sixth Congress*, III, 443–449 (quotations); TWW, Report to the President and Congress, Nov. 15, 1843, ESA (Early Letters Sent), roll 1, part 2, vol. 3, pp. 295–296; *Report of the Commissioner of the General Land Office. To the 9th Congress of the Republic of Texas* ([Washington, Tex.:] Vindicator Office, 1844), 5–8; Borden, Report to the President and Congress, Oct. 17, 1840, *Appendix to the Journals of the House of Representatives: Fifth Congress*, 253–254. Initially county surveyors were elected by Congress, but legislation enacted in February 1840 made the position an elective one in each county. See Gammel, *Laws of Texas*, I, 1406, II, 437.

36. James Harper Starr to TWW, Dec. 21, 1841, #143, Ward Papers; Randolph B. Campbell, *Gone to Texas: A History of the Lone Star State* (New York: Oxford University Press, 2003), 159.

37. Gammel, *Laws of Texas*, II, 684–686, 716; 777; Republic Claims, Audited Claims, TWW, Claims # 6610, 6724, 7036, H. L. Upshur, Claim #s 6561, 6704, 6860, 7064; TWW, Report to the President and Congress, Nov. 15, 1843, ESA (Early Letters Sent), roll 1, part 2, vol. 3, pp. 290–292; W. H. Abell to a friend, Apr. 11, 1843, in Hardy, "History of Travis County," 230 (quotation).

38. Seymour V. Connor, *Adventure in Glory* (Austin: Steck-Vaughn Co., 1965), 140–141 (1st quotation); Campbell, *Sam Houston*, 90, 92; Andrew Briscoe to TWW, May 5, 1841, #52, August 9, 1841, #54 (2nd quotation), Ward Papers.

39. James Reily to TWW, Aug. 4, 1841, #64.2, Ward Papers; Deed, Sept. 8, 1841, Harris County Deed Record, Book J, pp. 197–200; TWW to Andrew Briscoe, Nov. 26, 1841, Box 92, Briscoe Papers; Andrew Briscoe to TWW, Dec. 19, 1841, #59, Ward Papers.

40. Andrew Briscoe to TWW, Aug. 9, 1841, #54, Ward Papers; Campbell, *Sam Houston*, 92 (1st quotation); Mary Whatley Clarke, *David G. Burnet* (Austin: Pemberton Press, 1969),

204 (2nd quotation); Stanley Siegel, *A Political History of the Texas Republic, 1836–1845* (1956; reprint, New York: Haskell House Publishers, 1973), 179–180 (3rd, 4th, and 5th quotations); *Texas Centinel* (Austin), Sept. 23, 1841.

41. *Telegraph and Texas Register* (Houston), Jan. 19, 1842; *Land Commissioners of Texas*, 104–106.

NOTES TO CHAPTER 6

1. James Long to Matthew Woodhouse, July 5, 1842, Box 2-22L/10, Matthew Woodhouse Papers. Other 1842 letters using the nickname "Old Peg" and in one instance "Pegleg," addressed to Woodhouse by James Long, Joel Miner, and William Murrah, are in Box 2-23/904 of the Woodhouse Papers.

2. James Long to Matthew Woodhouse, July 5, 1842, Box 2-22L/10, Matthew Woodhouse Papers.

3. Ibid.

4. Ibid. (1st quotation); Aaron Bean to Marshall Pease, Oct. 17, 1855, P.1, Pease Papers (2nd quotation); TWW to M. P. Woodhouse, Sept. 1, 1842, #U176, Ward Papers (3rd quotation).

5. TWW to Sam Houston, Feb. 23, 1842, Houston Letters, Box 2-23/891, Hearne Collection; *Austin City Gazette*, Mar. 30, 1842.

6. *Daily Bulletin* (Austin), Jan. 8, 1842; Sam Houston, Message to Congress, Feb. 5, 1842, Williams and Barker (eds.), *Writings of Sam Houston*, II, 481–482; W. D. Miller to Sam Houston, Mar. 2, 1842, Box 1878/3-2, Washington D. Miller Papers (TSA).

7. W. H. Abell to a friend, Apr. 11, 1843, in Hardy, "History of Travis County," 231 (quotation); W. D. Miller to Sam Houston, Feb. 23, Mar. 2, 6, 1842, Box 1878/3-2, Miller Papers; Handbill, "To Arms! To Arms! Texians!!" Mar. 6 (but dated Mar. 5), 1842, #1713, Box 2-10/4, General Land Office Correspondence; Joseph Milton Nance, *Attack and Counter-Attack: The Texas-Mexican Frontier, 1842* (Austin, University of Texas Press, 1964), 55–57; Jacob Snively to James Harper Starr, Mar. 8, 1842, #762, Starr Papers.

8. W. H. Abell to a friend, Apr. 11, 1843, in Hardy, "History of Travis County," 231 (1st quotation); George Hockley to Sam Houston, Mar. 6, 1842 (2nd quotation), and Record of Vigilance Committee Meeting, Mar. 6, 1842, Smither (ed.), *Journals of the Sixth Congress*, III, 14–16; George Hockley, Special Order No. 137, Mar. 6, 1842, Republic Claims, Public Debt Claims, TWW, Claim #1649 (TSA); Joseph Waples to Anson Jones, Mar. 13, 1842 (misdated Feb. 13, 1842), Anson Jones, *Memoranda and Official Correspondence Relating to the Republic of Texas, Its History and Annexation* (New York: D. Appleton & Co., 1859), 171; W. D. Miller to Sam Houston, Mar. 9, 1842, Box 1878/3-2, Miller Papers; Nance, *Attack and Counter-Attack*, 64–67.

9. W. H. Abell to a friend, Apr. 11, 1842, in Hardy, "History of Travis County," 231 (1st quotation); Hockley, Declaration of Martial Law, Mar. 7, 1842, Smither (ed.), *Journals of the Sixth Congress*, III, 17; W. D. Miller to Sam Houston, Mar. 9, 1842, Box 1878/3-2, Miller Papers (other quotations).

10. George Hockley to TWW, Mar. 7, 1842, #U23, Ward Papers; Henry J. Jewett, "The Archive War of Texas," *DeBow's Review*, 26 (May, 1859), 515; Order Book of Col. T. William Ward, March 1842 (AHC); Nance, *Attack and Counter-Attack*, 69; Jacob Snively to James

Harper Starr, Mar. 8, 1842, #762, Starr Papers. The location on President's Hill was near East Eighth and San Jacinto Streets, the site today of St. David's Church. The location on Capitol Hill was near West Eighth and Colorado Streets, then the site of the capitol.

11. W. D. Miller to Sam Houston, Mar. 10 and 13, 1842, Box 1878/3-2, Miller Papers; Nance, *Attack and Counter-Attack*, 97. Nance states on page 93 that the two Bastrop companies together with a third mounted company raised by Colonel Louis P. Cooke left for San Antonio under General Edward Burleson's command on the morning of March 11, but Nance's source, W. D. Miller's letter to Sam Houston of March 13, states that Burleson and his force left Austin the morning of March 13, after conclusive news arrived of the retreat.

12. Sam Houston to George Hockley, Mar. 10, 1842, and George Hockley to Sam Houston, Mar. 16, 1842, Smither (ed.), *Journals of the Sixth Congress*, III, 17-18; W. D. Miller to Sam Houston, Mar. 16, 1842, Box 1878/3-2, Miller Papers; *The Encyclopedia of the New West* (Marshall, Tex.: United States Biographical Publishing Co., 1881), Texas Volume, 388.

13. TWW to James Harper Starr, July 31, 1843, #751, Starr Papers.

14. W. D. Miller to Sam Houston, Mar. 16, 1842, Box 1878/3-2, Miller Papers (1st quotation); Record of Public Meeting, Mar. 16, 1842, Smither (ed.), *Journals of the Sixth Congress*, III, 18-20; Marilyn McAdams Sibley, *Lone Stars and State Gazettes: Texas Newspapers before the Civil War* (College Station: Texas A&M University Press, 1983), 112–113, 120–122, 134–135, 138–139; *Austin City Gazette,* Aug. 17, 1842 (2nd quotation); Samuel Whiting to Mirabeau Lamar, Apr. 12, 1842, Gulick et al. (eds.), *Papers of Mirabeau Lamar*, IV, 5 (3rd quotation).

15. W. D. Miller to Sam Houston, Mar. 16, 1842, Box 1878/3-2, Miller Papers (quotation); Record of Public Meeting, 10 a.m., Mar. 16, 1842, Smither (ed.), *Journals of the Sixth Congress*, III, 18-20; W. D. Miller to Ashbel Smith, Apr. 6, 1842, Letters, April–June 1842, Ashbel Smith Papers (CAH). A record of the public meeting on March 16, 1842, that includes all ninety-six signatures on the letter to Hockley is in the Anson Jones Papers, Correspondence, 1809–1843 (CAH). Although Miller's March 16 letter to Houston leaves the impression he was not at the meeting, he was among "those present" who signed the letter to Hockley.

16. Record of Public Meeting, 4 p.m., Mar. 16, 1842, Smither (ed.), *Journals of the Sixth Congress*, III, 20-23 (quotation); Special Order No. 146, Mar. 16, 1842, Box 2-23/904, Woodhouse Papers.

17. W. D. Miller to Sam Houston, Mar. 17, 1842, Box 1878/3-2, Miller Papers; George Hockley, Special Order No. 147, Mar. 17, 1842, Box 2-23/904, Woodhouse Papers; George Hockley, Special Order No. 148, Republic Claims, Public Debt Claims, TWW, Claim #1649; Order Book of Col. T. William Ward, March 1842; George Hockley to William Pettus, Mar. 17, 1842, Smither (ed.), *Journals of the Sixth Congress*, III, 24. Four days prior to Hockley's order on March 17 dismissing Jones's troops, the two mounted companies from Bastrop County had joined an expedition against the Mexicans under General Edward Burleson.

18. Record of Public Meetings, Mar. 17, 1842, and Sam Houston to George Hockley, Mar. 22, 1842, Smither (ed.), *Journals of the Sixth Congress*, III, 24–28; Jewett, "Archive War of Texas," 516–517.

19. Joseph Waples to James Harper Starr, Mar. 23, 1842, #862, Starr Papers (1st quotation); W. D. Miller to Sam Houston, Mar. 16, 1842, Box 1878/3-2, Miller Papers (2nd quotation).

20. Joseph Waples to James Harper Starr, Mar. 23, 1842, #862, Starr Papers (1s quotation); W. D. Miller to Ashbel Smith, Apr. 6, 1842, Letters, April–June 1842, Ashbel Smith Papers (2nd quotation).

21. Sam Houston to George Hockley, Mar. 22, 1842, Smither (ed.), *Journals of the Sixth Congress*, III, 27–28; W. H. Abell to a friend, Apr. 11, 1843, in Hardy, "History of Travis County," 231 (quotation); *Morning Star* (Houston), Apr. 14, 1842; TWW to Sam Houston, Apr. 2, 1842, #2324, A. J. Houston Collection (TSA).

22. Anson Jones to Mary Jones, Apr. 4, 1842, Correspondence, 1809–1843, Jones Papers; Sam Houston to TWW, Apr. 4, 1842 (quotation), and Sam Houston to Henry Jones, Apr. 4, 1842, Smither (ed.), *Journals of the Sixth Congress*, III, 31; TWW to Sam Houston, Apr. 13, 1842, #2368, A. J. Houston Collection.

23. Julia Lee Sinks, who settled in Austin in 1840, made this comment in the seventh of a series of newspaper articles, "Early Days in Texas," published in the mid-1890s in Dallas and Galveston newspapers. Copies are in her papers at CAH.

24. Records of Public Meetings, Apr. 11, 13, 1842, Smither (ed.), *Journals of the Sixth Congress*, III, 35–42, 47; TWW to Sam Houston, Apr. 13, 1842, # 2368, A. J. Houston Collection; Henry Jones to TWW, Apr. 15, 1842, #U71, Ward Papers; TWW to Sam Houston, Apr. 18, 1842, General Land Office Correspondence, photocopy in Ward Papers. Ward's file copies of his letters of April 13 and 18 to Sam Houston are in the Ward Papers, #U173 and #U174.

25. *Telegraph and Texas Register* (Houston), Apr. 27, 1842; TWW to Sam Houston, Apr. 18, 1842, General Land Office Correspondence, photocopy in Ward Papers (1st and 3rd quotations); Walsh, "Austin in the Making," 7th installment, Vertical Files: Austin History (2nd quotation). Walsh moved to Austin in 1840 at age 4.

26. George Hockley to TWW, Apr. 4, 1842, #U65, and TWW to George Hockley, May 13, 1842, #U171 (quotation), Ward Papers; *Journals of the House of Representatives of the Eighth Congress of the Republic of Texas* (Houston: Cruger & Moore, 1844), 290; Sam Houston to Morgan C. Hamilton, Sept. 20, 1842, Williams and Baker (eds.), *Writings of Sam Houston*, III, 162.

27. TWW, Report to the President and Congress, Nov. 15, 1843, ESA (Early Letters Sent), roll 1, part 2, vol. 3, p. 302; *Journals of the House of Representatives of the Eighth Congress*, 282, 290; Proclamation to the Citizens of Texas, Mar. 7, 1843, #U183, Ward Papers. Testimony is conflicting as to the frequency with which the boxes of Land Office Records were opened during 1842 and why. In sworn testimony to the House of Representatives in January 1844, Ward stated that the records remained packed during 1842 "with the exception of the boxes being occasionally opened for the purpose of airing the contents." However, a House Committee stated that Ward had told them earlier that month that the boxes were "frequently opened for examination and airing." In his report to Congress in November 1843, Ward said that he wanted the boxes unpacked after every spell of damp weather and at least weekly and packed "separate and unmixed so that any record might be found without difficulty or confusion."

28. George M. Jimsey to TWW, Apr. 1, 1842, #1709 (1st quotation), and Musgrove Evans to TWW, June 27, 1842, #1697 (2nd quotation), Box 2-10/4, General Land Office Correspondence; W. H. Murrah to M. P. Woodhouse, May 30, 1842, Box 2-23/904, Woodhouse Papers (3rd quotation); *Telegraph and Texas Register* (Houston), Oct. 5, 1842; TWW to Sam Houston, Sept. 28, 1842, #U178, Ward Papers (4th quotation). In the General Land Office's record book of letters sent, there is no outgoing correspondence dated between February 17, 1862 and May 3, 1843. See ESA (Early Letters Sent), roll 1, part 2, vol. 3, pp. 242–243.

29. Francis Latham, *Travels in the Republic of Texas, 1842*, ed. Gerald S. Pierce (Austin: Encino Press, 1971), 22–25; W. H. Murrah to M. P. Woodhouse, May 30, 1842, Box 2-23/904, Woodhouse Papers.

30. James Long to M. P. Woodhouse, May 21 (1st and 3rd quotations), June 9 (4th quotation), 1842, W. W. Massie to M. P. Woodhouse, May 21, 1842 (2nd quotation), and W. H. Murrah to M. P. Woodhouse, May 30, 1842 (5th quotation), Box 2-23/904, Woodhouse Papers.

31. W. H. Murrah to M. P. Woodhouse, May 30, 1842, James Long to M. P. Woodhouse, May 2, 1842, and Joel Miner to M. P. Woodhouse, Aug. 25 (Miner's quotation), Oct. 17, 1842, Box 2-23/904, Woodhouse Papers; James Long to M. P. Woodhouse, July 5, 1842, Box 2-22L/10, Woodhouse Papers (Long's quotation).

32. W. H. Abell to a friend, Apr. 11, 1843, in Hardy, "History of Travis County," 232; TWW to Sam Houston, Apr. 18, 1842, General Land Office Correspondence, photocopy in Ward Papers (quotation); James Long to Matthew Woodhouse, July 5, 1842, Box 2-22L/10, Woodhouse Papers.

33. James Long to M. P. Woodhouse, May 2 (1st quotation), June 9 (2nd quotation), 1842, Box 2-23/1904, Woodhouse Papers; TWW to M. P. Woodhouse, Sept. 1, 1842, #U176 (3rd and 4th quotations), and TWW to Sam Houston, Sept. 28, 1842, #U178 (5th quotation), Ward Papers.

34. TWW to Sam Houston, Sept. 28, 1842, #U178 (quotation), and Samuel Whiting to TWW, Sept. 24, 1842, #U70, Ward Papers; TWW to Samuel Whiting, Sept. 23, 1842, typescript, Correspondence, 1842–1844, Concerning the "Archive War" (Tarleton Law Library, University of Texas at Austin).

35. Washington Miller to Ashbel Smith, Dec. 8, 1842, Letters, October–December 1842, Ashbel Smith Papers; Siegel, *Political History of Texas Republic*, 190; Sam Houston to TWW, Oct. 8, 1842, and Sam Houston to John Chenoweth, Oct. 9, 1842, Williams and Barker (eds.), *Writings of Sam Houston*, IV, 149–150.

36. Joel Miner to M. P. Woodhouse, Aug. 27, 1842, Box 2-23/904, Woodhouse Papers (1st quotation); *Telegraph and Texas Register* (Houston), Oct. 19, 1842 (2nd and 3rd quotations).

37. Authorization for James Shaw to open boxes of State, War, and Treasury Department records, Oct. 17, 1842, #U61, and TWW to Sam Houston, Oct. 30, 1842, #U179, Ward Papers; *Southern Intelligencer* (Austin), Mar. 22, 1866 (1st and 2nd quotations); Jewett, "Archive War of Texas," 521; *Telegraph and Texas Register* (Houston), Nov. 9, 1842 (3rd quotation).

38. George Teulon to Anson Jones, Dec. 9, 1842, Jones, *Memoranda and Official Correspon-*

dence, 180; Proclamation to the Citizens of Texas, Mar. 7, 1843, #U183, Ward Papers.

39. *Morning Star* (Houston), Oct. 27, 1842; Jewett, "Archive War of Texas," 520; Joel Miner to M. P. Woodhouse, Oct. 17, 1842, Box 2-23/904, Woodhouse Papers (quotation).

40. George Teulon to Anson Jones, Dec. 9, 1842, and Samuel Whiting to Anson Jones, Dec. 10, 1842 (quotation), Jones, *Memoranda and Official Correspondence*, 180–181; TWW to Sam Houston, Oct. 30, 1842, #U179, Ward Papers.

41. Spaw (ed.), *Texas Senate*, I, 118; Sam Houston to Thomas I. Smith and Eli Chandler, Dec. 10, 1842 (1st quotation), Proclamation Ordering the Removal of the Archives from Austin, Dec. 10, 1842, and Sam Houston to TWW, Dec. 10, 1842 (2nd quotation), Williams and Barker (eds.), *Writings of Sam Houston*, III, 226–230.

42. Marquis James, *The Raven: A Biography of Sam Houston* (Indianapolis: Bobbs-Merrill, 1929), 328–329. A. E. Skinner does an excellent job of reviewing the evidence and calling into question Eberly's role in "Mrs. Eberly and That Cannon: Myth-Making in Texas History," *Texas Libraries*, 43 (Winter, 1981), 155–163.

43. De Witt Clinton Baker, *A Texas Scrap-Book: Made Up of the History, Biography, and Miscellany of Texas and Its People* (1875; reprint, Austin: Texas State Historical Association, 1991), 143; *Mooney & Morrison's General Directory of the City of Austin, Texas, for 1877–78* (Houston: Eugene Von Boeckmann, [1877]), 17–18.

44. Alexander W. Terrell, "The City of Austin from 1839 to 1865," *Quarterly of the Texas State Historical Association*, 14 (Oct., 1910), 124–125, 125n. Terrell's cites as his source three longtime Austin residents. One of them, however, Frank Brown, a well-known chronicler of Austin history, never claimed any more for Eberly in his own writings than "It has been said that Mrs. Eberly applied the torch which discharged the piece." See Frank Brown, "Annals of Travis County and of the City of Austin (From the Earliest Times to the Close of 1875)" (15 vols.; typescript), ch. IX, 91 (AHC). The other two were James O. Rice and Steele Mathews, who, Terrell says, "then lived in Austin." The source of their information is not known. Nor can it be confirmed they were they were in Austin in late December 1842 or early 1843. Neither name appears in any records connected with the events of December 30–31, 1842.

45. TWW to Sam Houston, Jan. 8, 1843, Williams and Barker (eds.), *Writings of Sam Houston*, III, 230n–231n; *Telegraph and Texas Register* (Houston), Jan. 11, 1843.

46. *Journals of the House of Representatives of the Eighth Congress*, 295; Mark B. Lewis to William Cazneau and John Caldwell, Jan. 1, 1843, *Texas Times* (Galveston), Feb. 11, 1843; "The Growth and Decay of a Town," *Connecticut Courant, Supplement* (Hartford), Dec. 14, 1844. Lewis, an Austin resident, participated in the day's events.

47. Jewett, "Archive War in Texas," 521; TWW to Sam Houston, Jan. 8, 1843, Williams and Barker (eds.), *Writings of Sam Houston*, III, 230n (quotation). Jewett was an Austin resident at the time and an active participant in the Archives War starting in March 1842. Sources disagree as to whether the howitzer fired grape or canister or both. In a January 4 message to the House of Representatives, Sam Houston said it was charged with grape and canister. In his January 8 letter to Houston, Ward, an experienced artillerist who was at the scene, called it grape. Jewett, writing sixteen years later, called it canister, as did the account in the 1877–78 city directory.

48. TWW to Sam Houston, Jan. 8, 1843, Williams and Barker (eds.), *Writings of Sam*

Houston, III, 230n (1st and 3rd quotations); *Journals of the House of Representatives of the Eighth Congress*, 291 (2nd quotation); TWW, Proclamation to the Citizens of Texas, Mar. 7, 1843, #U183, Ward Papers.

49. Mark B. Lewis to William Cazneau and John Caldwell, Jan. 1, 1843, *Texas Times* (Galveston), Feb. 11, 1843.

50. "Growth and Decay of a Town," *Connecticut Courant, Supplement* (Hartford), Dec. 14, 1844.

51. "Names of the individuals who took possession of the Archives of the Gen'l Land Office in Brushy Creek Milam Co. Dec' 31 1842," #U191, Ward Papers; Brown, "Annals of Travis County," ch. IX, 92–94.

52. Mark B. Lewis to William Cazneau and John Caldwell, Jan. 1, 1843, *Texas Times* (Galveston), Feb. 11, 1843; Joshua Holden to TWW, Jan. 31, 1843, #U187, Ward Papers.

53. Statement of Clerks Wynn & Mitchell, Jan. 25, 1843, #U184, Ward Papers; "Growth and Decay of a Town," *Connecticut Courant, Supplement* (Hartford), Dec. 14, 1844; Mark B. Lewis to William Cazneau and John Caldwell, Jan. 1, 1843, *Texas Times* (Galveston), Feb. 11, 1843 (quotation); Sam Houston to the House of Representatives, Jan. 4, 1843, Williams and Barker (eds.), *Writings of Sam Houston*, VII, 8.

54. T. R. Fehrenbach, *Lone Star: A History of Texas and the Texans* (New York: Macmillan, 1968), 261 (quotation); "Growth and Decay of a Town," *Connecticut Courant, Supplement,* (Hartford), Dec. 14, 1844; Virginia Roberts Gilman, "Chalmers, John Gordon," and James Hays McLendon, "Lewis, Mark B.," *NHT*, II, 27, IV, 180; Smithwick, *Evolution of a State*, 206; Lorna Geer Sheppard, *An Editor's View of Early Texas: Texas in the Days of the Republic as Depicted in the Northern Standard (1842–1846)* (Austin: Eakin Press, 1998), 142–143.

55. "Growth and Decay of a Town," *Supplement to the Connecticut Courant (Hartford)*, Dec. 14, 1844; James Webb to Mirabeau Lamar, May 4, 1843, Gulick et al. (eds.), *Papers of Mirabeau Lamar*, IV, 20.

NOTES TO CHAPTER 7

1. John Nathan Cravens, *James Harper Starr: Financier of the Republic of Texas* (Austin: Daughters of the Republic of Texas, 1950), 73–74, 77–78, 82–85, 105–106, 111–112; Linda Sybert Hudson, "Starr, James Harper," *NHT*, VI, 66.

2. James Harper Star to TWW, July 9, 1843, #89.1, Ward Papers.

3. TWW to James Harper Starr, July 31, 1843, #751, Starr Papers (1st quotation); TWW, Report to the President and Congress, Nov. 15, 1843, ESA (Early Letters Sent), roll 1, part 2, vol. 3, pp. 287–289 (2nd and 3rd quotations).

4. *Texas State Gazette* (Austin), Dec. 29, 1849 (quotation); Carroll, *Homesteads Ungovernable*, xix, 163–164.

5. Sam Houston to the House of Representatives, Jan. 4, 1843, Williams and Barker (eds.), *Writings of Sam Houston*, III, 265–266; John Chenoweth to Sam Houston, Feb. 1, 1843 (TSA), photocopy in Ward Papers.

6. TWW, Postscript to letter to Matthew Woodhouse, Jan. 8, 1843, #2820, A. J. Houston Collection; TWW to the Committee of the People of Austin in possession of the Land Office Records, Jan. 24, 1843, #U186, Ward Papers (quotation).

7. Joshua Holden to TWW, Jan. 31, 1843, #U187, Ward Papers (quotation); *Telegraph and Texas Register* (Houston), Feb. 22, 1843.

8. TWW, Proclamation to the Citizens of Texas, Mar. 7, 1843, #U183 (1st quotation), Joshua Holden to TWW, Mar. 27, 1843, #U188 (2nd quotation), and TWW to the Committee in possession of the General Land Office records, Mar. 27, 1843, #U189, Ward Papers.

9. TWW to B. Menard, May 25, 1843, ESA (Early Letters Sent), roll 1, part 2, vol. 3, p. 244 (quotation); Walter Winn and Nathaniel Mitchell to TWW, Feb. 1, 1843, #279, Ward Papers; *Journals of the House of Representatives of the Eighth Congress*, pp. 288–293.

10. Joshua Holden to the People of Bastrop County, Apr. 12, 1843, General Land Office Correspondence, photocopy in Ward Papers.

11. Ben Procter, "Washington-on-the-Brazos, 1842–1845" in *Capitols of Texas* (Waco: Texian Press, 1970), 107–108; J. W. Scott to TWW, Apr. 16, 1845, #2508, Box 2-10/6, General Land Office Correspondence; Stanley Siegel, *Big Men Walked Here! The Story of Washington-on-the-Brazos* (Austin: Jenkins Pub. Co., 1971), 49 (quotations); Herbert Gambrell, *Anson Jones: The Last President of Texas* (2nd ed.; Austin: University of Texas Press, 1964), 265–268, 366; J. K. Holland, "Reminiscences of Austin and Old Washington," *Quarterly of the Texas State Historical Association*, 1 (Oct. 1897), 93.

12. Llerena B. Friend, *Sam Houston: The Great Designer* (Austin: University of Texas Press, 1969), 109; Siegel, *Big Men Walked Here*, 51–53.

13. TWW, Proclamation, Apr. 25, 1843, Ward Papers.

14. TWW to B. Gillespie, Oct. 5, 1843, ESA (Early Letters Sent), roll 1, part 2, vol. 3, p. 278 (quotation); TWW, Proclamation to the Citizens of Texas, Mar. 7, 1843, #U183. Ward stated in his proclamation that the seal was in the records held by the Austinites. There is no further evidence as to its fate. Even after getting his records back from the Austinites, Ward waited for a replacement before issuing patents. For more information, see Jesús F. de la Teja, "A Short History of the General Land Office Seals," *SHQ*, 90 (Jan., 1987), 296–299.

15. TWW, Report to the President and Congress, Nov. 15, 1843, ESA (Early Letters Sent), roll 1, part 2, vol. 3, p. 287 (1st quotation); TWW to Franklin Hardin, July 10, 1843, and TWW to E. Jones, Aug. 12, 1843 (2nd quotation), ESA (Early Letters Sent), roll 1, part 2, vol. 3, pp. 259, 271.

16. TWW to L. C. Stanley, Oct. 1, 1843 (quotation), and TWW to W. Y. M. Farlane, Oct. 11, 1843, ESA (Early Letters Sent), roll 1, part 2, vol. 3, pp. 277, 279–280.

17. TWW to A. Harper, May 31, 1843, and TWW to E. H. King, July 10, 1843 (quotation), ESA (Early Letters Sent), roll 1, part 2, vol. 3, pp. 245–246, 257–258.

18. James Harper Star to TWW, July 9, 1843, #89.1, Ward Papers; TWW to James Harper Starr, July 31, 1843, #751, Starr Papers (quotations).

19. James Reily to TWW, Mar. 21, 1843, #70, Ward Papers; TWW to Sam Houston, Jan. 1, 1844, #2803, A. J. Houston Collection.

20. James Reily to TWW, Nov. 23, # 79, Dec. 21, #80 (1st quotation), 1843, Ward Papers; De Cordova, *Texas*, 162 (2nd quotation). Regarding the source of the biographical information on Ward in De Cordova's *Texas*, 26.

21. Charles W. Brown, "Hamilton, James," *NHT,* III, 428–429 ; De Cordova, *Texas,* 162 (quotation).

22. TWW, Report to the President and Congress, Nov. 15, 1843, ESA (Early Letters Sent), roll 1, part 2, vol. 3, pp. 297–298 (quotations); Madge Evalene Pierce, "The Service of James Hamilton to the Republic of Texas" (M.A. thesis, University of Texas at Austin, 1933), 108–109.

23. James Reily to TWW, Nov. 23, #79 (1st quotation), Dec. 21, #80 (2nd quotation), Dec. 31, #71 (3rd quotation), 1843, Ward Papers; Winkler (ed.), *Secret Journals of the Senate,* 281, 283.

24. Sam Houston to TWW, Dec. 28, 1843, Williams and Barker (eds.), *Writings of Sam Houston,* III, 499; TWW to Emelie Simler, Jan. 11, 1844, ESA (Early Letters Sent), roll 1, part 2, vol. 3, pp. 328; *Journals of the House of Representatives of the Eighth Congress,* 281.

25. *Journals of the House of Representatives of the Eighth Congress,* 283 (quotations), 289–296; TWW to Sam Houston, Jan. 12 and 14, 1844, #U194, Ward Papers; TWW, Report to the President, Senate, and House, Oct. 2, 1844, pp. 1–2, typescript, Correspondence, 1842–1844, Concerning the "Archive War."

26. *Journals of the House of Representatives of the Eighth Congress,* 284–285 (2nd and 3rd quotations); TWW to Sam Houston, Jan. 12 and 14, 1844, #U194, Ward Papers (1st and 4th quotations).

27. *Journals of the House of Representatives of the Eighth Congress,* 286.

28. Greenberg, *Honor & Slavery,* xiii, 8 (1st quotation); Edwin Morehouse to TWW, Jan. 28, 1844, #127 (2nd quotation), and H. G. Catlett to TWW, Jan. 25, 1844, #124, Ward Papers; TWW to the Speaker of the House of Representatives, Jan. 25, 1844 (TSA), photocopy in Ward Papers; *Journals of the House of Representatives of the Eighth Congress,* 389.

29. *Journals of the House of Representatives of the Eighth Congress,* 286; TWW, A Card, Feb. 3, 1844, #U34, Ward Papers (quotations); Campbell, *Gone to Texas,* 231.

30. *Telegraph and Texas Register* (Houston), Apr. 17, 1844; TWW to James Shaw, Mar. 20, 1844, Connor (ed.), *Texas Treasury Papers,* III, 995–996 (quotation).

31. TWW, Report to the President, Senate, and House, Oct. 2, 1842, p. 1, typescript, Correspondence, 1842–1844, Concerning the "Archive War" (1st and 2nd quotations); TWW to G. W. Glasscock, Mar. 14, 1844, #1878, Box 2-10/5 General Land Office Correspondence (3rd quotation).

32. Mirabeau Lamar to TWW, Feb. 6, 1844, #U39, Ward Papers. A sketch of the Moreland House, together with the Quartermaster's Department, is in the Julia Lee Sinks Papers. One of Austin's original buildings, the Quartermaster's Department is building #7 in the sketch of Congress Avenue prepared by Edward Hall in 1840 and printed in *Austin & Travis County: A Pictorial History, 1839–1939* (Austin: Encino Press, 1975), 3.

33. *Southern Intelligencer* (Austin), Mar. 29, 1866 (1st quotation); TWW to James Shaw, Mar. 20, 1844, *Texas Treasury Papers,* III, 996 (2nd quotation); Sheppard, *An Editor's View of Early Texas,* 36.

34. W. Eugene Hollon and Ruth Lapham Butler (eds.), *William Bollaert's Texas* (Norman: University of Oklahoma Press, 1956), 195–198 (quotations); *Report of the Commissioner to the 9th Congress,* 22; TWW to Sam Houston, Apr. 23, 1844, #112, Ward Papers.

35. Stephen Cummings to TWW, Feb. 18, 1844, General Land Office Correspondence,

photocopy in Ward Papers (quotation); *Telegraph and Texas Register* (Houston), Apr. 17, 1844.

36. TWW to Sam Houston, Mar. 30, 1844, A. J. Houston Collection (quotation); TWW to B. F. Johnston, Apr. 26, 1844, TWW to B. J. White, July 22, 1844, and TWW to J. B. Miller, Aug. 8, 1844, ESA (Early Letters Sent), roll 1, part 2, vol. 3, pp. 353, 385, 393; De la Teja, "Short History of the General Land Office Seals," 296–299; *Northern Standard* (Clarksville), June 15, 1844.

37. *Telegraph and Texas Register* (Houston), Aug. 21, 1844 (1st quotation), Apr. 30, June 18, 1845; James O'Hara to Anson Jones, May 12, 1844, ESA (Early Letters Sent), roll 1, part 2, vol. 3, p. 338 (2nd quotation); *Report of the Commissioner to the 9th Congress*, 3–4.

38. *Report of the Commissioner to the 9th Congress*, 4–8; An Act amendatory to the various Land Laws and to establish Land Districts and for other purposes, Jan. 14, 1845, File 2921, 9th Congress, Congressional Bill Files (TSA); A. Ray Stephens and William M. Holmes, *Historical Atlas of Texas* (Norman: University of Oklahoma Pres, 1989), #30.

39. TWW to Lemuel D. Evans, Aug. 18, 1845, ESA (Early Letters Sent), roll 1, part 2, vol. 4, pp. 82–83 (1st quotation); *Report of the Commissioner to the 9th Congress*, 8–10; TWW to Surveyor of —— County (Circular), Feb. 21, 1845 (2nd quotation), and TWW to M. B. Lewis, Mar. 19, 1845, "Report of Commissioners, Feb. 15, 1845 to Jan. 19, 1891," pp. 14–19, 36 (TGLO). Following up Ward's recommendations in his 1843 annual report to Congress, a House committee introduced a bill in January 1844 to "produce more uniformity and system" in the General Land Office by granting the commissioner much more explicit and comprehensive authority over county surveyors, though they would still be elected, not appointed. The bill, however, died in committee. See the *Journals of the House of Representatives of the Eighth Congress*, 105–107, 150, and File 2796, Jan. 5, 1844, 8th Congress, Congressional Bill Files (quotation).

40. *Report of the Commissioner to the 9th Congress*, 12–14 (1st quotation); R. C. Trimble to TWW, Apr. 5, 1845, #2414 (2nd quotation), and David Hill to TWW, June 19, 1845, #2673, Box 2-10/6, General Land Office Correspondence. See also Starling, *Land Is the Cry*, 94–96.

41. Smithwick, *Evolution of a State*, 200 (quotation); Andrew Briscoe to TWW, Mar. 26, 1845, #64.1, Ward Papers.

42. TWW to Daniel Rowlett, May 3, 1845, ESA (Early Letters Sent), roll 1, part 2, vol. 4, pp. 55–56 (quotations); TWW to Thomas Rusk, Nov. 21, 1847, General Correspondence, Rusk Papers.

43. An Act amendatory of the various Land Laws and to establish Land Districts and for other purposes, Jan. 24, 1845, File 2937, 9th Congress, Congressional Bill Files; *Report of the Commissioner to the 9th Congress*, 8–9.

44. TWW to John M. Lewis, Jan. 4, 1845, and TWW to Daniel Rowlett, May 3, 1845, ESA (Early Letters Sent), roll 1, part 2, vol. 3, p. 482, vol. 4, p. 56; An Act amendatory to the various Land Laws and to establish Land Districts and for other purposes, Jan. 14, 1845, File 2921, 9th Congress, Congressional Bill Files; David Kaufman to TWW, Jan. 13, 1845, #2366, Box 2-10/6, General Land Office Correspondence (1st quotation); *Journals of the Senate of the Ninth Congress of the Republic of Texas* (Washington, Tex.: Miller & Cushney, 1845), 139, 141–142, 145; *Texas National Register* (Washington-on-the-Brazos), Feb. 8, 1845 (2nd quotation).

45. *Telegraph and Texas Register* (Houston), Dec. 25, 1844; David Kaufman to TWW, June 18, 1844, Box 2-10/5, and Jan. 13, 1845, #2366, Box 2-10/6 (quotations), General Land Office Correspondence.

46. *Texas National Register* (Washington-on-the-Brazos), Feb. 8, 1845 (1st quotation); TWW to James Harper Starr, Aug. 20, 1844, #762, Starr Papers (2nd quotation).

47. *Telegraph and Texas Register* (Houston), Jan. 22, 1845; David Kaufman to TWW, Jan. 13, 1845, #2366, Box 2-10/6, General Land Office Correspondence (1st quotation); TWW to Thomas Rusk, Nov. 21, 1847, General Correspondence, Rusk Papers; TWW to Daniel Rowlett, May 3, 1845, ESA (Early Letters Sent), roll 1, part 2, vol. 4, p. 56 (2nd quotation).

48. *Texas National Register* (Washington-on-the-Brazos), Feb. 8, 1845 (1st quotation); *Journals of the Senate of the Ninth Congress*, 219, 228, 234–235; TWW to James O'Hara, Jan. 27, 1845, General Land Office Correspondence, photocopy in Ward Papers (2nd quotation); TWW to George B. Erath, Mar. 25, 1845, ESA (Early Letters Sent), roll 1, part 2, vol. 4, p. 39 (3rd and 4th quotations).

49. *Journals of the Senate of the Ninth Congress*, 248; *Journals of the House of Representatives of the Ninth Congress of the Republic of Texas* (Washington, Tex.: Miller & Cushney, 1845), 350, 374; TWW to Daniel Rowlett, May 3, 1845 (quotation), and TWW to Lemuel Evans, Aug. 18, 1845, ESA (Early Letters Sent), roll 1, part 2, vol. 4, pp. 55, 83.

50. Gammel, *Laws of Texas*, II, 1145; TWW to Adolphus Sterne, Mar. 18, 1845, ESA (Early Letters Sent), roll 1, part 2, vol. 4, p. 30 (quotation); *Telegraph and Texas Register* (Houston), May 14, 1845; *Land Commissioners of Texas*, 104–106.

51. Ira Munson to Anson Jones, Mar. 8, 1845, Jones, *Memoranda and Official Correspondence*, 437–438.

NOTES TO CHAPTER 8

1. Nathan Washington Marston, *The Marston Genealogy in Two Parts* (South Lubec, Maine: n.p., 1888), 257; Petition of TWW and SLW, Mar. 27, 1858, Case No. 1522, DCTC.

2. SLW to TWW, June 20, #210 (1st quotation), July 8, #212 (2nd quotation), 1846, Ward Papers; Probate of Thomas Marston's Estate, Case #72, Probate Minutes, Travis County, vol. A, p. 382 (microfilm; AHC); Ashbel Smith to John Bauer, Mar. 22, 1845, Letters, Jan–June 1845, Ashbel Smith Papers.

3. John Farmer and Jacob B. Moore, *A Gazetteer of the State of New-Hampshire* (Concord, N.H.: Jacob B. Moore, 1823), 91; F. B. Eaton, *History of Candia: Once Known as Charmingfare; With Notices of Some of the Early Families* (Manchester, N.H.: Press of the Granite Farmer, 1852), 129, 137, 141; J. Bailey Moore, *History of the Town of Candia, Rockingham County, N. H., From Its First Settlement to the Present Time* (Manchester, N.H.: George W. Browne, 1893), 39, 220–221, 254, 294.

4. Thomas Lang, "Candia, N. H., Brief History: with Notices of the Early Families" (typescript, 1899), 59, 63–64 (Smyth Public Library, Candia); *Trow's New York City Directory for the Year Ending May 1, 1856* (New York: John F. Trow, 1855), 61, appendix, 61; Thomas Earle and Charles T. Congdon (eds.), *Annals of the General Society of Mechanics and Tradesmen of the City of New-York, from 1785 to 1880* (New York: Published by Order of the Society, 1882), 135, 140.

5. SLW to TWW, Nov. 8, 1846, #224, and Mary Curtis Bean to TWW, Mar. 26, 1847, #343 (quotation), Ward Papers.

6. *General Catalogue of Bowdoin College and the Medical School of Maine: A Biographical Record of Alumni and Officers, 1794–1950* (Portland, Maine: Anthoensen Press, 1950), 442; Marston, *Marston Genealogy*, 257; Elliot C. Cogswell, *History of Nottingham, Deerfield, & Northwood* (1878; reprint, Somersworth: New Hampshire Pub. Co., 1972), 429–430; SLW to TWW, Sept. 4, 1846, #217, Ward Papers; SLW to Lucadia Pease, Feb. 13, 1855, S.1, Pease Papers (quotation).

7. Mary Curtis Bean to TWW, Mar. 26, 1847, #343, and SLW to TWW, July 8, #212 (2nd quotation), Nov. 1, #223, 1846, Ward Papers; Moses Johnson to Olivia Johnson, Aug. 5, 1846, Personal Correspondence to Wife, Moses Johnson Papers (CAH) (1st quotation).

8. Aaron Bean to TWW, June 30, 1847, #392 (1st quotation), and SLW to TWW, Nov. 8, 1846, #224 (2nd quotation), Ward Papers.

9. Deeds, Feb. 11, Mar. 9, 1844, Harris County Deed Record, Book I, pp. 299–301, 306–308; United States Seventh Census (1850), Travis County, Texas, Population Schedules, City of Austin, #319 (microfilm; NA).

10. Mary Curtis Bean to TWW, Mar. 26, 1847, #343 (1st quotation), SLW to TWW, June 11, 1846, #209 (2nd quotation), and Charles B. Smyth, Deposition (Answers to Interrogatories), [May–June 1860], p. 11, Ward Papers.

11. SLW to TWW, June 20, #210 (1st quotation), Oct. 11 and 18, 1846, #222 (2nd and 3rd quotations), 1846, Ward Papers.

12. SLW to TWW, June 6, 1845, #366 (quotation), and John S. Ford, Medical Bill, Aug. 8, 1845, #252, Ward Papers.

13. TWW, Answers to Interrogatories, Jan. 16, 1861, attachment, pp. 13–14, Case No. 1958, DCTC; E. G. Perkins to TWW, May 28, 1846, #205, Jonathan Hull to TWW, June 19, 1846, #37, and SLW to TWW, Aug. 9, #213, Aug. 15, #214 (quotation), Sept. 27, #220, Nov. 1, #223, 1846, Ward Papers; Republic Claims, Audited Claims, TWW, Claim #2192; SLW, Complaint to Supreme Court, New York City, Mar. 22, 1859, p. 13 [26], NYCC.

14. Ashbel Smith to John Bauer, Mar. 22, 1845, Letters, Jan–June 1845, Ashbel Smith Papers (1st quotation); *Northern Standard* (Clarksville), Aug. 9, 1845 (2nd quotation); James K. Greer (ed.), *Buck Barry, Texas Ranger and Frontiersman* (1978; reprint, Lincoln: University of Nebraska Press, [1984]), 22–23; William A. McClintock, "Journal of a Trip Through Texas and Northern Mexico in 1846–1847," *SHQ*, 34 (July, 1930), 31 (3rd quotation).

15. Moses Johnson to Olivia Johnson, Aug. 26, 29 (1st quotation), 1845, Personal Correspondence to Wife, Moses Johnson Papers; Anson Jones to TWW, Sept. 24, 1849, #575 (2nd quotation), Dudley Bean to TWW, Mar. 26, 1846, #339 (3rd quotation), Stephen Crosby to TWW, Dec. 25, 1845, #581, and Jonathan Hull to TWW, Dec. 23, 1844, #15 (4th quotation), Ward Papers; W. B. Ochiltree to Anson Jones, Aug. 6, 1845, Jones, *Memoranda and Official Correspondence*, 483.

16. Aaron Bean to TWW, Oct. 30, 1845, #330, Feb. 1, 1847, #282 (2nd quotation), Ward Papers; SLW, Complaint to Supreme Court, New York City, Mar. 22, 1859, p. 6 [13], NYCC (1st quotation); Brown, "Annals of Travis County," ch. XII, 8. See note 26 below regarding the pagination of SLW's complaint.

17. *New-York City Directory for 1844 & 1845* (New York: John Doggett, Jr., 1844), 32; United States Seventh Census (1850), New York County, New York, Population Schedules, 15th Ward, Western Half, Dwelling #989, Family #1576 (microfilm; NA).

18. Mary Y. Bean to TWW, July 12, 1846, #132, SLW to TWW, June 11, #209, Sept. 20, #219, Nov. 8, #224 (1st quotation), 1846, and Joanna Bean to TWW, Nov. 15, 1846, #130 (2nd quotation), Ward Papers.

19. Joanna Bean to TWW, June 27, 1847, #383, and Aaron Bean to TWW, Oct. 30, 1845, #330, Feb. 8, 1847, #283, Ward Papers; *Texas Democrat* (Austin), Apr. 8, 1846.

20. *South Western American* (Austin), July 21, 1852 (quotation); Hafertepe, *Abner Cook*, 40–43.

21. SLW to TWW, Aug. 9, #213, Aug. 15, #214 (2nd quotation), Oct. 11 and 18, 1846, #222 (1st quotation), 1846, Ward Papers; *South Western American* (Austin), July 21, 1852. Ward stated that the house and grounds covered seven lots when advertising the property for sale in 1852, but at the time of the house's completion in 1847 the grounds may have covered no more than three or four lots.

22. SLW to TWW, Aug. 9, #213, Oct. 4, #221 (1st quotation), Oct. 11 and 18, #222, Nov. 8, #224 (2nd and 3rd quotations), 1846, Ward Papers; Joanna Bean to TWW, June 27, 1847, #383, and Jonathan Hull to TWW, Dec. 14, 1846, #296, Ward Papers; *South Western American* (Austin), July 21, 1852. Ward stated that the house had eleven rooms plus a kitchen and dark cellar in a "For Sale" notice placed in the July 21, 1852, edition of the *South Western American*.

23. Hafertepe, *Abner Cook*, 40–43; *South Western American*, July 21, 1852 (quotations); Lucadia Pease to Juliet Niles, July 12, Oct. 6, 1854, Katherine Hart and Elizabeth Kemp (eds.), *Lucadia Pease & the Governor, Letters: 1850–1857* (Austin: Encino Press, 1974), 198, 207; Henry Jewett to TWW, Nov. 24, 1847, #512, Ward Papers.

24. SLW to TWW, June 11, #209 (2nd quotation), Sept. 20, #219 (1st quotation), Nov. 16, #225.1 (4th quotation), 1846, and Joanna Bean to TWW, Nov. 15, 1846, #130, (3rd quotation), Ward Papers

25. SLW to TWW, Mar. 17, 1854, #U139, Ward Papers.

26. SLW, Complaint to Supreme Court, New York City, Mar. 22, 1859, pp. 1–40 [1–98], and TWW, Answer to SLW's Complaint of March 22, 1859, May 7, 1859, pp. 1–29 [1–74], NYCC; Norma Basch, *Framing American Divorce: From the Revolutionary Generation to the Victorians* (Berkeley: University of California Press, 1999), 6 (2nd quotation), 57 (1st quotation), 97, 103. The numbers in brackets for both SLW's complaint and her husband's answer are folio numbers and appear in the left hand margin of the documents.

27. SLW to TWW, June 11, #209 (1st quotation), July 8, #212 (2nd quotation), 1846, Ward Papers; SLW, Complaint to Supreme Court, New York City, Mar. 22, 1859, pp. 6–7 (3rd quotation), 19, 22–26 [14–17, 46, 53–63], and TWW, Answer to SLW's Complaint of March 22, 1859, May 7, 1859, pp. 5–6, 15–17, [11–14, 38–43], NYCC; SLW to Lucadia Pease, Sept. 29, 1856, S.1, Pease Papers.

28. Hendrik Hartog, *Man and Wife in America: A History* (Cambridge, Mass.: Harvard University Press, 2000), 29 (1st and 2nd quotations), 31, 64, 72, 101, 104, 113, 115, 136, 149–150; SLW to Lucadia Pease, May 14, 1854 (3rd quotation), Sept. 24, 1856 (4th quotation), S.1, Pease Papers.

29. Walsh, "Austin in the Making," 5th installment, Vertical File: Austin History; SLW to TWW, July 5, 1846 (on back of last page of letter of June 20), #210, Ward Papers.

30. SLW to Lucadia Pease, Sept. 24, 1855, S.1, Pease Papers.

NOTES TO CHAPTER 9

1. TWW, Answer to SLW's Petition of March 26, 1860, n.d., p. 10, Ward Papers (1st quotation); James Mayfield to TWW, Nov. 24, 1843, #102, Ward Papers (2nd quotation).

2. Gloria T. Sanders, *Lower Limb Amputations: A Guide to Rehabilitation* (Philadelphia, F. A. Davis Co., 1986), 18–19; Atha Thomas and Chester C. Haddan, *Amputation Prosthesis: Anatomic and Physiologic Considerations, with Principles of Alignment and Fitting Designed for the Surgeon and Limb Manufacturer* (Philadelphia: J. B. Lippincott., 1945), 5; Faries, *Limbs for the Limbless*, 32–33, 46–48.

3. Susan Bean to TWW, Aug. 9, 1846, #213, Aaron Bean to TWW, May 6, #325, July 25, Nov. 13, #429 (2nd quotation), 1847, Jan. 11, 1848, #483 (1st quotation), James Collins to TWW, June 3, 1847, #380.1, and William Selpho to TWW, Jan. 1, 1847, #299, Ward Papers; McDaid, "'How a One-Legged Rebel Lives,'" 122; Stephen Mihm, "'A Limb Which Shall Be Presentable in Polite Society': Prosthetic Technologies in the Nineteenth Century," 284.

4. Sanders, *Lower Limb Amputations*, 20–21; Charles F. Stansbury, *Testimony in the Matter of the Application of B. Frank Palmer for the Extension of His Patent for an Artificial Leg* (Philadelphia: C. Sherman & Son, 1862), 4–9; Aaron Bean to TWW, June 20, 1855, TWW's Accounts with Aaron Bean, Nov. 20, 1855 and "1846," and Patrick Rooney to TWW, Mar. 31, 1860, #652 (quotation), Ward Papers; Gammel, *Laws of Texas*, III, 1251.

5. Mihm, "'A Limb Which Shall Be Presentable in Polite Society,'" 288–289 (1st quotation); TWW, Circular, Apr. 1851, DB 1850–1853, Broadside Collection (CAH) (2nd quotation); TWW to SLW, Feb. 16, 1854, #U197, Ward Papers (3rd quotation); TWW to M. H. Bowers, Mar. 15, 1871, General Correspondence, 1870–1872, Marmion H. Bowers Papers (CAH); Vitali, *Amputations and Prostheses*, 6; B. Frank Palmer, *The Patent Palmer Arm and Leg: Adopted for the U. S. Army and Navy* ([Philadelphia?: American Artificial Limb Co.?], 1866), 4. The probable diagnosis of osteomyelitis is based on conversations with orthopedic surgeon Geraldine Richter, M.D., on May 4, 2001, and rheumatologist John Lawson, M.D., on May 23, 2004.

6. Adolphus Sterne to James Harper Starr, Mar. 1, 1848, #768, Starr Papers; John D. McLeod to Thomas Rusk, Mar. 26, 1848, General Correspondence, Rusk Papers.

7. Campbell, *Gone to Texas*, 184–185; Thomas Rusk to TWW, July 30, 1845, #2522, Box 2-10/6, General Land Office Correspondence; *Journals of the Convention, Assembled at the City of Austin on the Fourth of July, 1845, for the Purpose of Framing a Constitution for the State of Texas* (1845; reprint, Austin: Shoal Creek Publishers, 1974), 145.

8. Moses Johnson to Olivia Johnson, Aug. 23, 1845, Personal Correspondence to Wife, Moses Johnson Papers (quotation); *Northern Standard* (Clarksville), Aug. 9, 1845; *Journals of the Convention*, 145–47.

9. *Journals of the Convention*, 163–165, 362.

10. *South-Western American* (Austin), July 16, 1851 (1st quotation); TWW, Circular, Apr. 1851, DB 1850–1853, Broadside Collection (2nd quotation); TWW to John Gray, Aug. 4,

1847, "Report of Commissioners, Feb. 15, 1845 to Jan. 19, 1891," p. 224; *Northern Standard* (Clarksville), June 14, 1851 (3rd quotation); *Journals of the Convention*, 164; *Texas Democrat* (Austin), Aug. 4, 1849 (4th quotation).

11. Samuel Huffer to TWW, July 17, 1844, #2077, Box 2-10/5, and H. L. Upshur to TWW, Aug. 27, 1845, #2709, Box 2-10/7 (1st and 3rd quotations), General Land Office Correspondence; *Northern Standard* (Clarksville), Aug. 9, 1845 (2nd quotation), June 14, 1851. Red River County at the time included present-day Titus and Franklin Counties and part of Morris County.

12. Lack, *Texas Revolutionary Experience*, 91–92. Regarding eleven league claims, the constitution of the Republic of Texas (1836) stated that "all eleven league claims, located within twenty leagues of the boundary line between Texas and the United States of America, which have been located contrary to the laws of Mexico, are hereby declared to be null and void."

13. *Northern Standard* (Clarksville), Jan. 28, 1843 (quotation); Gammel, *Laws of Texas*, II, 641–643; TWW to John Harris, Apr. 13, 1847, "Report of Commissioners, Feb. 15, 1845 to Jan. 19, 1891," pp. 88–89.

14. TWW to Lemuel Evans, Aug. 18, 1845, ESA (Early Letters Sent), roll 1, part 2, vol. 4, p. 83; James Harper Starr to TWW, June 19, 1847, #388, Ward Papers (1st quotation); *Journals of the House of Representatives of the State of Texas, Second Legislature* (Houston: Telegraph Office, 1848), 528 (2nd quotation); *Northern Standard* (Clarksville), July 5, 1851. For an excellent discussion of conflicts over Spanish and Mexican land grants in South Texas and the strong emotions generated by the issue, see Galen D. Greaser and Jesús F. de la Teja, "Quieting Title to Spanish and Mexican Land Grants in the Trans-Nueces: The Bourland and Miller Commission, 1850–1852," *SHQ*, 95 (Apr., 1992), 445–464.

15. *Red-Lander* (San Augustine), Dec. 11, 1845 (all quotations except Sam Houston's); Sam Houston to TWW, June 1, 1848, #556, Ward Papers; *Northern Standard* (Clarksville), June 14, 1851.

16. Stephen Crosby to TWW, Dec. 25, 1845, #581, Ward Papers (quotation); Cravens, *James Harper Starr*, 84; An Act to establish the central Railway Company, March 1846, #398, Ward Papers.

17. *Texas Democrat* (Austin), Mar. 11, 1846 (quotations); Comer Clay, "The Colorado River Raft," *SHQ*, 52 (Apr. 1949), 419.

18. *Journals of the Convention*, 165; *Journals of the House of Representatives of the First Legislature of the State of Texas* (Clarksville, Tex.: Standard Office, 1848), 260. On February 17, two days before the republic came to an end and Texas became a state, Stephen Crosby, chief clerk of the Land Office, reported to President Anson Jones that since the last meeting of Congress, 3,735 patents had been issued for 5,710,575 acres. See Stephen Crosby to Anson Jones, Feb. 17, 1846, ESA (Early Letters Sent), roll 1, part 2, vol. 4, p. 105.

19. De Cordova, *Texas*, pp. 70–73; TWW, A Bill To be entitled an Act to establish a Genl Land Office for the State of Texas, #395, Ward Papers.

20. *Journals of the House of Representatives of the First Legislature*, 235–236; *Journals of the Senate of the First Legislature of the State of Texas* (Clarksville, Tex.: Standard Office, 1848), 178; Senate Bill No. 68, 1st Legislature, An act to establish a General Land Office of the State of Texas, Congressional Bill Files.

21. *Journals of the Senate of the First Legislature*, 202–203, 255, 259, 269, 274, 313–314, 318–319, 324–325, 327–328, 331–332 ; *Journals of the House of Representatives of the First Legislature*, 672–673; *Texas Democrat* (Austin), May 13 (quotations), Nov. 18, 1846; Gammel, *Laws of Texas*, II, 1538–1541.

22. *Journals of the House of Representatives of the First Legislature*, 711, 719; *Journals of the Senate of the First Legislature*, 330; *Northern Standard* (Clarksville), June 14, 1851 (quotation); Sheppard, *An Editor's View of Early Texas*, 15, 33; Ernest Wallace, *Charles DeMorse: Pioneer Editor and Statesman* (Lubbock: Texas Tech Press, 1943), 60.

23. James Reily to TWW, Apr. 2, 1847, #317, Ward Papers.

24. *Texas Democrat* (Austin), May 13, 1846; *Journals of the House of Representatives, Second Legislature*, 848; *Journals of the House of Representatives of the First Legislature*, 618 (quotation).

25. TWW to Asa Mitchell, July 24, 1846, ESA (Early Letters Sent), roll 1, part 2, vol. 4, p. 110 (1st quotation); Charles Pressler to his family in Germany, March–April 1847, Mrs. Harry Barnhart Collection (TSA) (other quotations); Charles Pressler to TWW, Dec. 12, 1847, #447, Ward Papers. Though known to Ward and others in Austin as Charles William Pressler, "Charles William" was actually an Anglicized form of his name, Karl Wilhelm Pressler.

26. In his December 1847 annual report Ward told the legislature that 6,429 patents had been issued since its previous meeting in February–May 1846. See TWW, Report to Governor Henderson and the Legislature, December 1847, *Journals of the House of Representatives, Second Legislature*, 129. However, the table of patents issued under each president and governor, prepared by the General Land Office, indicates that 4,813 patents were issued between February 18, 1846, and December 30, 1847. See *Land Commissioners of Texas*, 104–107.

27. *Texas Democrat* (Austin), Dec. 22, 1847 (quotation); J. Pinckney Henderson, Appointment of TWW as Commissioner of the General Land Office, Dec. 22, 1846, #407, Ward Papers.

28. James Harper Starr to TWW, July 5, 1846, #2859, Box 2-10/7, General Land Office Correspondence; Seymour V. Connor, *The Peters Colony of Texas: A History and Biographical Sketches of the Early Settlers* (Austin: Texas State Historical Association, 1959), 88–89.

29. TWW to William G. Banks, Feb. 15, 1845 (quotation), TWW to James Howlett, Apr. 3, 1845, TWW to A. A. Nelson, May 19, 1845, TWW to Jacob Snively, Apr. 20, 1847, and TWW to J. Tinkle, July 26, 1847, "Report of Commissioners, Feb. 15, 1845 to Jan. 19, 1891," pp. 1, 28, 35–36, 90, 103; TWW to James Harper Starr, May 26, 1845, #763, Starr Papers.

30. TWW, A Bill To be entitled an Act to establish a Genl Land Office for the State of Texas, #395, Ward Papers; Gammel, *Laws of Texas*, II, 1539; Charles A. Pressler, "Pressler, Karl Wilhelm," *NHT*, V, 334; TWW, Report to Governor Henderson and the Legislature, December 1847, *Journals of the House of Representatives, Second Legislature*, 130 (quotation); Moore, "Mapping Texas Public Lands," 9.

31. James Harper Starr to TWW, June 19, 1847, #388, Ward Papers; TWW to James Harper Starr, July 27, 1847, #766, Starr Papers (quotation); TWW, Report to Governor Henderson and the Legislature, December, 1847, *Journals of the House of Representatives, Second Legislature*, 120.

32. Hafertepe, *Abner Cook*, 74, 93; John McLeod to Thomas Rusk, Aug. 20, 1847, Gen-

eral Correspondence, Rusk Papers (quotation); TWW, Report to Governor Henderson and the Legislature, December, 1847, *Journals of the House of Representatives, Second Legislature*, 120–121.

33. Texas State Library & Archives Commission, "Bell to the Texas Senate, January 31, 1850," <http://www.tsl.state.tx.us/governors/earlystate/bell-to-senate.html> [Accessed Nov. 6, 2004]; *Texas State Gazette* (Austin), Mar. 29, 1851; Dorman Winfrey, "Austin, 1853–1881," in *Capitols of Texas*, 125 (quotation); Hafertepe, *Abner Cook*, 56–57.

34. John McLeod to Thomas Rusk, Aug. 20, Oct. 10 (1st quotation), Nov. 14 (2nd and 3rd quotations), 1847, General Correspondence, Rusk Papers.

35. *Northern Standard* (Clarksville), Mar. 4, 1848.

36. *Journals of the House of Representatives, Second Legislature*, 155–156, 188–190, 247, 267–272; John McLeod to Thomas Rusk, Jan. 1, 1848 (1st quotation), General Correspondence, Rusk Papers; *Northern Standard* (Clarksville), Jan. 29 (3rd quotation), Mar. 4, (2nd quotation), 1848; TWW to James Harper Starr, Jan. 14, 1848, #767, Starr Papers.

37. *Journals of the House of Representatives, Second Legislature*, 286 (1st quotation), 290–291, 536; Adolphus Sterne to James Harper Starr, Jan. 27, 1848 #768, Starr Papers (2nd quotation).

38. Adolphus Sterne to James Harper Starr, Jan. 27, 1848 #768, Starr Papers; John McLeod to Thomas Rusk, Feb. 20, 1848, General Correspondence Rusk Papers.

39. John McLeod to Thomas Rusk, Feb. 20, 1848, General Correspondence, Rusk Papers (1st and 3rd quotations); Adolphus Sterne to James Harper Starr, Mar. 1, 1848, #768 (2nd quotation), and TWW to James Harper Starr, Feb. 9, 1848, #767 (4th quotation), Starr Papers; R. J. White to Thomas Rusk, Feb. 28, 1847 [1848], General Correspondence, Rusk Papers. The commissioner had added reason to feel aggrieved by Reagan, beyond the impugning of his integrity. As chairman of the Committee on Public Lands, Reagan pushed through a law that threatened to undermine Ward's system of permanent land districts. Arguing that people needed more convenient access to local land records than was provided by district surveyor's offices (which in larger districts were remote from many residents) his legislation made it possible for any county to establish a surveyor's office, acquire copies of surveys and maps of county land, and even convert itself into a land district. As it turned out, however, virtually no counties used the law to convert themselves into land districts. See James Harper Starr to TWW, June 19, 1847, #388, Ward Papers; *Journals of the House of Representatives, Second Legislature*, 402, 602–604; Reagan, *Memoirs*, 54; Gammel, *Laws of Texas*, III, 153–155.

40. *Journals of the House of Representatives, Second Legislature*, 536–539, 646–658, 681, 690–691, 693; *Northern Standard* (Clarksville), Mar. 11, 1848 (quotations).

41. *Northern Standard* (Clarksville), June 14, 1851 (quotations); *Journals of the House of Representatives, Second Legislature*, 472, 513; TWW to Thomas Rusk, Mar. 13, 1848, General Correspondence, Rusk Papers.

42. *Journals of the House of Representatives, Second Legislature*, 536–539, 646–658 (quotation), 842–860; *Telegraph and Texas Register* (Houston), Mar. 4, 1846; Aaron Bean to TWW, Apr. 26 and May 7, 1848, Ward Papers; Statement of the Account of TWW for moneys drawn by him on Requisition, Dec. 18, 1848, Records of the Legislature: Memorials and

Petitions, Box 100-472 (TSA); Gammel, *Laws of Texas*, III, 698–699; TWW, Circular, Apr. 1851, DB 1850–1853, Broadside Collection.

43. TWW to A. McNeill, Feb. 11, 1848, "Report of Commissioners, Feb. 15, 1845 to Jan. 19, 1891," p. 328; *Journals of the House of Representatives, Second Legislature*, 655–656 (1st and 2nd quotations); R. J. White to Thomas Rusk, Feb. 28, 1847 [1848] (3rd quotation), and John McLeod to Thomas Rusk, Feb. 20, 1848 (4th quotation), General Correspondence, Rusk Papers.

44. *Journals of the Senate of the State of Texas, Second Legislature* (Houston: Telegraph Office, 1848), 413–433; R. J. White to Thomas Rusk, Feb. 28, 1847 [1848], General Correspondence, Rusk Papers (1st quotation); Gammel, *Laws of Texas*, III, 84–85; Sam Houston to TWW, June 1, 1848, #556, Ward Papers (2nd quotation).

45. TWW to Thomas Rusk, Mar. 13, 1848, General Correspondence, Rusk Papers (1st quotation); *Journals of the House of Representatives, Second Legislature*, 848–849; SLW to Lucadia Pease, Sept. 24, 1855, S.1, Pease Papers (2nd quotation).

NOTES TO CHAPTER 10

1. Jacob De Cordova to Lucadia Pease, May 10, 1854, and SLW to Lucadia Pease, May 14, 1854, S.1, Pease Papers.

2. Amy Hudock, "Overview of Southworth's Writing and Her Place in Literary History," <http://frodo.marshall.edu/~hudock1/overview.html> [Accessed Dec. 15, 2007]; E. D. E. N. [Emma Dorothy Eliza Nevitte] Southworth, *The Discarded Daughter: A Novel* (1852; reprint, Chicago: M. A. Donohue & Co., n.d.), 11 (2nd quotation), 41, 81, 87, 104, 106–107, 122–123, 137–139, 259 (1st quotation); SLW to Lucadia Pease, May 14, 1854, S.1, Pease Papers.

3. Aaron Bean to TWW, July 18, 1848, Ward Papers (1st quotation); TWW to Thomas Rusk, June 18, 1853, General Correspondence, Rusk Papers (2nd quotation).

4. *Texas Democrat* (Austin), Jan. 28, 1846; *Texas State Gazette* (Austin), June 1, 1850; John Riordan to TWW, Jan. 26, 1853, #U111, Ward Papers; United States Seventh Census (1850), Travis County, Texas, Population Schedules, City of Austin, #319; Randolph B. Campbell and Richard G. Lowe, *Wealth and Power in Antebellum Texas* (College Station: Texas A&M University Press, 1977), 95–96.

5. TWW to Thomas Rusk, Mar. 13, 1848, General Correspondence, Rusk Papers (1st quotation); Charles Richard Williams (ed.), *Diary and Letters of Rutherford Birchard Hayes, Nineteenth President of the United States* (5 vols.; [Columbus]: Ohio State Archeological and Historical Society, 1922–1926), I, 259 (2nd quotation); Mabelle Eppard Martin (ed.), "From Texas to California in 1849: Diary of C. C. Cox," *SHQ*, 29 (July, 1925), 40 (3rd quotation).

6. TWW to Thomas Rusk, Mar. 13, 1848, General Correspondence, Rusk Papers (quotation); TWW to Dudley Ward, June 26, 1859, #U124, and TWW to John Riordan, Sept. 21, 1848, #U117, Ward Papers.

7. SLW, Complaint to Supreme Court, New York City, Mar. 22, 1859, pp. 8–9 [18–20], NYCC.

8. TWW, Answer to SLW's Complaint of March 22, 1859, May 7, 1859, pp. 6–7 [15–17] NYCC (1st quotation); Aaron Bean to TWW, June 1, 1847, #387 (2nd quotation), and

Joanna Bean to TWW, June 1, #384, June 27 #383 (3rd quotation), 1847, Ward Papers.

9. SLW, Complaint to Supreme Court, New York City, Mar. 22, 1859, p. 32 [77], NYCC.

10. SLW, Complaint to Supreme Court, New York City, Mar. 22, 1859, pp. 1–2, 10–12 [3, 23–25, 29], NYCC; TWW, Circular, Apr. 1851, DB 1850–1853, Broadside Collection (quotation). Susan states in her 1859 complaint that she had two daughters by Thomas William Ward, only one of whom (Anna, born in 1851) was still alive. There is no mention of the other daughter in any other surviving records, but 1849 is the most likely year of her birth, and the absence of other references to her suggests she died at a very early age.

11. John Riordan to TWW, Apr. 2, 1849, #U27.1, Ward Papers (1st quotation); *Northern Standard* (Clarksville), July 28, 1849 (2nd quotation); *Texas Democrat* (Austin), July 14, 1849; *Texas State Gazette* (Austin), Sept. 29, 1849; Anson Jones to TWW, Sept. 24, 1849, #575, Ward Papers (3rd quotation). The vote count, with the returns in one county, Williamson, incomplete or unofficial, was 12,332 for Smith to 5,943 for Ward.

12. Connor, *Peters Colony*, 99n, 114–118, 126–127; Harry E. Wade, "Peters Colony," and David Minor, "Wardville," *NHT*, V, 167–168, VI, 823.

13. *Texas State Gazette* (Austin), Feb. 21, Sept. 6, 1851; TWW, Circular, Apr. 1851, DB 1850–1853, Broadside Collection (quotation); *Northern Standard* (Clarksville), June 14, Nov. 8, 1851.

14. *Journal of the House of Representatives of the State of Texas – Fourth Legislature* (Austin: Cushman & Hampton, 1852), 823.

15. *South Western American* (Austin), Dec. 15, 1852; Peter Bell to Franklin Pierce, Jan. 18, 1853, Thomas Rusk, Sam Houston, et al., to Franklin Pierce, Mar. 5, 1853, Note re General Rusk, undated (quotation), and Thomas Rusk to William Marcy, Mar. 31, 1853, roll 46, MP M967, RG 59.

16. Charles Stuart Kennedy, *The American Consul: A History of the United States Consular Service, 1776–1914* (New York: Greenwood Press, 1990), vii. Ward received a recess appointment on May 24, 1853, which was confirmed by the Senate on Feb. 13, 1854.

17. Kennedy, *American Consul*, 80, 83; *New York Times*, May 25, 1853 (1st quotation); Dudley Bean to TWW, May 24, 1853 (2nd quotation), and Aaron Bean to TWW, Mar. 4, and July 22, 1853, Ward Papers; *New York Herald*, May 24, 1853 (3rd quotation).

18. TWW to James Harper Starr, June 7, 1853, #777, Starr Papers; Aaron Bean to TWW, July 22, 1853, Ward Papers.

19. *Texas State Gazette* (Austin), Aug. 20, 1853; TWW to William Marcy, Sept. 4, 1853, ConDis, Panama, vol. 2, roll 2; Dudley Bean to TWW, Feb. 25, 1853, and Account-Receipt for Books, Sept. 22, 1853, Ward Papers; Anson Jones to Mary Jones, Oct. 7, 1853, Correspondence, 1851–1853, Jones Papers.

20. SLW to TWW, Mar. 25, #U140 (1st quotation), Mar. 17, #U139 (other quotations), 1854, Ward Papers.

21. Philip Gildersleeve to TWW, May 9, 1852, #547 (1st quotation), and Dudley Bean to TWW, Nov. 5, 1853, Ward Papers; Anson Jones to May Jones, Aug. 5, Dec. 19 (3rd quotation), 1853, Correspondence, 1851–1853, Jones Papers; Lucadia Pease to Juliet Niles, Jan. 13, 21, 1854, Hart and Kemp (eds.), *Lucadia Pease & the Governor*, 177–178, 180 (2nd quotation).

22. Mary Bean to Lucadia Pease, June 5, 1854, S.1, Pease Papers; Lucadia Pease to Maria Niles Moor, Dec. 19, 1853, and Lucadia Pease to Augusta Niles Ladd, Dec. 28, 1853 (quo-

tation), Hart and Kemp (eds.), *Lucadia Pease & the Governor*, 173, 176; Roger Griffin, "Connecticut Yankee in Texas: A Biography of Elisha Marshall Pease" (Ph.D. diss., University of Texas at Austin, 1973), 80; Vivian Elizabeth Smyrl, "Governor's Mansion," *NHT*, III, 268.

23. Lucadia Pease to Juliet Niles, Jan. 13, 1854 (1st quotation), and Lucadia Pease to Marshall Pease, June 5, 1854 (2nd quotation), Hart and Kemp (eds.), *Lucadia Pease & the Governor*, 177, 195; SLW to Lucadia Pease, May 14, 1854, S.1, Pease Papers.

24. TWW to SLW, Feb. 16, 1854, #U197, Ward Papers.

25. SLW, Complaint to Supreme Court, New York City, Mar. 22, 1859, pp. 3, 11–13, 15–17, 21 [6, 26–30, 35–41, 50–51], and TWW, Answer to SLW's Complaint of March 22, 1859, May 7, 1859, p. 3 [7], NYCC.

26. SLW, Petition to Travis County District Court, Mar. 26, 1860, p. 2, Case No. 1958, DCTC; SLW to Lucadia Pease, May 14, 1854 (quotation), Sept. 24, 1855, S.1, Pease Papers; SLW, Complaint to Supreme Court, New York City, Mar. 22, 1859, pp. 25, 33–34, [61, 80–81], NYCC.

27. SLW to Lucadia Pease, May 14, 1854 (1st and 2nd quotations), S.1, and SLW to Marshall Pease, July 14, 1855 (3rd quotation), P.1, Pease Papers; SLW to TWW, Mar. 17, #U139, Mar. 25, #U140, 1854, Ward Papers.

28. SLW, Complaint to Supreme Court, New York City, Mar. 22, 1859, p. 5 [12], NYCC (1st quotation); Aaron Bean to TWW, May 27, 1853, Feb. 25, 1854 (other quotations), Ward Papers.

29. Lucadia Pease to Juliet Niles and Augusta Niles Ladd, Feb. 27, 1854, Hart and Kemp (eds.), *Lucadia Pease & the Governor*, 184; SLW, Power of Attorney, Feb. 23, 1854, Galveston County Deed Record, vol. K, pp. 569–570 (microfilm; Sam Houston Regional Library and Research Center, Liberty, Texas) (quotations).

30. Lucadia Pease to Maria Niles Moor, May 1854, Hart and Kemp (eds.), *Lucadia Pease & the Governor*, 188–189 (1st quotation); SLW to Lucadia Pease, June 19, 1854, S.1, Pease Papers (2nd and 3rd quotations).

NOTES TO CHAPTER 11

1. *New York Times*, Apr. 30, May 1, 1856; John Haskell Kemble, *The Panama Route, 1848–1869* (1943; reprint, Columbia: University of South Carolina Press, 1990), 148. By 1856 the journey from New York to San Francisco by way of Panama routinely took twenty-three to twenty-six days.

2. Kemble, *Panama Route*, 206, 253–255; Roy F. Nichols, *Franklin Pierce: Young Hickory of the Granite Hills* (Philadelphia: University of Pennsylvania Press, 1931), 262 (quotation); De Cordova, *Texas*, 162. Regarding the number of people killed in the "Panama Massacre" (18 foreigners, almost all of them Americans, and at least 3 Panamanians), see endnote 7, chapter 13.

3. TWW to SLW, Feb. 16, 1854, #U197, and TWW to Dudley Bean, Apr. 26, 1854, Ward Papers; Lithograph of "Col. Thos. Wm. Ward, U.S. Consul at Panama," 1853, and message on reverse side, #CN 01248 (CAH).

4. *Panama Herald*, Nov. 8, 1853; Newspaper clipping, Second Steamer Edition, Oct. 18, 1853, Letters Received, 1850–1860, vol. 28, Records of the U.S. Consulate in Panama City, RG 84: Records of Foreign Service Posts of the Department of State (NA).

5. Kemble, *Panama Route*, 166–172, 187–189, 194–195; *Texas Democrat* (Austin), Mar. 3, 1849 (quotation); *New York Times*, Mar. 2, 1855; Joseph L. Schott, *Rails Across Panama: The Story of the Building of the Panama Railroad, 1849–1855* (Indianapolis: Bobbs-Merrill Co., 1967), 47, 55.

6. Robert Tomes, *Panama in 1855* (New York: Harper & Brothers, 1855), 136–137, 146–148; TWW to SLW, Apr. 20, 1855, #U158, Ward Papers; Schott, *Rails Across Panama*, 56; Mercedes K. Morris, "The *Star & Herald*—An Epitaph," <http://czbrats.com/Articles/S&H.htm> [Accessed Mar. 30. 2005].

7. *Daily Panama Star*, Oct. 19, 1853, Jan. 27, 1854; Kemble, *Panama Route*, 176; Schott, *Rails Across Panama*, 56–58, 185; *Weekly Panama Star*, Apr. 18, 1853; *Panama Herald*, Dec. 29, 1851, Jan. 26 (quotation), Feb. 9, 1852; Mrs. D. B. Bates, *Incidents on Land and Water, or Four Years on the Pacific Coast* (Boston: J. French and Co., 1857), 286–290. Contemporary estimates of Panama City's population in the period from 1853 to 1855 varied from a low of 4,000 to a high of 15,000. In its issue of October 12, 1853, the *Daily Panama Star*, commenting on the Government of New Granada's ignorance of statistics concerning the country, claimed that the government did not know whether Panama City's population was closer to 6,000 or 10,000.

8. *Panama Herald*, Oct. 12, 1852, Mar. 23, 1854; Fessenden N. Otis, *Illustrated History of the Panama Railroad* (New York: Harper & Brothers, 1861), 126 (1st quotation); *Panama Star and Herald*, July 19, 1855 (2nd quotation).

9. James B. Bowlin, to William Marcy, May 10, 1855, William R. Manning (ed.), *Diplomatic Correspondence of the United States: Inter-American Affairs, 1831–1860* (12 vols.; Washington, D.C.: Carnegie Endowment for International Peace, 1932–1939), V, 700 (1st quotation); Velma Newton, *The Silver Men: West Indian Labour Migration to Panama, 1850–1914* (rev. ed.; Kingston, Jamaica: Ian Randle Publishers, 2004), 39, 83; TWW to William Marcy, Oct. 24, 1854, ConDis, Panama, vol. 3, roll 3 (2nd quotation). The population figures reported by Bowlin applied to the four provinces of the Isthmus in the new State of Panama formed in 1855.

10. TWW to SLW, Feb. 16, 1854, #U197, Ward Papers (1st quotation); *Daily Panama Star*, Sept. 27, 1853, Mar. 14, 1854 (2nd quotation).

11. TWW to William Marcy, Jan. 1 (quotation), Jan. 14, 1854, Oct. 1, 1855, ConDis, Panama, vol. 3, roll 3; *Daily Panama Star*, Dec. 27, 1853; Thomas Rusk to TWW, Feb. 18, 1854, #569, Ward Papers.

12. *Weekly Panama Star*, Apr. 21, 1853.

13. Pedro A. Herrán to Lewis Cass, Mar. 14, 1859, Manning (ed.), *Diplomatic Correspondence*, V, 933.

14. TWW to James S. Green, Mar. 12, 1854, TWW to J. M. Urrutia Añino, Jan. 25, 1854, J. M. Urrutia Añino to TWW, Feb. 3, 1854, Consuls to J. M. Urrutia Añino, Jan. 26, 1854 (1st quotation), J. M. Urrutia Añino to Consuls, Feb. 15, 1854 (2nd quotation), ConDis, Panama, vol. 3, roll 3; *Daily Panama Star*, Mar. 10, 1854 (3rd quotation).

15. TWW to J. M. Urrutia Añino, Feb. 10, 1854 (quotation), and J. M. Urrutia Añino to TWW, Feb. 13, 1854, ConDis, Panama, vol. 3, roll 3.

16. *Panama Star and Herald*, May 11, Aug. 2, 20, 29, 30 (1st quotation), Sept. 15, Oct. 12, 1854, Mar. 13, 1855; Tomes, *Panama in 1855*, 122–124; *New York Times*, Aug. 14, 1854; James B.

Bowlin to TWW, Nov. 8, 1855, Ward Papers; TWW to William Marcy, June 5, 1855 (2nd quotation), and attached letters, ConDis, Panama, vol. 3, roll 3. Runnels later became a legendary figure celebrated for his Guard's supposed exploits during 1852 in rooting out a band of Isthmian thieves and cut-throats known as the Derienni and hanging most of them. Seventy-eight men were strung up in two mass executions that year, according to John Easter Minter in his 1948 book, *The Chagres: River of Westward Passage* (New York: Rinehart & Co., 1948), 246–249. References to the story and an elaboration of it have appeared in more recent publications, in particular Joseph Schott's *Rails Across Panama*, 60–63, 85–94, 97–100, 140–146, and on the Internet. It turns out that it is based on fictionalized and fabricated sources. Schott based his discussion of Runnels and his Guard on documents that purported to be the diary and memorabilia of Runnels' sister, Octavia Charity Marsden, but he learned after publishing his book that they were fakes (letter from Joseph L. Schott to the author, Dec. 2005). Runnels and his Guard were not active prior to 1854, and, while they were not averse to rough treatment, no evidence has turned up that hanging was their modus operandi.

17. William Marcy to James S. Green, Feb. 16, 1854, Manning (ed.), *Diplomatic Correspondence*, V, 373; *Daily Panama Star*, Mar. 9, 1854; *New York Times*, Apr. 10, 1854; *Panama Herald*, June 23, 1853.

18. TWW to James S. Green, Mar. 12, 1854 (quotation), J. M. Urrutia Añino to TWW, Mar. 29, Apr. 15, 1854, and TWW to William Marcy, May 23, 1854, ConDis, Panama, vol. 3, roll 3; *Daily Panama Star*, Mar. 1, 1854; *New York Times*, May 10, 1854.

19. James S. Green to William Marcy, Apr. 22, 1854, Manning (ed.), *Diplomatic Correspondence*, V, 695 (1st quotation); TWW to William Marcy, May 23 (2nd quotation), June 28 (3rd quotation), 1854, ConDis, Panama, vol. 3, roll 3.

20. TWW to William Marcy, May 23 (1st quotation), June 28 (2nd quotation), 1854, ConDis, Panama, vol. 3, roll 3.

21. TWW to SLW, Feb. 16, 1854, #U197, Ward Papers.

22. TWW to SLW, Apr. 20, 1855, #U158 (1st quotation), TWW to Dudley Bean, Apr. 4, 1854, and Dudley Bean to TWW, May 20, 1854, Ward Papers; *Panama Star and Herald*, July 6, 1854; Thomas Rusk to William Marcy, July 8, 1854, ConDis, Panama, vol. 3, roll 3 (2nd quotation).

Notes to Chapter 12

1. SLW to Lucadia Pease, Feb. 13 (2nd and 3rd quotations), Sept. 24 (1st quotation), 1855, S. 1, Pease Papers.

2. SLW to Lucadia Pease, Aug. 27, 1854 (2nd quotation), Feb. 13, 1855 (3rd quotation), and SLW to Marshall Pease, July 14, 1855 (1st quotation) P. 1, Pease Papers; TWW to SLW, Feb. 16, 1854, #U197, and Aaron Bean to TWW, Dec. 12, 1854 Ward Papers.

3. SLW to Lucadia Pease, Feb. 13, 1855, S. 1, Pease Papers; TWW to Aaron Bean, Dec. 17, 1854, #U292, and Aaron Bean, Current Account, Dec. 18, 1854, Ward Papers; De Cordova, *Texas*, 164.

4. SLW, Complaint to Supreme Court, New York City, Mar. 22, 1859, pp. 22–24 [53–57], and TWW, Answer to SLW's Complaint of March 22, 1859, May 7, 1859, pp. 15–16 [38–41] (quotation), NYCC.

5. TWW to SLW, Apr. 20, 1855, #U158, Ward Papers.

6. SLW to Lucadia Pease, Sept. 24, 1855, S.1, Pease Papers (quotation); Hancock and West, Cross Interrogatories to Harriet Bean Dinsmore, May 5, 1860, Case No. 1958, DCTC.

7. *New York Times*, Feb. 9 (1st quotation), Mar. 17, 1855; James B. Bowlin to TWW, Oct. 11, 1855, Ward Papers (2nd quotation); Kemble, *Panama Route*, 226.

8. Kemble, *Panama Route*, 181–182, 189–190; Schott, *Rails Across Panama*, 187–188; *New York Times*, Feb 9, Mar. 2, 17, Sept. 13, 1855; TWW to SLW, Feb. 28, 1855, #U198, Ward Papers; Stephen J. Randall, *Colombia and the United States: Hegemony and Interdependence* (Athens: University of Georgia Press, 1992), 33; *Panama Star and Herald*, Feb. 20, 24, Dec. 29, 1855, Jan. 12, 1856.

9. *Panama Star and Herald*, Mar. 10, 1855; TWW to William Marcy, Aug. 22, 1854, ConDis, Panama, vol. 3, roll 3; Commander William Mervine to TWW, May 9, 1855, Letters Received, 1850–1860, vol. 28, Records of U.S. Consulate in Panama City, RG 84; *Weekly Panama Star*, Jan. 30, 1854; Aaron Bean to TWW, Mar. 17, July 3, 1855, Ward Papers.

10. TWW to William Marcy, June 7, 1855, ConDis, Panama, vol. 3, roll 3 (1st quotation); TWW to SLW, Feb. 28, #U198 (2nd and 3rd quotations), Apr. 20, #U158, 1855, Ward Papers.

11. Aaron Bean to TWW, July 3, Aug. 20, 1855, and Frederick Dillout, Deposition, Dec. 1860, p. 7 (1st quotation), Ward Papers; SLW to Lucadia Pease, Sept. 24, 1855, S.1, Pease Papers (2nd and 3rd quotations).

12. SLW to Lucadia Pease, Nov. 12, 1855, S.1, Pease Papers; *New York Times*, Oct. 17, 1855 (quotation); TWW to William Marcy, Oct. 1, 1855, ConDis, Panama, vol. 3, roll 3; William Marcy to Pedro A. Herrán, Oct. 23, 1855, Colombia, 1835–1885, roll 15, MP M99 (Notes to Foreign Legations in the United States from the Department of State, 1834–1906), RG 59.

13. James B. Bowlin to William Marcy, May 17, 1855, and William Hunter to James B. Bowlin, July 31, 1855, Manning (ed.), *Diplomatic Correspondence*, V, 376, 701; James B. Bowlin to TWW, Oct. 11, 1855, Ward Papers (1st quotation); TWW to William Marcy, June 12, Aug. 8, 29, Sept. 18, Oct. 1 (2nd quotation), 1855, ConDis, Panama, vol. 3, roll 3.

14. Aaron Bean to TWW, July 3, Sept. 5, 1855, Ward Papers.

15. *New York Times*, Oct. 17, 1855.

16. Ibid.; Report by Two Members of the Board of Health in Panama City, Sept. 16, 1855, Letters Received, 1850–1860, vol. 28, Records of U.S. Consulate in Panama City, RG 84.

17. *New York Times*, Oct. 17, 1855 (quotations); Manuel M. Diaz to TWW, Aug. 20, 1855, and TWW to Manuel M. Diaz, Aug. 21, 1855, ConDis, Panama, vol. 3, roll 3; Aaron Bean to Marshall Pease, Oct. 17, 1855, P.1, Pease Papers; *Panama Star and Herald*, Oct. 2, 1855.

18. *New York Times*, Oct. 17, 18, 1855.

19. Pedro A. Herrán to William Marcy, Oct. 18, 1855, and William Marcy to TWW, Oct. 22, 1855, Instructions Received, 1853–1860, vol. 61, Records of U.S. Consulate in Panama City, RG 84.

20. TWW to William Marcy, Nov. 19, 1855, ConDis, Panama, vol. 3, roll 3; J. A. Thomas to TWW, Dec. 27, 1855, Instructions Received, 1853–1860, vol. 61, Records of U.S. Consulate in Panama, RG 84 (quotations); *New York Times*, Dec. 29, 1855, Jan. 8, Feb. 28, 1856.

21. E. Taylor Parks, *Colombia and the United States, 1765–1934* (Durham, N.C.: Duke University Press, 1935), 220n (quotation); Thomas Rusk to TWW, Mar. 31, 1856, #573, Ward Papers.

22. TWW to William Marcy, Mar. 28, 1856, ConDis, Panama, vol. 4, roll 4.

23. SLW to Lucadia Pease, Apr. 20 (1st quotation), July 31 (3rd quotation), 1856, S.1, Pease Papers; Mary Ward to Dudley Ward, Mar. 2, 1856, #U254 (2nd quotation), Ward Papers.

24. *New York Times*, Feb. 15, 1856; Theodore de Sabla to Dudley Ward, May 10, 1858, #U261, Ward Papers (quotation).

25. *Panama Star and Herald*, Feb. 21, 1856 (quotation); *The Panama Massacre: A Collection of the Principal Evidence and Other Documents* (Panama City, Panama: Office of the Star and Herald, 1857), 11–12, 20.

Notes to Chapter 13

1. John Castillo Kennedy, "Incident on the Isthmus," *American Heritage*, 19 (June, 1968), 66–67; *Panama Massacre*, 1–3, 22, 38, 47–48, 64–65, 68 (quotation). For a thoughtful analysis of the causes of the riot on April 15, 1856, see Mercedes Chen Daley, "The Watermelon Riot: Cultural Encounters in Panama City, April 15, 1856," *Hispanic American Historical Review*, 70 (Feb. 1990), 85–108.

2. *Panama Massacre*, 5–7, 22–23, 28, 31, 35, 38–39, 41–42, 52, 55, 57–58, 62, 66, 67; Testimony of James Johnson, enclosed in TWW to William Marcy, May 4, 1856, ConDis, Panama, vol. 4, roll 4 (quotation), and news clipping from the *Daily Picayune*, enclosed in Amos Corwine to William Marcy, Sept. 26, 1856, ConDis, Panama, vol. 5, roll 5.

3. Consul's Statement relative to the affairs of 15th April/56, Aug. 5, 1856, #U294, Ward Papers (2nd quotation); Theodore de Sabla to TWW, Apr. 18, 1856, and TWW to William Marcy, Apr. 18 (with addendum dated Apr. 19), 1856, ConDis, Panama, vol. 4, roll 4; *Panama Massacre*, 23–24, 28–29, 31–32, 34 (1st quotation), 40, 66. Eyewitness accounts of the events on April 15 are, to the say the least, inconsistent (Ward himself wrote varying accounts of what happened), making a definitive account impossible. Moreover, the testimony of both Americans and Panamanians was clearly influenced by their respective biases as to which group was responsible for the conflict. While there is extensive testimony by American participants and eyewitnesses supporting the contention that Ward and the rail and steamship company officials sought actively to restrain passengers from provoking an attack, it should be noted that such testimony also tended to absolve the Americans of responsibility for the debacle that followed.

4. Consul's Statement relative to the affairs of 15th April/56, Aug. 5, 1856, #U294, Ward Papers; *Panama Massacre*, 5, 29, 33, 34–35, 60 (quotations), 62, 64–65; TWW to William Marcy, Apr. 18, 1856, vol. 4, roll 4, and Theodore de Sabla to the Editors of *El Panameño*, Apr. 24, 1856, vol. 5, roll 5, ConDis, Panama.

5. *Panama Massacre*, 24–25 (1st quotation), 29, 33, 60, 63 (2nd quotation).

6. Consul's Statement relative to the affairs of 15th April/56, Aug. 5, 1856, #U294, Ward Papers (quotation); *Panama Massacre*, 25–26, 29–30, 34.

7. Statement of Emilio LeBreton, M.D., and Jose Kratochwil, M.D., Relative to the Riot at Panama, Sept. 6, 1856, #U296, Ward Papers; *Panama Massacre*, 61; TWW to William

Marcy, Apr. 18, 1856, ConDis, Panama, vol. 4, roll 4; Kennedy, "Incident on the Isthmus," 72. Drs. LeBreton and Kratochwil, who were on the scene during the riot and attended many wounded during it and for days afterwards, prepared a detailed report on American and other foreign casualties in September 1856 and concluded that fourteen were killed on April 15 and another four died later of their wounds. Ward told Marcy that upwards of 50 Americans were wounded, but he tended to be loose with numbers.

8. Commander T. Bailey to Amos Corwine, June 7, 1856 (1st quotation), TWW to William Marcy, May 4, 1856 (2nd quotation), and Claims for damage done to persons and property at Panama on the 15th April 1856, May 1856 (3rd quotation), ConDis, Panama, vol. 4, roll 4.

9. TWW to Francisco de Fábrega, Apr. 21, 1856, ConDis, Panama, vol. 4, roll 4 (1st quotation); Parks, *Colombia and the United States*, 223; Lino de Pombo to Isaac E. Morse and James B. Bowlin, Feb. 28, 1857, Manning (ed.), *Diplomatic Correspondence*, V, 861 (2nd quotation).

10. TWW to William Marcy, May 4, 1856, ConDis, Panama, vol. 4, roll 4 (1st and 2nd quotations); William Marcy to TWW, May 3 (3rd quotation), May 14 (4th quotation), 1856, Instructions Received, 1853–1860, vol. 61, Records of U.S. Consulate in Panama City, RG 84.

11. Amos Corwine, June 2, 1856, ConDis, Panama, vol. 4, roll 4; William Marcy to TWW, May 3, 1856, Instructions Received, 1853–1860, vol. 61, Records of U.S. Consulate in Panama, RG 84 (1st quotation); *Panama Massacre*, 1–21; *Panama Star and Herald*, Aug. 19, 1856 (2nd quotation); *New York Times*, Sept. 23, 1856; Parks, *Colombia and the United States*, 288–302.

12. Amos Boyd to TWW, May 31, 1856, Ward Papers (1st quotation); *New York Times*, Nov. 7, 1855, May 19, 1856 (2nd quotation).

13. Wheaton J. Lane, *Commodore Vanderbilt: An Epic of the Steam Age* (New York: Alfred A. Knopf, 1942), 69, 318; Cornelius Vanderbilt to William Marcy, June 16, 1856, ConDis, Panama, vol. 4, roll 4 (quotations).

14. TWW to William Marcy, June 18, 1856, ConDis, Panama, vol. 4, roll 4 (quotations); Kemble, *Panama Route*, 58–61, 253–254. Of the approximately 100,000 travelers who crossed the two isthmuses during 1853 and 1854, more than 40,000 went by way of Nicaragua. Passenger traffic across Nicaragua declined during 1855, in part due to completion of the Panama Railroad, and plummeted during 1856 and 1857, primarily due to warfare in the country.

15. Lane, *Commodore Vanderbilt*, 94, 108–109 (quotation), 114–119; David I. Folkman, Jr., *The Nicaragua Route* (Salt Lake City: University of Utah Press, 1972), 48, 73–78. The Accessory Transit Company was also known as the Nicaragua Transit Company.

16. Lane, *Commodore Vanderbilt*, 119–121.

17. TWW to Cornelius Vanderbilt, May 27, 1856 (attached to TWW to William Marcy, July 18, 1856), TWW to William Marcy July 17, 1856, vol. 5, roll 5, and TWW to William Marcy, June 18, 1856, vol. 4, roll 4, ConDis, Panama.

18. U.S. Department of State, *Regulations Prescribed by the President for Consular Officers of the United States* (Washington, D.C.: A. O. P. Nicholson, 1856), 112; TWW to William Marcy, June 18, 1856, vol. 4, roll 4, and TWW to William Marcy, Aug. 2, 1856, vol. 5, roll 5, ConDis, Panama.

19. Cornelius Vanderbilt to William Marcy, June 16, 1856 (2nd quotation), attached affidavit of Robert Horner, May 31, 1856 (1st quotation), and TWW to William Marcy, June 18, 1856, ConDis, Panama, vol. 4, roll 4; Department of State, *Regulations Prescribed by the President for Consular Officers*, 112; TWW to William Marcy, July 17, 1856, ConDis, Panama, vol. 5, roll 5 (3rd quotation).

20. Robert Horner to TWW, June 3, 1856 (quotation), and other documents attached to Cornelius Vanderbilt to William Marcy, June 16, 1856, and TWW to William Marcy, June 18, 1856, ConDis, Panama, vol. 4, roll 4; *New York Times*, Aug. 13, 1856.

21. William Marcy to TWW, June 18, 1856, Instructions Received, 1853–1860, vol. 61, Records of U.S. Consulate in Panama City, RG 84.

22. TWW to William Marcy, July 17, July 18 (quotation), Aug. 2, 1856, ConDis, Panama, vol. 5, roll 5.

23. William Marcy to TWW, Aug. 1, 1856, Ward Papers (1st quotation); *New York Times*, Aug. 11 (2nd quotation), 1856.

24. *Campbell et al. v The Uncle Sam*, 4 *Federal Cases*, 1196–1199, Case No. 2,371 (quotations). In his decision Judge Hoffman did not deal with the issue of possible confiscation of Vanderbilt's steamships if they landed in Nicaragua. The trial was reported in the *Alta California* (San Francisco), Aug. 7, 14, 15, 22, 1856. Judge Hoffman's decision (taken from the *Alta California*, Aug. 22, 1856) was reported verbatim in the *New York Day Book*, Dec. 27, 1856, a copy of which is in Ward Papers, attached to William Marcy to TWW, Aug. 1, 1856.

25. *Campbell et al. v The Uncle Sam*, 4 *Federal Cases*, 1199–1201, Case No. 2,372.

26. *New York Day Book*, Dec. 27, 1856; *De Cordova, Texas*, 164.

NOTES TO CHAPTER 14

1. SLW to Lucadia Pease, July 31 (3rd quotation), Sept. 29, (1st quotation), 1856, S.1, and SLW to Marshall Pease, July 14, 1856 (2nd quotation), P.1, Pease Papers; Lucadia Pease to Marshall Pease, Oct. 19, 1856, Hart and Kemp (eds.), *Lucadia Pease & the Governor*, 309.

2. SLW to Marshall Pease, July 14 (1st, 2nd, and 3rd quotations), July 15, 1855, P.1, and SLW to Lucadia Pease, Nov. 12, 1855, July 31, 1856 (4th quotation), S.1, Pease Papers.

3. SLW to Lucadia Pease, Sept. 29, 1856, S.1, Pease Papers.

4. Charles Smyth, Deposition (Answers to Interrogatories), [May–June 1860], 1–2, 15, Charles Smyth, Deposition (Answers to Cross-Interrogatories), [May–June 1860], pp. 4, Frederick Dillout, Deposition, Dec. 1860, pp. 9, 11, and Amedie Simonin, Deposition, Nov. 28, 1860, pp. 3–4, Ward Papers; Lucadia Pease to Marshall Pease, Oct. 19, 1856, Hart and Kemp (eds.), *Lucadia Pease & the Governor*, 309 (quotations).

5. Samuel Ward to Jacob De Cordova, Aug. 17, 1855, #626.2, and Samuel Ward to TWW, Nov. 15, 1855, #628 (quotation), Ward Papers.

6. Charles Smyth to TWW, Nov. 16, 1855, #U1.1, Ward Papers.

7. Amedie Simonin, Deposition, Nov. 28, 1860, pp. 7–9, and Charles Smyth to TWW, Mar. 17, 1857, #U1.6, Ward Papers; TWW, Answers to Interrogatories, Jan. 16, 1861, attachment, p. 3, Case No. 1958, DCTC.

8. Amedie Simonin, Deposition, Nov. 28, 1860, pp. 4, 7–8, Statement of Losses & Agreement to Divide Collections, 1860, #U154, and TWW to Jacob De Cordova, July 14, 1857,

#623, Ward Papers; Lucadia Pease to Juliet Pease, Dec. 30, 1857, Hart and Kemp (eds.), *Lucadia Pease & the Governor*, 347.

9. Jemima Rivington, Deposition, Oct. 22, 1860, pp. 3–6, and Charles Smyth, Deposition (Answers to Interrogatories), [May–June 1860], p. 11 (quotation), Ward Papers; SLW, Complaint to Supreme Court, New York City, Mar. 22, 1859, pp. 26–27 [63–65], NYCC.

10. Amedie Simonin, Deposition, Nov. 28, 1860, pp. 9–10, TWW, Answer to SLW's Petition of March 26, 1860, n.d., pp. 13, 16–18, and Jemima Rivington, Deposition, Oct. 22, 1860, p. 17, Ward Papers; SLW, Petition to Travis County District Court, Mar. 26, 1860, pp. 7–8, Case No. 1958, DCTC (1st quotation); TWW, Answer to SLW's Complaint of March 22, 1859, May 7, 1859, pp. 16 (2nd quotation), 25–27 [42, 64–70], NYCC; Deeds, May 4, 1854, Mar. 28, 1866, Galveston County Deed Record, Book K, pp. 554–555, Book U, pp. 284–285.

11. Jemima Rivington, Deposition, Oct. 22, 1860, p. 5 (1st quotation), TWW, Answer to SLW's Petition of March 26, 1860, n.d., pp. 6–7 (2nd quotation), and Frederick Dillout, Deposition, Dec. 1860, pp. 3–4 (3rd and 4th quotations), Ward Papers.

12. TWW to Dudley Ward, June 1, #U203, June 10, #U205, June 19, #U204, June 26, #U207 July 15, #U206, 1857, and Anna Ward to TWW, Sept. 26, 1870, #601, Ward Papers; Amedie Simonin, Deposition, Nov. 28, 1860, pp. 13–14.

13. Charles Smyth to TWW, June 27, 1857, #U1.13A, Oct. 14, #U1.36, Oct. 21, #U1.37, 1858, Caroline Smyth to TWW, Mar. 19, 1857, #535 (1st quotation), Robie Ward to Dudley Ward, Oct. 22, 1857, #U247 (2nd quotation), Ward Papers.

14. Jemima Rivington, Deposition, Oct. 22, 1860, pp. 6–7, 22, SLW to TWW, Feb. 7, 1858, #U141 (quotation), and Charles Smyth to TWW, May 24, 1858, #U1.12, Ward Papers.

15. Anson Jones to TWW, Oct. 2, 1857, #580, Ward Papers.

16. Jemima Rivington, Deposition, Oct. 22, 1860, pp. 7–14, and Patrick Rooney to TWW, May 17, 1860, #657 (quotation), Ward Papers; SLW, Complaint to Supreme Court, New York City, Mar. 22, 1859, pp. 28–30 [68–72], NYCC.

17. Center for Substance Abuse Treatment, *Substance Abuse Treatment and Domestic Violence*, Treatment Improvement Protocol (TIP) Series No. 25 (Rockville, Md.: Substance Abuse and Mental Health Services Administration, 1997), 3–5; Linda S. Labell, "Wife Abuse: A Sociological Study of Battered Women and Their Mates," *Victimology: An International Journal*, 4 (Number 2, 1979), 264.

18. Jemima Rivington, Deposition, Oct. 22, 1860, p. 7, and Charles Smyth, Deposition (Answers to Interrogatories), [May–June 1860], p. 12, Ward Papers; SLW, Complaint to Supreme Court, New York City, Mar. 22, 1859, pp. 34–35 [83], and TWW, Answer to SLW's Complaint of March 22, 1859, May 7, 1859, p. 21 [53], NYCC; SLW, Petition to Travis County District Court, Mar. 26, 1860, pp. 2–3, Case No. 1958, DCTC.

19. SLW, Complaint to Supreme Court, New York City, Mar. 22, 1859, pp. 31–33 [73–78] (1st quotation), and Benjamin W. Bonney, Judge's Findings, Dec. 3, 1860, NYCC; SLW, Petition to Travis County District Court, Mar. 26, 1860, p. 2, Case No. 1958, DCTC; Jemima Rivington, Deposition, Oct. 22, 1860, pp. 14–16, Ward Papers. There are inconsistencies in the testimony regarding the date of the incident and whether Ward hit Susan

with his fist or his pistol or something else. The June 9 date appears to be correct. Susan stated in her initial testimony that Ward used his fist after threatening her with a pistol. Jemima Rivington testified that while she was in Susan's bedroom after breakfast she heard Susan tell Carrie Smyth that he hit her with a pistol. In her petition to the Texas court Susan said Ward threatened her with a pistol and then struck her with it, then crossed out "it" and wrote, "some other hard substance." In his findings, Justice Bonney of the Supreme Court, City and County of New York, stated that Ward hit her with a pistol.

20. TWW to Dudley Ward, June 26, 1858, #212, Ward Papers; SLW, Complaint to Supreme Court, New York City, Mar. 22, 1859, pp. 33–35, 38–39 [80–84, 93–94], and TWW, Answer to SLW's Complaint of March 22, 1859, May 7, 1859, pp. 21–22 [53–56] (quotation), NYCC.

21. TWW to Dudley Ward, Aug. 25, 1858, #U213 (quotation), and Charles Smyth to TWW, Oct. 14, 1858, #U1.36, Ward Papers.

22. Marshall Pease to Lucadia Pease, Oct. 7, 1858, P, Pease Papers; SLW, Complaint to Supreme Court, New York City, Mar. 22, 1859, pp. 35–36 [85–86], and TWW, Answer to SLW's Complaint of March 22, 1859, May 7, 1859, p. 22 [57–58], NYCC; Hartog, *Man and Wife in America*, 22, 23, 34–35, 72–73; Nancy F. Cott, *Public Vows: A History of Marriage and the Nation* (Cambridge, Mass.: Harvard University Press, 2000), 48.

23. SLW, Complaint to Supreme Court, New York City, Mar. 22, 1859, pp. 5 (2nd quotation), 33 (3rd quotation), 36–40 [12, 79, 86–97], and Thomas Clerke, Injunction by Order, Mar. 26, 1859, NYCC; Aaron Bean to Marshall Pease, Mar. 20, 1860, P.1, Pease Papers (1st quotation).

24. TWW, Answer to SLW's Complaint of March 22, 1859, May 7, 1859, pp. 1–29 [1–74], NYCC.

25. TWW, Answer to SLW's Petition of March 26, 1860, n.d., pp. 14–15, Ward Papers. For records of Thomas Wood Ward's pay as an assistant clerk in the General Land Office, Nov. 1844–Feb. 1845 and May 1845–Jan. 1846, see Republic Claims, Audited Claims, Thomas Wood Ward, Claims # 2016, 2092, 215x, 2376, 2602, 2690, 2781, 2850, 2921, 2999.

26. SLW, Petition to Travis County District Court, Mar. 26, 1860, p. 5, Case No. 1958, DCTC; Charles Smyth to TWW, Oct. 10, 1859, #U1.47 (1st and 2nd quotations), Charles Smyth, Deposition (Answers to Interrogatories), [May–June 1860], pp. 8–9, 14–15, TWW, Answer to SLW's Petition of March 26, 1860, n.d., pp. 14–15, and Hooper Van Vorst to TWW, Oct. 25, 1860, Ward Papers; Carroll, *Homesteads Ungovernable*, 148, 153.

27. Dudley Ward to TWW, June 13 [?], #U78.5 (1st quotation), June 23, #U78.14 (2nd quotation), July 24, #U78.1, 1859, Ward Papers.

28. Order Issued by Justice Josiah Sutherland, Supreme Court, New York City, Jan. 26, 1860, Case No. 1958, DCTC.

29. TWW to John Balfe, Bill of Sale, Household Furniture Jan. 28, 1860, Amedie Simonin, Deposition, Nov. 28, 1860, p. 2–3, and Charles Smyth to TWW, Oct. 10, #U1.47, Nov. 3, #U1.50, 1859, Ward Papers.

30. SLW, Petition to Travis County District Court, Mar. 26, 1860, pp. 8–10, and Writ Issued by Travis County District Court, Mar. 29, 1860, Case No. 1958, DCTC; Aaron Bean to Marshall Pease, Mar. 20, 1860, P.1, Pease Papers (1st quotation); TWW to Henry L. Kin-

ney, Apr. 2, May 14, #U4, 1860, and Patrick Rooney to TWW, Apr. 21, 1860, #654 (2nd quotation), Ward Papers; SLW to TWW, Apr. 30, 1860, and TWW to Sheriff J. M. Blackwell, Apr. 30, 1860, Case No. 2262, DCTC (3rd quotation).

31. Patrick Rooney to TWW, Apr. 21, #654 (2nd quotation), May 23, #659, June 22, #665 (1st quotation), Dec. 6, #680 (3rd quotation), 1860, Ward Papers.

32. Charles Smyth to TWW, May 26, #U132 (4th and 5th quotations), May 28, #U1.53 (7th quotation), June 8, #U1.55 (6th quotation), Aug. 25, #U1.58 (2nd quotation), Aug. 30, #U1.59 (1st quotation), Oct. 13, #U1.60, Nov. 24, #U1.75 (3rd quotation), 1860, Mar. 18, 1861, #U1.97, and Charles Smyth, Deposition (Answers to Cross-Interrogatories), [May–June 1860], pp. 12, Ward Papers.

33. Patrick Rooney to TWW, Mar. 31, #652 (2nd quotation), and Dec. 6, #680 (1st quotation), 1860; Charles Smyth to TWW, Nov. 24, #U1.75 (5th quotation), Dec. 8, #U1.78 (3rd and 4th quotations), 1860, Ward Papers.

34. SLW to Lucadia Pease, May 14, 1854 (1st quotation), S.1, Pease Papers; SLW, Petition to Travis County District Court, Mar. 26, 1860, p. 2, Case No. 1958, DCTC (2nd quotation); Patrick Rooney to TWW, May 23, #658 (3rd quotation), May 23, #659 (4th quotation), Oct. 20, #674 (5th quotation), 1860, and Charles Smyth to TWW, Aug. 30, 1860, #U1.59, Ward Papers.

35 Patrick Rooney to TWW, May 15, #656, May 31, #661, Aug. 10, #668.1 (quotation), Oct. 19, #673, 1860, and Charles Smyth to TWW, Aug. 25, #U1.58, Oct. 21, #U1.61, Oct. 24, #U1.62, Oct. 25, #U1.63, Nov. 11, #U1.68, Nov. 17, #U1.72, 1860, Ward Papers.

36. Patrick Rooney to TWW, Oct. 17, #671, Oct. 18, #672, Oct. 20, #674 (quotations), 1860, and Bernard McMullen to Dudley Ward, Dec. 27, 1860, #U275, Ward Papers; Burrill, Davison, & Burrill, Bill of Costs, Dec. 5, 1860, NYCC.

37. Hooper Van Vorst to TWW, Oct. 25, 1860 (quotations), and Charles Smyth to TWW, Oct. 21, #U1.61. Oct. 27, #U1.64, 1860, Ward Papers.

38. Benjamin W. Bonney, Judge's Findings, Dec. 3, 1860, NYCC; Patrick Rooney to TWW, Dec. 6, 1860, #680, Ward Papers.

39. Lucadia Pease to Juliet Niles, Dec. 30, 1860, Jan. [1861], S, Pease Papers; SLW, Motion to Amend Petition, Jan. 2, 1861, Case No. 1958, DCTC; District Court Minutes (Civil), Jan. 2, 1861, Book H, p. 558, DCTC.

40. Larry Jay Gage, "The Texas Road to Secession and War: John Marshall and the *Texas State Gazette*, 1860–1861," *SHQ*, 62 (Oct., 1958), 206.

NOTES TO CHAPTER 15

1. *Southern Intelligencer* (Austin), Sept. 22, 1865; Patrick Rooney to TWW, Dec. 13, 1860, #642, Ward Papers; Griffin, "Connecticut Yankee in Texas," 165 (1st quotation); Gage, "Texas Road to Secession and War," 203 (2nd quotation).

2. Barkley, *History of Travis County and Austin*, 74, 218; Paul D. Lack, "Slavery and Vigilantism in Austin, Texas, 1840–1860," *SHQ*, 85 (July, 1981), 1n, 8; Royal T. Wheeler to Oran M. Roberts, Feb. 12, 1863, Correspondence (IV), Oran M. Roberts Papers (CAH) (quotation).

3. *Northern Standard* (Clarksville), May 18, 1861, AF-Chron (AHC) (1st quotation); *Southern Intelligencer* (Austin), May 17, 1866 (2nd quotation); Griffin, "Connecticut Yankee in Texas," 169 (3rd quotation); "Dudley Ward," Confederate Index (CAH).

4. Hafertepe, *Abner Cook*, 88.

5. Lucadia Pease to Juliet Niles, May 2, 1861, S, Pease Papers.

6. SLW to Dudley Ward, Aug. 16, 1862 [but marked 1863], #U78.23 (1st quotation), Mar. 30, 1864, #U78.34, Ward Papers; Dudley Ward to TWW, Apr. 18, 1864 (2nd quotation), Dudley Ward Letters (TGLO). A search of Compiled Military Service Records at the National Archives turned up no evidence of Robie Marston serving in either the Union or Confederate military.

7. Carroll, *Homesteads Ungovernable*, 80, 99, 129, 136–139; Jean Stuntz, "Spanish Laws for Texas Women: The Development of Marital Property Law to 1850," *SHQ*, 104 (Apr., 2001), 555–559.

8. Jane Lynn Scarborough, "George W. Paschal, Texas Unionist and Scalawag Jurisprudent" (Ph.D. diss., Rice University, 1972), 71–72; Mrs. T. P. O'Connor [Elizabeth Paschal O'Connor], *I Myself* (New York: G. P. Putnam, 1914), 11.

9. Patrick Rooney to TWW, Dec. 6, #680 (1st quotation), Dec. 7, #681 (2nd quotation), 1860, and Charles Smyth to TWW, Apr. 17, 1860, #U130 (3rd quotation), Ward Papers; William Rounseville Alger, *Life of Edwin Forrest, The American Tragedian* (2 vols., 1877; reprint, New York: Benjamin Blom, 1972), II, 496–499. According to Alger, Forrest ultimately paid his wife $64,000, but according to David Delman it was $68,000. See Delman, *The Bluestocking: The Story of the Famous Forrest Divorce Case* (New York: St. Martin's Press, 1994), 286.

10. Charles Smyth to TWW, Jan. 14, 1861, #U1.88, TWW, Answer to SLW's Petition of March 26, 1860, n.d., pp. 6–10 (1st–3rd quotations), 14–16 (4th quotation), and TWW to Henry L. Kinney, May 14, 1860, #U4, Ward Papers; Interrogatories for Henry L. Kinney, May 30, 1860, Case No. 1958, DCTC.

11. Jemima Rivington, Deposition, Oct. 22, 1860, p. 30 (1st quotation), Charles Smyth to TWW, Jan. 9, #U1.84 (2nd quotation), Jan. 14, #U1.88, 1861, and TWW, Answer to SLW's Petition of March 26, 1860, n.d., p. 18, Ward Papers; District Court Minutes (Civil), July 28, 1860, Book H, pp. 463–464, DCTC.

12. B. A. Shepherd to TWW, Jan. 18, 1859, #610, Ward Papers; Deed, Jan. 15, 1859, and Release, July 5, 1859, Harris County Deed Record, Book U, pp. 660–661, Book V, p. 482; *Tri-Weekly Telegraph* (Houston), Mar. 16, 1860; Lucadia Pease to Juliet Niles, Jan. [1861], S, Pease Papers (quotation). On secreting assets in recent years, see Larissa MacFarquhar, "So You Want a Divorce," *The New Yorker* (Apr. 20, 2001), 92.

13. TWW, Answers to Interrogatories, Jan. 16, 1861, attachment, pp. 5 (1st quotation), 7, Case No. 1958, DCTC; Henry L. Kinney to TWW, Mar. 26, 1860, and TWW to Henry L. Kinney, Apr. 2 (2nd and 3rd quotations), May 14, #U4, 1860, Ward Papers; Record Book, Estate of TWW, p. 11, Ward Papers.

14. District Court Minutes (Civil), Jan. 3, 1861, Book H, p. 564, DCTC; Note by John T. Price, Sheriff, Jan. 3, 1861, TWW, Answer of the Defendant, Jan. 8, 1861 (1st quotation), Rule to Show Cause Why Defendant Should Not be Adjudged Guilty of Contempt, Jan. 10, 1861 (2nd quotation), and Order of the Court with Accompanying Interrogatories, Jan. 10, 1861, Case No. 1958, DCTC.

15. TWW, Answers to Interrogatories, covering memorandum (1st quotation) and pp. 8–10 of attachment, Jan. 16, 1861, and TWW, Further Answer of the Defendant, Jan. 17,

1861, Case No. 1958, DCTC; M. W. Townsend to his brother, Feb. 11, 1861, Nathaniel Townsend Papers (CAH) (2nd quotation).

16. Order for TWW's Arrest, Jan. 17, 1861, and Notification by Sheriff John T. Price of TWW's Release, Jan. 17, 1861, Case No. 1958, DCTC; TWW, Answer to Motion for Attachment, p. 8, [March 1861], Ward Papers.

17. Charles Smyth to TWW, Jan. 14, #U1.88 (1st quotation), May 10, 1861, #1.98, Charles Smyth, "Passing Thoughts," #U1.89 (enclosed in Charles Smyth to TWW, Jan. 11, 1861, #U1.86) (2nd quotation), and Patrick Rooney to TWW, May 13, 1861, #690, Ward Papers; *State Gazette* (Austin), Apr. 27, 1861; Gammel, *Laws of Texas*, V, 350; TWW, Answers to Interrogatories, Jan. 16, 1861, attachment, pp. 2–5, 12–15, Case No. 1958, DCTC.

18. TWW, Answer to Motion for Attachment, pp. 2–11, [March 1861], Ward Papers; Order for the Jailing of TWW, June 17, 1861, Case No. 1958, DCTC; *Southern Intelligencer* (Austin), Sept. 29, 1865 (quotations); Edward A. Blackburn Jr., *Wanted: Historic County Jails of Texas* (College Station: Texas A&M University Press, 2006), 326.

19. TWW, Petition for a Writ of Habeas Corpus, June 18, 1861, and James H. Bell, Memorandum, June 21, 1861, Ward Papers.

20. SLW, Motion for Appointment of a Receiver, July 1861, TWW, Exceptions to the Motion for Appointment of a Receiver, [July 1861], and Orders for Alimony for the months June (quotation), July, and August 1861, Case No. 1958, DCTC; SLW, Answer of the Defendant, Dec. 8, 1864, pp. 3–4, Case No. 2262, DCTC; Lewis L. Gould, *Alexander Watkins Terrell: Civil War Soldier, Texas Lawmaker, American Diplomat* (Austin: University of Texas Press, 2004) 34–35; District Court Minutes (Civil), June 8–9, 1863, Book I, pp. 69–72, DCTC.

21. Amelia E. Barr, *All the Days of My Life: An Autobiography. The Red Leaves of a Human Heart* (New York: D. Appleton and Co., 1923), 243–244 (quotation); James Arthur Irby, "Confederate Austin, 1861–1865" (M.A. thesis, University of Texas at Austin, 1953), 104–109; Brown, "Annals of Travis County," ch. XXIII, 27–28, 67–69, ch. XXIV, 20–21.

22. Petitions of SLW and TWW to the District Court, Travis County, June 13, 1864, Case No. 1958, DCTC; Tax Receipt, Apr. 7, 1863, and Estimates of Tithes Due, Feb. 16, June 27, 1864, Ward Papers; Dudley Ward to TWW, Apr. 7, Dec. 1, 1863, Feb. 13, Feb. 22, May 4, 1864, Dudley Ward Letters.

23. David C. Humphrey, "A 'Very Muddy and Conflicting' View: The Civil War as Seen from Austin, Texas," *SHQ*, 94 (Jan., 1991), 398–401; SLW to Dudley Ward, Mar. 30, 1864, #U78.34 (quotations), and Dudley Ward to Colonel Ashbel Smith, Aug. 12, 1863, #U239, Ward Papers; Lieutenant J. S. Atchison to Dudley Ward, Nov. 16, 1863, and Dudley Ward to TWW, Nov. 26, 1863, Dudley Ward Letters.

24. TWW to Ashbel Smith, Sept. 16, 1864, Letters 1864, Ashbel Smith Papers (CAH); Dudley Ward to TWW, Sept. 14, 1864, Dudley Ward Letters; *Weekly State Gazette* (Austin), Sept. 28, 1864.

25. Irby, "Confederate Austin," 103; SLW, Answer of the Defendant, Dec. 8, 1864, p. 13, Case No. 2262, and TWW, Petition for Injunction, Aug. 5, 1864, p. 2, Case No. 1958, DCTC; District Court Minutes (Civil), June 10, 13, 1864, Book I, pp. 81–82, 84–85, DCTC.

26. TWW, Motion to Set Aside the Court's Judgment, June 11, 1864, and TWW, Protest

Against the Appointment of a Receiver, June 13, 1864, p. 5 (quotations), Case No. 1958, DCTC; TWW et al., Injunction Bond, Aug. 5, 1864, Case No. 2262, DCTC.

27. Dudley Ward to TWW, July 17, 1864 (quotation), and Dudley Ward to James Ward, Aug. 7, 1864, Dudley Ward Letters; Sheriff T. C. Collins, Report on Sale of Lots 23, 27, and 46, Nov. 8, 1864, Case No. 1958, Sheriff T. C. Collins, Report on Sale of Lot 45, Jan. 3, 1865, Case No. 2262, and Petition of N. G. Shelley to the Travis County District Court, Apr. 6, 1865, Case No. 2290, DCTC.

28. TWW, Answer to Plaintiff's Motion to Proceed to Trial, Dec. 9, 1864, and Judge A. D. McGinnis, Re Bill of Exception, Dec. 9, 1864, Case No. 1958, DCTC; *District Court Minutes (Civil)*, Dec. 9, 1864, Book I, p. 98, DCTC.

29. *Southern Intelligencer* (Austin), Sept. 22, 1865.

30. *Weekly State Gazette* (Austin), Nov. 23, 1864, Mar. 15, 1865 (2nd quotation); City Council Minutes, Dec. 3, 1864 through Mar. 6, 1865, Records of the Mayor's Office and Board of Aldermen, Nov. 15, 1862–Oct. 4, 1869 (City Clerk's Office, Austin); Barr, *All the Days of My Life*, 248–249 (1st quotation); Brad R. Clampitt, "The Breakup: The Collapse of the Confederate Trans-Mississippi Army in Texas, 1865," *SHQ*, 108 (Apr., 2005), 502; *Tri-Weekly Telegraph* (Houston), Apr. 5, 1865, AF-Chron.

31. City Council Minutes, Mar. 23, 25, 28, 30, 1865, Records of the Mayor's Office; *Weekly State Gazette* (Austin), Mar. 29, 1865 (quotation); Record of Mass Meeting, Apr. 1, 1865, #641.2, Ward Papers.

32. For an excellent overview of the plundering that followed the collapse of the Confederate trans-Mississippi army in Texas, see Clampitt, "The Breakup," 499–534.

33. Ibid., 515 (quotation), 517.

34. Barr, *All the Days of My Life*, 249–250; Baker, *Texas Scrap-Book*, 349–350. According to Frank Brown, chronicler of Austin's nineteenth-century history and an Austin resident from 1846 until his death in 1913, the account of the riots quoted here from Baker's *Texas Scrap-Book* first appeared in the August 18, 1865, issue of the Austin *Southern Intelligencer*, of which Brown was a publisher. Though the newspaper account was anonymous, according to Brown, the author "is believed to have been" Baker. Baker lived in Austin from about 1850 until his death in 1881. However, an account of the riots does not appear in the August 18 issue of the weekly *Southern Intelligencer*, nor has one been located in another issue. See Brown, "Annals of Travis County," ch. XXIV, 14.

35. TWW, Resolution, n.d., #641.1, Ward Papers. At a later date Ward mistakenly dated the resolution April 1, 1865, but his covering note (#640) makes it clear the resolution concerned "his efforts to protect the citizens against the aggressions of the Confederate Soldiers after Lee's surrender."

36. TWW, Tender of Services to Assist Civil Authorities, May 26, 1865 (with a note by Edward Clark and George Flournoy, [May 26, 1865], and a note by the committee appointed by the meeting at the capitol, May 27, 1865), #641.5, and TWW to George R. Freeman, June 14, 1865, #641.7, Ward Papers.

37. TWW, Tender of Services, May 26, 1865 (1st quotation), and TWW to George R. Freeman, June 14, 1865, #641.7 (2nd quotation), Ward Papers; *Southern Intelligencer* (Austin), Aug. 4, 1865.

38. *Southern Intelligencer* (Austin), July 21 (2nd quotation), Aug. 4, 1865; *Texas State*

Gazette (Austin), Extra, May 29, 1865 (1st quotation); City Council Minutes, June 2 (3rd quotation), 5, 1865, Records of the Mayor's Office.

39. City Council Minutes, June 2, 1865, Records of the Mayor's Office (1st quotation); Barr, *All the Days of My Life*, 250 (2nd quotation).

40. Patrick Cox, "Treasury Robbery," *NHT*, VI, 557; Irby, "Confederate Austin," 138–140; *Texas State Gazette* (Austin), July 18, 1865; *Southern Intelligencer* (Austin), July 7, 1865; Willis Robards to Ashbel Smith, June 15, 1865, Letters 1865, Ashbel Smith Papers (quotation). Freeman's company was limited by its contract with Robards and Randolph to thirty men, but over the course of the month the company was active about sixty men actually participated.

41. TWW to George R. Freeman, June 14, 1865, #641.7 (1st quotation), Ward Papers; *Southern Intelligencer* (Austin), July 7, 1865; City Council Minutes, June 27, 1865, Records of the Mayor's Office (2nd and 3rd quotations).

42. *Southern Intelligencer* (Austin), July 7, 1865 (1st quotation); *Texas State Gazette* (Austin), June 28 (2nd quotation), July 11 (3rd quotation), 1865;

43. City Council Minutes, June 27, 30, July 4, 1865, Records of the Mayor's Office; *Southern Intelligencer* (Austin), July 7, 1865. When the minutes for the July 4 city council meeting (at which the organization of a volunteer police force was authorized) were printed in the Austin *Southern Intelligencer* on July 7, the meeting was misdated June 4. Frank Brown used the June 4 date for the decision to organize a volunteer police force in his widely used "Annals of Travis County and Austin," ch. XXIV, 22. As a result, some have concluded that the decision to organize a volunteer police force was made in direct response to the riots of returning soldiers in late May, whereas it was actually made in response to emancipation.

44. *Texas State Gazette* (Austin), July 4, 1865.

45. Ibid., July 11, 1865 (quotations); *Southern Intelligencer* (Austin), Oct. 12, 1865.

46. *Southern Intelligencer* (Austin), July 7, 1865 (quotations); *Texas State Gazette* (Austin), July 11, 1865.

NOTES TO CHAPTER 16

1. Robert W. Shook, "Federal Occupation and Administration of Texas, 1865–1870" (Ph.D. diss., University of North Texas, 1970), 71; Elizabeth Bacon Custer, *Tenting on the Plains; or General Custer in Kansas and Texas* (3 vols.; Norman: University of Oklahoma Press, 1971), I, 217 (1st quotation); SLW to Carrie and Julie Pease, Dec. 23, 1865, R.1, Pease Papers (2nd and 3rd quotations).

2. SLW to Carrie and Julie Pease, Dec. 23, 1865, R.1, Pease Papers.

3. SLW to Carrie Pease, Feb. 27, 1866, C.1 (quotations), and Marshall Pease to Carrie Pease, May 18, 1866, D, Pease Papers; Custer, *Tenting on the Plains*, II, 266; *Southern Intelligencer* (Austin), May 17, 1866.

4. *Southern Intelligencer* (Austin), Oct. 6, 1865, May 17, 1866. The mayor and city council met three times in August and early September but only on the most routine of matters.

5. *Weekly State Gazette* (Austin), May 3, 1865; *Southern Intelligencer* (Austin), Sept. 22, 1865 (3rd and 4th quotations), Jan. 18, 1866 (1st quotation), Jan. 10, 1867 (2nd quotation).

6. *Texas State Gazette* (Austin), Oct. 10, 1865 (quotation); *Southern Intelligencer* (Austin), Sept. 15, Oct. 6, 1865, Jan. 11, 1866.

7. *Southern Intelligencer* (Austin), Nov. 2, 9, Dec. 7, 1865, Jan. 4, 11, 1866; *Texas State Gazette*, Oct. 17 (quotations), 19, 24, 1865; City Council Minutes, Oct. 12, 26, Dec. 5, 1865, Jan. 1, 1866, Records of the Mayor's Office.

8. *Southern Intelligencer* (Austin), Sept. 22, Oct. 26, Dec. 7, 14, 21, 1865; *Weekly State Gazette* (Austin), Dec. 23, 1865; City Council Minutes, Oct. 26 (quotation), Dec. 11, 1865, Jan. 1, 1866, Records of the Mayor's Office.

9. *Southern Intelligencer* (Austin), Feb. 1, May 17 (quotation), 1866; *Tri-Weekly State Gazette* (Austin), Feb. 10, 1866; Stuart A. MacCorkle, *Austin's Three Forms of Government* (San Antonio: Naylor Co., 1973), 63; TWW to William H. Seward, Aug. 23, 1867, Records re Custom House Nominations, box 440, Appointments Division, RG 56.

10. Marshall Pease to Carrie Pease, May 18, 1866, D, and Aaron Bean to Marshall Pease, Aug. 1, 1866, P.1 (quotation), Pease Papers.

11. District Court Minutes (Civil), June 11, 1866, Book I, pp. 288–289, DCTC; Marshall Pease to Carrie Pease, June 6, 1866, P, Pease Papers; Agreement between TWW and SLW in District Court, Case No. 1958, July 5, 1866, and Agreement in District Court Regarding the Judgment Rendered in the Supreme Court of the City and County of New York, July 5, 1866, Legal Affairs: General Correspondence, 1865–1870, Marmion Henry Bowers Papers (CAH); Deed, July 5, 1866, Travis County Deed Record, vol. Q, pp. 232–233 (microfilm; AHC).

12. Deeds, Apr. 9, 1870, June 28, 1872, Travis County Deed Record, vol. T, pp. 214–215, vol. W, p. 723; District Court Minutes (Civil), Nov. 16, 1866, Mar. 6, 1867, Book I, pp. 297, 384, DCTC; *Southern Intelligencer* (Austin), Nov. 22, 1866 (quotation); Anna Ward to Carrie Pease, Jan. 17, May 15, 1867, C.1, and Lucadia Pease to Marshall Pease, Aug. 27, 1867, S, Pease Papers.

13. Lucadia Pease to her children, Dec. 13, 1867 (1st and 2nd quotations), and Lucadia Pease to Marshall Pease, Nov. 27, 1870, S, Pease Papers; SLW, Amended Petition, [October 1871], document 28, Case No. 2262, DCTC (3rd quotation).

14. James Throckmorton to Hugh McCulloch, Sept. 22, 1866, and enclosure, Applications for Appointments as Custom Service Officers, 1833–1910, box 221, Records re Custom Service Appointments, Appointments Division, RG 56; Andrew Johnson, Appointment of TWW as Collector of Customs, District of Corpus Christi, Oct. 6, 1866, Ward Papers.

15. Hugh McCulloch to J. Warren Bell, Oct. 26, 1867, Letters Sent re Employees of the Customs Service (Entry 34), vol. 8, p. 130, OST, RG 56; J. C. Russell, *In the Supreme Court of Texas, at Austin, December, A.D., 1871. B. F. Neal, et al., Ex'rs of H.L. Kinney, dec'd, Appellants, versus Lucien Birdseye, Appellee* (Corpus Christi: Advertiser Office, 1872), 2–4; B. F. Neal to TWW, Dec. 30, 1867, and Rental Agreement between TWW and W. G. Denney, Jan. 14, 1867, Ward Papers.

16. Carl E. Prince and Mollie Keller, *The U.S. Customs Service: A Bicentennial History* (Washington, D.C.: Department of the Treasury, U.S. Customs Service, 1989), chart of "Receipts and Expenditures of the National Government, 1789 to 1940," following p. 76.

17. Act of July 28, 1866, ch. 293, 14 *Stat.* 308–309.

18. *Weekly Advertiser* (Corpus Christi), Apr. 17, 1869.

19. TWW to Hugh McCulloch, Feb. 17, Mar. 26, with enclosure from G. W. Spencer to TWW, Feb. 28 (quotation), 1867, Series G, OST, roll 85, MP M174A (Letters Received by the Secretary of the Treasury From Collectors of Customs, 1833–1869), RG 56.

20. TWW to Hugh McCulloch, Feb. 19, 1867, Series G, OST, roll 85, MP 174A, RG 56; TWW to Hugh McCulloch, Mar. 7, Sept. 1, 1867, Records re Customhouse Nominations, box 440, Appointments Division, RG 56.

21. Hugh McCulloch to Nathan Sargent, May 9, 1867, vol. 5 (1st quotation), Oct. 28, 1867, vol. 6, Letters Sent to Heads of Bureaus, 1861–1878 (Entry 7), OST, RG 56; Nathan Sargent to Hugh McCulloch, Apr. 11, 1867, Letters Received from Executive Officers, 1831–1869 (Entry 82), OST, RG 56; Nathan Sargent to Hugh McCulloch, Oct. 13, 1868, Letters Received from the Commissioner of Customs (Entry 161), box 3, OST, RG 56; George S. Boutwell to Thomas Kearney, July 8, 1869, Letters Sent re Employees of the Customs Service (Entry 34), vol. 12, p. 368, OST, RG 56 (2nd quotation).

22. TWW to Hugh McCulloch, June 23, 1867, Series G, OST, roll 85, MP M174A, RG 56 (quotation); Hugh McCulloch to TWW, July 24, Records re Customhouse Nominations, box 440, Appointments Division, RG 56; *List of Nominations Made to and Rejected by the Senate During the Second Session of the Thirty-Ninth Congress, Ending March 3, 1867,* pp. 4–5, Letters Received from the Senate re Appointments, 1861–1910 (Entry 138), box 1, OST, RG 56; Brooks D. Simpson, *The Reconstruction Presidents* (Lawrence: University of Kansas Press, 1998), 112–113, 123.

23. Hugh McCullogh to Daniel McIntyre, July 23, 1867, Letters Sent re Employees of the Customs Service (Entry 34), vol. 7, p. 273, OST, RG 56; TWW to William H. Seward, Aug. 23, 1867, and Daniel Layman to Hugh McCulloch, Feb. 25, 1868, Records re Customhouse Nominations, box 440, Appointments Division, RG 56; Nathan Sargent to Hugh McCullogh, Oct. 5, 1868, Letters Received from Executive Officers, 1831–1869 (Entry 82), OST, RG 56; Nathan Sargent to Thomas D. Eliot, Mar. 20, 1868, 40th Congress, SEN 40A-E3, Commerce, box 18, S. 504–S.755, RG 46: Records of the U.S. Senate (NA).

24. TWW to William H. Seward, Aug. 23, 1867, Records re Customhouse Nominations, box 440, Appointments Division, RG 56.

25. Ibid. (quotation); Charles Smyth to TWW, Aug. 27, 1868, #U1.106, Ward Papers; Nathan Sargent to Thomas D. Eliot, Mar. 20, 1868, 40th Congress, SEN 40A-E3, Commerce, box 18, S. 504–S.755, RG 46; Act of July 13, 1868, ch. 156, 15 *Stat.* 382–383; Appointment of TWW, July 1, 1868, Commissions Issued to Major Treasury Officers ("Presidential Appointments"), 1791–1909, vol. 14, p. 19, Records re Presidential Appointments and Commissions, Appointments Division, RG 56; J. F. Hartley to Daniel C. McIntyre, Dec. 24, 1868, vol. 33, roll 20, OST, MP M175 (Letters Sent by the Secretary of the Treasury to Collectors of Customs, 1789–1878), RG 56.

26. TWW to Hugh McCulloch, Oct. 28 (1st quotation), Nov. 21, 1868, and William Hipsley to William Chandler, Sept. 14, 1867, Records re Customhouse Nominations, box 440, Appointments Division, RG 56; Nathan Sargent to Hugh McCulloch, July 20, 1868, Letters Received from Executive Officers, 1831–1869 (Entry 82), OST, RG 56 (2nd quotation).

27. TWW to Hugh McCulloch, Aug. 31, Oct. 10, Nov. 21, 1868, Jan. 30, 1869, Records re Customhouse Nominations, box 440, Appointments Division, RG 56; Hugh McCulloch to J. Warren Bell, July 9, 1868, and Hugh McCullogh to TWW, Jan. 7, 21, 1869, Letters Sent re Employees of the Customs Service (Entry 34), vol. 10, p. 14, vol. 11, pp. 120, 163, OST, RG 56; Hugh McCulloch to TWW, Jan. 7, 1869, vol. 33, OST, roll 20, MP M175, RG 56; D. W. Hastings to TWW, Jan. 29, 1869, and George Spencer to TWW, Jan. 31, 1869, Series G, OST, roll 99, MP M174A, RG 56.

28. *Weekly Advertiser* (Corpus Christi), Apr. 17, 1869.

29. Will of TWW, Jan. 26, 1869, and Anna Ward to TWW, Sept. 26, 1870, #601 (quotation), Ward Papers. Although Ward was legal guardian for his two stepchildren, Robie and Mary, he had never adopted them and was not legally obligated to include them in his will.

30. Anna Ward to TWW, Dec. 25, 1870, #600 (quotation), James Ward to TWW, Dec. 21, 1870, #605, and Tom Ward to TWW, Jan. 21, 1871, #604, Ward Papers; Lucadia Pease to Marshall Pease, Nov. 27, 1870, S, Pease Papers.

31. Tom Ward to TWW, Jan. 21, 1871, #604, Ward Papers; TWW to M. H. Bowers, Mar. 15, 1871, General Correspondence, 1870–1872, Bowers Papers; *Houston Courier*, Nov. 29, 1872.

32. TWW to M. H. Bowers, July 10, 1871, General Correspondence, 1870–1872, Bowers Papers; W. H. Woodward to TWW, Aug. 29, 1871, and Record Book, Estate of TWW, pp. 14–23, Ward Papers; Russell, *In the Supreme Court of Texas, at Austin, December, A.D. 1871,* 2–4; District Court Minutes (Civil), Nueces County, June 23, 1871, vol. C, pp. 606–610 (microfilm; Texas A&M University–Kingsville); Neal v. Birdseye, 39 *Texas* 604–605 (1873).

33. *Democratic Statesman* (Austin), Sept. 5, 1871 (1st quotation); *Mercantile and General City Directory of Austin, Texas, 1872–1873* (Austin: S. A. Gray, 1872), 110; Charles Smyth to TWW, Nov. 23, 1871, #U1.108, Ward Papers (2nd quotation); Gammel, *Laws of Texas,* VII, 211. Ward had already been awarded a $500 annual pension in 1870 under legislation benefiting all surviving veterans of the Texas Revolution. See Pension Claim, Approved Dec. 22, 1870, Republic Claims, Republic Pensions, TWW, roll 244, frame #407; Gammel, *Laws of Texas,* VI, 292–293.

34. *Houston Courier*, Nov. 29, 1872; *Democratic Statesman* (Austin), Nov. 26, 1872 (quotation); Articles of Agreement, Feb. 7, 1878, Record Book, Estate of TWW, Ward Papers.

35. District Court Minutes (Civil), June 30, Oct. 7, 1873, Book K, pp. 421 (quotation), 453, DCTC.

36. George W. Paschal, *A Digest of the Laws of Texas: Containing Laws in Force, and the Repealed Laws on Which Rights Rest* (2nd ed.; Washington, D.C.: W. H. & O. H. Morrison, 1870), 310–311 (quotation); SLW, Answer of the Defendant, Dec. 8, 1864, pp. 11–12, Case No. 2262, and Decree of the Court, Feb. 8, 1859, Case No. 1522, DCTC.

37. Copy of Deed for Lots 2, 4, 5, and 6 in Block 81, Jan. 26, 1854, Ward Papers; James Ward, Memoranda Relative to Lots in Block 81, City of Austin, n.d., in possession of the author; Probate of TWW's Will, Case #517, Probate Minutes, Travis County, vol. F, pp. 18–19, 426–427, vol. G, p. 183 (microfilm; AHC). In 1877, three years after Susan's death, James changed the legal status of one of his father's lots from community property to separate property.

38. Deed, Mar. 31, 1873, Travis County Deed Record, vol. Y, p. 24; *Daily Democratic Statesman* (Austin), July 1, 1873.

39. Will of SLW, July 7, 1873, Ward Papers.

40. Anna Ward to James Ward, Dec. 26, 31, 1874, Ward Papers.

NOTES TO RETROSPECT

1. *Southern Intelligencer* (Austin), Sept. 22, 1865.

2. TWW to SLW, Feb. 16, 1854, #U197, Ward Papers.

3. J. H. Brower to TWW, June 1, 1857, #584 (1st and 3rd quotations), and Amos Corwine to TWW, Oct. 30, 1856 (2nd quotation), Ward Papers.

4. *Weekly Advertiser* (Corpus Christi), Apr. 17, 1869.

5. SLW to Lucadia Pease, Sept. 24, 1855, S.1, Pease Papers.

6. Lucadia Pease to Marshall Pease, Nov. 27, 1870 (1st quotation), S, and SLW to Lucadia Pease, Sept. 24, 1855, S.1 (2nd quotation), Pease Papers.

7. Nancy Woloch, *Women and the American Experience: A Concise History* (2nd ed.; Boston: McGraw-Hill, 2002), 80; Nancy Tomes, "Historical Perspectives on Women and Mental Illness," in *Women, Health, and Medicine in America: A Historical Handbook,* ed. Rima D. Apple (New York: Garland Publishing, 1990), 145–154; Carroll Smith-Rosenberg, *Disorderly Conduct: Visions of Gender in Victorian America* (New York: Oxford University Press, 1985), 197–216.

8. Tomes, "Historical Perspectives on Women and Mental Illness," 152; Jemima Rivington, Deposition, Oct. 22, 1860, pp. 20–21, Ward Papers.

9. SLW, Codicil to Will, Dec. 26, 1874, Ward Papers.

10. *Democratic Statesman* (Austin), Nov. 26, 1872.

NOTES TO APPENDIX

1. Joel Miner to Matthew Woodhouse, Oct. 17, 1842 (1st quotation) and other letters by Miner, James Long, and William Murrah to Matthew Woodhouse, Boxes 2-22L/10 and 2-23/904, Matthew Woodhouse Papers, TSA; News clipping, September 1869, #U159, Ward Papers (2nd quotation); *Democratic Statesman* (Austin), Sept. 5, 1871.

2. *Galveston News,* Jan. 25, 1879; Smithwick, *Evolution of a State,* 195; Brown, "Annals of Travis County and Austin," ch. XXXI, p. 72.

Bibliography

MANUSCRIPT AND ARCHIVAL SOURCES

Austin, Texas

Austin History Center, Austin Public Library
AF—A 8250
AF—Chron
Frank Brown, Annals of Travis County and of the City of Austin (From the Earliest Times to the Close of 1875)
Niles-Graham-Pease Papers
Order Book of Col. T. William Ward
Travis County Deed Record (microfilm)
Travis County Probate Minutes (microfilm)

City Clerk's Office
City Council Minutes, Records of the Mayor's Office and Board of Aldermen, Nov. 15, 1862–Oct. 4, 1869

Dolph Briscoe Center for American History, University of Texas at Austin
Marmion H. Bowers Papers
Broadside Collection
Confederate Index
Mary Austin Holley Papers
Moses Johnson Papers
Anson Jones Papers
Maverick Family Papers
Oran M. Roberts Papers
Thomas J. Rusk Papers
Julia Lee Sinks Papers
Ashbel Smith Papers

James Harper Starr Papers
Nathaniel Townsend Papers
Vertical File, William C. Walsh, "Austin in the Making"
Thomas William Ward Papers (see Appendix B)

Tarleton Law Library, University of Texas at Austin
Correspondence, 1842–1844, Concerning the "Archive War"

Texas General Land Office
Austin's Register of Families
ESA (Early Letters Sent) (microfilm)
Headright Grants and Military Land Grants
Lost Book of Harris County
Report of Commissioners, Feb. 15, 1845 to Jan. 19, 1891
Dudley Ward Letters

Texas State Archives
Mrs. Harry Barnhart Collection
Congressional Bill Files
General Land Office Correspondence
Houston Letters, Hearne Collection
A. J. Houston Collection
Washington D. Miller Papers
Swante Palm Collection
Records of the Legislature: Memorials and Petitions
Republic Claims: Audited Claims, Republic Debt Claims, Republic
    Pensions
Texas Adjutant General Service Records
Texas Secretary of State, Legislative and Executive Bodies Prior to the
    Republic Series, Committee Reports
Matthew Woodhouse Papers

Travis County Courthouse
Records of the District Court for Travis County, 1858–1873 (microfilm)
        Case No. 1522: *Thomas William Ward and Susan L. Ward v. Robie and
            Mary Marston*
        Case No. 1958: *Susan L. Ward v. Thomas William Ward*
        Case No. 2262: *Thomas William Ward v. Susan L. Ward*
        Case No. 2290: *N. G. Shelley v. Thomas William Ward*
        District Court Minutes (Civil)

Dublin, Ireland

Dublin City Archives
Minute Book of the Commissioners for the Making of Wide and Convenient Streets in the City of Dublin, 1822–1823

Registry of Deeds
Memorials, 1817–1833

Representative Church Body Library
Baptism Register, St. Mary's Parish, 1792–1815
Vestry Book, St. Mary's Parish, 1792–1828

Trinity College Library, Manuscripts Department
Documents concerning Botany Bay, MUN/P/2/119
Registry of Trinity College Board Minutes, 1813–1817, MUN/V/5/6

Houston, Texas

Harris County Courthouse
    County Clerk's Office
    Harrisburg County Court Minutes
    District Clerk's Office
    Civil Records, Records Library, File No. 7

Houston Public Library
District Court Minutes, Harris County (microfilm)
Harris County Deed Record (microfilm)
Vertical Files, Houston Town Lot Book

Kingsville, Texas

Texas A&M University-Kingsville
District Court Minutes, Nueces County (microfilm)

La Porte, Texas

San Jacinto Museum of History, Herzstein Library
Andrew Briscoe Papers
Tod Collection

Liberty, Texas

Sam Houston Regional Library and Research Center
Galveston County Deed Record (microfilm)

New Orleans, Louisiana

New Orleans Notarial Archives
Acts of William Christy, L. Feraud, and Carlile Pollock

Williams Research Center
Vieux Carré Survey

New York, New York

New York County Clerk, Division of Old Records
Index #GA 625 of 1860, *Susan L. Ward v. Thomas W. Ward*

Chapel Hill, North Carolina

Southern Historical Collection, University of North Carolina at Chapel Hill
Thomas Jefferson Green Papers

Washington, D.C.

National Archives and Records Administration
Record Group 36: Records of the U.S. Customs Service
 Passenger Lists of Vessels Arriving at New York, New York, 1820–1897,
 Microfilm Publication M237A
Record Group 46: Records of the U.S. Senate
 40th Congress, SEN 40A-E3, Commerce
Record Group 56: General Records of the Department of the Treasury
 Records of the Appointments Division
  Records re Custom House Nominations
  Records re Custom Service Appointments, Applications for
   Appointments as Custom Service Officers, 1833–1910
  Records re Presidential Appointments and Commissions,
   Commissions Issued to Major Treasury Officers ("Presidential
   Appointments"), 1791–1909
 Records of the Office of the Secretary of the Treasury
  Letters Received from Executive Officers, 1831–1869 (Entry 82)
  Letters Received from the Commissioner of Customs (Entry 161)
  Letters Received from the Senate re Appointments, 1861–1910 (Entry
   138)

Letters Received by the Secretary of the Treasury from Collectors of
Customs, 1833–1869, Series G, Microfilm Publication M174A
Letters Sent by the Secretary of the Treasury to Collectors of Customs,
1789–1878, Microfilm Publication M175
Letters Sent re Employees of the Customs Service (Entry 34)
Letters Sent to Heads of Bureaus, 1861–1878 (Entry 7)
Record Group 59: General Records of the Department of State
Consular Dispatches from Panama City, Panama, Microfilm Publication
M139
Notes to Foreign Legations in the United States from the Department
of State, 1834–1906, Colombia, 1835–1885, Microfilm Publication
M99
Letters of Application and Recommendation During the
Administrations of Franklin Pierce and James Buchanan, 1853–1861,
Microfilm Publication M967
Record Group 84: Records of Foreign Service Posts of the Department of
State
Records of the U.S. Consulate in Panama City
Letters Received, 1850–1860
Instructions Received, 1853–1860
United States Seventh Census (1850), Population Schedules, New York,
Texas

NEWSPAPERS

Alta California (San Francisco)
Austin City Gazette
The Bee (New Orleans)
Carlow Morning Post (Ireland)
Commercial Bulletin (New Orleans)
Connecticut Courant (Hartford)
Daily Bulletin (Austin)
Daily Democratic Statesman (Austin)
Daily Panama Star (Panama City, Panama)
Daily Texian (Austin)
Democratic Statesman (Austin)
Dublin Evening Post
Dublin Mercantile Advertiser
Freeman's Journal (Dublin)
Houston Courier

Louisiana Courier (New Orleans)
Morning Star (Houston)
New Orleans Daily Picayune
New York Herald
New York Times
Northern Standard (Clarksville, Tex.)
Panama Herald (Panama City, Panama)
Panama Star and Herald (Panama City, Panama)
Red-Lander (San Augustine, Tex.)
Southern Intelligencer (Austin)
South Western American (Austin)
Telegraph and Texas Register (San Felipe de Austin, Houston)
Texas Democrat (Austin)
Texas National Register (Washington-on-the-Brazos)
Texas Sentinel, Texas Centinel (Austin)
Texas State Gazette (Austin)
Texas Times (Galveston)
Tri-Weekly State Gazette (Austin)
Tri-Weekly Telegraph (Austin)
True American (New Orleans)
Weekly Advertiser (Corpus Christi)
Weekly Panama Star (Panama City, Panama)
Weekly State Gazette (Austin)

PRINTED PRIMARY SOURCES

"An Alphabetical List of the Freemen of the City of Dublin, 1774–1824."
  The Irish Ancestor, 15 (Nos. 1 and 2, 1983), 1–133.
Barker, Nancy Nichols, ed. *The French Legation in Texas.* 2 vols. Austin: Texas
  State Historical Association, 1971–1973.
Barr, Amelia E. *All the Days of My Life: An Autobiography. The Red Leaves of a
  Human Heart.* New York: D. Appleton and Co., 1923.
Barrington, Sir Jonah. *Personal Sketches and Recollections of His Own Times.*
  Dublin: Ashfield Press, 1997.
Bates, Mrs. D. B. *Incidents on Land and Water, or Four Years on the Pacific Coast.*
  Boston: J. French and Co., 1857.
Binkley, William C., ed. *Official Correspondence of the Texan Revolution,
  1835–1836.* 2 vols. New York: D. Appleton-Century Co., 1936.
Bryan, J. P., ed. *Mary Austin Holley: The Texas Diary, 1835–1838.* Austin: University of Texas Press, 1965.

Connor, Seymour V., ed. *Texas Treasury Papers: Letters Received in the Treasury Department of the Republic of Texas, 1836–1846.* 4 vols. Austin: Texas State Library, 1955.

Crimmins, M. L., ed. "The Storming of San Antonio de Bexar in 1835." *West Texas Historical Association Year Book,* 22 (Oct., 1946), 95–117.

Custer, Elizabeth Bacon. *Tenting on the Plains; or General Custer in Kansas and Texas.* 3 vols. Norman: University of Oklahoma Press, 1971.

Dresel, Gustav. *Houston Journal: Adventures in North America and Texas, 1837–1841.* Edited by Max Freund. Austin: University of Texas Press, 1954.

Ehrenberg, Herman. *The Fight for Freedom in Texas in the Year 1836.* In Natalie Ornish, *Ehrenberg: Goliad Survivor, Old West Explorer: A Biography.* Dallas: Texas Historical Press, 1997.

Field, Joseph E. *Three Years in Texas.* 1836. Reprint, Tarrytown, N.Y.: William Abbatt, 1925.

Ford, John Salmon. *Rip Ford's Texas,* edited by Stephen B. Oates. Austin: University of Texas Press, 1963.

Fulton, Maurice Garland, ed. *Diary & Letters of Josiah Gregg.* 2 vols. Norman: University of Oklahoma Press, 1941–1944.

Gamble, John. *Sketches of History, Politics, and Manners, in Dublin, and the North of Ireland, in 1810.* London: Baldwin, Cradock, and Joy, 1826.

Gammel, H. P. N. *The Laws of Texas, 1822–1897.* 10 vols. Austin: Gammel Book Co., 1898.

Gray, William F. *From Virginia to Texas, 1835: Diary of Col. Wm. F. Gray.* 1909. Reprint, Houston: Fletcher Young Pub. Co., 1965.

Green, Rena Maverick, ed. *Samuel Maverick, Texan, 1803–1870: A Collection of Letters, Journals, and Memoirs.* San Antonio: privately printed, 1952.

Green, Thomas J. *Journal of the Texian Expedition Against Mier.* 1845. Reprint, New York: Arno Press, 1973.

Greer, James K., ed. *Buck Barry, Texas Ranger and Frontiersman.* 1978. Reprint, Lincoln: University of Nebraska Press, [1984].

Gulick, Jr., Charles A., Katherine Elliott, Winnie Allen, and Harriet Smither, eds. *The Papers of Mirabeau Buonaparte Lamar.* 6 vols. Austin: Texas State Library, 1921–1927.

Hart, Katherine, and Elizabeth Kemp, eds. *Lucadia Pease & the Governor, Letters: 1850–1857.* Austin: Encino Press, 1974.

Hollon, W. Eugene, and Ruth Lapham Butler, eds. *William Bollaert's Texas.* Norman: University of Oklahoma Press, 1956.

Jenkins, John H., ed. *The Papers of the Texas Revolution, 1835–1836.* 10 vols. Austin: Presidial Press, 1973.

Jewett, Henry J. "The Archive War of Texas." *DeBow's Review*, 26 (May, 1859), 513–523.

Jones, Anson. *Memoranda and Official Correspondence Relating to the Republic of Texas, Its History and Annexation.* New York: D. Appleton & Co., 1859.

Latham, Francis. *Travels in the Republic of Texas, 1842,* edited by Gerald S. Pierce. Austin: Encino Press, 1971.

Lubbock, Francis R. *Six Decades in Texas.* Austin: B. C. Jones, 1900.

Manning, William R., ed. *Diplomatic Correspondence of the United States: Inter-American Affairs, 1831–1860.* 12 vols. Washington, D.C.: Carnegie Endowment for International Peace, 1932–1939.

Martin, Mabelle Eppard, ed. "From Texas to California in 1849: Diary of C. C. Cox." *Southwestern Historical Quarterly*, 29 (July, 1925), 36–50.

Martineau, Harriet. *Society in America.* 3 vols. 1837. Reprint, New York: AMS Press, 1966.

McClintock, William A. "Journal of a Trip Through Texas and Northern Mexico in 1846–1847." *Southwestern Historical Quarterly*, 34 (July, 1930), 20–37.

Minutes of the Board of Land Commissioners, Harris [Harrisburg] County, Texas. 2 vols.; typescript. Transcribed from the records of the Texas General Land Office for the Chambers County Historical Commission, 1980.

Muir, Andrew Forest, ed. "Diary of A Young Man in Houston, 1838." *Southwestern Historical Quarterly*, 53 (Jan., 1950), 276–307.

———, ed. *Texas in 1837: An Anonymous, Contemporary Narrative.* Austin: University of Texas Press, 1958.

Muster Rolls of the Texas Revolution. Austin: Daughters of the Republic of Texas, 1986.

O'Connor, Mrs. T. P. [Elizabeth Paschal O'Connor]. *I Myself.* New York: G. P. Putnam, 1914.

Otis, Fessenden N. *Illustrated History of the Panama Railroad.* New York: Harper & Brothers, 1861.

Palmer, B. Frank. *The Patent Palmer Arm and Leg: Adopted for the U.S. Army and Navy.* [Philadelphia?: American Artificial Limb Co.?], 1866.

The Panama Massacre: A Collection of the Principal Evidence and Other Documents. Panama City: Office of the Star and Herald, 1857.

Proceedings of the Grand Lodge of Texas. 2 vols. Galveston: Richardson & Co., 1857.

Reagan, John H. *Memoirs, With Special Reference to Secession and the Civil War.* 1906. Reprint, Austin: Pemberton Press, 1968.

Red, William S., ed. "Extracts from the Diary of W. Y. Allen, 1838–1839."

Southwestern Historical Quarterly, 17 (July, 1913), 43–60.

Report of the Commissioner of the General Land Office to the 9th Congress of the Republic of Texas. [Washington, Tex.]: Vindicator Office, 1844.

Russell, J. C. *In the Supreme Court of Texas, at Austin, December, A.D., 1871. B. F. Neal, et als., Ex'rs of H.L. Kinney, dec'd, Appellants, versus Lucien Birdseye, Appellee.* Corpus Christi: Advertiser Office, 1872.

Sheppard, Lorna Geer. *An Editor's View of Early Texas: Texas in the Days of the Republic as Depicted in the Northern Standard (1842–1846).* Austin: Eakin Press, 1998.

Sibley, Marilyn McAdams, ed. "Letters From the Texas Army, Autumn, 1836: Leon Dyer to Thomas J. Green." *Southwestern Historical Quarterly*, 72 (Jan., 1969), 371–384.

Smither, Harriet, ed. "Diary of Adolphus Sterne." *Southwestern Historical Quarterly*, 33 (July, 1929), 75–79.

Smithwick, Noah. *The Evolution of a State or Recollections of Old Texas Days.* Austin: University of Texas Press, 1983.

Southworth, E. D. E. N. [Emma Dorothy Eliza Nevitte]. *The Discarded Daughter: A Novel.* 1852. Reprint, Chicago: M. A. Donohue & Co., n.d.

Stansbury, Charles F. *Argument on Behalf of the Applicant: in the Matter of the Application of B. Franklin Palmer, for the Extension of Letters Patent, Granted to Him 4th November, 1846, for the Improvement in Artificial Legs.* [Washington, D.C.?: , n.p., 1860].

———. *Testimony in the Matter of the Application of B. Frank Palmer for the Extension of His Patent for an Artificial Leg.* Philadelphia: C. Sherman & Son, 1862.

Stiff, Edward. *The Texan Emigrant.* 1840. Reprint, Waco: Texian Press, 1968.

Texas in 1840, or the Emigrant's Guide to the New Republic. 1840. Reprint, New York: Arno Press, 1973.

Tomes, Robert. *Panama in 1855.* New York: Harper & Brothers, 1855.

U.S. Department of State. *Regulations Prescribed by the President for Consular Officers of the United States.* Washington, D.C.: A. O. P. Nicholson, 1856.

Viener, Saul. "Surgeon Moses Levy: Letters of a Texas Patriot." *Publications of the American Jewish Historical Society*, 46 (Dec., 1956), 101–113.

Williams, Amelia W., and Eugene C. Barker, eds. *The Writings of Sam Houston, 1813–1863.* 8 vols. Austin: University of Texas Press, 1938–1943.

Williams, Charles Richard, ed. *Diary and Letters of Rutherford Birchard Hayes, Nineteenth President of the United States.* 5 vols. [Columbus]: Ohio State Archeological and Historical Society, 1922–1926.

PRINTED PRIMARY SOURCES: TEXAS HOUSE AND SENATE JOURNALS

Appendix to the Journals of the House of Representatives: Fifth Congress. Austin: Gazette Office, n.d.

First Congress—First Session. An Accurate and Authentic Report of the Proceedings of the House of Representatives. Columbia, Tex.: G & T. H. Borden, 1836.

Journals of the Convention, Assembled at the City of Austin on the Fourth of July, 1845, for the Purpose of Framing a Constitution for the State of Texas. 1845. Reprint, Austin: Shoal Creek Publishers, 1974.

Journals of the House of Representatives of the Eighth Congress of the Republic of Texas. Houston: Cruger & Moore, 1844.

Journals of the House of Representatives of the First Legislature of the State of Texas. Clarksville, Tex.: Standard Office, 1848.

Journals of the House of Representatives of the Ninth Congress of the Republic of Texas. Washington, Tex.: Miller & Cushney, 1845.

Journal of the House of Representatives of the State of Texas—Fourth Legislature. Austin: Cushman & Hampton, 1852.

Journals of the House of Representatives of the State of Texas, Second Legislature. Houston: Telegraph Office, 1848.

Journals of the Senate of the First Legislature of the State of Texas. Clarksville, Tex.: Standard Office, 1848.

Journals of the Senate of the Ninth Congress of the Republic of Texas. Washington, Tex.: Miller & Cushney, 1845.

Journals of the Senate of the Republic of Texas, Adjourned Session—Second Congress. Houston: [Telegraph Power Press], 1838.

Smither, Harriet, ed. *Journals of the Fourth Congress of the Republic of Texas, 1839–1840.* 3 vols. Austin: Von-Boeckmann-Jones Co., [1931].

———, ed. *Journals of the Sixth Congress of the Republic of Congress, 1841–1842.* 3 vols. Austin: Von Boeckmann-Jones Co., 1940–1945.

Winkler, Ernest, ed. *Secret Journals of the Senate, Republic of Texas, 1836–1845.* Austin: Austin Printing Co., 1911.

SELECTED SECONDARY SOURCES

Listed below is a selection of the more important secondary sources cited in the footnotes. Included are about half the books and articles cited. Complete citations are given in the footnotes for all sources the first time each is cited.

The Architecture of Richard Morrison (1767–1849) and William Vitruvius Morrison (1794–1838). Dublin: Irish Architectural Archive, 1989.

Baker, De Witt Clinton. *A Texas Scrap-Book: Made Up of the History, Biography, and Miscellany of Texas and Its People*. 1875. Reprint, Austin: Texas State Historical Association, 1991.

Barkley, Mary Starr. *History of Travis County and Austin 1839–1899*. 3rd ed. Austin: Austin Printing Co., 1981.

Barr, Alwyn. *Texans in Revolt: The Battle for San Antonio, 1835*. Austin: University of Texas Press, 1990.

Basch, Norma. *Framing American Divorce: From the Revolutionary Generation to the Victorians*. Berkeley: University of California Press, 1999.

Beckham, Jean C., and Scott D. Moore. "Interpersonal Hostility and Violence in Vietnam Combat Veterans with Chronic Posttraumatic Stress Disorder: A Review of Theoretical Models and Empirical Evidence." *Aggression and Violent Behavior*, 5 (Sept.–Oct., 2000), 451–466.

Beerstecher, Jr., Ernest. "An Early Likeness of the Capitol at Houston." *Texana*, 5 (Fall, 1967), 232–237.

Binkley, William C. "The Activities of the Texan Revolutionary Army after San Jacinto." *Journal of Southern History*, 6 (Aug., 1940), 331–346.

Bishop, Curtis. *Lots of Land*. Austin: Steck Co., 1949.

Bowker, John H., and John W. Michael, eds. *Atlas of Limb Prosthetics: Surgical, Prosthetic, and Rehabilitation Principles*. 2nd ed. St. Louis: Mosby Year Book, 1992.

Brown, Gary. *Volunteers in the Texas Revolution: The New Orleans Greys*. Plano, Tex.: Republic of Texas Press, 1999.

Campbell, Randolph B. *Gone to Texas: A History of the Lone Star State*. New York: Oxford University Press, 2003.

———. *Sam Houston and the American Southwest*. New York: HarperCollins College Publishers, 1993.

Carroll, Mark M. *Homesteads Ungovernable: Families, Sex, Race, and the Law in Frontier Texas, 1823–1860*. Austin: University of Texas Press, 2001.

Cartwright, Frederick F. *The Development of Modern Surgery*. London: Arthur Barker Limited, 1967.

Chemtob, Claude M., Roger S. Hamada, Herbert L. Roitblat, and Miles Y. Muraoka, "Anger, Impulsivity, and Anger Control in Combat-Related Posttraumatic Stress Disorder." *Journal of Consulting and Clinical Psychology*, 62 No. 4, (1994), 827–832.

Clampitt, Brad R. "The Breakup: The Collapse of the Confederate Trans-Mississippi Army in Texas, 1865." *Southwestern Historical Quarterly*, 108 (April, 2005), 499–534.

Coles, Harry Lewis. *History of the Administration of Federal Land Policies and Land Tenure in Louisiana, 1803–1860.* New York: Arno Press, 1979.

Connor, Seymour V. *The Peters Colony of Texas: A History and Biographical Sketches of the Early Settlers.* Austin: Texas State Historical Association, 1959.

Cravens, John Nathan. *James Harper Starr: Financier of the Republic of Texas.* Austin: Daughters of the Republic of Texas, 1950.

Daley, Mercedes Chen. "The Watermelon Riot: Cultural Encounters in Panama City, April 15, 1856." *Hispanic American Historical Review,* 70 (Feb. 1990), 85–108.

D'Arcy, Fergus. "An Age of Distress and Reform: 1800–1860." In *Dublin Through the Ages.* Edited by Art Cosgrove. Dublin: College Press, 1988.

Dean Jr., Eric T. *Shook Over Hell: Post-Traumatic Stress, Vietnam, and the Civil War.* Cambridge: Harvard University Press, 1997.

De Cordova, Jacob. *Texas: Her Resources and Her Public Men.* Philadelphia: J. B. Lippincott, 1858.

De la Teja, Jesús F. "A Short History of the General Land Office Seals." *Southwestern Historical Quarterly,* 90 (Jan., 1987), 293–299.

Denham, James M. "New Orleans, Maritime Commerce, and the Texas War for Independence, 1836." *Southwestern Historical Quarterly,* 97 (Jan., 1994), 511–534.

Dick, Everett. *The Lure of the Land: A Social History of the Public Lands from the Articles of Confederation to the New Deal.* Lincoln: University of Nebraska Press, 1970.

Eaton, F. B. *History of Candia: Once Known as Charmingfare; With Notices of Some of the Early Families.* Manchester, N.H.: Press of the Granite Farmer, 1852.

Faries, John Culbert. *Limbs for the Limbless: A Handbook on Artificial Limbs for Layman and Surgeon.* New York: Institute for the Crippled and Disabled, 1934.

Folkman Jr., David I. *The Nicaragua Route.* Salt Lake City: University of Utah Press, 1972.

Friedmann, Lawrence W. *The Psychological Rehabilitation of the Amputee.* Springfield, Ill.: Charles C. Thomas, 1978.

Gambrell, Herbert. *Anson Jones: The Last President of Texas.* 2nd ed. Austin: University of Texas Press, 1964.

Gerber, David A. "Introduction: Finding Disabled Veterans in History." In *Disabled Veterans in History,* edited by David A. Gerber. Ann Arbor: University of Michigan Press, 2000.

Greaser, Galen D., and Jesús F. de la Teja. "Quieting Title to Spanish and

Mexican Land Grants in the Trans-Nueces: The Bourland and Miller Commission, 1850–1852." *Southwestern Historical Quarterly*, 95 (April, 1992), 445–464.

Greenberg, Kenneth S. *Honor & Slavery: Lies, Duels, Noses, Masks, Dressing as a Woman, Gifts, Strangers, Humanitarianism, Death, Slave Rebellions, the Proslavery Argument, Baseball, Hunting, and Gambling in the Old South.* Princeton: Princeton University Press, 1996.

Griffin, Roger. "Connecticut Yankee in Texas: A Biography of Elisha Marshall Pease." Ph.D. diss., University of Texas at Austin, 1973.

Hafertepe, Kenneth. *Abner Cook: Master Builder on the Texas Frontier.* Austin: Texas State Historical Association, 1992.

Hardin, Stephen L. *Texian Iliad: A Military History of the Texas Revolution.* Austin: University of Texas Press, 1994.

Hartog, Hendrik. *Man and Wife in America: A History.* Cambridge: Harvard University Press, 2000.

Hill, Jacqueline. *From Patriots to Unionists: Dublin Civic Politics and Irish Protestant Patriotism, 1660–1840.* Oxford: Clarendon Press, 1997.

Hogan, William Ransom. *The Texas Republic: A Social and Economic History.* Norman: University of Oklahoma Press, 1969.

Houston, Virginia H. Taylor. "Surveying in Texas." In *One League to Each Wind: Accounts of Early Surveying in Texas,* edited by Sue Watkins. Austin: Von-Boeckmann-Jones, 1964.

Humphrey, David C. "A 'Very Muddy and Conflicting' View: The Civil War as Seen from Austin, Texas." *Southwestern Historical Quarterly,* 94 (Jan., 1991), 369–414.

Irby, James Arthur. "Confederate Austin, 1861–1865." M.A. thesis, University of Texas at Austin, 1953.

Kemble, John Haskell. *The Panama Route, 1848–1869.* 1943. Reprint, Columbia: University of South Carolina Press, 1990.

Kennedy, Charles Stuart. *The American Consul: A History of the United States Consular Service, 1776–1914.* New York: Greenwood Press, 1990.

Kennedy, John Castillo. "Incident on the Isthmus." *American Heritage,* 19 (June, 1968), 65–72.

Labell, Linda S. "Wife Abuse: A Sociological Study of Battered Women and Their Mates." *Victimology: An International Journal,* 4 (Number 2, 1979), 258–267.

Lack, Paul D. *The Texas Revolutionary Experience: A Political and Social History, 1835–1836.* College Station: Texas A&M University Press, 1992.

The Land Commissioners of Texas: 150 Years of the General Land Office. Austin: Texas General Land Office, 1986.

Lane, Wheaton J. *Commodore Vanderbilt: An Epic of the Steam Age.* New York: Alfred A. Knopf, 1942.

MacFarquhar, Larissa. "So You Want a Divorce." *The New Yorker* (April 23, 2001), 88–96.

Marks, Paula Mitchell. *Turn Your Eyes Toward Texas: Pioneers Sam and Mary Maverick.* College Station: Texas A&M University Press, 1989.

McDaid, Jennifer Davis. "'How a One-Legged Rebel Lives': Confederate Veterans and Artificial Limbs in Virginia." In *Artificial Parts, Practical Lives: Modern Histories of Prosthetics,* edited by Katherine Ott, David Serlin, and Stephen Mihm. New York: New York University Press, 2002.

Mihm, Stephen. "'A Limb Which Shall Be Presentable in Polite Society': Prosthetic Technologies in the Nineteenth Century." In *Artificial Parts, Practical Lives: Modern Histories of Prosthetics,* edited by Katherine Ott, David Serlin, and Stephen Mihm. New York: New York University Press, 2002.

Miller, Edward L. *New Orleans and the Texas Revolution.* College Station: Texas A&M University Press, 2004.

Miller, Kerby A. *Emigrants and Exiles: Ireland and the Irish Exodus to North America.* New York: Oxford University Press, 1985.

Miller, Thomas Lloyd. *The Public Lands of Texas, 1519–1970.* Norman: University of Oklahoma Press, 1971.

Moore, Michael T. "Mapping Texas Public Lands, 1824–1900." Austin: Texas General Land Office, typescript, n.d.

Nance, Joseph Milton. *After San Jacinto: The Texas-Mexican Frontier, 1836–1841.* Austin: University of Texas Press, 1963.

———. *Attack and Counter-Attack: The Texas-Mexican Frontier, 1842.* Austin: University of Texas Press, 1964.

Newell, Ala May. "The Postal System of the Republic of Texas." M.A. thesis, St. Mary's University of San Antonio, 1940.

Nixon, Pat Ireland. *The Medical Story of Early Texas: 1528–1853.* Lancaster, Pa.: Lancaster Press, 1946.

Parks, E. Taylor. *Colombia and the United States, 1765–1934.* Durham: Duke University Press, 1935.

Paschal, George W. *A Digest of the Laws of Texas: Containing Laws in Force, and the Repealed Laws on Which Rights Rest.* 2nd ed. Washington, D.C.: W. H. & O. H. Morrison, 1870.

Pierce, Madge Evalene. "The Service of James Hamilton to the Republic of Texas." M.A. thesis, University of Texas at Austin, 1933.

Prince, Carl E., and Mollie Keller. *The U.S. Customs Service: A Bicentennial History.* Washington, D.C.: Department of the Treasury, U.S. Customs Service, 1989.

Randall, Stephen J. *Colombia and the United States: Hegemony and Interdependence.* Athens: University of Georgia Press, 1992.

Rozear, Marvin P., and Joseph C. Greenfield, Jr. "'Let Us Cross Over the River': The Final Illness of Stonewall Jackson." *Virginia Magazine of History and Biography,* 103 (Jan., 1995), 29–46.

Sanders, Gloria T. *Lower Limb Amputations: A Guide to Rehabilitation.* Philadelphia, F. A. Davis Co., 1986.

Scarborough, Jane Lynn. "George W. Paschal, Texas Unionist and Scalawag Jurisprudent." Ph.D. dissertation, Rice University, 1972.

Schott, Joseph L. *Rails Across Panama: The Story of the Building of the Panama Railroad, 1849–1855.* Indianapolis: Bobbs-Merrill Co., 1967.

Sibley, Marilyn McAdams. *Lone Stars and State Gazettes: Texas Newspapers before the Civil War.* College Station: Texas A&M University Press, 1983.

———. "Thomas Jefferson Green: Recruiter for the Texas Army, 1836." *Texas Military History,* 3 (Fall, 1963), 129–145.

Smith-Rosenberg, Carroll. *Disorderly Conduct: Visions of Gender in Victorian American.* New York: Oxford University Press, 1985.

Spaw, Patsy McDonald, ed. *The Texas Senate: Volume 1, Republic to Civil War, 1836–1861.* College Station: Texas A&M University Press, 1990.

Starling, Susanne. *Land Is the Cry! Warren Angus Ferris, Pioneer Texas Surveyor and Founder of Dallas County.* Austin: Texas State Historical Association, 1998.

Stuntz, Jean. "Spanish Laws for Texas Women: The Development of Marital Property Law to 1850." *Southwestern Historical Quarterly,* 104 (April, 2001), 543–559.

Tomes, Nancy. "Historical Perspectives on Women and Mental Illness." In *Women, Health, and Medicine in America: A Historical Handbook,* edited by Rima D. Apple. New York: Garland Publishing, 1990.

Tyler, Ron, Douglas E. Barnett, Roy R. Barkley, Penelope C. Anderson, and Mark F. Odintz, eds. *The New Handbook of Texas.* 6 vols. Austin: Texas State Historical Association, 1996.

Walsh, Eamon. "Sackville Mall: The First One Hundred Years." In *The Gorgeous Mask: Dublin, 1700–1850,* edited by David Dickson. Dublin: Trinity History Workshop, 1987.

Warburton, J., J. Whitelaw, and Robert Walsh. *History of the City of Dublin; From the Earliest Accounts to the Present Time.* 2 vols. London: T. Cadell and W. Davies, 1818.

Winchell, Ellen. *Coping with Limb Loss.* Garden City Park, N.Y.: Avery Pub. Group, 1995.

Winkler, Ernest W. "The Seat of Government of Texas: I. Temporary Location of the Seat of Government." *Quarterly of the Texas State Historical Association*, 10 (Oct., 1906), 140–171.

———. "The Seat of Government of Texas: II. The Permanent Location of the Seat of Government." *Quarterly of the Texas State Historical Association*, 10 (Jan., 1907), 185–245.

Woloch, Nancy. *Women and the American Experience: A Concise History.* 2nd ed. Boston: McGraw-Hill, 2002.

Wyatt-Brown, Bertram. *Honor and Violence in the Old South.* New York: Oxford University Press, 1986.

Index

Note: TWW stands for Thomas William Ward throughout the index.

and divorce)

marriage to Susan L. Ward, 4, 109, 114–16; reconciliation in Tarrytown, 192–96; spousal abuse during, 4, 120–23, 144–48, 153–54, 195–196, 199–202, 208–9, 252–53, 302n19; traditional roles and, 169, 172, 252–53 (*See also* lawsuits for legal separation and divorce)

as mayor of Austin, 4, 28, 57, 59, 122, 149–50, 151; at close of Civil War, 224–28; dealing with emancipation, 229–30, 233–34; during Federal occupation, 232–35

military career of: with Generals Green and Rusk, 34–40; New Orleans Greys, 19–30, 264n11; promotions and commissions, 21, 32, 35, 38–40, 41, 264n11; resumption of duties after amputation, 34, 36; role in defense of Austin, 75–76, 78

nicknames linked to amputation, 4, 72, 244, 255–56

personality of (*See* character of TWW; honor; reputation of TWW)

political career of (*See also* consulship in Panama; General Land Office, commissioner, TWW as; as mayor of Austin), 54–55; anti-secession stance and, 211, 232, 237; as chief clerk, House of Representatives, 59; as chief clerk, stock commissioner's office, 54; electoral defeats during, 50, 52–53, 59, 142, 148, 149, 235; financial motives and, 52, 53, 150, 160, 235, 237, 240; Houston civic affairs and, 49–50; as member Harrisburg County Board of Land Commissioners, 50–52; as notary public, 59; as postmaster of Houston, 53, 54; as special land commissioner, Peters Colony, 148–49; as U.S. customs official, 237–42

political patrons of: David Burnet, 41, 59, 70–71, *illus. following 180*; Sam Houston, 3, 55, 76–77, 97–98, 99, 107, 134, 142, 150; Thomas Rusk, 41, 92, 145–46, 150, 176, 198, 240, *illus. following 180*

suicide, thoughts of, and, 30

and Watermelon War (Panama Massacre), 179–81, 182–83

as wealthy, 3–4, 20, 115, 145, 235

Ward, Thomas William, Jr. (son), 200, 204, 209, 223, 242–43; death of, 255

Ward, Thomas Wood (no relation), 203

Ward Papers, 256–57

Wardville, Texas, 149

Washington-on-the-Brazos, 84, 85–86, 88, 90, 103, 117; character of town, 95; TWW and General Land Office located in, 94–97, 98, 249

Watermelon War (Panama Massacre), 156–57, 165, 178–84, *illus. following 180*; casualties during, 181, 299n7; inciting events of, 178–79; TWW's role in, 179–81, 182–83; U.S. military presence after, 183–84

Webb, James, 78, 91

Whiting, Samuel, 77, 83, 85

Wilson, Robert, 53

women, social and legal status of: ill health and, 251–53; legal separation and divorce and, 201, 203, 209, 214; marital obligations and, 122, 153, 201, 209; property rights and, 4, 155, 196, 204, 209, 214–15, 219, 244–45; social attitudes toward spousal abuse, 144–45; women's rights movement as context, 206–7

Woodhouse, Matthew, 83–84

Wyatt-Brown, Bertram, 49

Y

yellow fever, 53, 189, 222